D1609379

Lectures on Ideology and Utopia

Paul Ricoeur

LECTURES ON IDEOLOGY AND UTOPIA

Edited by George H. Taylor

COLUMBIA UNIVERSITY PRESS
NEW YORK
1986

Library of Congress Cataloging-in-Publication Data

Ricoeur, Paul.
Lectures on ideology and utopia.

Bibliography: p.
Includes index.
1. Ideology—History. 2. Utopias—History.
I. Taylor, George, H., 1951– II. Title.
B823.3.R48 1986 320.5 86-6813
ISBN 0-231-06048-3

Columbia University Press
New York Guildford, Surrey

Printed in the United States of America

Book design by Ken Venezio

Contents

Part II. Utopia

Editor's Acknowledgments

Preparation of Paul Ricoeur's lectures for publication has been assisted by a number of people, all of whom deserve recognition and thanks for their contributions. Though he had no idea at the time that his efforts would result in the lectures' publication, Paul Casey was the person who taped all the lectures and stored them for reserved access at Harper Library of the University of Chicago. Jim Burris compiled an abridged transcript based on his own taping of the lectures; those of us who heard the lectures in their original presentation knew they were important, but Jim's transcriptions made this evident in much greater detail. In a period when my own time constraints were great, Judy Vaughan gave freely from her own demanding schedule to help me retape the original reel-to-reel tapes onto cassettes, which made the transcription of the lectures a much easier task. Joel Guerra, John Monroe, and Rahner James all provided key technical assistance. Diane Luneau helped me gain access to some important secondary bibliographic material. David Pellauer located some otherwise inaccessible Ricoeur material and made helpful suggestions on the bibliography and my introduction. Candice Hoke's editorial acumen was, as ever, highly significant, especially in the early and late stages of my labors. I cannot imagine having a better editor or closer friend. Finally my thanks go to Paul Ricoeur, both for allowing me to undertake this project and for so generously giving of his time in order to review it. I greatly value the opportunity I have had to work with him.

Editor's Introduction

The breadth of Paul Ricoeur's work is unsurpassed by perhaps any other thinker's in the world today. Although he is best known for his writings on religious symbolism *(The Symbolism of Evil)* and psychoanalysis *(Freud and Philosophy)*,[1] his work in fact encompasses a wide range of diverse—and often seemingly disparate—spheres of discourse: theories of history, analytic philosophy of language, ethics, theories of action, structuralism, critical theory, theology, semiotics, psychology, biblical studies, literary theory, and phenomenology and hermeneutics. Readers can find keeping up with Ricoeur a difficult task as he ventures onto so many different kinds of terrain. Unusual as Ricoeur's breadth may be, though, perhaps more surprising is what is missing from his list of themes. Ricoeur is very much engaged—personally and professionally—in the social, cultural, and political life of his day, and yet we find in his work no sustained examination of this subject matter. Two volumes of collected essays, *History and Truth* and *Political and Social Essays,* do present Ricoeur's views on a number of social and political topics, but these essays are specific responses to particular times, circumstances, and occasions.[2] We have missed from Ricoeur an extended analysis of the implications of his hermeneutic approach for social and political theory. Publication of the present volume, Ricoeur's lectures on ideology and utopia, should go far toward addressing this need.[3]

These lectures were first delivered at the University of Chicago in the fall of 1975, and the passage of time has little reduced their importance. They are of significant interest because of the figures they discuss, the themes they address, and the contributions they make to Ricoeur's larger corpus. Ricoeur offers in these lectures his first detailed analysis of Karl

Mannheim, Max Weber, and Clifford Geertz, and he expands his published discussions of Louis Althusser and Jürgen Habermas.[4] Of particular interest is Ricoeur's treatment of Marx, who is the subject of five of the eighteen lectures. Ricoeur has long named Marx, Freud, and Nietzsche the three great "masters of suspicion,"[5] but while he is well known for his interpretation of Freud, the present volume marks Ricoeur's first systematic analysis of Marx.[6]

As for the themes of the lectures—ideology and utopia—Ricoeur is the first since Mannheim to attempt to discuss them within one conceptual framework. Typically, ideology has been a topic for sociology or political science, utopia for history or literature. Ricoeur's juxtaposition of ideology and utopia better defines and demarcates the two, and markedly differentiates them from earlier conceptual formulations, where ideology has been contrasted to both reality and science, and utopia has been viewed as a mere dream, a wishful fancy.

The lectures are also of interest because of their relation to Ricoeur's writings as a whole. Ricoeur speaks to this directly in the lectures, and I will approach the themes of ideology and utopia by discussing Ricoeur's larger work first. After then discussing the specific themes of the lectures, I will move back from part to whole and situate Ricoeur's analysis of ideology and utopia in relation particularly to his writings on imagination and metaphor.

RICOEUR'S PHILOSOPHIC PROJECT

When reading Ricoeur, it is easy to become immersed in the subject at hand, whether it be French historiography, the semantics of action, or Freud's topological model. It is easy to lose sight of the fact that these subjects are often part of larger projects. Sometimes Ricoeur may mention at the end of an essay that he has only now reached—and will stop at—the horizon of his inquiry; at other points he talks about the "detour"—a favorite term—that is the focus of an entire essay, one that allows him in the final paragraph to attain by an indirect route some desired end. A prominent example is Ricoeur's book on Freud, which is ultimately not so much about Freud as about the nature of interpretation.[7] These overarching projects are not always present or easily defined, but despite the apparent diffuseness of Ricoeur's corpus, they do persist and may be said to be finally not religious, psychological, religious, or linguistic but philosophic in nature.[8]

This point holds equally as well for Ricoeur's lectures on ideology and utopia as it does for a work like *Freud and Philosophy*. Readers who seek detailed analyses of specific ideologies or utopias will be disappointed.[9] For the most part, Ricoeur discusses ideology and utopia not as phenomena but as concepts. Ricoeur repeatedly states, for example, that he is not interested in whether Marx was accurate historically about the role of industry at the beginning of capitalism; his focus is the epistemological structure of Marx's work. And Weber is examined not so much for the sociological content of his analyses as for his conceptual framework. Yet to characterize the lectures as philosophic should not suggest that they are remote or inaccessible. They make clear reference to what it means for us to be human beings living in a social and political world. Perhaps, then, the larger project to which the lectures belong is best characterized not simply as philosophic but as a *philosophical anthropology*.

What Ricoeur means by philosophical anthropology is not a subcategory of a social science discipline, but the study of *anthropos*—humanity—from a philosophical perspective. This inquiry, Ricoeur writes, is "aimed at identifying the most enduring features of [our] temporal condition . . .—those which are the least vulnerable to the vicissitudes of the modern age."[10] In the lectures, Ricoeur uses social and political categories to discuss what it means to be human, an issue that concerns both our present and our persisting possibilities.

THE LECTURES

Most of the lectures are on ideology; utopia is the focus of only the final three, although it surfaces as a topic throughout. Ricoeur begins his analysis of ideology with a discussion of Marx. Marx's concept of ideology has been the dominant paradigm in the West, and it is the model to which the rest of the thinkers discussed—and Ricoeur's own proposals—respond. As is typical of his presentation in several of the lectures, Ricoeur does not begin immediately with Marx's concept of ideology. Instead, he spends three of the five Marx lectures examining the developments in Marx that lead up to this concept. Only when the basis for Marx's conceptual framework is well delineated does Ricoeur address Marx's concept of ideology itself. For readers who find it difficult to understand how the "detours" comprising the first Marx lectures relate to ideology, Ricoeur supplies several signposts along the way. For Ricoeur, this careful and patient building of Marx's conceptual framework is the best basis upon which to analyze Marx's concept of ideology.

The path of Marx's early works, Ricoeur suggests, is a progression toward characterizing what is "the real." Determination of the nature of reality affects the concept of ideology, because Marx ultimately defines ideology as what is not real. The contrast in Marx is between ideology and reality, and not, as in later Marxism, between ideology and science. Ricoeur claims that *The German Ideology* is the culmination of Marx's progression on this topic.[11] In this work, Ricoeur says, Marx comes to define reality by praxis—productive human activity—and thus ideology by its opposition to praxis. The German ideology Marx opposes is that of Feuerbach and the other Young Hegelians. Feuerbach's own methodological inversion had recaptured as human activity what previously had been viewed as the power of the divine, but this human activity was still a product of consciousness or thought. Marx himself undertakes another reversal—another methodological inversion—to establish that the real source of human activity is praxis and not consciousness. The Young Hegelians—and Marx himself as late as the *Economic and Philosophic Manuscripts*—had treated consciousness as the center of human activity and as such the reference point for all existence, but in *The German Ideology* Marx criticizes the idealistic overtones of this emphasis and replaces consciousness with the living individual. Ricoeur argues that Marx's position is a challenge not only to the idealism of the Young Hegelians but also to another extreme prominent in later Marxism that sees anonymous structural forces—class, capital—as the active agents in history. While a structuralist reading of *The German Ideology* is possible, Ricoeur acknowledges, a more comprehensive interpretation discerns that Marx mediates between objectivist and idealist perspectives. Marx's great discovery in *The German Ideology,* says Ricoeur, is the complex notion of individuals in their material conditions. Real individuals and material conditions are conjoined.[12]

Marx's concept of ideology calls into question the autonomy granted to the products of consciousness. Ricoeur quotes Marx at length on how ideology is the imaginary, the "reflexes" and "echoes" of the real process of life. For Marx ideology is *distortion.* It is from this characterization of ideology as distortion that the rest of the lectures proceed. Ricoeur calls his approach in the lectures a genetic phenomenology, "a regressive analysis of meaning," "an attempt to dig under the surface of the apparent meaning to the more fundamental meanings" (lecture 18). Marx's concept of ideology as distortion defines ideology at a surface level; the remaining lectures uncover the concept's meaning at progressively deeper levels. For Ricoeur, the problem of ideology is finally not a choice between false and true but a deliberation over the relation between representation *(Vorstellung)* and praxis (lecture 5). Distortion is the proper characterization of ideology when representations claim autonomy, but the concept of ideology is predicated more basically on its simply being representation. Thus, distortion is one of the levels within this model and not, as Marx would have it, the model for ideology itself. The lectures that follow attempt to determine whether the relationship between representation and practice is one of opposition or conjunction. Ricoeur argues against Marx for the latter, claiming that representation is so basic as to be a *constitutive* dimension of the realm of praxis. The conjunction of ideology and praxis will redefine our conceptions of both.

The implications of this argument become fully evident only at the end of the ideology lectures, when Ricoeur discusses Clifford Geertz. But the basis for this argument, Ricoeur claims, lies in Marx. At the same point in *The German Ideology* where Marx offers his most trenchant definition of ideology as distortion, he also allows that there may be a "language of real life" that exists prior to distortion: "The production of ideas, of conceptions, of consciousness, is at first directly interwoven with the material activity and the material intercourse of men, the language of real life."[13] The language of real life, Ricoeur observes, is the discourse of praxis; it is not language itself—linguistic representation—but the symbolic structure of action. Ricoeur's argument is that the structure of action is inextricably symbolic, and that it is only on the basis of this symbolic structure that we can understand either the nature of ideology as distortion or the meaning of ideology in general. Ricoeur's purpose, then, is not to deny the legitimacy of Marx's concept of ideology as distortion but rather to relate it to ideology's other functions. Ricoeur comments: "I am interested . . . in the range of possibilities preserved by Marx's analysis, a range extending from the language of real life to radical distortion. I emphasize that the concept of ideology covers this full range" (lecture 5).

The rest of the lectures pursue this argument in detail, but the basis for the analysis lies in Marx's interpretation of ideology as distortion, that is, the contrast between things as they appear in ideas and as they really are, between representation and praxis. Before Ricoeur can move to the deeper levels of the meaning of ideology, however, he must confront a more recent interpretation that still considers it distortion, this time as opposed not to reality but to science. Ricoeur finds the best expression of this perspective in later Marxism, in particular in the structuralist Marxism of Louis Althusser.

Examination of Althusser's work is especially appropriate for Ricoeur, because his approach contains the most radical consequences of the changes in the conception of ideology from Marx to orthodox Marxism. Ricoeur summarizes these changes in three points. First, Althusser stresses the role of Marxism as a science. No longer is the methodological model one of inversion; a science breaks with what is nonscience, and between the two there is fundamental discontinuity. Ideology is described as the nonscientific or prescientific.[14] Second, this science maintains that reality functions on the basis of anonymous, impersonal forces; endorsement of the role of human agents is itself ideological. Third, Marxist science asserts that a causal relation exists between base or infrastructure (the anonymous forces) and superstructure (culture, art, religion, law). This superstructure is ideological. Althusser improves upon the model of his predecessors by declaring that the infrastructure has a causal "effectivity" on the superstructure, but the superstructure has the capacity to react back on the infrastructure. An event is not the product of the base alone but is affected also by superstructural elements, and hence "overdetermined."

Ricoeur's responses to Althusser's opposition of ideology and science set the stage for the remaining ideology lectures. Before turning at greater length to these later lectures, I will anticipate their importance by briefly relating them to Ricoeur's three counterproposals to Althusser's model. First, Ricoeur wants to challenge Althusser's paradigm and substitute for its opposition of science and ideology the model Ricoeur finds available in Marx, a correlation of ideology and praxis. A lecture on Mannheim follows the ones on Althusser, and Ricoeur shows there how Mannheim exposes the paradox of the opposition between ideology and science. Subsequent lectures examine Habermas' proposal that a nonpositivistic science can be recovered, if only one based on a practical human interest. Second, Ricoeur wants to reject completely the causal model of infrastructure and superstructure. He argues that it is meaningless to maintain that something economic acts on ideas (the superstructure) in a causal way. The effects of economic forces on ideas must be described within a different—a motivational—framework. Max Weber is the main figure discussed in the development of this model. Finally, Ricoeur wants to replace the emphasis on anonymous structural forces as the basis of history with a reemphasis on real individuals under definite conditions. Ricoeur maintains that Althusser conjoins under one heading—anthropological ideology—two different notions. One is the "ideology of consciousness, which Marx and Freud have rightly broken." The second is the individual in his or her conditions, a notion that can rightfully be expressed in nonidealist terms. The "destiny of anthropology," Ricoeur claims, "is not sealed by that of idealism" (lecture 9). Pursuit of the motivational model is one step toward solidifying this argument; another is the developing exploration of the symbolic structure of action, a theme that surfaces constantly throughout the lectures and reaches its culmination in the lecture on Geertz.

The value of Mannheim for Ricoeur's project lies as much in his failures as in his successes. One of Mannheim's real achievements is that he expands the concept of ideology to the point where it encompasses even the one asserting it. The viewpoint of the absolute onlooker, the one uninvolved in the social game, is impossible, says Mannheim. As Ricoeur puts it, "To call something ideological is never merely a theoretical judgment but rather implies a certain practice and a view on reality that this practice gives to us" (lecture 10). Any perspective expressed is in some sense ideological. This circularity of ideology is Mannheim's paradox, something that he tried to escape by claiming that an evaluative standpoint could be achieved through understanding the nature of the historical process, and more particularly, the correlations at work in history. This process of "relationism" was supposed to supplant relativism. Yet construction of these correlations again called for an absolute onlooker who somehow had the criteria for determining what in history was and was not in correlation. Ricoeur calls this failure in Mannheim's theory the desperate attempt to reconstruct "the Hegelian Spirit in an empirical system."

Mannheim somewhat redresses this failure to overcome the paradox of ideology in his comparison of ideology and utopia. As previously mentioned, Mannheim is the first to place ideology and utopia in a common conceptual framework. Unfortunately, however, Mannheim does not take the comparison very far, nor does he perceive that it offers an alternative to the contrast between ideology and science, which his own investigations have undermined as a model for social analysis. Mannheim describes ideology and utopia as forms of noncongruence, vantage points in discrepancy with present reality. This highlights their representational qualities, which Ricoeur generally endorses, but it also perpetuates the scientific paradigm that ideology, because it is noncongruent, is deviation. "In contrast to someone like Geertz," Ricoeur comments, "Mannheim has no notion of a symbolically constituted order; hence an ideology is necessarily the non-congruent, something transcendent in the sense of the discordant or that which is not implied in humanity's genetic code." Ricoeur himself seizes upon the correlation between ideology and utopia in order both to contrast it to the opposition between ideology and science and to indicate the path that he thinks social theory must take.

> [W]hat we must assume is that the judgment on ideology is always the judgment from a utopia. This is my conviction: the only way to get out of the circularity in which ideologies engulf us is to assume a utopia, declare it, and judge an ideology on this basis. Because the absolute onlooker is impossible, then it is someone within the process itself who takes the responsibility for judgment. . . . It is to the extent finally that the correlation ideology-utopia replaces the impossible correlation ideology-science that a certain solution to the problem of judgment may be found, a solution . . . itself congruent with the claim that no point of view exists outside the game. If there can be no transcendent onlooker, then a practical concept is what must be assumed. (lecture 10)[15]

This core insight receives expanded treatment in the rest of the lectures. Ricoeur will return to discussion of Mannheim in the first lecture on utopia.

Ricoeur moves next to an analysis of Max Weber, replacing the causal model informing orthodox Marxism with Weber's motivational model. Marxism emphasizes that the ruling ideas of an epoch are those of the ruling class. Ricoeur contends, however, that this domination cannot be understood as a causal relation of economic forces and ideas but only as a relation of motivation. Here ideology attains what is for Ricoeur its second level; it moves from functioning as distortion to functioning as *legitimation*. The question of legitimacy is ineradicable in social life, says Ricoeur, because no social order operates by force alone. Every social order in some sense seeks the assent of those it rules, and this assent to the governing power is what legitimates its rule. Two factors are involved here, then: the *claim* to legitimacy by the ruling authority, and the *belief* in the order's legitimacy granted by its subjects. The dynamics of this interaction can only be comprehended within a motivational framework, and this is what Weber helps to unfold.

While Weber raises the role of claim and belief, he does not address what from Ricoeur's perspective is the most significant aspect of their interrelation—the discrepancy between them. Ideology assumes its function as legitimation to compensate for this discrepancy. Weber himself does not develop a theory of ideology, and it is on this point that Ricoeur makes a significant addition to Weber's model.[16] Ricoeur's thesis about ideology as legitimation has three points. First, the problem of ideology here concerns the *gap* between belief and claim, the fact that the belief of the ruled must contribute more than is rationally warranted by the claim of the governing authority. Second, ideology's function is to fill this gap. And third, the demand that ideology fill the gap suggests the need for a new theory of surplus value, now tied not so much to work—as in Marx—as to power. The discrepancy between claim and belief is a permanent feature of political life, Ricoeur maintains, and it is ideology's permanent role to provide the needed supplement to belief that will fill this gap.

Ricoeur next discusses Habermas. Habermas reappropriates and transforms themes present in previous figures, and Ricoeur's discussion of him anticipates and helps lay the ground for the consideration of Geertz and the concept of utopia. Habermas is especially significant because he reorients the concept of praxis in a direction that Ricoeur strongly recommends. Habermas claims that one of Marx's key mistakes is his failure to distinguish between relations of production and forces of production. Emphasis on the latter alone gives rise to the objectivist interpretation of Marx. Recognition of the relations of production, on the other hand, acknowledges that praxis includes a certain institutional framework. By an institutional framework Habermas means "the structure of symbolic action" and "the role of cultural tradition" through which people apprehend their work. "Once again," Ricoeur observes, "we see that the distinction between superstructure and infrastructure is not appropriate, because we include something of the so-called superstructure within the concept of praxis. . . . [P]raxis incorporates an ideological layer; this layer may become distorted, but it is a component of praxis itself" (lecture 13). Only when we distinguish between forces of production and relations of production may we speak of ideology; ideology is a question for the latter alone. Habermas affirms the concept of praxis that Ricoeur has been trying to establish; the role of "the structure of human interaction" in praxis corresponds with Ricoeur's persistent theme of the symbolic mediation of action.

Habermas also resurrects the possibility of a science that avoids the false opposition with ideology. Habermas speaks of three sciences: instrumental, historical-hermeneutic, and critical social. He emphasizes the third and claims that psychoanalysis is its model. Within this third, critical science, the psychoanalytic concept of resistance is the paradigm for ideology, and the effort in psychoanalysis to overcome resistance, to achieve self-understanding, is the prototype for the critique of ideology. For Habermas ideology is a mode of distorted communication, the systematic distortion of the dialogic relation. Someone like Weber may note the gap between claim and belief in matters of political legitimacy, but the power of Habermas' analysis lies in its recognition that this gap is the product of distorted relations and that bridging the gap is a result possible only at the end of a process of critique.

Ricoeur applauds Habermas' development of a critical science, and yet he differs with Habermas over the latter's separation of the critical social sciences from the hermeneutic sciences. Ricoeur maintains that Habermas' second and third sciences cannot and should not be finally distinguished. Ricoeur's argument, set forth both in the present text and at greater length elsewhere,[17] is that the critical sciences are themselves hermeneutic, because the ideological distortions they attempt to overturn are processes of desymbolization. "The distortions belong to the sphere of communicative action" (lecture 14). The critique of ideology is part of the communicative process, its critical moment; we may say that it represents what in other terminology Ricoeur calls the moment of explanation within the process that moves from understanding to explanation to critical understanding.

Habermas has replied to criticism about *Knowledge and Human Interests,* the main text addressed by Ricoeur in the lectures, and his theory has moved in some new directions. But *Knowledge and Human Interests* remains central for discussion of Habermas' theory of ideology, and Ricoeur's response in the lectures to the newer proposals is consistent with the criticism he has already advanced. Psychoanalysis continues to be an important model for the critical social sciences in Habermas,[18] and one way to specify the inadequacy of his theory, says Ricoeur, is to demonstrate the extent to which the parallelism between the two fails. Ricoeur's criticism bears both on the stance of the theorist engaged in critical social science and on the results this science intends to achieve. On the first point, Ricoeur maintains that, unlike the psychoanalyst, the critical theorist does not transcend the polemical situation. "The status of ideology-critique itself," he contends, "belongs to the polemical situation of ideology" (lecture 14). On the second point, while psychoanalysis does help the patient to attain the experience of recognition, this experience has no existing parallel in the critical social sciences.

To take the second point further, we may say that in psychoanalysis recognition is the restoration of communication, either with the self or with others. For the critical social sciences, Habermas states, this communicative ability may be termed communicative competence. Ricoeur's criticism is that the analogy between recognition and communicative competence may not be as complete as Habermas intends, and more particularly, that he uses the notion of competence ambiguously. According to Chomsky's terminology, competence is the correlate of performance; it is an ability at our disposal. Communicative competence, however, is an ability that is not at our disposal but rather an unfulfilled *ideal,* a regulative idea. The notion of communication without boundary or constraint is one of an ideal speech act. Therefore, communicative competence does not have the same standing as recognition in psychoanalysis. While recognition is an actual experience, communicative competence is a utopian ideal.

We may summarize Ricoeur's two criticisms of Habermas as follows. First, the critical theorist cannot and does not stand outside or above the social process. Second, the only possibility for judgment is one that contrasts ideology to utopia, for it is only on the basis of a utopia—the viewpoint of the ideal—that we can engage in critique.

Ricoeur's model correlating ideology and praxis is finally completed when he describes the concept of ideology at its third level, ideology as *intergration.* Here the lectures turn to the long-anticipated discussion of Geertz. Ricoeur finds in Geertz confirmation of his own emphasis on the symbolic structure of action. All social action is already symbolically mediated, and it is ideology that plays this mediating role in the social realm. Ideology is integrative at this stage; it preserves social identity. At its deepest level, then, ideology is not distortion but integration. It is, in fact, only on the basis of ideology's integrative function that its legitimative and distortive functions may appear. "Only because the structure of human social life is already symbolic can it be distorted" (lecture 1). Distortion would not be possible without this prior symbolic function. Ideology becomes distortive at the point "when the integrative function becomes frozen, . . . when schematization and rationalization prevail" (lecture 15). Ricoeur leads us to a nonpejorative concept of ideology; ideology as symbolic mediation is *constitutive* of social existence. "The distinction between superstructure and infrastructure completely disappears, because symbolic systems belong already to the infrastructure, to the basic constitution of human being."

Ricoeur also cites a second, related insight of Geertz's analysis: ideology can be profitably compared to the rhetorical devices of discourse. As we saw earlier, Ricoeur uses Weber's motivational model to consider how the interests of the ruling class can be transformed into society's ruling ideas. The relation between interests and ideas is motivational, not causal. In Geertz the emphasis is no longer on the motives themselves but on how they become expressed in signs. There is a need, Ricoeur quotes Geertz, to analyze " 'how symbols symbolize, how they function to mediate meanings.' "[19] In this situation, Ricoeur contends, a positive meaning of rhetoric joins the integrative meaning of ideology, because ideology is "the rhetoric of basic communication." Just as with ideology, rhetorical devices cannot be excluded from language; they are instead an intrinsic part of language. Symbolic mediation is fundamental both to social action and to language. *The Rule of Metaphor* shows Ricoeur's abiding interest in this topic.

In the final three lectures, Ricoeur shifts his attention to the subject of utopia, building on the analysis of ideology already set forth. Each of the utopia lectures focuses on a different figure (Mannheim, Saint-Simon, and Fourier), but they maintain a common theme. Ricoeur begins his analysis by considering why the relationship between ideology and utopia is usually not explored, and he emphasizes that the differentiation between the two tends to disappear in Marxist thought. Whether Marxism views ideology to be in opposition to the real (the Marx of *The German Ideology*) or in opposition to science (orthodox Marxism), utopia is placed in the same category as ideology: it is the unreal or the unscientific. The lectures return to Mannheim here, because he places ideology and utopia in a common framework without reducing their differences.

Mannheim's analysis proceeds in three steps: first, by a criteriology—a working definition of utopia; second, by a typology; and third, by a temporal dynamics—the historical direction of the typology. Ricoeur's response to Mannheim's first step, the criteriology, orients his assessment as a whole. For Mannheim, both ideology and utopia are noncongruent with reality, but ideology legitimates the existing order while utopia shatters it. Ricoeur criticizes Mannheim because of the predominance granted to utopia as noncongruence rather than as that which shatters. The implications of Mannheim's choice become apparent in his discussion of utopia's temporal dynamics. Mannheim sees in the modern period in which he writes the dissolution of utopia, the end of noncongruence, a world no longer in the making. Ricoeur argues that this determination is not only based upon certain sociological and historical evaluations but is also grounded within a particular conceptual framework. Mannheim seems bound to a way of thinking that defines reality by a scientific—even if not positivistic—perspective. Instead of developing a model founded on the tension between ideology and utopia, which would permit a more dynamic sense of reality, his model opposes first ideology, and then utopia, to a reality determined by rationalistic and scientific criteria: ideology and utopia are noncongruent to, deviant from, reality. Because he does not include in his analysis the symbolic structure of life, Mannheim cannot incorporate into his model the permanent and positive traits of either ideology or utopia.

What are these permanent and positive traits? If the best function of ideology is integration, the preservation of the identity of a person or group, the best function of utopia is exploration of the possible. The utopia puts in question what presently exists; it is an imaginative variation on the nature of power, the family, religion, and so on. We are forced to experience the contingency of the social order. The utopia is not only a dream, though, for it is a dream that wants to be realized. The intention of the utopia is to change—to shatter—the present order. One of the chief reasons Ricoeur discusses Saint-Simon and Fourier is that they exemplify this perspective; they are representative of a type neglected by Mannheim—non-Marxist socialist utopians—who made strenuous efforts to have their utopias realized. Even while the utopia's intent is to shatter reality, though, it also maintains a distance from any present reality. Utopia is the constant ideal, that toward which we are directed but which we never fully attain. Here Ricoeur builds on a sentiment of Mannheim's that the latter was not able to incorporate into his theory, that the death of utopia would be the death of society. A society without utopia would be dead, because it would no longer have any project, any prospective goals.

If at a first level the correlation is between ideology as integration and utopia as the "other," the possible, at a second level ideology is the legitimation of present authority while utopia is the challenge to this authority. Utopia attempts to confront the problem of power itself. It may offer either an alternative to power or an alternative kind of power. It is on the question of power that ideology and utopia directly intersect. Because a "credibility gap" exists in all systems of legitimation, all forms of authority, a place for utopia exists also. "If . . . ideology is the surplus-value added to the lack of belief in authority," says Ricoeur, "utopia is what finally unmasks this surplus-value" (lecture 17). Utopia functions to expose the gap between the authority's claims for and the citizenry's beliefs in any system of legitimacy.

If, as Ricoeur maintains, ideological legitimation must be linked to a motivational model, the utopian confrontation of power raises questions about the sources of motivation. This question runs throughout the lectures on Saint-Simon and Fourier. Ricoeur is particularly interested in the way utopias, even the most rationalistic, attempt to reintroduce the emotional impulse found prototypically in the "chiliastic"—or messianic—form of utopia described by Mannheim. Part of Ricoeur's interest is that the persistence of this need counters the dynamics envisaged by Mannheim, where the movement is away from the chiliastic. The problem is how to "impassionate society," to move it and motivate it. At times the answer is to call into prominence, as does Saint-Simon, the role of the artistic imagination. Another response is to call upon "the political educator." This role, which Ricoeur has described at greater length in other writings,[20] is that of "intellectual midwifery"; it is the role of the creative mind who begins a "chain reaction" in society. Saint-Simon, for example, thought that he himself played this part. Another way to raise this problematic of motivation is to see how utopias appropriate the language and claims of religion. On the basis of his discussions of Saint-Simon and Fourier, Ricoeur raises the question "whether all utopias are not in some sense secularized religions that are also always supported by the claim that they found a new religion" (lecture 18).[21]

Utopia functions at a third level also. At the stage where ideology is distortion, its utopian counterpart is fancy, madness, escape, the completely unrealizable. Here utopia eliminates questions about the transition between the present and the utopian future; it offers no assistance in determining or in proceeding on the difficult path of action. Further, utopia is escapist not only as to the means of its achievement, but as to the ends to be achieved. In a utopia no goals conflict; all ends are compatible. Ricoeur calls this pathological side of utopia "the magic of thought" (lecture 17).

Ricoeur concludes the lectures by observing that the correlation between ideology and utopia forms a circle, a practical circle: the two terms are themselves practical and not theoretical concepts. It is impossible for us to get out of this circle, for it is the unrelieved circle of the symbolic structure of action. A circle it may be, but one that challenges and transcends the impossible oppositions of ideology versus science or ideology versus reality. Within this circle, Ricoeur says, "we must try to cure the illnesses of utopias by what is wholesome in ideology—by its element of identity . . .—and try to cure the rigidity, the petrification, of ideologies by the utopian element." Yet it is too simple, Ricoeur adds, to let it be thought that the circle is merely continuous. We must try to make the circle a spiral. "We wager on a certain set of values and then try to be consistent with them; verification is therefore a question of our whole life. No one can escape this" (lecture 18).

Ricoeur's lectures on ideology and utopia have their own autonomy and develop masterfully the logic of their argument. By enlargening our perspective, though, and turning from the lectures to an evaluation of their place within Ricoeur's work as a whole, we can better define both their import for this corpus and the view they open to its larger significance.

RICOEUR'S CORPUS AS A WHOLE

In the space of a few pages the scope of Ricoeur's work can be at best merely sketched. My intention is to focus on the past decade, with particular attention to Ricoeur's writings on metaphor and on imagination; this work forms a central context for the present lectures.

The most appropriate beginning is with *The Rule of Metaphor,* whose parallels with the lectures are striking. It seems no accident that the lectures were delivered in 1975, the same year the original French version of *The Rule of Metaphor* first appeared. To begin with this volume is apt in yet another sense, because it is part of a project still very much current in Ricoeur's thought. Ricoeur notes a direct connection between *The Rule of Metaphor* and *Time and Narrative,* his latest text, saying that the two "form a pair." Though published several years apart, "these works were conceived together."[22] As we shall see, then, the lectures share a conceptual framework with some of Ricoeur's most recent thinking.

One of the basic aims of *The Rule of Metaphor* is to counter the popular view that metaphor is a deviation or substitution in naming, an ornamental addition that can be reduced to some "proper"—that is, literal—meaning. Ricoeur argues instead that "the denotation-connotation distinction has to be maintained to be entirely problematic . . ." (RM:148).[23] In contrast, Ricoeur says, "a more precise semantics . . . shatters the illusion that words possess a proper, i.e. primitive, natural, original . . . meaning in themselves. . . . [L]iteral does not mean proper in the sense of originary, but simply current, 'usual.' The literal sense is the one that is lexicalized" (RM:290–91). No primordial relation exists between a word and that which it represents. The meaning of a word is not a given but rather something that must be established. The literal is not that with which we begin but the result of usage that has become customary. Ricoeur bases this analysis on his characterization of metaphor. A metaphor is not a product of naming but of predication; it is the result of a semantic interaction—a tension—between a word and the sentence in which it appears. A literal meaning is then the product of an interaction between word and sentence that invokes no tension; the usage is accepted, "current, 'usual.' "

This reversal—that metaphor is not deviation from the literal but rather that the literal is itself a product of the relational—causes Ricoeur to propose that a basic "metaphoric" may be in fact the source of categorial order.

> Certainly, the only functioning of language we are aware of operates within an already constituted order; metaphor does not produce a new order except by creating rifts in an old order. Nevertheless, could we not imagine that the order itself is born in the same way that it changes? Is there not, in Gadamer's terms, a "metaphoric" at work at the origin of logical thought, at the root of all classification? . . . The idea of an initial metaphorical impulse destroys [the] oppositions between proper and figurative, ordinary and strange, order and transgression. It suggests the idea that order itself proceeds from the metaphorical constitution of semantic fields, which themselves give rise to genus and species. (RM:22–23)[24]

The affinity of Ricoeur's analysis here with the lectures on ideology is patent. Just as it is incorrect to portray metaphoric representation as a deviation from literal representation, so it is incorrect to portray ideological representation as a deviation from scientific representation. In both cases Ricoeur reverses the relationship, granting priority to the metaphoric and the ideological. The literal and the scientific exist only within the larger metaphoric and ideological fields.

If an underlying "metaphoric" characterizes the nature of language, the parallel in social life is the symbolic mediation of human action. "[T]he so-called 'real' process already has a symbolic dimension. . . . In other words, a pre-symbolic, and therefore preideological, stage of real life can nowhere be found. Symbolism in general is not a secondary effect of social life; it constitutes real life as socially meaningful."[25] As Ricoeur says elsewhere, "ideology is always an unsurpassable phenomenon of social existence. . . ."[26] Ricoeur also returns to this symbolic mediation of action in *Time and Narrative*. If ideology as distortion makes no sense without an underlying symbolic structure of action that can be distorted, similarly "literature would be incomprehensible if it did not give a configuration to what was already a figure in human action" (TN:64).[27] An essential aspect of this prefiguration, Ricoeur says, is the symbolic mediation of action; this mediation is an "implicit or immanent symbolism" (TN:57). "Before being submitted to interpretation, symbols are interpretants internally related to some action" (TN:58).[28]

To maintain that action is symbolically mediated or that ideology is insuperable seems to leave human beings caught in an unyielding circle, unfailingly determined by our culture, our class, our ethnic heritage, our nation. Yet, as his discussion of Habermas reveals, Ricoeur believes that a critical moment is still possible. We begin with an experience of belonging or participation in the culture, class, time, and so on that give us birth, but we are not completely bound by these factors. Instead, we are involved in a dialectic of understanding and explanation. Understanding—indicator of the relation of belonging—"precedes, accompanies, closes, and thus envelops explanation." But in return, "explanation develops understanding analytically."[29] In *The Rule of Metaphor* Ricoeur identifies the tension at work here as "the most primordial, most hidden dialectic—the dialectic that reigns between the experience of belonging as a whole and the power of distanciation that opens up the space of speculative thought" (RM:313). This dialectic lies at the heart of the interpretive process. "Interpretation is . . . a mode of discourse that functions at the intersection of two domains, metaphorical and speculative. . . . On one side, interpretation seeks the clarity of the concept; on the other, it hopes to preserve the dynamism of meaning that the concept holds and pins down" (RM:303).[30]

The possibility of distance—this position of "distanciation"—that Ricoeur points to has two dimensions: it can both expand and criticize a given understanding. Of greater significance, though, is the very existence of distance and its dialectic with belonging. While we are caught in ideology, we are not caught completely. At the same time, the moment of critique does not establish a science autonomous from ideology. As the lectures argue at greater length, science cannot be placed in absolute opposition to ideology. "[D]istanciation," Ricoeur writes, "as the dialectical counterpart of participation, is the condition of the possibility of a critique of ideologies, not without, but within hermeneutics."[31]

This tension between belonging and distanciation illuminates the nature of Ricoeur's general theory of hermeneutics. For Ricoeur, hermeneutics is a product of historical understanding. Because we can never entirely escape our cultural and other conditioning, our knowledge is necessarily partial and fragmentary. As in his criticism of Mannheim in the lectures, Ricoeur argues against the possibility of the uninvolved or absolute onlooker. No human being can attain the perspective of what Hegel called Absolute Knowledge. The human condition of "pre-understanding," our situation of belonging, "excludes the total reflection which would put us in the advantageous position of non-ideological knowledge."[32] A social theory cannot escape from ideology, "because it cannot reach the perspective which would dissociate it from the ideological mediation to which the other members of the group are submitted."[33] Ricoeur's hermeneutics positions itself against the stance—previously quite in vogue—that speaks of "the end of ideology" as a historical possibility.

In his defense of the ineradicably situated and historical character of human understanding, Ricoeur's hermeneutics supports Gadamer's and challenges the claims of objectivist hermeneutics, as found in the writings of Emilio Betti and E. D. Hirsch.[34] Hirsch, for example, has argued that in a text we can separate its meaning—what the text actually says—from its significance—what the text is about, its larger implications. Ricoeur responds, however, that this demarcation "cannot be maintained without equivocation." Hirsch may want "to subordinate the unstable realm of value to the stable realm of meaning," but Ricoeur finds that Hirsch has "undermined the stability of this realm by showing that all textual meaning has to be constructed, that all construction requires choice, and that all choice involves ethical values."[35] A figure parallel to Hirsch in the social sciences might be Max Weber. Ricoeur proclaims that no neutral, nonideological stance is available.

Hermeneutics is bound by the unrelieved hermeneutic circle. Yet as both the lectures and Ricoeur's more general comments on distanciation note, the possibility of critique persists. Because it includes critique, the hermeneutic situation is not nonrational—allowing endorsement only of whatever lies within the circle—but rational in a sense different from formal rationality. Ricoeur attempts to recover the idea and possibility of practical reason, here in the Aristotelian rather than Kantian sense of the term. "We must speak less," Ricoeur says, "of the critique of practical reason than of practical reason as critique." Practical reason is located in the ethical and political realms, and there the degrees of rigor and truth are different from that which we have come to expect elsewhere. To attempt critique on the basis of "objective" reason is only to fall back into the "ruinous opposition of science and ideology." It is only from within the sphere of ideology that critique arises.[36]

Ricoeur in fact argues that hermeneutics does not so much fall simply on the side of practical reason, because it attempts to go beyond the very opposition between the "theoretical" and the "practical." Perpetuation of this opposition, Ricoeur says, leads only to a subtraction of belief from knowledge, while "Hermeneutics claims instead to generate a crisis within the very concept of the theoretical as expressed by the principle of the connectedness and unity of experience."[37] The effort of practical reason is to distinguish between objectification—the positive transformation of values into discourses, practices, and institutions—and alienation—the distortion of these values, the reification of discourses, practices, and institutions.[38] The task of practical reason is therefore to balance between the metaphoric and speculative moments, between the originative value-laden impulse and the ordering response at work in social life. Because social action is mediated symbolically, ideology cannot be avoided, but the effort is to promote ideology at its integrative—and not distortive—level.

Up to this point, I have located ideology and utopia in Ricoeur's work at large by stressing his emphasis on the situated character of human existence. The focus has been on the basic "metaphoric," the possibility of critical distance, the historical character of the hermeneutic situation, and the fundamental need to revive practical reason. As the vocabulary suggests, these factors relate to existing sources of symbolic mediation and so correlate much more with the function of ideology than that of utopia. I will now turn to themes that correspond more to the function of utopia and begin by discussion of Ricoeur's philosophy of the imagination. A brief return to Ricoeur's theory of metaphor lays the foundation for this topic.

In speaking earlier of the basic "metaphoric," I drew attention to *The Rule of Metaphor*'s "most extreme hypothesis, that the 'metaphoric' that transgresses the categorial order also begets it" (RM:24). To unfold the import of imagination, we must reorder this characterization and emphasize that what begets the categorial order also transgresses it. In the act of transgression, metaphor destroys an old order but it does so "only to invent a new one"; the category-mistake that is metaphor "is nothing but the complement of a logic of discovery" (RM:22). This logic of discovery introduces Ricoeur's philosophy of the imagination. Ricoeur speaks of "the conception of imagination, first set out in the context of a theory of metaphor centered around the notion of semantic innovation. . . ."[39] Elsewhere he draws an even more direct comparison between metaphor and imagination: "It seems to me, it is in the moment of the emergence of a new meaning from the ruins of literal predication that imagination offers its specific mediation."[40] The logic of discovery at work in imagination is our particular interest. The notion of innovation is central both to Ricoeur's concept of utopia and to his philosophic project as a whole.

It is somewhat artificial, however, to point only to the innovative side of imagination, because both ideology and utopia are processes of imagination. Ricoeur both begins and ends the lectures by maintaining that the correlation of ideology and utopia typifies what he calls the social and cultural imagination. In order to ascertain more precisely the character of utopia as imagination, we should first consider how ideology and utopia together form the social imagination. Ricoeur discusses this relation at several points in the lectures. In social life, imagination functions in two different ways:

> On the one hand, imagination may function to preserve an order. In this case the function of the imagination is to stage a process of identification that mirrors the order. Imagination has the appearance here of a picture. On the other hand, though, imagination may have a disruptive function; it may work as a breakthrough. Its image in this case is productive, an imagining of something else, the elsewhere. In each of its three roles, ideology represents the first kind of imagination; it has a function of preservation, of conservation. Utopia, in contrast, represents the second kind of imagination; it is always the glance from nowhere. (lecture 15)

If ideology is imagination as picture, utopia is imagination as fiction. "In a sense all ideology repeats what exists by justifying it, and so it gives a picture . . . of what is. Utopia, on the other hand, has the fictional power of redescribing life" (lecture 18). Ricoeur builds on Kant to say that the comparison between picture and fiction may be characterized as one between *reproductive* and *productive* imagination.[41]

I will leave aside commentary on the reproductive or ideological side of the imagination, whose characteristics were anticipated in discussing the situated nature of human existence and the "basic metaphoric" that "begets order." Instead, I turn to the imagination's productive or utopian side. For Ricoeur, the utopian quality of the imagination moves us from the constituted to the constituting. The new perspective opened up by the utopian has two effects, effects that are finally not separable: it offers a vantage point from which to perceive the given, the already constituted, and it offers new possibilities above and beyond the given. Utopia is the view from "nowhere"—the literal meaning of the word—that ensures that we no longer take for granted our present reality. Ricoeur says that we may call utopia what in Husserlian terms is an imaginative variation regarding an essence. Utopia "has a constitutive role in helping us rethink the nature of our social life." It is "the way in which we radically rethink" the nature of the family, consumption, authority, religion, and so on; it is "the fantasy of an alternative society and its exteriorization 'nowhere' " that works "as one of the most formidable contestations of what is" (lecture 1). Utopia acts not only to de-reify our present relations but to point to those possibilites that may yet be ours.[42]

In our earlier discussion, we saw that for Ricoeur distanciation affords us the moment of critique within social life. Explanation is the critical stance within understanding; the critique of ideologies is possible. When the focus is on utopia instead of ideology, the point of critical distance is rather different. Instead of a confrontation of ideology by critique, ideology is opposed by utopia.[43] While ideology-critique allows a reintegration of the critical moment within hermeneutics and so provides an alternative to the failed model that opposes ideology and science, the correlation of ideology and utopia offers the alternative to the failed model that opposes ideology and reality. Because social action is ineluctably mediated through symbols, simple recourse to the "objective facts" is not determinative; what is a fact or what is the nature of this fact may be in dispute because of the varying interpretive schemata in which the fact is perceived and analyzed. At this level, the problem is not primarily one of facts but of "the conflict of interpretations," to cite Ricoeur's well-known phrase and title of one of his books. To put it in another language, we may say that the conflict is between metaphor and metaphor.[44] "We must destroy a metaphor," Ricoeur says, "by the use of a contrary metaphor; we therefore proceed from metaphor to metaphor" (lecture 9).[45] No unmediated reality exists to which we can appeal; disagreement remains the conflict of interpretations.

> My inclination is to see the universe of discourse as a universe kept in motion by an interplay of attractions and repulsions that ceaselessly promote the interaction and intersection of domains whose organizing nuclei are off-centered in relation to one another; and still this interplay never comes to rest in an absolute knowledge that would subsume the tensions. (RM:302)

So far, I have described the side of utopia that offers us distance from present reality, the ability to avoid perceiving present reality as natural, necessary, or without alternative. What we must evaluate now is the character of the alternative that utopia proposes. Again our aim is to determine how this concept correlates with themes within Ricoeur's wider investigations. We may begin by expanding a point only briefly mentioned before, that the utopian quality of the imagination moves us from the instituted to the instituting. We return, therefore, to the productive character of the imagination. This capacity, Ricoeur says, may be termed "poetic." With the use of this term, Ricoeur indicates that he has begun his long-anticipated investigation of the "poetics of the will," itself one part of a project he has called a "philosophy of the will."[46]

The poetic has the function of "making" and of change, and is a concept addressed in both *The Rule of Metaphor* and *Time and Narrative*. The "meaning-effects" of metaphor and narrative "belong to the same phenomenon of semantic innovation" (TN:ix). Both metaphorical utterance and narrative discourse are included in "one vast poetic sphere" (TN:xi). If metaphor and narrative involve semantic innovation, the implications extend to innovation in social existence as a whole. At one point Ricoeur goes so far as to say that the problem of creativity has been the single issue guiding the entire course of his reflections.[47] Ricoeur's work may have focused on the status of language, but his conclusions have much larger implications. "[T]hrough this recovery of the capacity of language to create and recreate, we discover reality itself in the process of being created." Poetic language "is attuned to this dimension of reality which itself is unfinished and in the making. Language in the making celebrates reality in the making."[48] The nature of this relation can be made more precise by looking, once again, to the role of metaphor.

> If this analysis is sound, we should have to say that metaphor not only shatters the previous structures of our language, but also the previous structures of what we call reality. When we ask whether metaphorical language teaches reality, we presuppose that we already know what reality is. But if we assume that metaphor redescribes reality, we must then assume that this reality as redescribed is itself novel reality. My conclusion is that the strategy of discourse implied in metaphorical languages is . . . to shatter and to increase our sense of reality by shattering and increasing our language. . . . With metaphor we experience the metamorphosis of both language and reality.[49]

At the social level, utopia has this metaphoric quality. As productive imagination its task is "exploration of the possible." It is true, Ricoeur says, that "A model may reflect what is, but it also may pave the way for what is not" (lecture 18). This capacity of utopia to change reality brings out the argument of the lectures in greater force. Utopia is not simply a dream but one that wants to be actualized. "The utopia's intention is surely to change things, and therefore we cannot say with Marx's eleventh thesis on Feuerbach that it is a way only of interpreting the world and not changing it" (lecture 17). The model that sets ideology in opposition to reality is inadequate, because reality is symbolically mediated from the beginning. Similarly, a model that sets utopia in opposition to reality is inadequate because reality is not a given but a process.

Reality is always caught in the flux of time, in the processes of change that utopia attempts to bring about. In *Time and Narrative,* Ricoeur considers at length the function of time and emphasizes the "dynamic aspect which the adjective 'poetic' imposes on . . . [his] analysis." His defense of "the primacy of our narrative understanding" in relation to explanation in history and narrative fiction is a defense of "the primacy of the activity that produces plots in relation to every sort of static structure, achronological paradigm, or temporal invariant" (TN:33).[50] The juxtaposition of understanding and explanation gains a temporal dimension. The poetic nature of reality receives its most emphatic characterization in *The Rule of Metaphor,* where Ricoeur speaks of "the revelation of the Real as Act." The poetic capacity, the capacity for creativity and change, is a most fundamental characteristic of reality in general and the human condition in particular. "To present [human beings] 'as acting' and all things 'as in act'—such could well be the ontological function of metaphorical discourse . . ."(RM:43).

One of the most significant results of Ricoeur's emphasis on the real as act is that the very nature of truth can no longer be taken for granted. Actually, Ricoeur says, the nature of truth is put in question by both the temporal and the symbolic dimensions of human existence. On the one hand, because human life is symbolically mediated, any concept of the real is interpretive. The model of truth as adequation is inadequate; we can no longer maintain that an interpretation corresponds with or represents some unmediated, "literal" fact. Instead, poetic language breaks through to "a pre-scientific, ante-predicative level, where the very notions of fact, object, reality, and truth, as delimited by epistemology, are called into question . . ." (RM:254).[51] We cannot finally separate the real from our interpretation; the very nature of the real retains a metaphoric quality. The metaphor is also at work in the temporal dimension, because "the reference of metaphorical utterance brings being as actuality and as potentiality into play" (RM:307). At the social level the role of potentiality is assumed by utopia.

Ricoeur's response to this challenge to the notion of reality is to call for a "radical reformulation of the problem of truth."[52] Ricoeur will develop this topic in volume 3 of *Time and Narrative,* but anticipates his treatment by speaking in earlier works of a "metaphorical" or "prospective" concept of truth.[53] The task, says Ricoeur, is to "go so far as to metaphorize the verb 'to be' itself and recognize in 'being-as' the correlate of 'seeing-as,' in which is summed up the work of metaphor" (TN:80). What we understand to be the real is symbolically mediated from the beginning, and the real is also always in process. Therefore, Ricoeur claims, "the real is everything already prefigured that is also transfigured." The boundary line between invention and discovery can no longer be maintained. "[I]t is vain . . . to ask whether the universal that poetry 'teaches,' according to Aristotle, already existed before it was invented. It is as much found as invented."[54]

The possibilities of creativity and change opened by Ricoeur's metaphoric theory of truth are perhaps the culmination of his philosophic enterprise. Yet as ever in Ricoeur, to appreciate fully these possibilities we must reintroduce the dialectic and reemphasize the sources out of which these possibilities arise. We must reclaim the dialectic of utopia and ideology. This move is anticipated in the quotation above on the dynamic relation between prefiguration and transfiguration. If utopia opens the possible, it does so on the basis of a metaphoric transformation of the existing. We earlier used the concept of ideology to orient our discussion of the fact that we have always already begun, that we always find ourselves within a situation of symbolic mediation—of class, nation, religion, gender, and so forth. As the lectures demonstrate, ideology here is the nonpejorative figure of identity and integration.

This dialectic between the prefigured and the transfigured takes several forms in Ricoeur's work. He describes religious faith, for example, as rooted in the tension between memory and expectation.[55] Another example may be found in the character of ethical life: "Freedom only posits itself by transvaluating what has already been evaluated. The ethical life is a perpetual transaction between the project of freedom and its ethical situation outlined by the given world of institutions."[56] More generally we may say that the dialectic between the prefigured and the transfigured provides an enlarged sense of the meaning of tradition. A tradition is "not the inert transmission of some already dead deposit of material but the living transmission of an innovation always capable of being reactivated by a return to the most creative moments of poetic activity. . . . In fact, a tradition is constituted by the interplay of innovation and sedimentation" (TN:68).

If the dialectic of ideology and utopia functions in one sense as the conjunction of prefiguration and transfiguration, it also operates at another level, one described by a theory of interpretation. Here the emphasis on utopia points to possibilities, but this metaphoric movement must be counterbalanced by the response of speculative thought.

> Interpretation is . . . a mode of discourse that functions at the intersections of two domains, metaphorical and speculative. It is a composite discourse, therefore, and as such cannot but feel the opposite pull of two rival demands. On one side, interpretation seeks the clarity of the concept; on the other, it hopes to preserve the dynamism of meaning that the concept holds and pins down. (RM:303)

We may incorporate this tension as the final result of the analyses advanced thus far. Earlier I spoke of the possibility of the critical moment within ideology. Ideology is a symbolic formulation from which we can achieve some distance. This model is Ricoeur's response to the inadequate paradigm that placed ideology and science in basic opposition. Later I showed how Ricoeur disputes the model opposing ideology to reality and invokes instead the dialectic between ideology and utopia. There is no possibility of attaining a nonideological layer of reality, but ideologies as paradigms are still open to the criticism coming from the "nowhere" of utopia. I then went on to explore the dimensions of possibility the utopia allows. Ricoeur's theory of interpretation, or hermeneutics, confirms that we must maintain the dialectic and move back from a criticism of ideology by utopia to what we may call a criticism of utopia by ideology. This revives the critical moment within interpretation, but now it is no longer criticism as a moment within ideology but the critique of the utopian—the open, the possible—by the drive for identity—the ideological. We must confront who we may be by who we are.[57] A hermeneutics like Ricoeur's, attuned to "the mythopoetic core of imagination," must face the challenge of the "hermeneutics of suspicion."

> [A] reference to Freud's "reality principle" and to its equivalents in Nietzsche and Marx—eternal return in the former, understood necessity in the latter—brings out the positive benefit of the ascesis required by a reductive and destructive

interpretation: confrontation with bare reality, the discipline of Ananke, of necessity.[58]

To some extent this is to reiterate that we are caught in a conflict of interpretations. Yet, as Ricoeur's statement on interpretation demonstrates, conflict is not simply opposition. We recall a comment quoted earlier, where Ricoeur says that he sees "the universe of discourse as a universe kept in motion by an interplay of attractions and repulsions that ceaselessly promote the interaction and intersection of domains whose organizing nuclei are off-centered in relation to one another . . ." (RM:302). If we may use the imagery of metaphor once more, we may say that the conflict of interpretations is a play of both similarity and difference and not merely difference. The hermeneutic circle is not a vicious circle, endlessly circling only around itself. Instead, differing interpretations react and respond to one another, and attempt to incorporate or subsume one another. As Ricoeur observes in the lectures, the task is to make the circle a spiral (lecture 18).

There is also another implication of Ricoeur's definition of interpretation. He defines interpretation not as a response merely to the metaphoric but as something that functions at the intersection of the metaphoric and the speculative. Ricoeur's hermeneutics cannot be defined merely as a theory of understanding—as can Gadamer's philosophical hermeneutics, for example—but as a theory of understanding that includes the dimension of explanation, the dimension of critical distance.[59] In this sense, we may say that Ricoeur's "detours" through the hermeneutics of suspicion—through psychoanalysis, through structuralism, and now through Marx—are the critical moments within, and not over against, his own hermeneutic theory. The conflict between the metaphoric and the speculative may persist, and yet interpretation attempts to encompass them both within an envisaged whole.[66]

Metaphor is living not only to the extent that it vivifies a constituted language. Metaphor is living by virtue of the fact that it introduces the spark of imagination into a "thinking more" at the conceptual level. This struggle to "think more," guided by the "vivifying principle," is the "soul" of interpretation. (RM:303)

Ricoeur summarizes his analysis of ideology and utopia by saying: "Ideology and utopia have ultimately to do with the character of human action as being mediated, structured and integrated by symbolic systems."[61] The conjunction of ideology and utopia typifies the social imagination, and

Ricoeur's argument is that "social imagination is constitutive of social reality itself" (lecture 1). Interpretation and practice cannot be divorced. The task of interpretation in its relation to this nexus is to "think more." It is a task that Ricoeur takes for his own and that his work unceasingly exemplifies.

A NOTE ON THE TEXT

As I mentioned above, Paul Ricoeur delivered the ideology and utopia lectures in the fall of 1975 at the University of Chicago. The lectures were taped in their entirety, and a verbatim transcript was created from these tapes. My editing of the lectures was based on these transcripts and on Ricoeur's own lecture notes, which he graciously provided to me. Ricoeur's lecture notes were available for all except for the first, introductory lecture, the two lectures on Marx's *The German Ideology,* and the lecture on Geertz. Each lecture was developed from approximately four tightly written pages of notes; Ricoeur wrote the notes in English. The aim in the editing was to incorporate the notes where they added to the presentation in lecture, whether as a point of clarification or as a section left out in lecture because of time limitations.

A few other changes were made in the process of transforming the lectures into a printed text. Several of the original lectures began or ended with discussion periods. All questions asked of Ricoeur have been deleted, but Ricoeur's responses have been integrated into the text. Introductory comments on Mannheim that originally appeared at the end of lecture 9 have been moved to the beginning of lecture 10. The quotations of Weber in lectures 11 and 12 were originally taken from the Parsons translation, *The Theory of Social and Economic Organization*. Because the two-volume edition of *Economy and Society* is both the translation Ricoeur prefers and the standard Weber translation currently, all Weber citations now refer to this text. Ricoeur's responses to discussion questions on Weber at the beginning of lecture 13 have been moved to lecture 12. Because this left lecture 13 rather abbreviated, and because the original division between lectures 13 and 14 was arbitrarily forced because of time constraints, the text recombines the original lectures 13 through 15 (all on Habermas) into two lectures in print. As a result, while there were 19 original lectures, the present volume has 18.

The published text preserves the lecture quality of Ricoeur's original presentation. Ricoeur's discursive style in lecture should make this work more accessible, and readers may find his commentary and other parenthetical remarks of interest. The lecture format has also been maintained to indicate the status of this text. Though he has reviewed the lectures extensively in preparation for their publication, Ricoeur has not reworked them. This text should therefore be distinguished from other works of Ricoeur's specifically written for publication.

All notes to the lectures are the editor's and have been discussed with Ricoeur; they have intentionally been kept to a minimum. Several notes contain direct quotations of Ricoeur, based on taped conversations with the editor. These conversations took place in May 1984 at the National Humanities Center, North Carolina, and in December 1984 at the University of Chicago. Full bibliographic citations to works mentioned in the text or in the notes appear at the end of the volume.

Lectures on Ideology and Utopia

I

Introductory Lecture

In these lectures I examine ideology and utopia. My purpose is to put these two phenomena, usually treated separately, within a single conceptual framework. The organizing hypothesis is that the very conjunction of these two opposite sides or complementary functions typifies what could be called social and cultural *imagination*.[1] Thus, most of the difficulties and ambiguities met in the field of a philosophy of imagination, which I am exploring now in a separate set of lectures,[2] will appear here but within a particular framework. In turn, my conviction, or at least my hypothesis, is that the dialectic between ideology and utopia may shed some light on the unsolved general question of imagination as a philosophical problem.

Inquiry into ideology and utopia reveals at the outset two traits shared by both phenomena. First, both are highly ambiguous. They each have a positive and a negative side, a constructive and a destructive role, a constitutive and a pathological dimension. A second common trait is that of the two sides of each, the pathological appears before the constitutive, requiring us to proceed backwards from the surface to the depths. Ideology, then, designates initially some distorting, dissimulating processes by which an individual or a group expresses its situation but without knowing or recognizing it. An ideology seems to express, for example, the class situation of an individual without the individual's awareness. Therefore the procedure of dissimulation does not merely express but reinforces this class perspective. As for the concept of utopia, it frequently has a pejorative reputation too. It is seen to represent a kind of social dream without concern for the real first steps necessary for movement in the direction of a new society. Often a utopian vision is treated as a kind of schizophrenic attitude toward society, both a way of escaping the logic of action through a construct outside history and a form of protection against any kind of verification by concrete action.

My hypothesis is that there is a positive as well as negative side to both ideology and utopia and that the polarity between these two sides of each term may be enlightened by exploring a similar polarity between the two terms. My claim is that this polarity both between ideology and utopia and within each of them may be ascribed to some structural traits of what I call cultural imagination. These two polarities encompass what are for me the main tensions in our study of ideology and utopia.

The polarity *between* ideology and utopia has scarcely been taken as a theme of research since Karl Mannheim's famous book *Ideology and Utopia*. This book, on which I shall rely heavily, was first published in 1929. I think that Mannheim is the one person, at least until very recently, to have tried to put ideology and utopia within a common framework, and he did this by considering them both as deviant attitudes toward reality. It is within their common aspect of noncongruence with actuality, of discrepancy, that they diverge.

Since Mannheim, most attention to these phenomena has focused on either ideology or utopia, but not both together. We have, on the one hand, a critique of ideology, mainly in Marxist and post-Marxist sociologists. I think particularly of the Frankfurt School, represented by Habermas, Karl-Otto Apel, and others. In contrast to this sociological critique of ideology, we find a history and sociology of utopia. And the latter field's attention to utopia has little connection with the former's attention to ideology. The separation between these two fields may be changing, however; there is at least some renewed interest in their connections.

The difficulty in connecting ideology and utopia is understandable, though, because they are presented in such different ways. Ideology is always a polemical concept. The ideological is never one's own position; it is always the stance of someone else, always *their* ideology. When sometimes characterized too loosely, an ideology is even said to be the fault of the other. People thus never say they are ideological themselves; the term is always directed against the other. Utopias, on the other hand, are advocated by their own authors, and they even constitute a specific literary genre. There are books which are called utopias, and they have a distinct literary status. Thus, the linguistic presence of ideology and utopia is not at all the same. Utopias are assumed by their authors, whereas ideologies are denied by theirs. This is why it is at first sight so difficult to put the two phenomena together. We must dig under their literary or semantic expressions in order to discover their functions[3] and then establish a correlation at this level.

In my own attention to this deeper, functional level of correlation, I take Karl Mannheim's suggestion of the concept of noncongruence as the starting point of my inquiry. I do so because the possibility of noncongruence, of discrepancy, in many ways already presupposes that individuals as well as collective entities are related to their own lives and to social reality not only in the mode of a participation without distance but precisely in the mode of noncongruence; all the figures of noncongruence must be part of our belonging to society. My claim is that this is true to such an extent that social imagination is *constitutive* of social reality. So the presupposition here is precisely that of a social imagination, of a cultural imagination, operating in both constructive and destructive ways, as both confirmation and contestation of the present situation. Therefore, it may be a fruitful hypothesis that the polarity of ideology and utopia has to do with the different figures of noncongruence typical of social imagination. And perhaps the positive side of the one and the positive side of the other are in the same relation of complementarity as the negative and pathological side of the one is to the negative and pathological side of the other.

But before trying to say anything more here about this overarching complementarity which is the horizon of my inquiry, I want briefly to present the two phenomena separately. I shall start from the pole of ideology and then consider the second pole, the opposite pole, of utopia.

The most prevalent conception of ideology in our Western tradition stems from the writings of Marx, or more precisely, from the writings of the young Marx: the *Critique of Hegel's "Philosophy of Right,"* the *Economic and Philosophic Manuscripts of 1844,* and *The German Ideology.* In the title and content of this last book, the concept of ideology comes to the forefront.

I mention only in passing an earlier, more positive use of the word "ideology," since it has disappeared from the philosophical scene. This usage derived from a school of thought in eighteenth-century French philosophy, people who called themselves *idéologues,* advocates of a theory of ideas. Theirs was a kind of semantic philosophy, saying philosophy has not to do with things, with reality, but merely with ideas. If this school of thought is of any remaining interest, it is perhaps because the pejorative use of the word "ideology" started precisely in reference to it. As opponents of the French Empire under Napoleon, this school's members were treated as *idéologues*. Therefore, the negative connotation of the term is traceable to Napoleon and was first applied to this group of philosophers. This perhaps warns us that there is always some Napoleon in us who designates the other as *idéologue*. Possibly there is always some claim to power in the accusation of ideology, but we shall return to that later. As for any relation between this French concept of *idéologie* and the pejorative use of ideology in the left Hegelians, the group from which Marx sprang, I do not see any direct transition, though others may have better information on this than I.

Turning to Marx himself, how is the term "ideology" introduced in his early writings? I shall return to this topic in following lectures with the support of texts, but let me offer now a short survey, a mapping, of the different uses of the word. It is interesting to see that the term is introduced in Marx by means of a metaphor borrowed from physical or physiological experience, the experience of the inverted image found in a camera or in the retina. From this metaphor of the inverted image, and from the physical experience behind the metaphor, we get the paradigm or model of distortion as reversal. This imagery, the paradigm of an inverted image of reality, is very important in situating our first concept of ideology. Ideology's first function is its production of an inverted image.

This still formal concept of ideology is completed by a specific description of some intellectual and spiritual activities which are described as inverted images of reality, as distortions through reversal. As we shall see, here Marx depends on a model put forth by Feuerbach, who had described and discussed religion precisely as an inverted reflection of reality. In Christianity, said Feuerbach, subject and predicate are reversed. While in reality human beings are subjects who have projected onto the divine their own attributes (their own human predicates), in fact the divine is perceived by human beings as a subject of which we become the predicate. (Notice all this is expressed by Feuerbach in Hegelian categories.) The typically Feuerbachian paradigm of inversion thus involves an exchange between subject and predicate, between human subject and divine predicate, that results in the substitution of a divine subject having human predicates for a human subject. Following Feuerbach, Marx assumes that religion is the paradigm, the first example, the primitive example, of such an inverted reflection of reality which turns everything upside down. Feuerbach and Marx react in opposition to Hegel's model, which turns things upside down; their effort is to set them right side up, on their feet. The image of reversal is striking, and it is the generating image of Marx's concept of ideology. Enlarging the concept borrowed from Feuerbach of religion as inversion between subject and predicate, the young Marx extends to the whole realm of ideas this paradigmatic functioning.

Perhaps here the French concept of *idéologie* can be recaptured within a post-Hegelian framework. When separated from the process of life, the process of common work, ideas tend to appear as an autonomous reality; this leads to *ideal*ism as *ideol*ogy. A semantic continuity exists between the claim that ideas constitute a realm of their own autonomous reality and the claim that ideas provide guides or models or paradigms for construing experience. Therefore it is not only religion but philosophy as idealism that appears as the model of ideology. (As a cautionary note, we should point out that the picture of German idealism presented here—that is, the claim that reality proceeds from thought—is more accurate as a description of a popular understanding of idealism than of the supposed locus of this idealism, Hegelian philosophy itself. Hegelian philosophy emphasized that the rationality of the real is known through its appearance in history, and this is contrary to any Platonic reconstruction of reality according to ideal models. Hegel's philosophy is much more neo-Aristotelian than neo-Platonic.) In any case, the popular interpretation of idealism prevailed in the culture of Marx's time, and as a result not only religion but idealism, as a kind of religion for lay people, was elevated to the function of ideology.

The negative connotation of ideology is fundamental because ideology, according to this first model, appears as the general device by which the process of real life is obscured. I insist, therefore, that the main opposition in Marx at this point is not between science and ideology, as it becomes later, but between reality and ideology. The conceptual alternative to ideology for the young Marx is not science but reality, reality as praxis. People do things, and then they imagine what they are doing in a kind of cloudy realm. Thus we say first there is a social reality in which people fight to earn their living, and so on, and this is real reality, as praxis. This reality is then represented in the heaven of ideas, but it is falsely represented as having a meaning autonomous to this realm, as making sense on the basis of things which can be thought and not only done or lived. The claim against ideology therefore comes from a kind of realism of life, a realism of practical life for which praxis is the alternate concept to ideology. Marx's system is materialist precisely in its insistence that the materiality of praxis precedes the ideality of ideas. The critique of ideology in Marx proceeds from the claim that philosophy has inverted the real succession, the real genetic order, and the task is to put things back in their real order. The task is a reversal of a reversal.

Starting from this first concept of ideology, in which I insist that ideology is not opposed to science but to praxis, the second stage of the Marxist concept arises after Marxism has been developed in the form of a theory and even a system. This stage comes into view in *Capital* and subsequent Marxist writings, especially the work of Engels. Here Marxism itself appears as a body of scientific knowledge. An interesting transformation of the concept of ideology follows from this development. Ideology now receives its meaning from its opposition to science, with science identified as the body of knowledge and *Capital* as its paradigm. Thus, ideology implies not only religion in Feuerbach's sense or the philosophy of German idealism as seen by the young Marx, but includes all prescientific approaches to social life. Ideology becomes identical to all that is prescientific in our own approach to social reality.

At this point the concept of ideology engulfs that of utopia. All utopias—and particularly the socialist utopias of the nineteenth century, those of Saint-Simon, Fourier, Cabet, Proudhon, and so on—are treated by Marxism as ideologies. As we shall see, Engels radically opposes *scientific* socialism to *utopian* socialism. In this approach to ideology, therefore, a utopia is ideological because of its opposition to science. Utopia is ideological to the extent that it is nonscientific, prescientific, and even counterscientific.

Another development in this Marxist concept of ideology arises because of the meaning given to science by later Marxists and post-Marxists. Their concept of science can be divided into two main strands. The first originates in the Frankfurt School and involves the attempt to develop science in the Kantian or Fichtean sense of a critique such that the study of ideology is linked to a project of liberation. This connection between a project of liberation and a scientific approach is directed against the treatment of social reality found in any positivistic sociology that merely describes. Here the concept of an ideology-critique presupposes a stand taken against sociology as merely an empirical science. The empirical science of sociology is itself treated as a kind of ideology of the liberal, capitalistic system, as developing a purely descriptive sociology so as not to put into question its own presuppositions. It seems that step by step everything becomes ideological.

What is most interesting, I think, in this German school represented by Horkheimer, Adorno, Habermas, and so on is the attempt to link the critical process of *Ideologiekritik* to psychoanalysis. The Frankfurt School claims that the project of liberation which its sociological critique offers for society parallels what psychoanalysis achieves for the individual. A measure of exchange of conceptual frameworks occurs between sociology and psychoanalysis. This is typical of the German school.

A second concept of science developed by Marxism features a conjunction not with psychoanalysis, which takes care of the individual, but with structuralism, which brackets any reference to subjectivity. The kind of structuralist Marxism developed mainly in France by Louis Althusser (on whom we shall dwell in some detail) tends to put all humanistic claims on the side of ideology. The claim of the subject to be the one who makes sense of reality *(Sinngebung)* is precisely the basic illusion, Althusser contends. Althusser is arguing against the claim of the subject in the idealistic version of phenomenology, which is typified by Husserl's *Cartesian Meditations.* The comparison is to Marx's critique of capitalism, where he did not attack the capitalists but analyzed the structure of capital itself. For Althusser, therefore, the writings of the young Marx must not be considered; it is rather the mature Marx who presents the main notion of ideology. The young Marx is still ideological, since he defends the claim of the subject as individual person, as individual worker. Althusser judges the concept of alienation in the young Marx as the typically ideological concept of pre-Marxism. Thus, all the work of the young Marx is treated as ideological. According to Althusser, *la coupure,* the break, the dividing line between what is ideological and what is scientific, must be drawn within the work of Marx itself. The concept of ideology is extended so far as to include a portion of Marx's own work.

So we see the strange result of this continuing extension of the concept of ideology. Starting from religion for Feuerbach, the concept of ideology progressively covers German idealism, prescientific sociology, objectivist psychology and sociology in their positivistic forms, and then all the humanistic claims and complaints of "emotional" Marxism. The implication seems to be that everything is ideological, although this is not exactly the pure doctrine of Marxism! I shall discuss some late articles by Althusser which present finally a kind of apology for ideology. Since very few people live their lives on the basis of a scientific system, particularly if we reduce the scientific system only to what is said in *Capital,* then we may say that everyone lives on the basis of an ideology. The very extension of the concept of ideology acts as a progressive legitimation and justification of the concept itself.

My own attempt, as perhaps has already been anticipated, is not to deny the legitimacy of the Marxist concept of ideology, but to relate it to some of the less negative functions of ideology. We must integrate the concept of ideology as distortion into a framework that recognizes the symbolic structure of social life. Unless social life has a symbolic structure, there is no way to understand how we live, do things, and project these activities in ideas, no way to understand how reality can become an idea or how real life can produce illusions; these would all be simply mystical and incomprehensible events. This symbolic structure can be perverted, precisely by class interests and so on as Marx has shown, but if there were not a symbolic function already at work in the most primitive kind of action, I could not understand, for my part, how reality could produce shadows of this kind. This is why I am seeking a function of ideology more radical than the distorting, dissimulating function. The distorting function covers only a small surface of the social imagination, in just the same way that hallucinations or illusions constitute only a part of our imaginative activity in general.

One way to prepare this more radical extension is to consider what some writers in the United States have called Mannheim's paradox. Mannheim's paradox results from his observation of the development of the Marxist concept of ideology. The paradox is the nonapplicability of the concept of ideology to itself. In other words, if everything that we say is bias, if everything we say represents interests that we do not know, how can we have a theory of ideology which is not itself ideological? The reflexivity of the concept of ideology on itself provides the paradox.

Importantly, this paradox is not at all a mere intellectual game; Mannheim himself lived and felt the paradox most acutely. As for myself, I consider Mannheim a model of intellectual integrity for the way he confronted this problem. He began with the Marxist concept of ideology and said, but if it is true, then what I am doing is ideology too, the ideology of the intellectual or the ideology of the liberal class, something which develops the kind of sociology I am now engaged in. The extension of Marx's concept of ideology itself provides the paradox of the reflexivity of the concept according to which the theory becomes a part of its own referent. To be absorbed, to be swallowed by its own referent, is perhaps the fate of the concept of ideology.

We should note that this extension, this generalization, is not linked merely to the internal history of Marxism but has parallels in what the Marxists call bourgeois sociology, particularly American sociology. Take, for example, Talcott Parsons in his article "An Approach to the Sociology of Knowledge," or in his book *The Social System;* or read Edward Shils's key essay, "Ideology and Civility."[4] Parsons and Shils argue for a strain theory, according to which the function of a social system is to correct sociopsychological disequilibrium. According to this hypothesis, every theory is part of the system of strain which it describes. Just as in the case of Marxist theory, therefore, the concept of strain, which formerly dominated American sociology, also comes to swallow its own exponents.

These excesses in theory are precisely what nourish the paradox discerned by Mannheim, a paradox Mannheim himself reached by a mere epistemological extension of Marxism. Put in general epistemological terms, the paradox of Mannheim may be expressed in the following ways: what is the epistemological status of discourse about ideology if all discourse is ideological? How can this discourse escape its own exposition, its own description? If sociopolitical thought itself is entwined with the life situation of the thinker, does not the concept of ideology have to be absored into its own referent? Mannheim himself, as we shall see later, fought for a nonevaluative concept of ideology, but he ended with an ethical and epistemological relativism.[5] Mannheim claims to present the truth about ideology, and yet he leaves us with a difficult paradox. He destroys the dogmatism of theory by establishing its relativistic implications (as situationally bound), but he fails to apply this relativity self-referentially to his own theory. Mannheim's claim to truth about ideology is itself relative. This is the difficult paradox that we are forced to confront.

One way to contend with this paradox, however, may be to question the premises on which it is based. Perhaps the problem of Mannheim's paradox lies in its epistemological extension of a Marxism founded upon the contrast between ideology and science. If the basis of sociopolitical thought is grounded elsewhere, perhaps we can extricate ourselves from this paradox of Mannheim's. I wonder, then, whether we need not set aside the concept of ideology as opposed to science and return to what may be the most primitive concept of ideology, that opposed to praxis. This will be my own line of analysis, to establish that the opposition between ideology and science is secondary in comparison to the more fundamental opposition between ideology and real social life, between ideology and praxis. In fact, I want to claim not only that the latter relation is prior to the former, but that the very nature of the ideology-praxis relationship must be recast. Most basic to the ideology-praxis contrast is not opposition; what is most fundamental is *not* the distortion or dissimulation of praxis by ideology. Rather, most basic is an inner *connection* between the two terms.

I anticipated these remarks earlier in considering the concrete example of people living in situations of class conflicts. How can people live these conflicts—about work, property, money, and so on—if they do not already possess some symbolic systems to help them interpret the conflicts? Is not the process of interpretation so primitive that in fact it is *constitutive* of the dimension of praxis? If social reality did not already have a social dimension, and therefore, if ideology, in a less polemical or less negatively evaluative sense, were not constitutive of social existence but merely distorting and dissimulating, then the process of distortion could not start. The process of distortion is grafted onto a symbolic function. Only because the structure of human social life is already symbolic can it be distorted. If it were not symbolic from the start, it could not be distorted. The possibility of distortion is a possibility opened up only by this function.

What kind of function can precede distortion? On this question I must say I am very impressed with an essay by Clifford Geertz, "Ideology as a Cultural System," which appears in his book, *The Interpretation of Cultures.* I first read this essay after having written on ideology myself,[6] and I am thus greatly interested in the conjunction of our thought. Geertz claims that Marxist and non-Marxist sociologists have in common an attention only to the determinants of ideology, that is, to what causes and promotes it. What these sociologists avoid asking, however, is how ideology operates. They do not ask how ideology functions, they do not question how a social interest, for example, can be "expressed" in a thought, an image, or a conception of life. The deciphering of whatever strange alchemy there may be in the transformation of an interest into an idea is for Geertz, then, the problem evaded or overlooked by Marxists and non-Marxists alike. Geertz's explicit comments about one of these approaches may be applied to both: while the Marxist theory of class struggle and the American conception of strain may be diagnostically convincing, functionally they are not (207).[7] I think Geertz's distinction is accurate. These sociologies may offer good diagnoses of social illness. But the question of function, that is, how an illness really works, is finally the most important issue. These theories fail, says Geertz, because they have overlooked "the autonomous process of symbolic formulation" (207). Again the question to be raised, therefore, is how can an idea arise from praxis if praxis does not immediately have a symbolic dimension?

As I shall discuss more fully in a subsequent lecture, Geertz himself attempts to address this problem by introducing the conceptual framework of rhetoric within the sociology of culture or, as the German tradition would put it, the sociology of knowledge. He thinks that what is lacking in the sociology of culture is a significant appreciation of the rhetoric of figures, that is to say, the elements of "style"—metaphors, analogies, ironies, ambiguities, puns, paradoxes, hyperboles (209)—which are at work in society just as much as in literary texts. Geertz's own aim is to transfer some of the important insights achieved in the field of literary criticism to the field of the sociology of culture. Perhaps only by attention to the cultural process of symbolic formulation may we avoid giving ourselves over to the pejorative description of ideology merely as "bias, oversimplification, emotive language, and adaption to public prejudice," descriptions all taken not from Marxists but from American sociologists.[8]

The blindness of both Marxists and non-Marxists to what precedes the distorting aspects of ideology is a blindness to what Geertz calls "symbolic action" (208). Geertz borrows this expression from Kenneth Burke,[9] and as we have seen, it is not by chance that the expression comes from literary criticism and is then applied to social action. The concept of symbolic action is notable because it emphasizes description of social processes more by tropes—stylistic figures—than by labels. Geertz warns that if we do not master the rhetoric of public discourse, then we cannot articulate the expressive power and the rhetorical force of social symbols.

Similar understandings have been advanced in other fields, for example, in the theory of models (which I studied earlier within the framework of another set of lectures).[10] In a basic sense these developments all have the same perspective, namely that we cannot approach perception without also projecting a network of patterns, a network, Geertz would say, of templates or blueprints (216) through which we articulate our experience. We have to articulate our social experience in the same way that we have to articulate our perceptual experience. Just as models in scientific language allow us to see how things look, allow us to see things *as* this or that, in the same way our social templates articulate our social roles, articulate our position in society *as* this or that. And perhaps it is not possible to go behind or below this primitive structuration. The very flexibility of our biological existence makes necessary another kind of informational system, the cultural system. Because we have no genetic system of information for human behavior, we need a cultural system. No culture exists without such a system. The hypothesis, therefore, is that where human beings exist, a nonsymbolic mode of existence, and even less, a nonsymbolic kind of action, can no longer obtain. Action is immediately ruled by cultural patterns which provide templates or blueprints for the organization of social and psychological processes, perhaps just as genetic codes—I am not certain[11]—provide such templates for the organization of organic processes (216). In the same way that our experience of the natural world requires a mapping, a mapping is also necessary for our experience of social reality.

Our attention to the functioning of ideology at this most basic and symbolic level demonstrates the real constitutive role ideology has in social existence. Another step remains, however, in our investigation of the nature of ideology. We have followed the Marxist concept of ideology to the paradox of Mannheim and have then tried to extricate ourselves from the paradox by returning to a more primitive function of ideology. We still need to determine, however, the connecting link between the Marxist concept of ideology as distortion and the integrative concept of ideology found in Geertz. How is it possible that ideology plays these two roles, the very primitive role of integration of a community and the role of distortion of thought by interests?

I wonder whether the turning point is, as Max Weber has suggested, the use of authority in a given community. We may agree with Geertz, at least as a hypothesis, that the organic processes of life are ruled by some genetic systems (216). As we have seen, however, the flexibility of our biological existence makes necessary a cultural system to help organize our social processes. The guidance of the genetic system is most lacking and the need for the cultural system consequently most dramatic precisely at the point where the social order raises the problem of the legitimation of the existing system of leadership. The legitimation of a leadership confronts us with the problem of authority, domination, and power, the problem of the hierarchization of social life. Ideology has a most significant role here. While it may be diffused when considered merely as integrative, its place in social life is marked by a special concentration. This privileged place of ideological thinking occurs in politics; there the questions of legitimation arise. Ideology's role is to make possible an autonomous politics by providing the needed authoritative concepts that make it meaningful (218).

In analyzing this question of the legitimation of authority, I use the work of Max Weber. No other sociologist has meditated to such a degree on the problem of authority. Weber's own discussion focuses on the concept of *Herrschaft*. The concept has been translated into English as both authority and domination, and its cogency stems precisely from the fact that it means the pair. In a given group, says Weber, as soon as a differentiation appears between a governing body and the rest of the group, the governing body has both the power of leadership and the power to implement order by means of force. (Weber typifies the latter in particular as the essential attribute of the state.) Ideology enters here because no system of leadership, even the most brutal, rules only by force, by domination. Every system of leadership summons not only our physical submission but also our consent and cooperation. Every system of leadership wants its rule to rest not merely on domination, then; it also wants its power to be granted because its authority is legitimate. It is ideology's role to legitimate this authority. More exactly, while ideology serves, as I have already said, as the code of interpretation that secures integration, it does so by justifying the present system of authority.

Ideology's role as a legitimating force persists because, as Weber has shown, no absolutely rational system of legitimacy exists. This is true even of those systems claiming to have broken completely with both the authority of tradition and that of any charismatic leader. Possibly no system of authority can break completely with such primitive and archaic figures of authority. Even the most bureaucratized system of authority constitutes some code to satisfy our belief in its legitimacy. In a later lecture, I shall give specific examples of the way Weber describes the typology of authority according to the system of legitimacy each type describes.

To maintain that no totally rational system of authority exists is not merely historical judgment or prediction, however. The very structure of legitimation itself ensures the necessary role of ideology. Ideology must bridge the tension that characterizes the legitimation process, a tension between the claim to legitimacy made by the authority and the belief in this legitimacy offered by the citizenry. The tension occurs because while the citizenry's belief and the authority's claim should correspond at the same level, the equivalence of belief with claim is never totally actual but rather always more or less a cultural fabrication. Thus, there is always more in the authority's claim to legitimacy than in the beliefs actually held by the group members.

This discrepancy between claim and belief may mark the real source of what Marx called surplus-value *(Mehrwert)*. Surplus-value is not necessarily intrinsic to the structure of production, but it is necessary to the structure of power. In socialist systems, for example, although no private appropriation of the means of production is permitted, surplus-value still exists because of the structure of power. This structure of power poses the same question as all others, a question of belief. Believe in me, the political leader exhorts. The difference between the claim made and the belief offered signifies the surplus-value common to all structures of power. In its claim to legitimacy, every authority asks for more than what its members offer in terms of belief or creed. Whatever role surplus-value may have in production is not at all denied; the point is rather to expand the notion of surplus-value and demonstrate that its most persisting location may be in the structure of power.

The problem we are facing descends to us from Hobbes: what is the rationality and irrationality of the social contract; what do we give and what do we receive? In this exchange, the system of justification, of legitimation, plays a continuing ideological role. The problem of the legitimation of authority places us at the turning point between a neutral concept of integration and a political concept of distortion. The degradation, the alteration, and the diseases of ideology may originate in our relation to the existing system of authority in our society. Ideology moves beyond mere integration to distortion and pathology as it tries to bridge the tension between authority and domination. Ideology tries to secure integration between legitimacy claim and belief, but it does so by justifying the existing system of authority as it is. Weber's analysis of the legitimation of authority reveals a third, mediating role for ideology. The legitimation function of ideology is the connecting link between the Marxist concept of ideology as distortion and the integrative concept of ideology found in Geertz.

This concludes the summary of the problems of ideology to be explored in the balance of my lectures. The lectures on ideology proceed in the following order.[12] My starting point is the role of ideology as distortion as expressed in the writings of the young Marx. This inquiry is shaped by sections from the *Critique of Hegel's "Philosophy of Right,"* the *Economic and Philosophic Manuscripts,* and *The German Ideology.* I then explore the writings of the contemporary French Marxist Louis Althusser; my principal texts are his books *For Marx* and *Lenin and Philosophy.* Attention to a portion of Karl Mannheim's *Ideology and Utopia* follows, although part of our investigation of Mannheim's book awaits the discussion of utopia. In turning to Max Weber and parts of his *Economy and Society,* my chief consideration is the role of ideology in the legitimation of systems of authority. Discussion of Jürgen Habermas, mainly through readings in *Knowledge and Human Interests,* follows Weber. The ideology section of the lectures ends with an analysis of ideology's integrative function. Here I rely on Geertz, principally his article "Ideology as a Cultural System," and also offer some comments of my own.

In shifting from ideology to utopia,[13] I want in this first lecture only to sketch the landscape of utopia's conceptual framework. As I said at the beginning of this lecture, there seems to be no transition from ideology to utopia. An exception may be the treatment of utopia afforded by a scientific sociology, particularly the orthodox Marxist version. Because it is nonscientific, utopia is characterized by Marxists as itself ideological. This reduction is atypical, however. When ideology and utopia are considered phenomenologically, that is, when a descriptive approach takes into account the meaningfulness of what is presented, then ideology and utopia belong to two distinct semantic genres.

Utopia in particular distinguishes itself by being a declared genre. Perhaps this is a good place to commence our comparison of ideology and utopia: works exist which call themselves utopias while no author claims that his or her work is an ideology. Thomas More coined the word "utopia" as a title for his famous book written in 1516. As we know, the word means what is nowhere; it is the island which is nowhere, the place which exists in no real place. In its very self-description, therefore, the utopia knows itself as a utopia and claims to be a utopia. The utopia is a very personal and idiosyncratic work, the distinctive creation of its author. In contrast, no proper name is affixed to an ideology as its author. Any name joined to an ideology is anonymous; its subject is simply *das Man,* the amorphous "they."

Nevertheless, I wonder whether we cannot structure the problem of utopia exactly as we structured the problem of ideology. That is to say, can we not start from a quasi-pathological concept of utopia and proceed downward to some function comparable precisely to the integrative function of ideology? To my mind, this function is achieved exactly by the notion of the nowhere. Perhaps a fundamental structure of the reflexivity we may apply to our social roles is the ability to conceive of an empty place from which to look at ourselves.

To unearth this functional structure of utopia, however, we must go beyond or below the specific contents of particular utopias. Utopias speak to so many divergent topics—the status of the family, the consumption of goods, the appropriation of things, the organization of public life, the role of religion, and so on—that it is extremely difficult to fit them within a simple framework. In fact, if we consider utopias according to their contents, we even find opposing utopias. Concerning the family, for example, some utopias legitimate all kinds of sexual community, while others endorse monasticism. With regard to consumption, some utopias advocate asceticism, while others promote a more sumptuous lifestyle. So we cannot define utopias commonly by their concepts. In the absence of utopia's thematic unity, we must seek unity in its function.

I thus propose to move beyond the thematic contents of utopia to its functional structure. I suggest that we start from the kernel idea of the nowhere, implied by the word "utopia" itself and by the descriptions of Thomas More: a place which exists in no real place, a ghost city; a river with no water; a prince with no people, and so on. What must be emphasized is the benefit of this special extraterritoriality. From this "no place" an exterior glance is cast on our reality, which suddenly looks strange, nothing more being taken for granted. The field of the possible is now open beyond that of the actual; it is a field, therefore, for alternative ways of living.

This development of new, alternative perspectives defines utopia's most basic function. May we not say then that imagination itself—through its utopian function—has a *constitutive* role in helping us *rethink* the nature of our social life? Is not utopia—this leap outside—the way in which we radically rethink what is family, what is consumption, what is authority, what is religion, and so on? Does not the fantasy of an alternative society and its exteriorization "nowhere" work as one of the most formidable contestations of what is? If I were to compare this structure of utopia with a theme in the philosophy of imagination, which I am now studying elsewhere,[14] I would say it is like Husserl's imaginative variations concerning an essence. Utopia introduces imaginative variations on the topics of society, power, government, family, religion. The kind of neutralization that constitutes imagination as fiction is at work in utopia. Thus I propose that utopia, taken at this radical level, as the function of the nowhere in the constitution of social or symbolic action, is the counterpart of our first concept of ideology. There is no social integration without social subversion, we may say. The reflexivity of the process of integration occurs by means of the process of subversion. The nowhere puts the cultural system at a distance; we see our cultural system from the outside precisely thanks to this nowhere.

What confirms this hypothesis that the most radical function of utopia is inseparable from the most radical function of ideology is that the turning point of both is in fact at the same place, that is to say, in the problem of authority. If every ideology tends finally to legitimate a system of authority, does not every utopia, the moment of the other, attempt to come to grips with the problem of power itself? What is ultimately at stake in utopia is not so much consumption, family, or religion but the use of power in all these institutions. Is it not because a credibility gap exists in all systems of legitimation, all authority, that a place for utopia exists too? In other words, is it not the function of utopia to expose the credibility gap wherein all systems of authority exceed, as I tried to say earlier, both our confidence in them and our belief in their legitimacy? Quite possibly, then, the turning point of ideology from its integrative to its distorting function is also the turning point of the utopian system. So I am very attentive to the function of power, authority, and domination in utopia; I question who has power in a given utopia and how the problem of power is subverted by the utopia.

Though a more uncertain hypothesis, it is also quite possible that ideology and utopia become pathological at the same point, in the sense that the pathology of ideology is dissimulation whereas the pathology of utopia is escape. The nowhere of utopia may become a pretext for escape, a way of fleeing the contradictions and ambiguity both of the use of power and of the assumption of authority in a given situation. This escapism of utopia belongs to a logic of all or nothing. No connecting point exists between the "here" of social reality and the "elsewhere" of the utopia. This disjunction allows the utopia to avoid any obligation to come to grips with the real difficulties of a given society. All the regressive trends denounced so often in utopian thinkers—such as the nostalgia for the past, for some paradise lost—proceed from this initial deviation of the nowhere in relation to the here and now. So my problematic, which I do not want to anticipate any further, is: does not the eccentric function of imagination as the possiblity of the nowhere imply all the paradoxes of utopia; further, is not this eccentricity of the utopian imagination at the same time the cure of the pathology of ideological thinking, which has its blindness and narrowness precisely in its inability to conceive of a nowhere?

The next lecture begins with the young Marx and discusses passages from the *Critique of Hegel's "Philosophy of Right"* and the *Economic and Philosophic Manuscripts*. My interest as we enter the section of lectures on ideology is in exploring the opposition between ideology and praxis in the young Marx that precedes the opposition prevailing in later Marxism between ideology and science.

Part I

IDEOLOGY

2

Marx: The *Critique of Hegel* and the *Manuscripts*

In this lecture I want to start my discussion of the first concept of ideology in the young Marx. I shall develop the general theme that the first concept of ideology in Marx is determined not by its opposition to science, as will be the case in the later development of Marxist doctrine, but by its opposition to *reality*. (We might say an opposition to Marxist science is actually impossible at this time, because during the 1843–44 period we are discussing, Marxist science does not yet even exist!) In his early works, Marx's task is to determine what is the real. This determination will affect the concept of ideology, since ideology is all that is not this reality. The development in these early works encompasses the difficult progression, completed only in *The German Ideology,* toward the identification between *reality* and human *praxis*. So Marx's early writings are a movement toward this identification between reality and praxis and, consequently, toward the constitution of the opposition between praxis and ideology.

A principal element in the development of the first Marxist concept of ideology is its extrication from a Feuerbachian anthropology. Feuerbach centered his anthropology around the concept of *Gattungswesen,* which has been translated into English as "generic essence" or "species being." Marx's struggle to extricate himself from the Feuerbachian anthropology is most significant, because as long as the concept of human reality as *Gattungswesen,* as species being, has not been reduced to empirical praxis, the concept of ideology itself will not have received its appropriate contrary and consequently its own appropriate content. The writings of the early Marx may be seen, then, as a progressive reduction of the Hegelian "Spirit" *(Geist)* through the Feuerbachian concept of species being to the properly

Marxist concept of praxis. Thus we have already a good example of what Marx will consider an ideological critique of a concept: the critique is a reduction, a reduction of the concept to its basis, to its concrete basis of existence. The question of what is this concrete basis is the problem at stake in these early works. Ideology will appear as the shadow world that praxis both expels from its sphere and at the same time generates from within itself. As we shall see, this is the difficulty of the Marxist concept of ideology: on the one hand ideology is excluded from the concrete basis of existence, but on the other hand it is somehow ineluctably generated from this basis at the same time.

In my initial lectures on Marx, I shall survey the progression in Marx's texts that leads to the development of his concept of ideology, a concept itself not reached until *The German Ideology.* The first important writing for this inquiry is the *Critique of Hegel's "Philosophy of Right,"* written in 1843. This manuscript has had a very strange history, becoming known only in 1922 and first published only in 1927. The excellent English translation we use is by Joseph O'Malley, who offers a very good introduction to the work also. The text as a whole is a discussion of paragraphs 261–313 of Hegel's *Philosophy of Right.*

In addition to this originally unpublished manuscript, Marx wrote an important introduction to a proposed revision of the *Critique,* an essay actually published during Marx's lifetime. This essay appeared in 1844 in the *Deutsch-französische Jahrbücher* under the title, "A Contribution to the Critique of Hegel's 'Philosophy of Right'—Introduction." The book edited by O'Malley includes both this proposed introduction and the longer, originally unpublished essay. The intended introduction was well known and is one of the most famous of Marx's writings. In fact I shall start from this introduction and then return to the text itself, because it gives us the clue to the philosophical program of Marx.

Marx begins this introduction with the famous sentence: "For Germany the critique of religion is essentially completed; and the critique of religion is the prerequisite of every critique" (131). In saying this, Marx is supported by previous work—the work of Feuerbach. In claiming that "the critique of religion is essentially completed," Marx is referring directly to Feuerbach. So in Marx the critique of religion is something imported. He considers this critique complete and something to which he need not return. What is even more important, though, is the second part of the first sentence: "the critique of religion is the prerequisite of every critique."

This striking declaration provides us with a most appropriate starting point. Here we have the model for any critique of ideology. For Feuerbach religion is the paradigm of all reversal, and as I mentioned in my introductory lecture, the first concept of ideology in Marx is constituted precisely according to this model. Something has been inverted in human consciousness, and we have to invert the inversion; this is the procedure of the critique.

This paradigm of inverted consciousness is clearly evident on the first page of the introduction:

> The foundation of irreligious criticism is this: man makes religion; religion does not make man. Religion is, in fact, the self-consciousness and self-esteem of man who has either not yet gained himself or has lost himself again. But man is no abstract being squatting outside the world. Man is the world of man, the state, society. This state, this society, produce religion, which is an inverted world consciousness. . . .

I emphasize those last few words. While the word "ideology" is not yet pronounced and will not be used by Marx before *The German Ideology,* the model of reasoning is already present. Marx continues:

> This state, this society, produce religion, which is an inverted world consciousness, because they are an inverted world. Religion is the general theory of this world, its encyclopedic compendium, its logic in popular form, its spiritualistic *point d'honneur,* its enthusiasm, its moral sanction, its solemn complement, its universal basis of consolation and justification. It is the fantastic realization of the human being. . . .

Notice this idea of the "fantastic realization." But of what? —"The human being." So at this stage Marx has a very abstract concept of human reality.

> [Religion] is the fantastic realization of the human being because the human being has attained no true reality. Thus, the struggle against religion is indirectly the struggle against that world of which religion is the spiritual aroma. (131)

This text is typically Feuerbachian. It is not yet Marxist except for its practical conclusion: a "call to abandon a condition which requires illusions." So already there is some displacement toward the social conditions which really make human reality possible.

I think we must insist on the vocabulary, the semantic gradients of this text which says: "man *makes* religion." Marx already has the model of a praxis that has been inverted. Yet while Marx transfers the problem from the sphere of representation to that of production, at this point production is still a matter of "self-consciousness," "world consciousness," "self-esteem," which all imply an idealistic concept of consciousness, a remnant of the Hegelian Spirit. Nevertheless, at this stage in Marx's work consciousness is the appropriate locus, because it is there, Marx says, that the fabulous production, the "fantastic realization of the human being," takes place.

Thus within this framework Marx has already raised his major oppositions, using a type of thought and even a rhetoric that is striking. Notice the abrupt antitheses in the text between "man . . . [as] abstract being" and "man . . . [as] the world of man, the state, society," between "fantastic realization" and "true reality." These antitheses are strengthened a few lines later in the following famous image: "Criticism has plucked the imaginary flowers from the chain, not so that man shall bear the chain without fantasy or consolation, but so that he shall cast off the chain and gather the living flower" (131–32). The living flower of real life is juxtaposed to the illusory flowers, the merely decorative function, of religious symbols.

Sometimes this reversal is even presented in Kantian terms, as a kind of continuance, a development, of the Copernican revolution. For example, Marx says, "The critique of religion disillusions man so that he will think, act, and fashion his reality as a man who has lost his illusions and regained his reason, so that he will revolve about himself as his own true sun." Reason is still an important counterpoint to fantasy; the invocation of reason is an appeal to rationalism. This is typically Kantian in its language. The quotation concludes, "Religion is only the illusory sun about which man revolves so long as he does not revolve about himself" (132). Human individuals have to center themselves once more around themselves. Marx's orientation is still in the shadow of German idealism, which put human consciousness and autonomy at the top of the universe. In fact, the ultimate stage of this recovery of the autonomy and self-assertion of consciousness is a kind of atheism. It is an idealistic atheism, since human self-consciousness is the center of this reassertion of human being. We may say that a humanistic anthropology is being expressed. The concept of human being presented here remains abstract in a way *The German Ideology* will call ideological.

This, then, is Marx's starting point, given to him by Feuerbach. Marx takes up a problem that he was not the first to identify, but he understands his particular task as the extension of this critique from religion to law and politics.

> It is the task of history, therefore [i.e., what Marx finds to be his own task after Feuerbach], once the other-world of truth has vanished, to establish the truth of this world. It is above all the task of philosophy, which is in the service of history, to unmask human self-alienation in its secular forms, once its sacred form has been unmasked. Thus, the critique of heaven is transformed into the critique of the earth, the critique of religion into the critique of law, the critique of law into the critique of politics. (132)

Why, though, this shift from the critique of theology to the critique of politics, from heaven to earth? Because for Marx, German politics was anachronistic, especially in comparison with France and England, where bourgeois revolutions had already developed. In Germany's political situation, where its people did not change and seemingly could not change their politics and economics, philosophy became the retreat in which the Germans did their reflective work. They elaborated a philosophy which was both the expression of this anachronism and its reinforcement.

> Just as ancient peoples lived their past history in their imagination, in mythology [we see the word imagination which interests me here], so we Germans have lived our future history in thought, in philosophy. We are philosophical contemporaries of the present day without being its historical contemporaries. German philosophy is the ideal prolongation of German history. (135)

Notice the phrase "ideal prolongation." Again, while the world "ideology" is not uttered, the elements of the concept are already gathered.

Marx applies this idea of the "ideal prolongation" to the relations of Germans to their history. It is the same structure that Feuerbach applied to Christianity in its relation to the Western world as a whole. The kernel of Germany's anachronistic philosophy, says Marx, is the philosophy of the state, political philosophy, in particular the political philosophy of Hegel. This political philosophy is the source of nourishment for what Marx called Germany's "dream history": "Thus, the German nation is obliged to connect its dream history with its present circumstances, and subject to criticism not only these circumstances but also their abstract continuation" (136). While Marx's philosophical vocabulary may be loose in equating such terms as "mythology," "dream history," "imagination," and "ideal prolongation," these terms do reinforce one another. They are set out not because of their differences, their distinctions, but because of their accumulative power. These phrases have an unmistakable accumulative power.

What is under attack in Marx's political philosophy is a speculative philosophy of right in which we proceed from the idea of the state toward its components. For Marx this will be the model of ideological thinking, a movement from the idea to reality and not from reality toward the idea.

> If it was only in Germany that the speculative philosophy of right was possible—this abstract and extravagant thought about the modern state, whose reality remains in another world (even though this is just across the Rhine) [Marx is speaking here of the development of the French Revolution]—the German thought-version *(Gedankenbild* [the world view]) of the modern state, on the other hand, which abstracts from actual man [this is ideology], was only possible because and in so far as the modern state itself abstracts from actual man, or satisfies the whole man only in an imaginary way. In politics the Germans have thought what other nations have done. Germany was their theoretical conscience. (137)

Marx's statement is a very good approach to the concept of ideology, since the abstraction of the state in a speculative philosophy of right expresses the fact that the existing state is itself an abstraction from life. A kind of historical ideology is at work, something the philosopher merely reflects in a theory of the state. Once again the oppositions are clarified: "abstract thought" versus "reality"; "thought-version" *(Gedankenbild)* versus "actual man"; imaginary abstraction versus what Marx calls the "actual man" or the "whole man." As we shall see, this notion of the "whole man" is basically derived from the concept of *Gattungswesen* in Feuerbach.

I shall not discuss in any detail the conclusion of this introduction, but it is important to see how the turning point of the analysis is resolved. Marx concludes that the only critique which can change reality is a critique not by means of words and ideas, such as the critique made by the left Hegelians, who remain speculative thinkers, but a critique involving concrete praxis. More particularly, Marx claims, this concrete, practical critique is actualized only when supported by a class of the society which represents universality. The dimension of universality is transferred from the sphere of thought to an actual class, that class which is universal because it has nothing; having nothing, it is everything. The first Marxist concept of the proletariat is constructed in this way. Here, we should note, the concept is abstract, since the proletariat is said to be the class which has no particular interests but, because deprived of everything, therefore represents the real interests of society as a whole.

This concept of the proletariat is abstract in a way that will appear ideological for the mature Marx. At this stage, the proletariat is a construct; Marx claims a place for the needs of the universal class that succeeds the place occupied by universal thought. "Revolutions require a passive element, a material basis. Theory will be realized in a people only in so far as it is the realization of their needs" (138). A page further: "A radical revolution can only be a revolution of radical needs, whose preconditions and birthplaces appear to be lacking" (139). The concept of need, which was already in a sense Hegelian, replaces that of universal thought. Radical need replaces radical thought. Once more, the opposition is between the abstract activity of thought and actual struggle. This emphasis leads to the famous development of a "class with radical chains, a class in civil society that is not of civil society, an estate that is the dissolution of all estates, a sphere of society having a universal character . . ." (141). As we can see, the concept is basically a construct; it is not at all a sociological description. Despite the claim that the proletariat replaces universal thought, the proletariat is still a philosophical concept. Marx ends this dense and strenuous introduction by linking the real emancipation of the whole society, its "positive possibility," to a class which would be a class with radical chains, a class "that can claim no traditional title but only a human title . . ." (141). The abstract idea of humanity, taken from Feuerbach, is the continuing anthropological support for the entire analysis.

From this introduction we may derive the main method that Marx will apply in the body of the *Critique* itself. Joseph O'Malley defines this method as transformative.[1] The expression is a good one. Marx's method is close to that applied by Feuerbach to religion: it is a reductive method, a reduction of the abstract world of representation, of thoughts, to its concrete, empirical basis, an overthrow of mystical speculation. The reduction is the reversal of a reversal, since it proceeds by taking all those entities that have been falsely projected upwards—the eternal, the logical, the transcendent, the abstract, the divine, whatever they may be—and reducing these projections to their initial basis. The model is Feuerbachian, expressed in the logic of Hegel as the substitution of the subject for the predicate. While in actuality humanity is the subject and the divine a predicate—that is, a projection of human thought—religion transforms this divine predicate into a subject, a god, and the human becomes a predicate of this absolute subject. The reductive process transforms this false subject into the predicate of the real subject. Exactly who is the real subject, though, is precisely the problem faced by the young Marx. The whole work of the young Marx is a fight for the real subject of this predicate which has been projected upwards. We shall see later that Marx's concept of ideology depends on just this model of projection. The reversal becomes the general method for dissolving illusions, and the transformative method will expose ideology as an illusory reversal itself needing to be reversed and so dissolved. Marx's task is to achieve in his critique of philosophy what Feuerbach accomplished in his critique of theology: the reestablishment of the primacy of the finite, the concrete, the real.

Turning from Marx's published introduction to his longer, unpublished essay, I shall take a small section of this text as paradigmatic of Marx's critique of Hegel. I shall focus on Marx's critique of paragraph 262 of the *Philosophy of Right.* Marx quotes this paragraph, which reads:

> The actual Idea is mind *[Geist],* which, sundering itself into the two ideal spheres of its concept, family and civil society, enters upon its finite phase, but it does so only in order to rise above its ideality and become explicit as infinite actual mind. [We see a movement of the idea in its finite expression. The "actual Idea" finishes its circle and returns to itself in the constitution and in the self-consciousness of the citizens who adhere to the spirit of the constitution.] It is therefore to these ideal spheres that the actual Idea assigns the material of this its finite actuality, viz., human beings as a mass, in such a way that the function assigned to any given individual is visibly mediated by circumstances, his caprice and his personal choice of his station in life. (7)[2]

This paragraph is easy to fight against, since it is abstracted from the development of Hegel's text. Nevertheless it appeared to Marx as the model of all speculative thinking, since Hegel derives the institutions of existing political bodies from an idea. We perhaps should be more careful than Marx, though, in determining what Hegel means by the "actual idea." (Unlike the given translation, I translate "idea" without the capital "I." I am not sure it deserves the capitalization.) Particularly we should decipher the meaning of the word "actual." Hegel calls the idea *wirkliche,* actual, but in what sense? Not in the sense of empirical, but in the sense of working, of effective. In German, *wirklich* is built on *wirken,* which is to be active, to be efficient. Therefore the English "actual" translates *wirkliche* rather well, meaning not that being there, which would be *Daseinde,* but that being at work in history. In Hegel, then, the "actual idea" is neither an ideal, as in Plato, nor an empirical given, as say for Machiavelli; it is rather something working through history as a germ, which has both reality and rationality. The idea is not an ideal; on the contrary, as the quotation above suggests, only the family and civil society are ideal in the sense that they are abstractions of this concrete entity, which in Hegel is the state, as the institutional embodiment of the *Volksgeist.*

Marx, though, did not recognize this very complex status of the idea in Hegel. For Marx, to speak of the *wirkliche Idee,* the actual idea, is to project something somewhere above us (like for Feuerbach the god of religion) as an infinite actual mind or "Spirit." As a consequence, Marx says, the *real* institutions of *actual* human life—the family and civil society—become mere receptacles or appearances of the idea, incarnations of an alien reality which floats above it. Let us read the part of Marx's critique that gives the flavor of the whole:

> The so-called "actual Idea" (mind as infinite and actual) is described as though it acted according to a determined principle and toward a determined end. It sunders itself into finite spheres, and does this "in order to return to itself, to be for itself"; moreover it does this precisely in such a way that it is just as it actually is.
>
> In this passage the logical, pantheistic mysticism appears very clearly. (7)

I should add to this that Marx's critique here starts with the sentence, "Let us translate this into prose." He takes Hegel's commentary as a kind of poetic text, something that must be translated. (The emphasis on the need for translation recurs frequently; see, for example, page 16: "Now let's translate this entire paragraph into common language as follows. . . .") Marx attempts a reduction of speculation. At this time, though, the reduction is not to political economy but to ordinary experience. Ordinary experience itself tells us that the state is not (as it was for Hegel) some embodiment of the "actual idea" but that in fact citizens live in states which have censorship, torture, and so on. The movement is from the idea to ordinary experience, even if ordinary experience is not yet framed within a new theoretical framework. Marx's objection to "pantheistic mysticism" (another word for ideology) is therefore this:

> Actuality is not expressed as itself but as another reality. Ordinary empirical existence does not have its own mind *(Geist)* but rather an alien mind as its law, while on the other hand the actual Idea does not have an actuality which is developed out of itself, but rather has ordinary empirical existence as its existence. (8)

The word for existence here is *Dasein,* which means what is there, *Da-sein.* In contrast to what is only thought, Marx emphasizes what is actually *there*.

The kinship with Feuerbach is transparent. Marx has no difficulty transposing his own language into that of the subject-predicate relation.

> The Idea is given the status of a subject [i.e., the one who bears the predicate], and the actual relationship of family and civil society to the state is conceived to be

its inner imaginary activity. Family and civil society are the presuppositions of the state; they are the really active things; but in speculative philosophy it is reversed.

Again notice the concept of reversal, which I put as the central, leading thread of all these analyses: "but in speculative philosophy it is reversed." Once more we have the reversal of a reversal. The quotation concludes:

But if the Idea is made subject [by Hegel], then the real subjects—civil society, family, circumstances, caprice, etc.—become unreal, and take on the different meaning of objective moments of the Idea. (8)

Though its name is not raised, ideology already means this reversal of reality. The implications for our inquiry into the concept of ideology are not yet obvious, however, to the extent that the counterpart of ideology itself remains somewhat abstract: here the family and civil society appear as the active forces. At this stage Marx focuses more on the notion of reversal alone: "the conditions are established as the conditioned, the determining as the determined, the producing as the product of its [own] product." "The actual becomes phenomenon, but the Idea has no other content than this phenomenon" (9).

Marx allows me to conclude my presentation of the *Critique* at this point, since he closes this discussion with the following sentence: "The entire mystery of the *Philosophy of Right* and of Hegelian philosophy in general is contained in these paragraphs" (9). Abstract though the model may be, the *Critique* establishes both the paradigm of reversal and the transformative method that Marx will utilize, in increasingly concrete fashion, throughout his development of the concept of ideology. The vocabulary of the *Critique* may not be cautious; terms like "mystery," "mysticism," "abstraction," and "imaginary activity" are blended together. But what we must appreciate here is the cumulative power, not the discriminating function, of Marx's analysis.

I have said enough, I believe, to present some of the major issues in Marx's *Critique of Hegel's "Philosophy of Right."* I would now like to provide an introduction to the text we shall examine in the next two lectures, the *Economic and Philosophic Manuscripts of 1844*. Like the *Critique,* the *Manuscripts* became known only fairly recently, being first published in 1932. Also like the *Critique,* the *Manuscripts* do not directly consider the concept of ideology. In the German index, the word "ideology" does not even appear. The *Manuscripts* are of interest not for any depiction of the concept of ideology but rather for the elaboration of the opposite concept, for what is the concrete basis of human life as opposed to the ideological construct. The concept of ideology will not be complete as long as we do not know to what we oppose it, to what we have to contrast it.

Most decisive here will be the struggle in the *Manuscripts* both with and against the Feuerbachian concept of *Gattungswesen,* species being. I shall in fact limit my discussion to those passages which wrestle with the concept of *Gattungswesen.* This wrestling is most important because if the concept of species being is a construct, then it must be treated as ideological itself. Recognition of this problem, finally, governs the emergence of the concept of ideology in *The German Ideology,* to which we shall turn in the fifth lecture. The German ideology Marx attacks there is no longer Hegel; that critique is done, it is over. Instead, Marx attacks precisely the left-wing Hegelians, including among them, Feuerbach. So a split occurs within the left wing of Hegelianism. We shall examine how Marx both uses, and at the same time dissolves from within, the Feuerbachian concept of humanity as a universal species present in every individual (perhaps as God is said to be in all creatures). The concept of reality, which provides the basic contrast for that of ideology, therefore remains uncertain as long as the species being of Feuerbach has not been unmasked as itself a shadow concept and as in fact a mere and poor rephrasing of the Hegelian Spirit, the Hegelian *Geist.*

In *The Poverty of Philosophy* Marx says that Feuerbach finally is poorer than Hegel (164). This is true to the extent that Hegel is surely richer in content than Feuerbach. The critique of religion and the kind of atheism advocated by Feuerbach are in a basic sense the culmination of idealistic thought; they ultimately give to human consciousness divine power. Self-consciousness becomes the support of all predicates developed by the culture, predicates developed mainly through the fabric of religion. As the cornerstone of the whole structure and superstructure of culture, self-consciousness is the foremost idealistic concept. In Feuerbach everything happens within human consciousness, both its alienation and its emancipation; everything occurs, therefore, in the field of ideas, the field of representation. We have not left but instead have reinforced the Kantian and Fichtean assertion of the autonomy of consciousness.

The fight against heteronomy, which started with Kant, finds its culmination in and so belongs to the same circle as Kantian philosophy. The claim that the human being is the measure of all things—a claim for autonomy versus heteronomy—is finally the central contention. Because of this emphasis, sometimes I think that the idealistic concept of consciousness is by construction an atheistic concept. When placed in contrast to the assertion of radical autonomy, dependence is perhaps the only possible truth of religion, an avowal of an element of passivity in my existence, an avowal that in some ways I receive existence. As soon as I put autonomy at the top of the philosophical system, as soon as I promote to such an extent this Promethean dimension of autonomy, then surely autonomy becomes godlike itself. Because of Feuerbach's promotion of autonomy, heteronomy becomes evil by construction. Consequently, everything which is not autonomy is alienation. What is in fact the mystery here, to speak like Marx, is first, how a self-positing consciousness could lose its own control, could have its control alienated, and second, how this power, once alienated, could ever be reintegrated. A kind of magical history occurs, we may say.

In the *Manuscripts* Marx preserves an ambiguous relation to Feuerbach. This ambiguity is especially acute in Marx's usage of the concept of human being. Stressing this usage will be key for our reading of Marx's text. Sometimes Marx describes the human being as the living individual, but at the same time he also maintains the properties that Feuerbach assigns to human being, that is to say, as the universal, the bearer of all conceivable qualities and their ideal representation. For Feuerbach, human being as species being is infinite, whereas individuals are only its finite expressions. We may say, therefore, that Feuerbach has gathered and concentrated in the concept of human being the collection of predicates of perfection, claiming that this collection of perfection is at the same time a subject which asserts itself. As we can see, the characterization is not so far from the Hegelian *Geist*. Feuerbach's presentation is a bit more ambiguous than this picture represents, however. He in fact hesitated between a super-idealism concentrated in human being and a form of philosophical materialism. For example, when Feuerbach says, "Der Mensch ist was er isst," the play of words on *ist* and *isst*—to be and to eat—emphasizes the materialist relation, "man is what he eats." Yet "man" as species being is also the actual infinite. Thus in Feuerbach the human being is sometimes a god and sometimes a living and eating being.

The *Manuscripts* represent an attempt by Marx to naturalize, and in that sense to dissolve from within, this Feuerbachian humanism and all its idealistic overtones. The relation of human being to nature and of human being to human being will absorb the idealistic predicates, and Marx will speak of these relationships as, respectively, natural and generic. (Attention to natural relationships becomes the more Marxist terminology; talk of generic relationships remains more Feuerbachian.) This ambiguous terminology allows the *Manuscripts* to preserve the dignity of a natural being who is at the same time the bearer of the universal. The immanence of the "species" to the individual lessens the isolation of individual subjects. At the same time, particular intersubjective relations support the basic generic function; they nourish the sense of species being or generic essence. Always, though, this interrelation carries a specifically Marxist flavor of naturalism. This strange mixture of naturalism and humanism permeates the *Manuscripts.*

Reacting to this mixture, critics who deny the final Marxist significance of the *Manuscripts* are in this sense correct: something fundamentally Hegelian rules the whole process of its thought, that is, the role of consciousness in objectifying itself and so negating itself in its product. Human beings produce themselves as objects. We recognize in operation here the work of the negative by which the Hegelian Spirit differentiates itself, ojectifies itself, and produces itself as self. This process of objectification and of efficient negativity will become more and more identical to the process of work. We might say that in the work of the young Marx a certain reciprocity obtains: just as Marx claims that economics grounds the orientations of philosophy, so German metaphysics also invades Marx's own depiction of the economic process.

To conclude this lecture, let me set aside the methodological significance of this last remark in order that I may emphasize its more general import: we must observe the persistence in the young Marx of the categories of his predecessors. As the following quotation makes even more evident, the *Manuscripts* manifest a strong and as yet undifferentiated conjunction between Hegelian, Feuerbachian, and what will become specifically Marxist concepts:

> The outstanding achievement of Hegel's *Phenomenology* and of its final outcome, the dialectic of negativity as the moving and generating principle, is thus first that Hegel conceives the self-creation of man as a process, conceives objectification as loss of the object, as alienation and as transcendence [*Aufhebung,* the suppression, the overcoming] of this alienation; that he thus grasps the essence of labor and comprehends objective man—true, because real man—as the outcome of man's own labor. The real, active orientation of man to himself as a species being, or his manifestation as a real species being (i.e., as human being), is only possible by the utilization of all the powers he has in himself and which are his as belonging to the

species—something which in turn is only possible through the cooperative action of all of mankind, as the result of history—is only possible by man's treating these generic powers as objects: and this, to begin with, is again only possible in the form of estrangement. (177)

Major concepts of Hegel (estrangement, objectification) and of Feuerbach (species being, generic powers) are here reformulated and placed within the structure of labor. Marx's project is a reconstruction, a philosophical reconstruction, of the concept of labor. He reconstructs the concept of labor not as a descriptive phenomenon but as a process made meaningful through the species being objectifying itself in an object, in a product, and then recognizing itself in the product; this is the process of objectification and alienation.

We see that a basic theme in German philosophy is recapitulated in Marx. The idea of the self-emptying of oneself in something else in order to become oneself is a theme running back from Marx through Hegel to at least the age of German mystics such as Jakob Boehme. (Perhaps the antecedents stretch back historically even to Paul; his *Epistle to the Philippians* talks of God's self-emptying in Christ.) What Marx calls "treating these generic powers as objects" continues a long line in German history reflecting on the creative function of emptying oneself in order to reassert and recapture oneself. Marx's continuity and discontinuity with his intellectual predecessors is, then, highly significant. In the *Manuscripts,* such Hegelian and Feuerbachian concepts as objectification, realization, alienation, and estrangement are employed in a loose fashion to describe the underlying structure of the relation of human beings to their labor, to the products of their labor, to the activity of labor, to the other laborer, and to money as depriving individuals of the meaning of their labor. All the reversals at work here prefigure Marx's development of our main theme, the concept of ideology.

What I want to prepare us for in the *Manuscripts,* therefore, is the identification of this strange mixture of a metaphysics of the universal, coming from Hegel, a humanistic view of species being, dependent on Feuerbach, and the truly Marxist problematic of human beings as workers alienated in their labor. Our aim is to continue extracting from Marx's development what is of interest for the concept of ideology, and in the next lecture we shall return to the *Manuscripts* for that purpose.

3

Marx: The "First Manuscript"

In this lecture I shall discuss the "First Manuscript" of the *Economic and Philosophic Manuscripts of 1844*. I shall concentrate on the section entitled "Estranged Labor." My choice of texts will be selective, depending on their relevance for our main topic, the concept of ideology.

How can we relate the *Manuscripts* to an inquiry on ideology? The term ideology does not appear in the text, and the problem that will come to the forefront in *The German Ideology,* the complete reduction to the life of the individual worker as the counterpart of all ideological systems, is not yet elaborated. Nevertheless, the *Manuscripts* are important to our inquiry for two reasons. First, the type of reality to be contrasted to ideology is becoming more and more specific. Ideological evocation of abstract transcendent entities is now differentiated from recourse to human individuals as living and acting beings in social settings. Second and most important, the *Manuscripts* offer a framework to account for the genesis of the ideological entities being repudiated. The *Manuscripts* provide a model for construing the concept of ideology as the reversal of a relation to things, a relation to works, and so on. As we shall see in subsequent lectures, the concept of ideology will be an extension of this process of inversion to such spheres as law, politics, ethics, art, and religion; for Marx these domains will be precisely the ideological spheres. The model which the *Manuscripts* provide is the inversion of human labor into an alien, foreign, seemingly transcendent entity: private property, or more specifically, capital. Therefore, the transformation by which the subjective essence of labor (still very Hegelian language) is abolished and lost in a power that seems to rule human existence becomes the paradigm for all similar processes. Something human is inverted into something which seems to be exterior, external, superior, more powerful, and sometimes supernatural.

In this concept of inversion, which will take on a very technical meaning in the *Manuscripts,* we may observe all kinds of exchanges between the Feuerbachian concept—explored in the previous lecture—of the individual emptying himself or herself into the divine and human labor inverting itself into the foreign power of money. It is as if each type of alienation is reflected in and reinforced by the other. As we shall see, this relationship is more an analogy than a derivation in the *Manuscripts*. The increasingly dogmatic trend in Marxism is to speak of a derivation of all alienations from one fundamental, economic alienation. But in the *Manuscripts* the argument always remains analogical; it is never a systematic deduction, reduction, or derivation. We may say, therefore, that the *Manuscripts* speak nowhere directly of ideology, but it is everywhere indirectly addressed.

In beginning the section of the "First Manuscript" called "Die Entfremdete Arbeit" (Estranged Labor), we are faced immediately with the semantic difficulty of translating the German *entfremdete* with its root *-fremd,* foreign, alien. *Entfremdete* has been translated as "estranged," which is a good translation. *Entfremdete* is one of two key words in the text which are somewhat distinguishable in Hegel but synonymous in Marx. The other word is *entäusserte* whose root, *-äusserte,* means externalized. *Entäusserte* has usually been translated as alienated. *Entfremdung* and *Entäusserung,* estrangement and alienation, are rigorously synonymous in Marx, at least in these early texts. As we shall discover, the significance of these two terms gains greater clarity in their opposition to objectification *(Vergenständlichung),* the transformation into an object, which is the good process that Marx wants to recover.

In "Estranged Labor" as in the "First Manuscript" as a whole, Marx's method is to start from what he calls the *premises* of political economy (106). Marx speaks of premises—the German is *Voraussetzungen,* so presuppositions, assumptions—he talks of what has been taken as a fact, and so on. And what are these premises? ". . . The fact of private property." Note that the German word for fact here is very strong: it is *das Faktum,* not *Tatsache,* therefore something well established.

This means that Marx takes for granted a previous analysis, that of the British economists. He credits these economists with a major discovery: that wealth is created not by the fertility of the soil, as the physiocrats had claimed, but by human labor. For Marx, this *Faktum* of political economy includes in particular several consequences identified by Adam Smith.

First, agriculture is now a part of industry; there is a shift from the productivity or fertility of the soil to the productivity of human labor. The soil is productive only because human labor is applied to it. A second consequence is that with the rise of the profit of mobile capital, the profit of the land as land disappears. (For classical economy, this was the land's rent.) Third, the land, the ground, becomes a form of capital since it has the same relation as mobile, mutable capital to its owner's profits. We may say, then, either that the value of land as land disappears, or that it is absorbed as a particular instance of capital.

This transformation is what Marx characterizes in the "Third Manuscript" as the universalization of private property (132). This does not mean that everyone becomes an owner; rather, private property is universalized in the sense that all the different kinds of property now become abstract. The argument is Hegelian in its orientation. Property has value only in its ability to be exchanged as capital. Thus landed property loses the status of being a particular and becomes a part, an aspect, of universal property. Marx explains this transformation in a section of the "First Manuscript" called "Rent of Land." Let me quote for our purposes only a few sentences of this important text:

> The final consequence [of this evolution] is thus the abolition of the distinction between capitalist and landowner, so that there remain altogether only two classes of the population—the working class and the class of capitalists. This huckstering with landed property, the transformation of landed property into a commodity, constitutes the final overthrow of the old and the final establishment of the money aristocracy. (100)

The result of this transformation is that labor appears as the only source for any kind of property. The concept of property is unified on the basis of the notion of labor. This is the important conclusion drawn. Marx closes the section on "Rent of Land" by arguing that the old French slogan, "l'argent n'a pas de maître"—money has no lord—is now true since "the complete domination of dead matter over mankind" (102) has been achieved. For Marx this "complete domination of dead matter" is the great discovery of British political economy. This discovery, therefore, is not Marxist in origin.

The starting point of the section on "Estranged Labor" is that this "domination of dead matter" is taken as a fact by British political economy but nevertheless is not understood. Even more, this discovery is self-defeating. The claim of political economy is that human labor, human industry, alone generates all wealth, all capital, but it is actually the case that capital hires and fires human labor. For Marx this is the great contradiction of political economy: it has discovered that there is nothing sacred in property, that property is merely accumulated labor, and yet property—capital—has the power of hiring and firing human labor. These two discoveries remain scattered effects of political economy's analysis. When brought together, however, these effects engender a contradiction that forces us to go further than the British economists and to question the meaning of what has been taken as fact. Marx proceeds by attempting to decipher the meaning of something taken to be merely a fact.

> Political economy starts with the fact of private property, but it does not explain it to us. It expresses in general, abstract formulas the material process through which private property actually passes, and these formulas it then takes for laws. It does not comprehend these laws, i.e., it does not demonstrate how they arise from the very nature of private property. (106)

The word "nature" is not a good translation here. In using the word "nature," the translator mistakenly does not preserve the German *Wesen,* which means essence. Marx wants to oppose an essential analysis to a factual analysis. There is no doubt; here Marx is using the Hegelian *Wesen.*

Analysis of the process of estrangement or alienation is Marx's answer to the silence of British political economy regarding the contradiction between the theory that labor is the source of property—wealth—and the theory that the wage is the power of money over labor. Marx appropriates the two Hegelian concepts *Entfremdung* and *Entäusserung,* estrangement and alienation, and claims that they express in common precisely the inversion that interests us as the model of all ideological processes.

> This fact expresses merely that the object which labor produces—labor's product—confronts it as something alien *[fremdes],* as a power independent of the producer. The product of labor is labor which has been embodied in an object, which has become material: it is the objectification *[Vergegenständlichung]* of labor. (108)

As I mentioned briefly before, the objectification of labor is contrasted to the alienation of labor and is a desirable result. Objectification is a key concept in Marx, and in this emphasis he follows Hegel. Objectification is the process by which something interior externalizes itself and in that way becomes actual, a very Hegelian motif. When I first enter the world, I have only an inner life. Only when I do something is there a work, a deed, something public and common to others, such that I realize or actualize myself. Only then do I really come to exist. Objectification is this process of actualization. "Labor's realization is its objectification" (108). This is the fundamental concept.

"In the sphere of political economy," however, and that means in the sphere of the capitalist economy, "this realization *[Verwirklichung]* of labor appears as loss of realization *[Entwirklichung]*. . . ." English and French lose the fruits of the wordplay between *Verwirklichung* and *Entwirklichung;* we would have to speak of realization and "de-realization." The translator says "loss of realization," which is a good choice. "In the sphere of political economy this realization of labor appears as loss of realization for the workers; objectification as loss of the object and bondage to it; appropriation as estrangement, as alienation" (108). Appropriation and estrangement are opposed to one another because appropriation means not to become an owner but to make proper to oneself *(propre),* to make one's own, what was foreign. (This is also the main opposition in Gadamer's *Truth and Method,* although admittedly in quite a different context. To read a text is also to overcome a kind of alienation, a cultural distance, and to make one's own what was foreign.) So this differentiation between appropriation and estrangement or alienation has strong philosophical overtones. To recapitulate, the process of objectification is not something bad. On the contrary, it is the meaning of work as such that we deposit our meaning in something exterior.

As I have observed before, Marx proceeds here just as Hegel did: not by the discrimination but by the accumulation of terms. This is the reason why a rich semantics exists around Marx's concepts. The terms to become actual, to become efficient, and to become objective are all more or less synonymous. This accumulative procedure also generates a rich span of opposite terms. In contrast to efficient is deficient, in contrast to foreign is appropriation, in contrast to estrangement is reappropriation, and so on.

What Marx's analysis reveals, therefore, is that the reversal taken as a "fact" by political economy is in actuality the loss of human essence. What properly should be the objectification—the essence—of human labor appears in political economy as instead the loss—the estrangement—of its realization. Without the insights gained through an analysis of alienation, the "facts" of political economy remain meaningless. We may say, very cautiously, that Marx's analysis here is a hermeneutics of political economy. It is a critical hermeneutics, since political economy conceals the alienation native to the labor process. "Political economy conceals the estrangement inherent in the nature of labor by not considering the direct relationship between the worker (labor) and production" (109–10).

Marx extends his analysis further by comparing what happens in alienation to what occurs in religion. He uses religion as a metaphor. Marx does not claim that what happens in religion proceeds from what happens in labor; he says only that the two processes are parallel. "It is the same in religion. The more man puts into God, the less he retains in himself [a very Feuerbachian statement]. The worker puts his life into the object; but now his life no longer belongs to him but to the object" (108). In religion and labor the processes of alienation are parallel; they share the image of estrangement, whether it be estrangement in the divine or estrangement in capital.

Marx follows this parallelism in different ways throughout the *Manuscripts*. A striking example, to which we shall return, occurs in the "Third Manuscript" when Marx calls Adam Smith the Luther of economy (128–29). Marx interprets Luther as having interiorized the external obedience required by the Catholic church. (This was the perception of Catholicism at the time.) Marx goes on to say that Luther accomplished this transformation without lifting the burden of transcendence, the burden of being under the reign of a transcendent power. This burden is simply changed from being a call of external obedience to one of internal obedience. In the same way, says Marx, Adam Smith discovered the subjective essence of capital; the workings of capital become internalized in the process of labor. The burdens of this new transcendence are maintained in the power of capital over what actually generates it. Marx's argument is very powerful; a process of internalized transcendence occurs in both cases.

We shall return to this example of Luther and Adam Smith later; I mention it now to emphasize a methodological point. At this stage of Marx's writings there is no claim that religious alienation proceeds from economic alienation; the interplay is one of analogy, and it is not necessary to press the interpretation further. We should view the degradation and perversion that is alienation through a system of analogies rather than as a system of derivation. The theory of derivation may seem a more powerful argument, but it is also easier to refute. Recourse to analogy, on the other hand, is a good instrument for self-criticism. The same observations may be made about other thinkers such as, for example, Freud. When Freud claims that religion is a kind of private neurosis and neurosis a public religion,[1] here too a very powerful analogy exists, but it is one that must not be pressed further in the sense of an identity. The analogy says more.

Returning to the remaining pages of the section on "Estranged Labor," which end the "First Manuscript," Marx does not add anything further to the general concept of alienation, but he articulates it in several figures. The basic framework of the concept of alienation has been delineated and Marx now proceeds as did Hegel in the *Phenomenology:* analyzing a figure, a shape, by construing its different "moments." Marx demarcates this progression within the concept of alienation in four moments. I shall not develop each of these four aspects equally but only as each pertains to the construction of a good paradigm for ideology. For our purposes, the most significant moments are the third and fourth.

The first form of alienation occurs in one's relationship to one's own labor (110). Alienation of the products of one's labor is the model for Marx's depiction of the concept of alienation as a whole. The second aspect is alienation in the act of production, in the producing capacity itself. Joining Hegel in the capacity to invert expressions, Marx summarizes these first two forms of alienation in the following play on words: they represent, respectively, the alienation of the activity and the activity of alienation, *Entäusserung der Tätigkeit* and *Tätigkeit der Entäusserung.*

> If then the product of labor is alienation, production itself must be active alienation, the alienation of activity, the activity of alienation. In the estrangement of the object of labor is merely summarized the estrangement, the alienation, in the activity of labor itself. (110)

The alienation of labor signifies that labor is external to the worker; it is not voluntary but coerced or forced labor. The analogy with religion is developed once again.

> Just as in religion the spontaneous activity of the human imagination, of the human brain and the human heart, operates independently of the individual . . . so is the worker's activity not his spontaneous activity. It belongs to another; it is the loss of his self. (111)

(Again I note my interest in the use of the word imagination, here not *Einbildung* but *Phantasie,* so imagination more as fancy than as fiction.) The humanism of the young Marx, rejected by the structuralists as we shall see in future lectures, is clear in this passage. Marx's portrayal makes no sense if it is not the individual in his or her spontaneous activity who is affected, infected, and destroyed by alienation. At least at this stage of his writing, Marx claims an underlying role for individual spontaneity.

More important for our purposes than the first two figures, however, is the third form of estrangement. This stage will be the most revealing for our primary purpose, the identification of the real basis from which ideologies are abstracted by transcendence. This third form moves beyond estrangement in the product and in the activity to the estrangement of the worker's humanity itself. The worker is affected and infected in his or her *Gattungswesen,* species being. I reemphasize the importance of this concept in Feuerbach. Feuerbach never said that it is each human being who advances on the gods; rather, it is something in humanity as a whole that is the bearer of the divine predicates. Species being represents humanity both in extension—as a collective group—and in intension—as a comprehensive nature. Species being is then a collective being, and it is this collective being that has all the attributes of universality, infinity, and so on. Given this characterization, it is less absurd to say that humanity invents the gods, since in fact it is a kind of human god or divine human being. For Feuerbach to argue that humanity produces the gods, he must artificially elevate the species being of humanity to the level of gods, and this is no real theoretical advance in our understanding of religion. In any case, Marx preserves the concept of species being in the *Manuscripts.* Possibly this is to reinforce emphatically the extensiveness of the concept of estrangement, but it is surely also to bring estrangement to the level of what Marx called precisely the *essence.* This was Marx's purpose: to proceed from the fact of economy of the *essence* of estrangement. For Marx the influence of estrangement on the human essence is critical.

Marx typifies the third aspect of estranged labor in the following way:

> Man is a species being, not only because in practice and in theory he adopts the species as his object . . . but . . . also because he treats himself as the actual, living species; because he treats himself as a universal and therefore a free being. (112)

The first part of this quotation is Feuerbachian. Human beings are species beings not only because they consider or contemplate what is essential but because *they* are essential. This identity of essence and existence in species being is one of the continuing problems in a reading of Feuerbach. This Feuerbachian emphasis is followed, in the latter part of the quotation, by a Hegelian motif. Human freedom occurs not in the mere assertion of individuality but when this assertion has been transposed into the sphere of universality. Before this transposition occurs, the assertion is only arbitrariness. Freedom must traverse all the stages of universalization. This is the tradition of autonomy in German philosophy: to assert oneself as the universal. It is this capacity for being the universal that is affected by estrangement. "[E]stranged labor estranges the species from man" (112). In his later writings, as we shall see, Marx grafts the concept of the division of labor onto this dispersion of species being. If I react as a worker, as an individual of the city, or as an individual of the country, I am no longer a universal. The division of labor will become a dramatic element in Marx because of its relation to this central concept of species being.

Several important consequences derive from the fact that human beings are species beings, and these Feuerbachian influences persist even through Marx's writing of *Capital*. The first consequence is the dividing line between animals and human beings. Marx always affirms this difference very strongly. In *Capital,* for example, Marx will say that because bees always build their hives each in the same way, their activity is not work. Only human beings work. For Marx this difference remains a fundamental dividing line between animal life and human life. The distinction, says Marx, proceeds from the fact that human beings not only conceive the universal, they have a vocation for being universal, and this gives them a certain distance from their needs. Human consciousness is superior to mere awareness; in its fundamental capacity for reflection, consciousness is identified with species being. In the *Manuscripts* Marx will even claim:

> Just as plants, animals, stones, air, light, etc., constitute theoretically a part of human consciousness [this is subjectivist idealism], partly as objects of natural sciences, partly as objects of art—his spiritual inorganic nature [again a strongly idealistic expression], spiritual nourishment which he must first prepare to make palatable and digestible—so also in the realm of practice they constitute a part of human life and human activity. (112)

The capacity of human beings to submit nature to their own needs proceeds from the "spiritual" superiority of human beings over nature.

This difference between human life and animal life is not, however, the most significant implication of the fact that human beings are species beings, this universal essence. The main consequence is the ability of human beings to produce themselves by the process of objectification.

> [T]he productive life is the life of the species. It is life-engendering life. The whole character of a species—its species character—is contained in the character of its life activity; and free, conscious activity is man's species character. Life itself appears only as a means to life. (113)

Human beings work, therefore, not only to eat but in order to become this species being.

In creating a world of objects by his practical activity, in his work upon inorganic nature, man proves himself a conscious species being, i.e., as a being that treats the species as its own essential being, or that treats itself as a species being. (113)

It is just in his work upon the objective world, therefore, that man first really proves himself to be a species being. This production is his active species life. Through and because of this production, nature appears as his work and his reality. The object of labor is, therefore, the objectification of man's species life. . . . (114)

The concept of objectification and the idea of life producing life are superimposed. The way humanity produces itself is by objectifying itself. Once more this is very Hegelian, since only in deed, in action, does the self-assertion of humanity occur.

Because of the human vocation to be self-creative, self-asserting, the fact of alienation cuts very deeply. To be submitted to the power of another is the contrary of the creation of oneself. Estrangement is fundamentally the reversal, the inversion, of the human capacity for the creative process of objectification. Humanity's species being is the depository of the identity between objectification and self-creation. In estrangement this essential being is transformed, becoming merely the means to existence in the sense of survival. What was formerly the means for self-assertion becomes the "end": to exist physically.

In tearing away *[entreisst]* from man the object of his production, therefore, estranged labor tears from him his species life, his real objectivity as a member of the species, and transforms his advantage over animals into the disadvantage that his inorganic body, nature, is taken away from him. (114)

Following the three prior stages of alienation in the product, alienation within production, and alienation at the core of species being, the fourth and final dimension of alienation is the estrangement of human being from human being, estrangement at the level of intersubjectivity. This dimension of alienation is important because it reorients in a more concrete way the concept of species being. Delineation of this aspect of alienation provides us with the transition to the "Third Manuscript." There is no leap from the third to the fourth stage of alienation, because for Feuerbach the concept of *Gattungswesen* already had this relational aspect. *Gattungswesen* is human being for human being. This other-directedness represents in each of us our participation in the species. I am part of the species to the extent that I recognize the same humanity in others.

In fact *[überhaupt]*, the proposition that man's species nature is estranged from him means that one man is estranged from the other, as each of them is from man's essential nature.

The estrangement of man, and in fact *[überhaupt]* every relationship in which man stands to himself, is first realized and expressed in the relationship in which a man stands to other men. (114–15)

Why does Marx say *überhaupt,* which means not "in fact" but "in general"? At issue is why there is estrangement "in general" at all. Attention to this problem provides Marx with the fundamental transition to the question: for whose benefit does estrangement occur? Until this point we have considered *from what* human beings are estranged—from nature, and so on. But if the intersubjective dimension is introduced, then we must ask *for the sake of whom* are we estranged? "If the product of labor is alien to me, if it confronts me as an alien power, to whom, then, does it belong?" (115). This question is a powerful transition. The problem of wages, the relation between capital and wages, is implied in the question of estrangement for the sake of whom. The two parts of the contradiction of political economy—that labor produces all property and yet is hired in the form of the wage—are related precisely by the answer to this question. We must understand that estrangement is itself an intersubjective process in order to acknowledge that in estrangement the power of the one is transferred, yielded to the other.

This transformation in our understanding of estrangement is a decisive step in dissolving the prestige of private property. Private property seems a thing having power over human beings. Marx's reversal establishes that private property is in fact a power of one person over another. There is a complete reduction to the human dimension not only of work but also of capital. Marx reveals on both sides what has been concealed: both the one who labors and the one who enjoys the fruits of this labor. We might say that Marx tries to put the relationship between capital and wage within the framework of the Hegelian master-slave relationship. The economic relation between money and wage or property and wage seems to be a relation between things or, as some contemporary Marxists will say, between processes or structures. For at least the young Marx, however, these apparently "objective" enigmas must be reduced to subjective processes. The allusion to the master-slave relation is significant, because the master and the slave do not stand in the same relation to things. The slave forms the thing whereas the master enjoys it. It is precisely this relationship which appears in our text: "If the worker's activity is a torment to him, to another it must be delight and his life's joy. Not the gods, not nature, but only man himself can be this alien power over man" (115).

Thus everything is now contained in the relation of one person to another. All the magic in the relationship between wage and capital is exposed. Marx closes his discussion by equating to the practical the whole process which appears as the work of human beings, including their estrangement. Even human estrangement has to appear as a human activity. "The medium through which estrangement takes place is itself practical" (116). The concept of the practical is enlarged to include not only simple actions but the generation of the whole process of objectification and estrangement. Marx insists that we may transform something which is our work, because if it were a given or a law of nature, a law which escaped us, then the prospect of revolution would be completely insane. If alienation is itself our work, however, then so also is the abolition of alienation—the topic of the "Third Manuscript."

In a quasi-Fichtean sense, Marx equates the practical to a creative act. Estrangement becomes a medium through which we create without recognizing that we are creating. What we are doing through estrangement is obscure for ourselves; this is why we have to unconceal it. We must uncover, says Marx, the act of creation and concealment that is political economy itself.

> Thus through estranged labor man not only creates his relationship to the object and to the act of production as to men that are alien and hostile to him [these are three of the shapes of estrangement]; he also *creates* the relationship in which other men stand to his production and to his product, and the relationship in which he stands to these other men. Just as he *creates* his own production as the loss of his reality, as his punishment; his own product as a loss, as a product not belonging to him; so he *creates* the domination of the person who does not produce over production and over the product. Just as he estranges his own activity from himself, so he confers to the stranger an activity which is not his own. (116; emphases added)

Marx's usage of the concept of creation is extremely important because it provides a scope to the concept of production that is much broader than mere economics. I sometimes wonder whether orthodox Marxism's dogmatic reduction of everything to production does not proceed from a failure either to know or remember that for the young Marx at least the concept of production was defined by creation, and not the contrary. It is because human beings create their lives and the conditions for their lives that they produce. The concept of production here does not initially have an economic meaning. What some schools of Marxism, those most opposed to this reduction, have called economism in Marxism proceeds from this leveling, this flattening, of the concept of production. Thanks to its origin in Hegel and Feuerbach, though, the concept of production preserves a broader intention. The later division in the Marxian use of the word production will be very unfortunate. Sometimes production will be opposed to consumption, and then it is merely an economic process; on the other hand, sometimes production will be opposed to estrangement, and then it has a broader meaning. The hesitation between the two uses of the word production will be a dramatic adventure within the Marxist school. This is one reason why the return to the young Marx is most significant.

Marx concludes his argument in "Estranged Labor" and the "First Manuscript" as a whole by saying: "we have derived the concept of private property from the concept of estranged, alienated labor by analysis. . . ." (118). Marx summarizes his argument as having been derived by analysis. "Just as we have derived the concept of private property from the concept of estranged, alienated labor by analysis, so we can develop every category of political economy with the help of these two factors. . . ." Because the concept of private property has been derived, we may say that what appeared as a starting point, as a "fact" of political economy, has now become a result of the analysis. "[I]t is as a result of the movement of private property that we have obtained the concept of alienated labor . . . from political economy" (117). What was a fact now appears a result: "on analysis of this concept [of alienated labor] it becomes clear that though private property appears to be the source, the cause of alienated labor, it is rather its consequence, just as the gods are originally not the cause but the effect of man's intellectual confusion" (117). To a static fact Marx opposes a dynamic process, the process of estrangement, and the static fact is determined to be the frozen result of this dynamic process. In actuality alienation is the source, the cause, the ground of private property, not as a positivistic cause but as the fundamental meaning which rules a fact. The relation between meaning and fact is dominant: "We have accepted the estrangement of labor, its alienation, as a fact, and we have analyzed this fact" (118). A mystery, an enigma is dissolved by this reduction of the origin to the status of an effect. This is the model of all *Ideologiekritik*.

This conclusion is most powerful. Marx establishes that the fact of private property, the domination of dead matter—capital—over human beings, is in actuality a product of the estrangement of human essence, humanity's species being. The "First Manuscript" demarcates the different forms of estrangement and demonstrates most importantly that estrangement is at bottom a result of human activity itself. In this manuscript Marx not only reaffirms the model of inversion, of reversal; he also extends this model by offering a more precise account of the genesis of ideological entities, that is to say, by analyzing to a greater depth the real basis from which ideologies are abstracted.

Despite these powerful insights, however, Marx expresses at the very end of the "First Manuscript" some dissatisfaction with his results. Unresolved by the analysis of the "fact" of political economy is the question "how": how do human beings come to alienate their labor? Marx determines that he must change his attention from the analysis of human essence to the question of history. This transition introduces the problem not only of the "Third Manuscript" but also of *The German Ideology*. Marx sees that he must pursue the implications of his discovery that estrangement is a *movement,* a movement of private property. The problem is to transform a concept—essence—into a historical force. In Hegel the concept was not static but dynamic. Nevertheless, it is always difficult in Hegel to correlate what happens in the field of shapes, figures, with historical examples. A certain gap exists between the examples and the concept, the work of the concept. In his own raising of the question of the historical, Marx may have wanted to be very cautious not to become trapped in this difficulty. This is why Marx ends the "First Manuscript" by raising the following points:

> We have accepted the estrangement of labor, its alienation, as a fact, and we have analyzed this fact. How, we now ask, does man come to alienate, to estrange, his labor? How is this estrangement rooted in the nature of human development? We have already gone a long way to the solution of this problem by transforming the question of the origin of private property into the question of the relation of alienated labor to the course of humanity's development. For when one speaks of private property, one thinks of dealing with something external to man. When one speaks of labor, one is directly dealing with man himself. This new formulation of the question already contains its solution. (118–19)

Unfortunately, the manuscript breaks off unfinished soon after this statement, but we see that the problem is the need to pass from an essential analysis to a historical analysis. We shall follow this problem and its implications for the concept of ideology when we turn in the next lecture to the "Third Manuscript."

4

Marx: The "Third Manuscript"

In this lecture I shall discuss the "Third Manuscript" of Marx's *Economic and Philosophic Manuscripts*. I leave aside the "Second Manuscript," because most of it has been lost; only a few pages survive. This discussion will complete my presentation of the *Manuscripts* as a whole.

The distinctiveness of the "Third Manuscript," in comparison with the first, lies much more at the level of method than content. The "Third Manuscript" does not add anything important to the concept of alienation as such. Alienation remains the inversion of the different modes of objectification. In this manuscript we find the same fundamental approval of the insights of British political economy regarding the complete reduction of all property, particularly landed property, to capital. At its ultimate stage, the structure of property is manifested in a relation to money and not to the land itself. Not only has British political economy established the complete reduction of all property to capital, though, for it has also established the complete reduction of capital to labor, and therefore to a subjective factor. In the first lines of the "Third Manuscript" this latter reduction is expressed as a reduction to the "subjective essence": "The subjective essence of private property—private property as activity for itself, as subject, as person—is labor" (128). Labor is the sole essence of wealth. This is a summary of what was said in the "First Manuscript." The language is quite Hegelian; the internalization of something exterior—in this case, depiction of the subjective essence of private property—is a typical Hegelian procedure.

Another way Marx expresses the role of "subjective essence" is by saying that political economy has taken modern industry and "made it a power in the realm of consciousness" (128). The word "consciousness" is not used in the sense that we give to the word now, that is, as awareness, as being aware of. Instead, consciousness takes on the much stronger sense found in German philosophy of being the center of production. As such, consciousness is then the center of reference of all existence. The philosophical accent is strong. This emphasis on "a power in the realm of consciousness" marks precisely the great difference between the *Manuscripts* and *The German Ideology*. In the latter text, the function of consciousness as the ultimate reference of analysis is replaced by the notion of the real, living individual, the working and suffering individual. The concept of consciousness recedes exactly on the side of ideology; it becomes one of the concepts belonging to the ideological sphere. In the *Manuscripts,* however, consciousness is still the instance to which ideology is reduced. Only in *The German Ideology* is consciousness reduced in turn to something more primitive, more radical: the real, living individual. The individual takes the place of consciousness.

Marx's comparison of Adam Smith and Luther in the "Third Manuscript," which I anticipated in the last lecture, is a commentary on this reduction to consciousness. As I explained before, just as Luther is credited with having interiorized religious alienation, so Adam Smith has interiorized the power of property as in fact that of labor. What Adam Smith has failed to point out, however, says Marx, is that this power of human labor has been alienated. The human being

> no longer stands in an external relation of tension to the external substance of private property, but has . . . become this essence of private property. What was previously being external to oneself—man's externalization in the thing—has merely become the act of externalizing—the process of alienating. (129)

Again, this is a summary of the "First Manuscript." Another similar expression Marx uses is that the human being as "essence" has become "unessential" (130). The German is stronger here; the comparison is between *Wesen* and *Unwesen.* The alienation of the labor process makes the human being, as essence, the non-essence.

The "Third Manuscript" does not improve, then, the *concept* of alienation, but it is nevertheless important for several reasons. First, it provides a historical dimension to a concept which in the "First Manuscript" remained abstract and ahistorical. Development of the history of property and therefore of the history of the division of labor provides a history for alienation itself. Alienation becomes less and less a concept than a process.

The manuscript speaks of the evolution from ground rent to abstract property, the reduction of agriculture to industry. "All wealth has become industrial wealth, the wealth of labor; and industry is accomplished labor, just as the factory system is the essence of industry . . ." (131). The language of essence persists, even as it becomes more historical. As I mentioned in the last lecture, the Hegelian concept of essence establishes how an essence can be historical. For Hegel the essence is not static but rather the germinal kernel of an evolution. The language of essence and the language of historical development can both be preserved, since the essence is itself the germ of a historical development. Therefore for Marx, "industry is accomplished labor, just as the factory system is the essence of industry—of labor—brought to its maturity, and just as industrial capital is the accomplished objective form of private property" (131).

Marx's stress not only on essence but on an essence "brought to its maturity" yields yet another comparison with Hegel. As Emil Fackenheim has shown in his book *The Religious Dimension in Hegel's Thought,* Hegel thought that he was able to philosophize because certain fundamental historical developments had occurred: the Enlightenment, liberal Protestantism, the rise of the liberal state. Similarly, Marx believes that another historical plateau has been achieved. With the rise of the English factory, the essence of industry is "brought to its maturity." The meaning of an event becomes clear and a theory of it becomes possible when it has been brought to its maturity by history. This emphasis in Marx helps explain the following methodological remarks, a remark significant also as a transition from a Hegelian to a properly Marxist approach: "We can now see how it is only at this point that private property can complete its dominion over man and become, in its most general form, a world-historical power" (131). Exactly as in the Hegelian system, only when a form has reached its maturity may we speak of its essence. The essence recaptures the movement from inchoate to mature form. This is Marx's answer to the question left unsolved in the "First Manuscript," when he said, "We have accepted the estrangement of labor. . . . How, we now ask, does man come to alienate, to estrange, his labor" (118)? The answer is that there is a historical expansion of an essence, the essence of industry.

The second contribution of the "Third Manuscript," and for us the most interesting, is the introduction of an approach looking at the suppression of the contradiction of estrangement. We may say, and this too is very Hegelian, that we understand a contradiction when it is in the process of being overcome. We regard the contradiction from the point of view of its overcoming. Hegel's *Logic,* for example, starts with the concepts of being, nonbeing, and becoming, and it is only because of the concept of becoming that the pair being/nonbeing becomes a creative contradiction and not merely a dead opposition. A look backward occurs from the process of suppression to the contradiction itself. This perspective changes decisively how the problems of the "First Manuscript" are approached. The "First Manuscript" started from the "facts," the facts discerned by British political economy, and it analyzed these facts to extract their essence. The analysis was regressive from fact to essence, but always within, always on the basis of, the "facts." In the "Third Manuscript," however, the approach proceeds from the movement of the overcoming of suppression to the contradiction itself. The "Third Manuscript" says: "The transcendence of self-estrangement follows the same course as self-estrangement" (132). Because it "follows the same course," we may read the meaning of estrangement in the meaning of its suppression.

In the "Third Manuscript," therefore, Marx reformulates the Hegelian concept of *Aufhebung* in relation to self-estrangement. Our text's translation of *Aufhebung* as "transcendence" is unfortunate; I do not think that in English we hear the movement of transcending in transcendence. But there is no good translation of the German word. In Hegel, *Aufhebung* means the overcoming of a contradiction but an overcoming, a suppression, that preserves the positive meaning of the first term. The first term is said to become itself in its overcoming. Thus the *Aufhebung* both suppresses and preserves the strength of the contradiction within the solution that overcomes the first term. As we can see, the Hegelian concept is very complex. In the *Manuscripts,* though, there is no doubt that *Aufhebung* means simply abolition. From Hegel to Marx the meaning of *Aufhebung* is reduced to that of abolition, more specifically, practical abolition. In Marx the role of *Aufhebung* as preservation disappears, and it is replaced by an emphasis on *Aufhebung* as suppression alone. For this reason I think that in the *Manuscripts* the best translation of *Aufhebung* would be suppression and not transcendence.

In the "Third Manuscript" communism will be the name for the *Aufhebung*—the transcendence, the suppression—of self-estrangement. The word "communism" does not yet have the specific political and organizational meaning it will have later. At this point the word designates in a vague way only the stage of history in which the contradiction will have disappeared. We have no right, therefore, to say communism here represents anything like the Soviet Union. We must forget completely that there is now somewhere a country called communist. This distinction is important for our relation to Marx in general. It is not that our relation to Marx should be neutral but rather that it must be nonpolemical, just like our relation to such other thinkers as Freud, Nietzsche, and so on.

How, then, is the *Aufhebung,* the suppression, of self-estrangement to occur? As I have already quoted, Marx says: "The transcendence [suppression] of self-estrangement follows the same course as self-estrangement" (132). To say that it "follows the same course" means that the process of overcoming will proceed from partial to total stages. Just as the course of estrangement moved from a partial stage—the relation of the agricultural worker to the landowner—to a total stage—the relation of the worker to abstract, universal capital—so the overcoming of estrangement will proceed from a partial, scattered overcoming to an abstract and universal overcoming. Marx will develop the different aspects of the overcoming in the same way as he analyzed the forms of estrangement.

Because the process of *Aufhebung* must move from a partial to a total overcoming, we can better explain Marx's harsh and in many respects surprising attack on what he calls crude communism. He speaks of the "as yet completely crude and thoughtless communism" (133). Marx issues this brutal condemnation because he thinks a partial break with the system—for example, a return to nature or a return to a previous relation to the land—would not identify the full consequences of the abstractness of labor and consequently could not bring about liberation at a level equal to that of the estrangement. To respond to an abstract estrangement by concrete liberation is not the solution. The solution must respond to the level of the problem. (An interesting comparison could be made here between Marx and those in the United States and Europe who argue that to find a solution to the industrial system we must precisely get out of the industrial system.) For Marx, we must push the industrial system to its last consequences in order to achieve a solution at the level of the illness. The nostalgia of romantics for an earlier labor situation is thus misplaced. The craft worker who made a complete work still did not control the market; the value of the work was determined by someone else. Marx's condemnation of crude communism is so strong, then, because there the relation to property in the form of "envy" and "greed" (133)—unfair terms, I would say—has not been subverted.

Marx's position here surely involves the question of humanity's *Gattungswesen,* its species being. For Marx the preservation of humanity's species being necessarily entails, as we saw in the last lecture, a strong opposition between human being and animals, between culture and nature. If the break with property does not preserve this dichotomy—for example, by a return to nature, which would obscure the difference between human being and animal—then the solution is regressive. The annulment of private property by universal private property is an abstract negation of the world of culture. Even if an equality of wages is paid out by communal capital, the community as a whole becomes "the universal capitalist" (134). By "the universal capitalist" Marx means that what is universalized is only the relation of estrangement: everyone becomes alienated, instead of just the working class. It might be proper, in fact, to call this universalization ideological. Marx says, "Both sides of the relationship [labor and capital] are raised to an imagined universality . . ." (134). The German original for "imagined" is *vorgestellte;* therefore, the universalization occurs in representation only. For Marx the solution is an imaginary one.

As a test case of his argument Marx takes the relation between man and woman. This relation is a test case because it exists on the borderine between nature and culture. In this kind of relation it is most crucial to preserve the difference between nature and culture since it is not a given. The question is reminiscent of Hegel, who says that the relation between man and woman is the "natural" access to community life. True sexuality belongs both to nature and, through the kinship system, to culture. If we read Marx here with Lévi-Strauss' eyes, the relation between man and woman is very striking, since it is a natural species relationship which has to remain at the same time a relation of species being. Marx is horrified by the notion of a "community of women," where "a woman becomes a piece of communal and common property" (133) for men; the community of women blurs the distinction between culture and nature, between humanness and animal life.

This direct, natural, and necessary relation of person to person is the relation of man to woman. In this natural species relationship man's relation to nature is immediately his relation to man, just as his relation to man is immediately his relation to nature—his own natural destination. In this relationship, therefore, is sensuously manifested, reduced to an observable fact, the extent to which the human essence has become nature to man, or to which nature to him has become the human essence of man. From this relationship one can therefore judge man's whole level of development. From the character of this relationship follows how much man as a species being, as man, has come to be himself and to comprehend himself. . . . (134)

The English is poor here, using only one word for "man" as human and for man as distinct from woman. The example of the relation between man and woman shows, therefore: "The first positive annulment of private property—crude communism—is thus merely one form in which the vileness of private property, which wants to set itself up as the positive community, comes to the surface" (134–35). Marx emphasizes that to generalize this property relation is still to remain within a property relation. This is the situation of the universal capitalist. In future years Marx fights strongly against all attempts to make everyone a small capitalist, to distribute ownership, for these are efforts that would prevent the abolition of property. This is why the Communist Party and many other branches of Marxism will fight against any kind of reformism which would distribute or enlarge the field of property without abolishing the relation as such.

The fight against crude communism and its reformism leads to the third contribution of the "Third Manuscript": development of the concept of accomplished communism. Accomplished communism plays the same role in the "Third Manuscript" 's discussion of the suppression of self-estrangement as accomplished alienation does in the "First Manuscript" 's analysis of the course of self-estrangement. The parallelism is not complete, however, since in the British factory of Marx's time there exists the figure, the symbol, of accomplished alienation, while the concept of accomplished communism floats, we may say, above the analysis. In light of this difference, I propose to say—though it is an interpretation, and I do not want to read it into the text—that the notion of accomplished communism in this text plays the role of a utopia. Could we not say, then, that we have another perspective on alienation: may we not look at alienation and judge it from this nowhere of utopia? Does not all judgment on ideology proceed from the nowhere of utopia? I know the Marxists' response to this view—my position is not a criticism but an attempt to understand—they will reject the utopian characterization, and for one fundamental reason. All utopias depend on a leap of the imagination "nowhere," "elsewhere," whereas the Marxists contend they rely on the *inner* movement proceeding from estrangement itself toward its own overcoming. For Marx, no fantastic leap onto the island of utopia need occur; the suppression of the contradiction proceeds from the contradiction itself. The accusation of the utopian characterization is escaped by reinforcing the Hegelian character of the analysis: the claim is that the contradiction has a dynamism which by necessity pushes forward its own overcoming.

This is the general Marxist approach to the question of the last stage. The claim is that this last stage is not invented; rather, it is ascertained by looking at the movement of estrangement's self-overcoming. The result, Marx says, is the following:

> Communism as the positive transcendence [overcoming, suppression] of private property, as human self-estrangement, and therefore as the real [not imagined but real, *wirkliche*] appropriation of the human essence by and for man; communism therefore as the complete return of man to himself as a social (i.e., human) being—a return become conscious, and accomplished within the entire wealth of previous development. This communism, as fully developed naturalism, equals humanism. . . . [This is the famous text which says that naturalism equals humanism in the last stage, since nature becomes human and humanity becomes natural.] [I]t is the genuine resolution of the conflict between man and nature and between man and man—the true resolution of the strife between existence and essence, between objectification and self-confirmation, between freedom and necessity, between the individual and the species. Communism is the riddle of history solved, and it knows itself to be this solution. (135)

The last sentence is typically Hegelian; that the riddle of history is solved is the perspective of the *Phenomenology of Spirit*. The final stage overcomes and subsumes the contradictions of the earlier ones. This final solution, because it is rooted in the contradiction itself, also "knows itself to be this solution," says Marx. This knowledge is exactly the equivalent of Hegel's Absolute Knowledge. The process is one of overcoming the series of contradictions, and Absolute Knowledge is nothing other than the self-reflection of the whole process. (The issue of the self-reflection of the whole process is discussed at length in Jean Hyppolite's book *Genesis and Structure of Hegel's Phenomenology of Spirit*.) Marx may transpose Hegelianism, but he raises the same questions. At issue is the locus of the one who engages in self-reflection. For Hegel the distinction is always between the "for us," for us philosophers who know the end, and in the "in itself" of the process. We may say that in the same way as the "for us" of the philosophers leads the interpretive process of the figures "in themselves," resolution of the problem of estrangement enlightens the deciphering of the contradiction itself. In the "Third Manuscript" the concept of accomplished communism has the same role as the "for us" of Hegel.

This similarity has some implications that are not only intriguing but highly attractive. I want to emphasize one of these implications in particular. The concept of accomplished communism has as its principal and concrete achievement the restoration of a sense of wholeness, of totality. In the division of labor humanity itself is divided; one person is an owner, another is a worker, and so on. In contrast, the concept of totality looks to the reconstruction of a whole; the integrity and integrality of humanity becomes the leading concept. This emphasis is intimated when Marx says: "The entire movement of history is, therefore, both its actual *[wirklicher]* act of genesis . . . and also for its thinking consciousness the comprehended and known process of its becoming" (135). Here is the same equation as in Hegel between what is real and what is thought. Because the act of genesis is *wirklich,* therefore actual in the sense of efficacious, it can be *begriffne und gewusste,* comprehend and known. There is a reflection of the process in thought.

This equation between actual and comprehended at the level of the totality is developed mainly by Lukács and the Austro-Hungarian branch of Marxism. In *History and Class Consciousness* Lukács places a great reliance on the concept of totality, arguing that emphasis of this concept distinguishes a Marxist approach from a positive approach. In contrast to the latter position, which proceeds by analysis alone, by analysis of parts, Lukács says we must consider the parts from the point of view of the whole and then rebuild the whole by use of the parts. A similar perspective is apparent in Sartre. In the *Critique of Dialectical Reason,* Sartre opposes the analytical relation to belonging to a whole. It is this belonging to a whole which is, finally, destroyed by alienation. Sartre provides a new concept of alienation, then, as an analytical process destroying the synthetic movement of humanity. The emphasis in the "Third Manuscript" on the notion of totality reinforces the difference between this manuscript and the first. No longer does the investigation move from fact to concept; instead, a circular relation is established between "the riddle of history" and the solution which "knows itself to be this solution."

This circular approach, a consideration of the process of alienation from the point of view of its suppression, also has important methodological implications. First, to observe that the beginning is interpreted by the end is to claim that here Marx is very philosophical. As Heidegger has observed, every good philosophical work is circular in the sense that the beginning belongs to the end; the problem is to enter correctly into the circular movement.[1] We cannot argue against Marxism, then, by saying that if its analysis is defined by the projection of a finite state, this is not good philosophizing.

A second methodological implication of Marx's circular approach has special appeal for those of us interested in the problem of the text and hermeneutics. The following remark of Marx is most significant: "A psychology for which this, the part of history most contemporary and accessible to sense, remains a closed book, cannot become a genuine, comprehensive and real science" (142). Marx criticizes those who approach political economy by an analytical approach, giving first a theory of salary, then a theory of property, and so on, chapter after chapter, without seeing the contradictions. What is destroyed by this process of analysis, says Marx, is the concept of society; humanity becomes a "closed book." What is needed, therefore, is the unconcealment or unsealing of the closed book. This emphasis is developed mainly by the post-Heideggerian Marxists, Habermas and others, who put Marxism more on the side of interpretation that on the side of explanation. If explanation is American sociology, then German *Ideologiekritik* is a kind of comprehension. Marx says that in the closed book all that is described constitutes nothing more than vulgar need. The text of action is viewed to be a mute text. In contrast, says Marx:

> We see how the history of industry and the established objective existence of industry are the open book of man's essential powers, the exposure to the senses of human psychology. Hitherto this was not conceived in its inseparable connection with man's essential being, but only in an external relation of utility, because, moving in the realm of estrangement, people could only think of man's general mode of being—religion or history in its abstract-general character as politics, art, literature, etc.—as the reality of man's essential powers and man's species activity. (142)

For the method which regards everything from the outside, in an external relation, the history of industry is a closed book. This concept of the closed book may be a source of the opposition, prevalent in orthodox Marxism, between ideology and science. Science becomes the reading of the closed text of industry. I would argue, however, that only when we view the text as open may we get out of the realm of estrangement. Perhaps science needs to be supported by utopia in order to unseal the sealed book. I do not want to expect too much of these passages in Marx, but it is a reward for the reader to find sections of this sort.

A fourth contribution of the "Third Manuscript" takes us beyond the retrospective use of the final stage to enlighten the previous stages and brings forth a most important implication of the all-comprehensive concept of suppression. Marx's concept of suppression *(Aufhebung)* embraces the material and spiritual aspects of estrangement as two *separable* forms. Again the contrast with orthodox Marxism is revealing. In orthodox Marxism the claim is that alienation in religion proceeds from alienation in economics. If, however, we follow Lukács and Sartre and recognize that Marx's position here incorporates the category of totality, then the claim is rather that we have partial figures constituting a whole. This change in orientation transforms the basis of the analogy between figures. We may make good use of the analogy between figures but must do so without claiming that one merely relies on or proceeds from the other.

> The positive transcendence [positive suppression] of private property, as the appropriation of human life [this is a global concept], is therefore the positive transcendence of all estrangement—that is to say, the return of man from religion, family, state, etc., to his human, i.e., social existence. Religious estrangement as such occurs only in the realm of consciousness, of man's inner life, but economic estrangement is that of real life. . . . (136)

Thus, economic estrangement and spiritual estrangement are analogous figures. We may view their unity from the perspective of the concept of the whole human being, an entity liberated precisely as a whole. We may regard the partial estrangements from the perspective of a total appropriation.

Does Marx express in this context more than an analogy, though? Immediately preceding the quotation just cited Marx writes: "Religion, family, state, law, morality, science, art, etc., are only particular modes of production, and fall under its general law" (136). The analogy between figures seems transformed into a reduction of all figures to the economic. This is not, however, an accurate reading of the quotation. In German the word *Producktion* has the same amplitude as objectification; thus, Marx's statement does not express an economism. The reductionism of classical Marxism is nevertheless nourished by the word's ambiguity. *Produktion* means both creative activity in general, activity as realization, and economic activity in particular, the material, perceptible form of estrangement. Under the influence of both Engels and Lenin, the category of totality is forgotten, and the economic concept of production swallows all the other dimensions of the concept of production in general, the concept still powerful in the *Manuscripts.* A shift occurs, moving away from the sense of the whole, away from the broad scope of the word "production," which has the same scope as the concept of appropriation itself, an appropriation covering all aspects of human life. Instead, the concept of production narrows to an economic basis and all human activities are related to this basis. We must hold on carefully, therefore, to those texts where this reduction has not yet appeared. Only the category of totality allows us to prevent the reduction to a mere economic concept of production. The unfortunate distinction that will prevail in Marxism between infrastructure and superstructure is the result of this reduction of the concept of production to a merely economic concept.[2]

In contrast, the notion of human being producing human being is the limit opposed to this reduction. Elaboration of this notion, the fifth major contribution of the "Third Manuscript," is linked to the circular relation described earlier between human activity and the assumption of an accomplished end to this activity. Here the emphasis is not so much the end itself (the abolition of estrangement) but that the notion of human being producing human being makes sense only upon the assumption of this end. "We have seen," says Marx, "how on the assumption of positively annulled private property man produces man—himself and the other man . . ." (136). This is not an economic concept but rather an anthropological concept, an anthropological concept in its preeconomic stage. I emphasize Marx's use of the word "assumption," which relates to my interpretation that the end is a kind of utopia. The word for assumption in the German original is *Voraussetzung,* so presupposition. We shall read in *The German Ideology* that the kind of anthropology Marx develops is not *Voraussetzungslos,* is not without presupposition. The presupposition is precisely that of a liberated human being. It is not, therefore, an objective description. The description is motivated by the process of liberation. It is "on the assumption of positively annulled private property [the *Voraussetzung*] [that] man produces man. . . ."

If we take objectification to be the process whereby "man produces man," then we have a better sense now of what this concept means. As I discussed in the last lecture, objectification is the form of externalization that Marx both contrasts to estrangement and also wants to reconstitute. What Marx establishes here is that the theory of appropriation logically precedes that of alienation, even if appropriation appears only as a historical result, a result of alienation's overcoming. The logical point of departure is the actual historical result. It is anticipation of the end of alienation which says something about the origin of the process in objectification. Only on the assumption of appropriation do we understand the proper human activity, that "man produces man." Thus, it is on the assumption of the abolition of estrangement that the fundamental concept of objectification is revealed.

This perspective allows me to raise again one of my hypotheses in these lectures: that a use of utopia is the tool for the critique of ideology. Is it not from the nowhere of an unalienated human being that we may speak of alienation? More precisely, how could we suffer from alienation if we had no anticipation of a state in which we would not be alienated? The anticipation of the end is therefore projected backwards. As long as we use only the method of the "First Manuscript," which is to dig under the fact of political economy, to proceed, as Marx says, by analysis of a fact, we cannot say much about objectification. But behind this analysis of the fact exists an anticipation of the end; we thus have to introduce the *Aufhebung,* the suppression of alienation, as a critical concept that uncovers what Marx already meant by the process of objectification. It is only after alienation has ended, whatever that may mean—the state of nonalienated labor if that is possible, the end of the wage, the end of the market, and so on—that we may say that now human beings objectify themselves.

The notion of objectification, that "man produces man," alerts us to the importance in Marx of the social dimension. Recourse to this dimension is one way Marx preserves the concept of totality. When Marx says that something is social, he invariably means that it makes a whole, whether of human being with human being or of the different human activities and faculties. It is the concept of a bond. To say that human beings are social is, therefore, more than a platitude; the ascription is a dynamic, all-embracing concept. "The human essence of nature first exists only for social man. . . . Thus society is the unity of being of man with nature—the true resurrection of nature—the naturalism of man and the humanism of nature both brought to fulfillment" (137). The word "social" must be interpreted in light of the concept of humanity as a totality, as a whole, and not in a Durkheimian or sociologist sense. Society designates this wholeness. I shall continually use the concept of the whole as the key.

Although the term is not used, ideology appears here as one aspect of this all-embracing production that is the social. In describing the functioning of ideology, Marx uses the word *Tätigkeit,* activity. *Tätigkeit* is the key concept in Fichte, where being human is a *streben,* a striving, aspiring, productive activity. The allusion to Fichte in this text is no mistake. The French thinker Roger Garaudy, for example, strongly maintains that the

Manuscripts must be interpreted in the light of Fichte, whose influence on Marx has been all but forgotten in the attention given to the role of Hegel.[3] The Fichtean character of Marx's description of human activity is plain.

> My general consciousness is only the theoretical shape of that which the living shape is the real community, the social fabric, although at the present day general consciousness is an abstraction from real life and as such confronts it with hostility. The activity *[Tätigkeit]* of my general consciousness, as an activity, is therefore also my theoretical existence as a social being. (137)

Intellectual life is not reduced to economic life; instead, Marx attempts to lift the abstraction which opposed one to the other. Once more, it is the scope given to rebuilding the totality that presides over this analysis.

To say that intellectual life is an abstraction is true. We all know what it means to have a relation only to books and not to real people, real life. This is the kind of abstraction Marx denounces when he speaks—if still not by name—of ideology. It is not the negation of the worth of intellectual life, but the disease which affects its separation from work, from labor. "In his consciousness of species man confirms his real social life and simply repeats his real existence in thought, just as conversely the being of the species confirms itself in species-consciousness and exists for itself in its generality as a thinking being" (138). This text has been used sometimes by orthodox Marxism to depict the concept of consciousness as merely a reflection—a mirror—of real life. The concept of ideology as reflection derives from this type of argument. My interpretation of the text quoted is somewhat different, however. When Marx says that "man . . . simply repeats his real existence in thought," the word "repeats" means that nothing could appear in the intellectual sphere if it had no roots in praxis, in practical life. The repetition occurs, therefore, not in the sense of a mirror but in the sense of having no roots in itself. "Thinking and being are thus no doubt distinct," Marx writes, "but at the same time they are in unity with each other" (138).

To summarize this development we could say with Marx: 'Man appropriates his total essence in a total manner, that is to say, as a whole man" (138). I propose that this is the kernel of the development articulated here by Marx. When Marx says, "Man appropriates his total essence . . . ," the German for "total essence" is *Allseitiges Wesen,* therefore an all-sided essence. It is the all-sided as opposed to the one-sided. The one-sided is an abstraction, and we could not have a concept of the one-sided if we did not have a certain anticipation of what would be the all-sided, the total. What prevails is not dogmatic reductionism but the category of totality. If there is room for utopia, it is the utopia of totality. Perhaps this is not far from Hegel's concept of reconciliation.

Need we say that Marx's attention to the totality of appropriation is reminiscent of religious thinking? I do not want to emphasize this aspect, because it would offer too easy a way for theologians to deal with Marx, as if he set forth a laicization of religious thought. We must accept Marx precisely in his attempt to speak in new terms of what he calls emancipation.[4] I have already quoted the expression, "the true resurrection of nature" (137); surely embedded here is a reminiscence of the Christian theology of Easter. Redemption, as Jürgen Moltmann has suggested, is the Easter of humanity. We must not make a mixture of Marxism and Christianity but perhaps think with both in a creative way. Just as Heidegger observes that poetry and philosophy sit on two different peaks and do not see the same thing,[5] we should say the same about Marxism and Christianity.

The lyricism of Marx's quasi-religious language on emancipation encourages us to read this section as utopian. Marx speaks of the emancipation of all senses *qua* human senses from the tyranny of having (139). A contemporary of Marx, Moses Hess, introduced this category of having into philosophy (a category that will return in Gabriel Marcel). In the *Twenty-One Sheets,* Hess says that humanity now has no being, it has only having; the opposition is between having and being. For Marx the relation of having, of possession, means something very precise: the relationship that dominates when private property reigns. Marx borrows from Hess the idea that having is estrangement not in an abstract form but as an actual alienation of all human senses. Only the suppression of private property will emancipate all human senses and qualities. As Marx will point out in *The German Ideology,* criticizing Feuerbach, even the character of nature is a product of industry and of the state of society (62). Where are there trees that human beings have not yet felled or planted? Perhaps only in the desert may we find nature before humanity. What we know, therefore, is a humanized—or dehumanized—nature. Consequently, our eye is itself estranged by seeing the ugly alterations of nature by humanity itself. The human eye is what it sees, and what it sees is already altered by the relation to property. To look at things displayed in a shop window is different depending on whether we can or cannot buy them. There is nothing like pure sight; that is the meaning of this passage. Once again we have to put even the human senses within the process of totality to ward off the abstraction of a Feuerbach, the abstraction of a psychology of perception, and so on.

Put in subjective terms, emancipation means the recovery of all human forces, all essential human powers, including all the human senses. Importantly, Marx incorporates among the human senses "not only the five senses but also the so-called mental senses" (141). The translation here is too modest; the German says *geistigen Sinne,* spiritual senses. The spiritual senses are "the practical senses (will, love, etc.)—in a word, human sense. . . ." Through the category of totality we deliver the concept of sense from its narrowness by rebuilding the human framework of which it is merely an abstraction. The category of totality not only preserves us from reductionism; it also is professed against reductionism. Reductionism reduces humanity to ideas, work, property, or something else. The concept of a humanized nature or naturalized humanity—the concept of the emancipation of all human senses and qualities—becomes a critical tool by which to read reality.

A corollary of this position is that the natural sciences, as an exercise of our spiritual senses, are themselves abstractions if separated from industry.

> [N]atural science has invaded and transformed human life all the more practically through the medium of industry; and has prepared human emancipation, although its immediate effect had to be the furthering of the dehumanization of man. Industry is the actual, historical relationship of nature, and therefore of natural science, to man. (142–43)

This quotation is very striking for a reading of Marcuse, Habermas, and all those who say that at the center of each epistemological sphere lies an "interest." Those who have read Habermas know he says that we have several interests, among them an interest in controlling nature, and that the latter governs the empirical sciences. The empirical sciences are not without presupposition; they presuppose a nature that we exploit by industry. For Habermas industry is the presupposition of the natural sciences. We would not be interested in the natural sciences if we did not have this practical relation to them through industry. The question of the real status of epistemology in relation to praxis is raised. As many current trends argue, there is no autonomy to the sciences; they all belong to this totality of interest. "Industry is the actual, historical relationship of nature . . . to man." This historical relationship is based on a history of needs.

The problem *The German Ideology* confronts is how everything is mediated by the history of our needs through the process of labor. Apart from the history of our needs established in labor, in industry, we do not know what nature is. To say that there is one basis for human life and another for science is, says Marx, a lie. The nature which develops in human history, nature as it develops through industry, has an anthropological status itself (143). The natural sciences are not autonomous; they do not exist simply unto themselves.

Another corollary of the emphasis on totality is that the division of labor is one key to the concept of ideology. The division of labor is itself a figure of estrangement. "The division of labor is the economic expression of the social character of labor within the estrangement" (159). The fragmentation of labor is the fragmentation of human being. This fragmentation explains why we do not know the meaning of objectification, the expression of oneself in a work. As we have seen, ideology represents the division of labor that abstracts intellectual life from the rest of human existence.

In conclusion, one of the issues remaining after a reading of the "Third Manuscript" is the status of the concept of totality as the anticipation of the appropriation by humanity of its scattered forces. In question, therefore, is the status of the concept of appropriation as itself the critical tool. This issue will be raised mainly by the Frankfurt School. These thinkers ask whether we can have critical social sciences without a project of emancipation. We may take this question as at least the content of a project. Without this project, human beings are merely like ants or bees; they simply observe, describe, analyze, and so on. Without a certain historical movement toward reappropriation, human beings are nothing more. It is the concept of appropriation which finally gives sense to the concept of creation. We rediscover that we are creative to the extent that we have a project of appropriation.

I think the fundamental discussion between Christianity and Marxism should be put at the level described here. Marx's claim is that the project of appropriation is in fact the most atheistic project conceivable, because the appropriation of humanity's strength, its forces, is at the same time the abolition of the concept of creation as a religious concept. Marx is most adamantly atheist, therefore, not when he is a materialist but when he is a humanist, that is, to the extent that he is a complete humanist. In his very interesting discussion on this topic (144–46), Marx says that when accomplished humanism and communism are achieved, people will no longer need to be atheist. They will no longer need to negate something, but will rather assert themselves positively. Atheism, as the protest against something, will be abolished along with religion. The utopian character of this section is enhanced by the anticipation of a time when the negation of estrangement will no longer be part of human beings' self-assertion. The concept of creation will be reappropriated in a way consonant with its use in describing the process of objectification. Once more in Marx, the end result enlightens the starting point.

Marx goes on to claim that abolition of the religious concept of creation and abolition of atheism also entail abolition of the question raised by religion, the question of origins. Marx says that the question of origins proceeds from an abstraction. He argues—and I do not know whether it is a fallacy or not—that the question itself must be canceled. To raise the question of what existed before human beings is to imagine that I do not exist, and I cannot do that. Because human beings are the center of all questions, I cannot raise a question which supposes that humanity does not exist.

> You postulate them [nature and human being] as non-existent, and yet you want me to prove them to you as existing. Now I say to you: Give up your abstraction and you will also give up your question [the abstraction from nature]. Or if you want to hold on to your abstraction, then be consistent, and if you think of man and nature as non-existent, then think of yourself as non-existent, for you too are surely nature and man. Don't think, don't ask me, for as soon as you think and ask, your abstraction from the existence of nature and man has no meaning. (145)

Therefore the question itself is ideological as an abstraction from the fact that I am now existent and a part of nature.

It seems, then, that we must go so far as to suppress the question of Leibniz, why is there something rather than nothing. Marx's position also counters that of Heidegger who, in *The Essence of Reasons,* says that the question of the principle of reason, that something in fact exists, is *the* philosophical question. Marx's argument confirms my claim that his stance here is very Fichtean. Fichte's entire philosophy is based on the reduction of the question of the origin to human self-assertion. For Marx, the question why is there something rather than nothing is finally the problem overcome by accomplished communism.

Marx's concept of the creation of humanity through labor is the ultimate point of a movement starting with the concept of autonomy in Kant and including the self-positing self-assertion in Fichte, Hegel's concept of Spirit certain of itself, and Feuerbach's species being *(Gattungswesen)*. The whole movement is atheistic, or rather it points toward a state where the negation of God would no longer be needed, where human self-assertion would no longer imply the negation of a negation. Religion may still have a claim here to the extent that this movement implies not merely an atheistic humanism but something else. In the same way that this movement incorporates an atheism beyond atheism, perhaps it is also with some god beyond god that the ultimate debate should be braved. There may be some connection between the two claims. This, however, is another matter. I want only to allude to the question of religion here. We must not transform Marxism into an apologetics for Christianity; that is the worst thing we could do. We must preserve the sense of conflict and not try to mix things together falsely.

In the next lecture we shall turn to *The German Ideology*. We shall focus the analysis on the concept of the real individual, a concept which takes the place of self-consciousness in Feuerbach. As we shall see, the conflict with Feuerbach will center precisely on this change in emphasis from consciousness to the real individual.

5

Marx: *The German Ideology* (1)

In this and the following lecture we shall examine *The German Ideology*. These two lectures will complete my analysis of Marx. We shall then turn to discuss the interpretation of ideology as it has unfolded within the Marxist movement as a whole. I am especially interested in the controversy that has developed in Marxism between the structuralist and the so-called humanist interpretations of ideology. I had hoped to spend more time analyzing the humanistic perspective—people like Lukács and Garaudy—but my discussion will focus on the structuralist approach as exemplified in the work of Louis Althusser. Following this review, we shall move to Mannheim and then to Weber, and in particular to Weber's problem of the legitimation of authority. After Weber we shall examine Habermas, and we shall finally conclude the discussion of ideology by reference to Geertz, at which point I shall also offer a few thoughts of my own.

In *The German Ideology* we have a Marxist and no longer a pre-Marxist text. Because of this, it is extremely important to locate precisely the text's conceptual framework. Even for those like Althusser who tend to discard the writings of the early Marx, this is a text of transition. We may say, then, that *The German Ideology* is at least a text of transition if not the basis for all Marx's properly Marxist writings. The question is to situate correctly the gap or, as Althusser will say, the epistemological break between Marx's early ideological and anthropological texts on the one hand, and his mature writings on the other, so as to decide on which side of the break *The German Ideology* lies. (For purposes of discussion, we shall refer to Marx alone as author of *The German Ideology,* even though the work was a joint effort of Marx and Engels.)

This question of the break is critical because *The German Ideology* opens two perspectives at the same time, and Marxist interpretation will vary decisively depending on which of these two alternatives is ranked more highly. What *The German Ideology* shifts away from is clear: entities like consciousness, self-consciousness, and species being, concepts all belonging to the Feuerbachian mode of thought and therefore to the Hegelian trend in German philosophy. If these concepts are now overcome, however, it is less obvious for which new concepts the battle is waged. The first alternative presented by *The German Ideology* is that the old concepts are replaced by such entities as modes of production, forces of production, relations of production, and classes, the typical Marxist vocabulary. According to this approach, these objective entities may be defined without any allusion either to individual subjects or, consequently, to the alienation of these subjects. If this alternative is chosen, the real starting point of Marxism involves the emergence of the notion of the real basis. The real basis becomes the infrastructure, and ideology is related to this basis as a superstructure. As we shall see, the major trend in orthodox Marxism focuses on these concepts of real basis and superstructure, of infrastructure and superstructure. The emphasis is on objective entities to the exclusion of the individuals involved in these processes. From this perspective, *The German Ideology* is Marxist in the sense that it pushes to the forefront a material basis of anonymous entities instead of idealistic representations and fantasies centered around consciousness. Consciousness is regarded as completely on the side of ideology; no implication of consciousness is said to exist in the real material basis as such.

The second perspective opened by *The German Ideology* has a rather dissimilar orientation. Classes and all other collective entities—modes of production, forms of production, forces, relations, and so on—are not considered to be the ultimate basis but rather only the basis for an objective science. In this more radical approach, this perspective argues, the objective entities are supported by the real life of actual, living individuals. The concept of real life as led by real individuals is given a central position. In this case, the epistemological break in Marx occurs not between the world of consciousness as ideological and some collective, anonymous entities but within the notion of humanity itself. The distinction is said to be between the Young Hegelians' emphasis on humanity as consciousness and Marx's emphasis in *The German Ideology* on humanity as real, living individuals. If the dividing line in Marx is placed here, the interpretation of the whole meaning of Marxism is quite different. No longer is the structure of *Capital* the ultimate basis; instead, *Capital* reflects a methodological abstraction ultimately rooted in the lives of individuals. It is particularly important to take a stand on this interpretation, because the concept of ideology Marx utilizes in this text is not opposed to science but to the real. (We shall leave for the later lectures on the forms of Marxism coming after Marx how the conception of ideology is changed when opposed to science instead of reality.) In *The German Ideology* the ideological is the imaginary as opposed to the real. Consequently, the definition of the concept of ideology depends on what is the reality—class or individual—to which it is contrasted.

In this and the following lecture, we shall stay as close as possible to the text of *The German Ideology,* and by preserving the possibility of the two readings we shall see in fact the ambiguity the text allows. This work is like Wittgenstein's duck/rabbit image (although I don't know which would be the rabbit in this case!): we may read it as a text about real individuals in their real lives or as a text about classes, a vocabulary of production and no longer a vocabulary of life. My own analysis of *The German Ideology* will proceed in the following manner: I shall first make some additional introductory comments to clarify the problem of ideology raised by the text and then consider the work's six or seven basic concepts. Finally, I will discuss the two threads of thought that appear in the text. In the present lecture I shall concentrate on presentation of the concepts; I reserve more for the next lecture comparison of the two alternate readings.

Regarding the text itself, the edition we are discussing is a translation only of part 1 of the German original. I should make one comment about the translation: the order of passages is not always the same as in the German text. The editor has chosen a more didactic order of presentation, although this loses the import of some passages which are better read following others, as in the original. The text itself was prepared for publication by Marx but never actually published during his lifetime. Lost for many years, the text was recovered and published for the first time only in 1932. I shall not spend much if any time on the so-called "Theses on Feuerbach," which are added to our volume as a supplementary text, even though these theses are so cryptic that they must really be read in coordination with the book's section on Feuerbach. One of these theses is helpful, however, in situating our problematic as we begin. The "Theses" end with the following renowned thesis: "The philosphers have only interpreted the world, in various ways; the point is to change it" (123). Can we change without interpreting, this is the problem. This is precisely the problem of our investigation of ideology.

In the preface which opens *The German Ideology,* we have the first suggestion of ideology's meaning in the text. Fundamentally the term designates the Young Hegelians and therefore all that proceeded from the decomposition of the Hegelian system. It is from this basis that the concept is extended to all forms of production which are not properly economic, such as law, the state, art, religion, and philosophy. We must never forget, then, the initial basis of this concept as a polemical term addressed to a certain school of thought. Marx begins: "Hitherto men have constantly made up for themselves false conceptions about themselves, about what they are and what they ought to be. They have arranged their relationships according to their ideas. . . ." The German for "conceptions" and also for "ideas" is *Vorstellungen,* representations. The *Vorstellungen* are the way in which we look at ourselves and not the way in which we do, we act, we are. "They have arranged their relationships according to their ideas of God, of normal man, etc. The phantoms of their brains have got out of their hands. They, the creators, have bowed down before their creations." Once more we have the image of reversal. What was the product becomes the master. The model of alienation is present without the term being used. We must not forget this, because some commentators maintain that the concept of alienation has disappeared from this work. Marx continues:

> Let us liberate them from the chimeras, the ideas, dogmas, imaginary beings under the yoke of which they are pining away. Let us revolt against the rule of thoughts. Let us teach men, says one, to exchange these imaginations for thoughts which correspond to the essence of man; says the second, to take up a critical attitude to them; says the third, to knock them out of their heads; and—existing reality will collapse. (37)

The ideology criticized here claims that in order to change people's lives, it is enough to change their thoughts. The figures challenged in the final sentence of the quotation are, repectively, Feuerbach, Bruno Bauer, and Stirner.

In part 1 of Marx's text, Feuerbach is the test case for German ideology to the extent that, as we remember, he claimed to reduce religious representations to the ideas of human beings. Marx contends that Feuerbach's reduction remains in a sense a religious idea, since consciousness is provided with all the attributes retained from the religious framework of ideas. What Marx calls the Young Hegelians' demand to interpret reality involves a use of critique on their part in which they always move within the realm of thought; they reduce one type of thought to another, but they remain within the framework of thought. "This demand [of the Young Hegelians] to change consciousness amounts to a demand to interpret reality in another way, i.e. to recognise it by means of another interpretation" (41). Thus, interpretation always moves among interpretations. Marx's perspective here helps to explain further his eleventh thesis on Feuerbach, already quoted, that the philosophers have only interpreted the world while the point is to change it (123). Interpretation is a process that occurs within representation, and it therefore remains ideological in that sense. For Marx the problem is that before moving to change the answers, the mode of questioning must be changed, the questions must be shifted. "It has not occurred to any one of these philosophers to inquire into the connection of German philosophy with German reality, the relation of their criticism to their own material surroundings" (41).

The occurrence of the word "material" in this passage allows me to introduce an inquiry into the basic concepts of *The German Ideology*. I want to survey the vocabulary of the text before considering the alternative ways it may be interpreted. The central term is "material," which is always opposed to "ideal." In this work the material and the real are exactly synonymous, as are the ideal and the imaginary. The following statement highlights Marx's orientation:

> The premises from which we begin are not arbitrary ones, not dogmas, but real premises from which abstraction can only be made in the imagination. They are the real individuals, their activity and the material conditions under which they live, both those which they find already existing and those produced by their activity. These premises can thus be verified in a purely empirical way. (42)

Note first that the adjective "real" modifies premises. The premises are *Voraussetzungen,* presuppositions. In opposition to these real premises are abstraction and imagination. When Marx continues that the real premises from which he begins are "the real individuals, their activity and material conditions under which they live . . . ," the two possibilities of interpreting *The German Ideology* are already present. Real individuals and material conditions are put together; perhaps the basis finally is individuals in their material conditions. Possibly this is a way of preserving the two readings. In any event, material conditions and real individuals are the two fundamental concepts. A final observation I should make about Marx's statement is that when he maintains that these real premises can be verified empirically, we should notice that they are first premises and then verified.

On the basis of Marx's declaration, one point must be emphasized from the outset: anonymous structures, such as material conditions, are coupled immediately by Marx with the support given to them by real individuals. Material conditions are always conditions for individuals. Marx underlines the inextricable role of living human individuals: "The first premise of all human history is, of course, the existence of living human individuals" (42). Marx enriches this role by noting the contribution humans make to their material conditions; this observation acts also to enlarge the notion of the material condition itself. "By producing their means of subsistence men are indirectly producing their actual material life" (42). The subject is still human beings. Material conditions cannot be defined without a certain sphere of human activity.

From the beginning, therefore, a subtle reciprocity exists between human activity and human dependence. On the one hand human beings act to produce their material conditions, and on the other hand they are also dependent on these conditions. Importantly, there obtains here neither an idependence of consciousness, which would be idealism, nor an autonomy of the conditions. A condition is always a condition for a certain way of acting. When Marx says, "The nature of individuals thus depends on the material conditions determining their production" (42), it is nevertheless the nature of individuals which remains even in this relation of dependence. As we can see, this concept of individual human life is quite different from the rather metaphysical and abstract concept of an objectification which is then alienated. The concept of objectification, which was still Hegelian, is replaced by the notion of an individual life producing under conditions which are themselves a given for this activity. There is a relation between the voluntary side of the activity and the involuntary side of the condition. The break with a sovereign self-consciousness arises precisely in this dependence on material conditions, determining conditions; still, conditions are always coupled with the concept of activity. Perhaps this is enough, though, about the first concept under consideration, the material and real and its connection either with individuals or conditions. We thus preserve the two possible readings of this text.

The next concept we shall discuss is that of productive forces. This concept is of consequence since it introduces history into the whole argument. History affects the anthropological basis we have just examined through what Marx calls the development of productive forces. The role of this concept has important implications for the concept of ideology; in an extreme and very strong statement, to which we shall return later in more detail, Marx says that there is no history of ideology (47). The process of history always comes from below, and for Marx this is precisely from the development of productive forces. Life in general has no history; living beings like bees and ants always build their homes in the same way. There is, however, a history of human production.

Connected to this concept of productive forces is the concept of the modes of production, what later works will call the relations of production. The relationship between productive forces and the modes of production is significant because the structuralist and anti-humanist interpretation of Marx will rely principally on this interplay between forces and forms, between forces of production and relations of production. The relations of production are mainly the juridical framework, the system of property, of salary, and so on; they are therefore the social rules according to which the technological process proceeds. Marx's claim is that technology, which involves only the productive forces, cannot be described as existing in and of itself; productive forces do not exist as such "nowhere." They are always caught in a certain juridical framework, a state, and so forth. Consequently, productive forces and forms are always interconnected. The evolutionary schema typical of Marx applies also at this level. Marx describes the whole process of history as an evolution of productive forces conjoined with an evolution of corresponding forms. In characterizing the division of labor and the forms of ownership—the consecutive evolutionary development of tribal, communal, feudal, and then capitalistic property—the status of the regime of property constitutes the form within which the forces develop (43–46). One trend that develops in orthodox Marxism is the claim that the only problem needing resolution is the discrepancy between forms and forces. The argument is that the capitalist structure is an obstacle to the development of productive forces, and therefore revolution will be the process by which forms and forces become harmonious.

The third concept we shall consider is that of class, the mode of union, of association, resulting from the interplay between forces and forms. This concept is critical for our study, since the problem is whether class is the ultimate requisite for a theory of ideology. Some texts say that an ideology is always an ideology of class. In this case, it is the concept underlying a theory of ideology. For another kind of analysis, however, there may be a genealogy of class. Therefore, determination of the role of class depends on how we locate the concept in Marx's analysis. In *The German Ideology* Marx introduces the concept of class in the following way:

The fact is, therefore, that definite individuals who are productively active in a definite way enter into these definite social and political relations. . . . The social

> structure and the State are continually evolving out of the life-process of definite individuals, but of individuals, not as they may appear *[erscheinen]* in their own or other people's imagination *[Vorstellung]*, but as they really are; i.e. as they operate, produce materially, and hence as they work under definite material limits, presuppositions and conditions independent of their will. (46–47)

I would amend the translation slightly. *Vorstellung* is not imagination but rather conception, idea, or representation. Marx contrasts the way certain things appear *(erscheinen)* as phenomena, that is, in representations, with the way they actually are. We must preserve the term *Vorstellung,* since it is the basic notion for what ideology really means.

On the basis of the statement just quoted, I again surmise that the key concept at work is the individual under certain conditions, but where the conditions belong to the structure of the individual. The class structure belongs to what people are and not to what they "imagine," not to what they merely conceive themselves to be. Therefore, we could say that this structure is an ontological structure; it is a mode of being together which precedes the way in which people represent their situation. The text of the original German makes this point even more strongly. When Marx says "as they really are," the German for "really" is *wirklich,* and *wirklich* has the same root as *wirken,* which has been translated by "as they operate." So in German to be real and to operate are the same thing. To be is to be operating, and the class is a way of operating together. Once more the concept of operating individuals supports the concept of class; necessary to the structure is "the life-process of definite [*bestimmter,* determinate or determined] individuals." Here is an initial anticipation of the relation between the so-called superstructure and the so-called infrastructure; the class is an infrastructure, but as a mode of being together it is also an activity under certain conditions.

The text then leads us to the important concept of historical materialism, although the term itself is not used and in fact is not found in Marx but only in later Marxism.[1] This concept proceeds from the description of the set of material conditions without which there would be no history. For *The German Ideology,* historical materialism is the description of the material conditions which give a history to humanity. The editor of the English translation has entitled this section "History: Fundamental Conditions" (48). Historical materialism is not yet a philosophy, a theory, a doctrine, a dogma; instead, it is a way of reading human life on the basis of the material conditions of its activity.

Marx summarizes the nature of historical development articulated by historical materialism in three points. Historical materialism incorporates first the production of the means to satisfy human material needs (48). When economists speak of need, says Marx, they speak of an entity which is an abstraction. They neglect the fact that needs receive their historical dimension only from the production of the means of satisfy them. More precisely, then, the production of material life itself is historical, but needs as such are not. This is true to such an extent that the second stage of this history is the production of new needs (49). When we produce only the means to satisfy existing needs, this production is limited to the horizon of these given needs. The second basic element of historical consequence arises only in the production of new needs. Only then is there a history of desire, as we know well in the present age of advertising, this permanent creation of needs in order to sell and so on.

The third moment which enters into historical development is the reproduction of humanity through the family (49). Comparison of Marx and Hegel on this topic is instructive. In Hegel's *Philosophy of Right,* the family represents the social structure in its most natural and immediate phase; economic life is considered later. For Marx, however, the structure of the family proceeds from the history of needs as part of the history of production. Here the history of the family is that it is first an economic cell, then it is destroyed by industry, and so on. The family is kept in the stream of the productive forces. Should we say, therefore, that historical materialism breaks completely with human beings, with the humanistic basis? We cannot if we keep in mind this fundamental declaration: "By social we understand the co-operation of several individuals, no matter under what conditions, in what manner and to what end" (50). *Zusammenwirken,* cooperation, is always behind a collective entity. The collective entities which are the object of historical materialism are constantly referred by Marx to the individuals who produce them.

We shall introduce as the fifth main concept of this text the concept of ideology itself. For Marx the ideological is that which is reflected by means of representations. It is the representational world as opposed to the historical world, the latter having a consistency of its own thanks to activity, the conditions of activity, the history of needs, the history of production, etc. The concept of reality covers all the processes that can be described under the title of historical materialism. Once more, ideology is not yet opposed to science, as will be the case in modern Marxism, but to reality.

I take as a central text on ideology some lines that we have already mentioned: "The social structure and the State are continually evolving out of the life-process of definite individuals, but of individuals not as they may appear in their own or other people's imagination *[Vorstellung]*, but as they really are . . ." (46). The concept of ideology may be large enough to cover not only distortions but all representations, all *Vorstellungen.* Ideology may sometimes be a neutral concept, so neutral that, for example, Eastern Communism speaks of communist ideology as opposed to bourgeois ideology. Therefore, the term ideology has no necessarily negative overtone. It is merely contrasted to what is real, actual, *wirklich.* We can see how close this is to distortion, since not to be real is the possibility of being distorted. Nevertheless, the difference between these two moments must be preserved.

If we preserve this difference, we realize that we cannot exclude the possibility that distortion is ideology in an inadequate form. This leads to the question whether there could be a language of real life which would be the first ideology, the most simple ideology. Marx responds in a paragraph I shall read almost line by line: "The production of ideas, of conceptions, of consciousness *[der Ideen, Vorstellungen, des Bewusstseins]* is at first directly interwoven with the material activity and the material intercourse of men, the language of real life" (47). This concept of the language of real life is fundamental to our analysis; the problem of ideology is only that it is representation and not real praxis. The dividing line is not between false and true but between real and representation, between praxis and *Vorstellung.*

In concord with Geertz here, I myself shall graft the entire analysis of ideology on this concession—on what will at least become a concession in Marxist language—that there is a language of real life which exists before all distortions, a symbolic structure of action that is absolutely primitive and ineluctable. Marx continues,

> Conceiving, thinking, the mental intercourse of men, appear at this stage as the direct efflux [*Ausfluss,* e-menation] of their material behavior. The same applies to mental production as expressed in the language of politics, law, morality, religion, metaphysics, etc. of a people. Men are the producers of their conceptions, ideas, etc.—real, active men, as they are conditioned by a definite development of their productive forces and of the intercourse *[Verkehrs]* corresponding to these, up to its furthest forms. (47)

"Intercourse" is the translation in this text of the German *Verkehr. Verkehr* is a word that will disappear from Marx's vocabulary and be replaced by *Verhältnis,* which has been translated by "relation" or "relationship." The paragraph goes on: "Consciousness can never be anything else than conscious existence, and the existence of men is their actual life-process." Here in German there is a play on words that neither the English nor the French translation can duplicate. Marx stresses that consciousness *(Bewusstsein)* is conscious *existence (bewusstes Sein).* Once more, consciousness is not autonomous but is instead connected with human beings' "actual life-process."

The distortions of ideology appear to the extent that we forget that our thoughts are a production; at this point the reversal occurs. Marx explains, in his famous lines on the *camera obscura,* which close the paragraph we have been discussing: "If in all ideology men and their circumstances appear upside-down, as in a *camera obscura,* this phenomenon arises just as much from their historical life-process as the inversion of objects on the retina does from their physical life-process" (47). This is the sort of text that plays a great role in orthodox Marxism. The image is a physical one—we can do nothing about that—and indeed the image in a camera is inverted. There appears, therefore, a mechanicistic approach to the problem of ideology in what is really only a metaphor. It is a metaphor of the reversal of images, but it proceeds as a comparison involving four terms. The ideological reversal is to the life-process as the image in perception is to the retina. But what is an image on the retina, I cannot say, since there are images only for consciousness. Hence, this metaphor is intriguing but also possibly deceiving.

Later we shall see how Louis Althusser tries in fact to get rid of this comparison to the inversion of the camera image. When an image is inverted, he maintains, it is still the same. Thus, Althusser goes so far as to say that the inverted image belongs to the same ideological world as its original. As a result, he claims, we must introduce a notion quite different from inversion, that of an epistemological break. (Althusser cites Spinoza as a good example of someone whose work articulated this perspective.) Althusser's imagery is that we must *break* with the ordinary perception of the sun rising and proceed to the astronomically accurate observation that there is no sunrise or sunset, except in the narrow perceptual sense. The change is not an inversion but a break, a *coupure.* (The word *coupure* was introduced in French by Gaston Bachelard to represent his claim that all scientific progress occurs through epistemological breaks.) For Althusser, therefore, the notion of an epistemological break must be substituted for that of the *camera obscura,* since an inverted image is always the same. To invert Hegelianism may be anti-Hegelian, but this inversion remains nevertheless within a Hegelian framework.

This Althusserian insight is not what I want to stress about Marx's text, however. I am interested here not so much in the false clarity of the image of reversal but in the range of possibilities preserved by Marx's analysis, a range extending from the language of real life to radical distortion. I emphasize that the concept of ideology covers this full range. Also of interest is that which ideology is being related to, what Marx calls the actual life-process; this is the ultimate point of reference. Human beings are always the point of reference, but they are human beings under historical conditions.

In any event, this unfortunate image of the camera, the *camera obscura,* brings forth some other unfortunate characterizations also. In the text they are no more than images, but they have been frozen in orthodox Marxism. I think particularly of the terms "reflex" and "echo." "We set out from real, active men, and on the basis of their real life-process we demonstrate the development of the ideological reflexes and echoes of this life-process. The phantoms formed in the human brain are also, necessarily, sublimates of their material life-process . . ." (47). People live but they have echoes of this life-process in their brains. Here ideology appears as a kind of smoke or fog, something that is secondary in terms of production. Notice also the word "sublimates" that appears in the text. This word has become popular through Freud, but just like the *camera obscura,* the retinal image, it has a physical origin. The sublimate is what evaporates in some chemical processes (more those of alchemy than chemistry); it is a deposit at the upper part of the vessel. Therefore the sublimate is the evaporation of the product. The expressions reflexes, echoes, sublimates, and retinal image all entail something evolving out of something else.

In later Marxism, the relation established between reality and the echo or reflex leads to a permanent disparaging of all autonomous intellectual activity. Evidence of this perspective is also available in Marx's own famous statement that intellectual activities have no history.

> Morality, religion, metaphysics, all the rest of ideology and their coresponding forms of consciousness, thus no longer retain the semblance of independence. They have no history, no development; but men, developing their material production and their material intercourse *[Verkehr],* alter, along with this their real existence, their thinking and the products of their thinking. (47)

By his use of the phrase "all the rest of ideology," Marx includes all the spheres involving representations in general, all cultural productions—art, law, and so on; the scope is extremely wide. The text is less strong than it may appear, however, since Marx says, "men, developing their material production—alter, along with this their real existence, their thinking and the products of their thinking." There is, therefore, a shadow history.

Marx's statement oscillates between a truism that people first live and then speak, think, and so on, and a fallacy that there is finally, for example, no history of art, to say nothing of a history of religion. The truism is the famous and, I would say, wonderful assertion that follows immediately the lines just cited: "Life is not determined by consciousness, but consciousness by life" (47). This is a classic assertion in Marxism. If we call consciousness not the modern English sense of consciousness, more or less synonymous with awareness, but the capacity for projecting objects, then it signifies the Kantian and Hegelian world of having objects, of organizing an objective world in representation; it is the whole phenomenal world as construed mentally. This is the sense of consciousness preserved by Freud; when he speaks of consciousness, it is as reality-testing. Marx's claim is that reality-testing is not something autonomous but rather a part of the whole process of the living individual. In analyzing this contrast between life being determined by consciousness and consciousness being determined by life, Marx says: "In the first method of approach the starting point is consciousness taken as the living individual; in the second method, which conforms to real life, it is the real living individuals themselves, and consciousness is considered solely as their consciousness" (47). Thus, if we take Marx's statement in a more narrow sense, as saying that nothing happens in consciousness, then it is not too interesting; on the other hand if we take it more broadly, as saying that it is the consciousness of the real individual, then perhaps the statement is less striking.

Later Marxist theory of ideology continues to struggle with this ambiguity; as we shall see in future lectures, it attempts to find a position of equilibrium in the famous proposition by Engels that the economic situation is the cause in the last instance, but the superstructure also reacts on the infrastructure. The autonomy of the ideological spheres is preserved, but the primacy of the economic is still asserted. The Marxists therefore try to find their way between two statements: that there is no history of consciousness, of ideology, but only a history of production, and that nevertheless the ideological spheres have a certain autonomy.

That ideology covers much more ground than religion, in the sense of

Feuerbach, is proved by the fact that science too is a part of the ideological sphere. For science the issue is the same as that which we have already discussed: there is the possibility of a real science when it is involved in real life. Science is real when it is the science of real life; at that point it is not a representation, a *Vorstellung,* but the presentation of the practical activity, the practical process, of human beings. Marx's comments on this matter are most important, because they define the status of his own book. The book is itself an ideological work in the sense that it is not life but the presentation of life. Marx writes: "Where speculation ends—in real life—there real, positive science begins: the representation of the practical activity, of the practical process of development of men" (48). We may thus relate this real, positive science to what Marx called, one page earlier, "the language of real life" (47).

We must correct one important mistake in the translation of the present passage, however. Where the translation has "the representation of practical life," the word "representation" is incorrect. In the original German the word is no longer *Vorstellung* but *Darstellung,* the exposé of life. Marx's utilization of *Darstellung* has its antecedent in Hegel. In the famous preface to the *Phenomenology of Spirit,* Hegel says that the task of philosophy is to give the *Darstellung,* the presentation, of the whole process. Marx here retains, then, the important Hegelian concept that beyond distorted representation there exists real presentation. Marx must leave room for such a concept because a book like *Capital* must justify its epistemological status in relation to ideology; its status is that of the presentation, the *Darstellung,* of the practical activity, the practical processes. "Empty talk about consciousness ceases, and real knowledge has to take its place. When reality is depicted, philosophy as an independent branch of knowledge loses its medium of existence" (48). The word "depicted" is the translation of the German verb form for *Darstellung.* I am not sure whether in English depiction may be too close to fiction. Still, the word is also used in the English translation of Wittgenstein's *Tractatus.* So there is something which may replace philosophy, at least to the extent that philosophy is the philosophy of consciousness, as in the German ideologies Marx criticizes. A place exists for a science of real life, which therefore must assume the status of the language of real life, the status of the discourse of praxis.

This issue will lead us in future lectures to the question whether we may construe a concept of praxis that does not have from the beginning a symbolic dimension so that it might have and receive its own language. If this language is not already constitutive of action, to appropriate Kenneth Burke's concept of symbolic action, then we cannot have this positive concept of ideology. We must leave room not only for a language of real life, for real science as *Darstellung,* though; we must also leave room for some logical activity that occurs in relation to this reality, namely, the necessity of building some abstractions, mythological abstractions. We must leave room for these mythological abstractions because all the concepts in a work—in Marx's case, production, conditions of production, and so on—are constructs.

In *The German Ideology* this logical activity is anticipated if not by an explicitly transcendental language then at least by a language of the condition of the possibility of description itself. "At the best [philosophy's] place can only be taken by a summing-up of the most general results, abstractions which arise from the observation of the historical development of men" (48). For my part I would say that this statement typifies the epistemological status of what Marx called the "premises" of his materialist method (42). Premises are inevitable; we cannot start merely by looking at things. We must read other phenomena, and we need some keys in order to read them. Marx continues: "Viewed apart from real history, these abstractions have in themselves no value whatsoever. They can only serve to facilitate the arrangement of historical material, to indicate the sequence of its separate strata" (48). This is not that far from what Max Weber calls ideal types. In sociology we cannot proceed by means of the naked eye alone. We must have such notions as forces and forms, and these are not given in reality but are constructs. Therefore, Marx as the ideologist of real life must rely first on a language of real life, second, on a real science of praxis, and third, on some abstractions allowing him to construe this science. And Marx insists that all these factors must be referred back to their origin in human beings. His methods has premises and "Its premises are men . . ." (47).

After discussing at such length the concept of ideology, let us now turn to the concept of consciousness, which is the central concept of German ideology. Marx wrote *The German Ideology* to oppose the import granted this concept. If the first part of the text is on Feuerbach, it is because Feuerbach made self-consciousness—the self-production of human beings by means of consciousness—the key. For Marx, consciousness is not a concept from which we depart but one at which we must arrive. The question of consciousness arises only after having considered four prior moments: the production of material life, the history of needs, the reproduction of life, and the cooperation of individuals in social entities (48–50). Consciousness is therefore not the ground but an effect.

Only now, after having considered four moments, four aspects of the primary historical relationship, do we find that man also possesses "consciousness," but, even so, not inherent, not "pure" consciousness. From the start the "spirit" is afflicted with the curse of being "burdened" with matter, which here makes its appearance in the form of agitated layers of air, sounds, in short, of language.

Language appears, we may say, as the body of consciousness. (A similar passage in the *Manuscripts*, which I passed over in lecture, makes the same point [143].)

Language is as old as consciousness, language *is* practical consciousness that exists also for other men, and for that reason alone it really exists for me personally as well; language, like consciousness, only arises from the need, the necessity, of intercourse with other men. (50–51)

This is language as discourse. To my mind Marx's whole description of language here does not belong to a theory of class but to a fundamental anthropology, because all human beings speak, and they all have language. This proves that the concept of intercourse itself, of exchange, belongs to this radical anthropological layer, no longer in the sense of consciousness but of life, of living individuals. "Where there exists a relationship it exists for me: the animal does not enter into 'relations' with anything, it does not enter into any relation at all" (51). The break between animal and humans typical of the *Manuscripts* can be raised here also on the basis of language. I wonder what Marx would say now about the discovery of some kind of language in bees and so on?

The final concept I would like to consider is that of the division of labor. Our entire enumeration of the basic concepts leads us to this concept; it is a term that takes the place of alienation in this text. What we need to discuss is whether the division of labor takes the place of alienation as a synonym or as a substitute. This question is still controversial among Marxists. Louis Althusser, for example, claims that the concept of alienation has disappeared from *The German Ideology;* he maintains that it has been replaced by the division of labor and that the latter concept belongs to the same sphere as modes of production, and so on. I myself shall attempt to show that the concept of the division of labor in fact provides the connecting link here in Marx between the more anthropological concepts and the abstract structures such as class and modes of production, because it is through the division of labor that objectified entities arise. Therefore, I content, this concept plays the role of alienation and perhaps is alienation under another name.

In the *Manuscripts* the division of labor is considered more as an effect than as a cause. It is principally the effect of the process rendering property abstract. Labor has forgotten its power of creating private property, and private property crushes the worker under its weight. Labor is scattered when hired by capital, it is hired for this or that task; this fragmentation of labor's tasks is an effect of the abstraction of property. The division of labor becomes the central concept because it is the fragmentation of the activity of labor itself. We may follow the evolution from the *Manuscripts* to *The German Ideology* if we consider the concept of alienation at what the *Manuscripts* calls its second stage: alienation of the activity. The division of labor is the synonym of this second stage. I would maintain, in fact, that the problem of the division of labor would not be of interest if it were not a fragmentation of human being. Otherwise, the division of labor would be merely a technological phenomenon: people work in special ways, and these special ways of working are part of the system of production. Because labor is what people do, however, it is their activity which is in division, decomposition, and fragmentation. The division of labor is the fragmentation of humanity itself as a whole. Therefore, the concept of the division of labor must be understood, it seems to me, from the point of view of humanity as a whole, and thus still on the basis of the category of totality.

Marx's principal text on the division of labor comes as part of a long paragraph, which I quote in detail:

> finally, the division of labour offers us the first example of how, as long as man remains in natural society, that is, as long as a cleavage exists between the particular and the common interests, as long, therefore, as activity is not voluntarily, but naturally, divided, man's own deed becomes an alien power opposed to him, which enslaves him instead of being controlled by him. For as soon as the distribution of labour comes into being, each man has a particular, exclusive sphere of activity *[Tätigkeit]*, which is forced upon him and from which he cannot escape. He is a hunter, a fisherman, a shepherd, or a critical critic, and must remain so if he does not want to lose his means of livelihood; while in communist society, where nobody has one exclusive sphere of activity but each can become accomplished in any branch he wishes, society regulates the general production and thus makes it possible for me to do one thing today and another tomorrow, to hunt in the morning,

> fish in the afternoon, rear cattle in the evening, criticise after dinner, just as I have a mind, without ever becoming hunter, fisherman, shepherd or critic. This fixation of social activity, this consolidation of what we ourselves produce into an objective power above us, growing out of our control, thwarting our expectations, bringing to naught our calculations, is one of the chief factors in historical development up till now. (53)

On the basis of this text, I do not see how we could say that the concept of alienation has disappeared. On the contrary, I would say that now the concept is more concretely described; it appears less as a metaphysical process, objectification inverted. The concept of the division of labor gives a material basis to the concept of alienation. The role of human activity *(Tätigkeit)* is central; that the result of the division of labor is opposed to our activity is exactly what is at stake.

In the German edition, the lines suggesting that the concept of alienation has disappeared in this text begin the paragraph following the one just cited in part. (They appear a few pages later in the English version.) Marx writes: "This 'alienation' (to use a term which will be comprehensible to the philosophers) can, of course, only be abolished given two practical premises" (56). (I shall consider the two premises in a moment.) The word "alienation" disappears from the vocabulary of *The German Ideology* because it is a philosophical word; it belongs to the intellectual world of Feuerbach. If the word is now put within quotation marks, it is nevertheless the same concept expressed in different terms. One term is substituted for another, not as an exclusion of the concept but rather as a more concrete approach to it. All the features of estrangement are present in the way we are divided in our activity. Therefore, the alienation that occurs in the division of labor is something that affects us as individuals. It is not merely a process in society but a form of mutilation of the real individual. *The German Ideology* may deny the word "alienation" because it is idealistic, but it does not deny this concept's meaning. All the descriptions of the abolition of estrangement recur in this text.

If the concept of alienation is not idealistic when transposed into the language of the division of labor, the same is true for the notion of a communist society. In Marx's previous writings, a communist society was more or less a dream; here it is still a dream, but now at least it is considered as a real possibility because defined by its real conditions. When Marx says, "This 'alienation' . . . can . . . only be abolished given two practical premises," the two premises are the development of a world market and the constitution of a universal class throughout the world. These premises are sufficient for Marx to say that the concept of a communist society is not a utopia, because what characterizes a utopia is that it provides no clue for its introduction into history. Here the overcoming of the division of labor is the required historic condition.

> Communism is for us not a state of affairs which is to be estabished [for Marx this would be utopian], an ideal to which reality [will] have to adjust itself. We call communism the real movement which abolishes the present stage of things. The conditions of this movement result from the premises now in existence. (56–57)

Once again the concept of the real is central: real conditions are requisite for the abolition of the division of labor, and they "result from the premises now in existence."

In the next lecture I shall return briefly to the concept of the division of labor as a way of introducing the major issue of the session, the question of the two possible readings of the text. We may read *The German Ideology* by taking as a leading thread either the material conditions or the real individuals, and I shall try to arbitrate between them. It will be a personal way of reading, of course. In subsequent lectures, we shall turn to later Marxist texts. Unfortunately, I have read only recently in Gramsci, because finally he is the most interesting Marxist for our topic of ideology. He avoids the crude mechanicism which has prevailed in orthodox Marxism. In any event, though, these lectures are not a course in Marxism; they are only a reading of some Marxist texts.

6

Marx: *The German Ideology* (2)

In the previous lecture, my principal goal was to enumerate the basic concepts of *The German Ideology*. This enumeration allowed me generally to postpone questions about the interpretation of the text, the topic that is our main theme in the present lecture. A brief return to the concept of the division of labor will provide us with the entryway to this discussion.

Let me reiterate first that in the hierarchy of concepts in *The German Ideology*, the concept of the division of labor takes the exact place granted earlier in the *Manuscripts* to the concept of alienation. As Marx observes, we may say that even the concept of ideology is introduced by that of the division of labor. Marx's strong statement on this point is the remark with which I want to begin. "Division of labour only becomes truly such from the moment when a division of material and mental labour appears" (51). The division between real life and representation is itself a case of the division of labor. Thus, this concept has an extremely large field of application. In fact, one of the reasons I think that the division of labor has the same field of application as alienation is that we replace the latter by the former on the same semantic surface, the same grid of meaning. Marx continues, "From this moment onward consciousness can really flatter itself that it is something other than consciousness of existing practice, that it really represents something without representing something real. . . ." This characterization is comparable to the definition of the sophist in Plato; the sophist is the one who says something without saying something which is. In the present case we have the possibility of bracketing reality in the world of representation, of consciousness. "[F]rom now on consciousness is in a position to emancipate itself from the world and to proceed to the formation of 'pure' theory, theology, philosophy, ethics, etc." (51–52).

The concept of the division of labor between work and thought may not explain completely the concept of the inversion of an image, but the condition for having an inverted image of reality is provided by means of the seclusion of the realm of thought from that of praxis.

Recognition of the double relation between reality and ideology—that ideology is at once separated and secluded from reality and yet also generated by it—leads us to the crucial question to which the rest of this session will be devoted: to what real basis is the ideological process reduced? As I have said before, the text seems to allow two possible readings. On the one hand, we may take as the real basis the anonymous entities such as class, forces of production, and modes of production. On the other hand, we may ask whether these entities are themselves reducible to something more primitive. Perhaps it is only in the state of our society that these entitites have autonomy. In other words, perhaps the autonomy of the general, so-called economic condition is itself a product of the state of alienation, even if we do not use that word.

Of the two different readings of *The German Ideology,* we may call the first an objectivist, structuralist interpretation. This interpretive path leads to Althusser and others, people for whom the individual disappears at least from the level of the fundamental concepts. The fundamental concepts pertain instead to the functionings of the anonymous structures. With someone like Engels there is no doubt that the relation between reality and ideology is one between infrastructure and superstructure and not between individual and consciousness. In the second approach to the text, on the other hand, the real basis is ultimately what Marx calls the real individual living in definite conditions. Here class is an intermediary concept isolable only for the sake of methodological abstractions, constructs that Marx allows real science will utilize, but only with the knowledge that they in fact remain abstractions. The argument is that these constructs are more appropriate to the stage of estrangement, where anonymous structures do appear to rule. We can summarize the alternative readings, then, by asking whether concepts like classes are epistemological abstractions or the real basis.

In my presentation of these alternatives, I shall first follow the structural line of interpretation. We may acquire an initial sense of this reading from the following fundamental statement on ideology, which I have reserved until this point:

> The conditions under which definite productive forces can be applied are the conditions of the rule of a definite class of society, whose social power, deriving

> from its property, has its practical-idealistic expression in each case in the form of the State; and, therefore, every revolutionary struggle is directed against a class, which till then has been in power. (94)

The concept of the ruling class is the immediate support for a theory of ideology. Thus, to unmask an ideology is to uncover and expose the structure of power behind it. Lying behind an ideology is not an individual but a structure of society.

The connection between the ruling class and ruling ideas is raised in the following text:

> The ideas of the ruling class are in every epoch the ruling ideas, i.e. the class which is the ruling material force of society, is at the same time its ruling, intellectual force. The class which has the means of material production at its disposal, has control at the same time over the means of mental production, so that thereby, generally speaking, the ideas of those who lack the means of mental production are subject to it. The ruling ideas are nothing more than the ideal expression of the dominant material relationships, the dominant material relationships grasped as ideas. . . . (64)

There is no doubt in this passage that material relationships are the basis for mental production. I leave for future lectures what we can glean from this notion that a dominant interest becomes a dominant idea; the relationship is not so clear, there seems a radical obscurity. To anticipate briefly, the question will resurface principally in our discussion of Max Weber. For Weber, every system of power, authority, or whatever it may be, always strives to legitimate itself. Therefore, he says, the place where ideology arises is in the system of legitimation of an order of power. My own question, building on Weber, is whether we can put the question of legitimation in terms of causation—the causality of the infrastructure on the superstructure—or must we express it through another conceptual framework, that of motivation. Is not a system of legitimation a form of motivation and not causation? This is the problem to which we shall return. In contrast, at least in the text I have quoted, ideologies are as anonymous as their basis, since "The ruling ideas are nothing more than the ideal expression of the dominant material relationships . . . grasped as ideas. . . ." This relationship between the dominant material relationships and the ruling ideas becomes the leading thread of the theory of ideology in orthodox Marxism, and it is increasingly interpreted in mechanistic terms and not at all in terms of a process of legitimation, which is still a kind of intellectual procedure. Thus, a first argument for reading the text on the basis of anonymous entities derives from the role played by the concept of the ruling class as the support for ruling ideas.

A second argument is that the ruling position in turn refers to a factor which Marx calls the real ground or real basis of history. This basis is expressed as an interplay between forces and forms or between forces and intercourse *(Verkehr),* what in later texts will be relations *(Verhältnisse).* Marx examines "The form of intercourse determined by the existing productive forces . . . and in its turn determining these . . ." (57). Therefore it is quite possible to write a history of the society without mentioning individuals but instead relying only on recourse to forces and forms. Another word Marx uses for the notion of the basis is circumstances *(Umstände).* Marx speaks of

> a mass of productive forces, capital funds and conditions, which, on the one hand, is indeed modified by the new generation, but also on the other prescribes for it its condition of life and gives it a definite development, a special character. It shows that circumstances make men just as much as men make circumstances. (59)

In the last sentence we have a more balanced expression; the relationship is circular rather than in one direction only. Orthodox Marxism will try to preserve this reciprocity by saying that while the infrastructure remains the dominant factor in the last instance, the superstructure may also react on the infrastructure. As we shall see more fully in following lectures, ascertaining what the phrase "in the last instance" really entails is the kernel of many of the theoretical conflicts within later Marxism. In the present context, the notion is that circumstances make human beings, but human beings also make circumstances. Marx also says that these circumstances are in fact what the philosophers have called "substance" (59). Philosophy wants to relate all changes to something that exists fundamentally, and the concept of substance plays this role. What the philosophers call substance, says Marx, is what he calls the concrete basis.

A third argument favoring the structural reading derives from the enormous place granted in Marx's empirical descriptions to such collective entities as the city and country. For Marx the city/country relationship is an aspect of the division of labor. This relationship plays a great role in Chinese Marxism; there it is one of the fundamental oppositions central to the division of labor. At one time Stalin also tried to attack this problem of the division between country and city. Marx himself writes: "The greatest division of material and mental labour is the separation of town and country" (68–69). This division may be superimposed on the division between the material and the mental, since we may say that the more mentally oriented activities are concentrated in the town. So the two divisions reinforce one another. This convergence is itself one more reason to read history at the level of an encounter and conflict between city and country.

We can follow this third line of argument further by noting that the great actors of this history are collective entities. Perhaps the principal structural agent—along with the proletariat as a class—is what Marx calls manufacture or industry. (We recall Marx's great admiration for the analysis of the English economists, who made the birth of the factory the birth of modern times.) Marx makes such statements as: "With guild-free manufacture, property relations also quickly changed" (73). "The expansion of trade and manufacture accelerated the accumulation of movable capital . . ." (74). Present is a dramaturgy of economic structures; one structure crumbles and is replaced by another, such as by the anonymous phenomenon the accumulation of movable capital (later a key concept in *Capital*). In quoting these sentences, my question is not at all whether Marx's description is accurate; I am neither interested in that problem nor competent to make that judgment. Instead, my concern is the epistemological structure of the work; I want to uncover the historical agents in the text. When Marx writes about collective entities being the actors of history, he always has in mind that the entities that have a history are not ideas but trade, commerce, property, labor, and so on. Thus, if I speak of these collective entities as historical agents, it is to do justice to all those texts where these entities act, they do something. There is a kind of dramatization associated with the activity of manufacture or industry.

> Big industry universalised competition in spite of these protective measures. . . . It destroyed as far as possible ideology, religion, morality, etc. and where it could not do this, made them into a palpable lie. It produced world history for the first time, insofar as it made all civilised nations and every individual member of them dependent for the satisfaction of their wants on the whole world, thus destroying the former natural exclusiveness of separate nations. It made natural science subservient to capital. . . . It destroyed natural growth in general. . . . It completed the victory of the commercial town over the countryside. . . . Generally speaking, big industry created everywhere the same relations between the classes of society. . . . Big industry makes for the worker not only the relation to the capitalist, but labour itself, unbearable. (77–78)

Big industry, a faceless structure, is the historical actor, the logical subject.

Even the division of labor, which we presented before as a fragmentation of human being, appears now as an aspect of the industrial class structure.

The division of labour, which we already saw above . . . as one of the chief forces of history up till now, manifests itself also in the ruling class as the division of mental and material labour, so that inside this class one part appears as the thinkers of the class (its active, conceptive ideologists, who make the perfecting of the illusion of the class about itself their chief source of livelihood), while the others' attitude to these ideas and illusions is more passive and receptive, because they are in reality the active members of this class and have less time to make up illusions and ideas about themselves. (65)

Perhaps the strongest argument for the structural reading of the text is a fourth claim: the necessity of political struggle places the stress on conflicts not between individuals but between classes. Here the concept of the proletariat appears precisely as a collective entity. To the extent that the proletariat becomes the second major historical agent, along with industry, we may write history as the conflict between big industry and the proletariat without mentioning individuals but only structures and forms.

And if these material elements of a complete revolution are not present (namely, on the one hand the existing productive forces, on the other the formation of a revolutionary mass, which revolts not only against separate conditions of society up till then, but against the very "production of life" till then, the "total activity" on which it was based), then, as far as practical development is concerned, it is absolutely immaterial whether the idea of this revolution has been expressed a hundred times already, as the history of communism proves. (59)

A revolution is a historical force and not a conscious production. Any consciousness of the need for change is supported by a class, "a class which forms the majority of all members of society, and from which emanates the consciousness of the necessity of a fundamental revolution . . ." (94). Orthodox Marxism will develop this conflict between structures in terms of what Freud calls, in relation to the struggle between life and death described in *Civilization and Its Discontents,* a gigantomachy, a conflict of giants. We may read and write history as the clash between capital and labor, a polemical relation between entities, a conflict of historical ghosts.

We may close this structural reading by a fifth and final characteristic, the methodological decision not to read history according to its own consciousness but according to the real basis. The claim that the historian is not to share the illusions of the epoch studied is advanced at several points. The following text is an example of Marx's critique:

The exponents of this [classical] conception of history have consequently only been able to see in history the political actions of princes and States, religious and all sorts of theoretical struggles, and in particular in each historical epoch have had to share the illusion of that epoch. For instance, if an epoch imagines itself to be actuated by purely "political" or "religious" motives, although "religion" and "politics" are only forms of its true motives, the historian accepts this opinion. (59–60)

In writing about the political actions of princes and states and various religious and theoretical struggles, the classical approach attends only the surface of history. It neglects that behind the king of Norway, to cite the familiar example, there is the herring and the history of herring trade. Historians fail when they assume the illusions of the epoch examined. It is on the basis of this kind of critique that I have elsewhere linked Marxism to what I call the school of suspicion.[1] Not to share the illusion of an epoch is precisely to look behind or, as the Germans say now, *hinterfragen,* to question behind.

This concludes my presentation of the structural reading of *The German Ideology,* with the exception of one final quotation. I have kept for the end perhaps the most pointed statement supporting the structural interpretation of this text: "Thus all collisions in history have their origin, according to our view, in the contradiction between the productive forces and the form of intercourse" (89). This statement defines what will become the classical orthodox Marxist position. The productive forces change on the basis of technological development, but the forms of intercourse resist. Indeed, resistance obtains not only in the productive relations—the juridical form of property is a good example—but also in the system of ideas grafted onto these structures. A revolutionary situation is created when this conflict, this contradiction, between productive forces and forms of intercourse constitutes a tension close to the point of rupture. For our purposes the most salient point here is the complete bracketing of the individuals bearing the contradiction.

Having amassed some of the passages upholding the objectivist reading of *The German Ideology,* I now would like to turn to those sections where real individuals in their conditions are emphasized and underlined as the ultimate basis. We shall see that Marx provides the tools for an inner criticism of any approach treating as ultimate explanatory factors such categories as the ruling class. Let us return first to the apparently clear statement that a ruling class is always behind a ruling idea. We recall the sentence that introduces Marx's discussion: "The ideas of the ruling class are in every epoch the ruling ideas, i.e. the class which is the ruling material force of society, is at the same time its ruling intellectual force" (64). For Marx, though, this link between ruling class and ruling idea is not mechanical; it is not a mirror image like an echo or a reflection. This relationship requires an intellectual process of its own.

> For each new class which puts itself in the place of one ruling before it, is compelled, merely in order to carry through its aim, to represent its interest as the common interest of all the members of society, that is, expressed in ideal form: it has to give its ideas the form of universality, and represent them as the only rational, universally valid ones. (65–66)

A change occurs in the ideas themselves. (I leave what it might mean for an interest to be "expressed" in ideal form until the discussion of Geertz and others who maintain that in any interest there is already a symbolic structure.) A process of idealization takes place, since an idea linked to a particular interest must appear as a universal idea. This means that a process of legitimation also occurs which claims acceptance by the rest of the society. Therefore, a real work of thought is implied in the transposition of particular interests into universal interests.

Not only does this transposition require a real effort of thought, but it may proceed in a number of different ways. If, for instance, we say that rationalism in the eighteenth century represented the interests of the rising class, the bourgeoisie, we cannot deduce from this statement the differences between Descartes, Spinoza, and Kant. Thus, the manner in which an interest is represented in an ideal sense is in fact the summary of a huge and complex process of thought. Lucien Goldmann, a student of Lukács, struggled his entire life with this problem. He tried to refine the Marxist model by distinguishing within the French society of the seventeenth century, for example, the competing interests of such groups as the military and the judiciary. Goldmann claimed the enterprise of the latter had specific contradictions which could be represented by the hidden god of Pascal. As we can see, this is very difficult work to undertake, but it is one of the great challenges of a Marxist history of ideas to make more plausible the connections between a system of interests and a system of thought.

I myself would argue that there are many intermediary links or stages between a crude assertion of an interest and the refined form of a philosophical or theological system. We may take as another example the Reformation conflict between Calvinists and Jesuits on predestination and free will. To a certain extent we may say that this conflict is a way of dealing with forces not mastered in economic life, but there are so many steps between the economic contradictions and their theological expression that their direct linkage becomes either a truism or a fallacy, especially if the model used is borrowed from a mechanical kind of physics. We would have to speak, like later Marxism, of the efficiency of the basis, but I shall leave that discussion for our reading of Althusser. It makes more sense, I think, if we interpret the relationship between an interest and its expression in ideas by means of a system of legitimation. (Again, I use the term as advanced by Max Weber.) If we utilize this framework, then we must introduce the notion of motive and also the role of the individual agents who have these motives, because a system of legitimation is an attempt to justify a system of authority. The process is a complex interplay of claims and beliefs, claims on the part of the authority and beliefs on the part of the society's members. The motivational process is so complex that it is extremely difficult to incorporate it within the crude relationship between infrastructure and superstructure. The orthodox model may have to be refined to such an extent that finally it breaks.

Let us turn now to the role of class. As before I do not discuss Marx as a historian of society; my question is not whether he is correct to say that this class has replaced that one. Instead, my question is what does Marx mean by class; in particular, to what extent is class an ultimate category? There are many passages in which Marx suggests that class actually has a history of its own and that its autonomy in relation to the individual is itself a process similar to the one that isolates ideas from their basis. We may say, therefore, that a theory of history which utilizes the concept of class as an ultimate cause is in fact the victim of the illusion of autonomy, exactly as the ideologist falls victim to the illusion of the independence of ideas. Marx writes, "The separate individuals form a class only insofar as they have to carry on a common battle against another class. . . ." A genealogy is offered for what in another kind of discourse becomes an ultimate factor. Two discourses are intertwined, one for which class is the historical agent and another for which an anthropological reduction or genealogy of the sociological entity occurs. Marx continues:

On the other hand, the class in its turn achieves an independent existence over against the individuals, so that the latter find their conditions of existence predestined, and hence have their position in life and their personal development assigned to them by their class, become subsumed under it. This is the same phenomenon as the subjection of the separate individuals to the division of labour and can only be removed by the abolition of private property and of labour itself. We have already indicated several times how this subsuming of individuals under the class brings with it their subjection to all kinds of ideas, etc. (82)

The same process that severs ideas from real life has severed the class from the individual. Therefore, class itself has a history.

In several other passages Marx speaks of the class as a circumstance or condition. What we must recognize is that there are conditions or circumstances only for individuals. Conditions and circumstances always refer to the individuals found in these situations. Thus, we must apply the same reduction from class to individual as from ideology to class; an anthropological reduction supports the economic reduction. An anthropological reduction is implied in Marx's continual claim that real individuals are the ones who enter into relations.

If from a philosophical point of view one considers this evolution of individuals in the common conditions of existence of estates and classes, which followed on one another, and in the accompanying general conceptions forced upon them, it is certainly very easy to imagine that in these individuals the species, or "Man," has evolved, or that they evolved "Man"—and in this way one can give history some hard clouts on the ear. One can conceive these various estates and classes to be specific terms of the general expression, subordinate varieties of the species, or evolutionary phases of "Man." (83)

Marx makes an anthropological interpretation of class structure. In fact, Marx's argument is even more forceful than that. To claim that the aim of the communist revolution is the abolition of class presupposes that class is not an inviolable structure, not a given, but rather a product of history. Just as it has been created, so it can also be destroyed. The notion of the abolition of class makes sense only if class is not an irreducible, historical factor but the result of a transformation of personal powers into objective powers. "The transformation through the division of labour, of personal powers (relationships) into material powers, cannot be dispelled by dismissing the general idea of it from one's mind, but can only be abolished by the individuals again subjecting these material powers to themselves and abolishing the division of labour" (83). The true victims of the division of labor, of the class structure, are individuals. Individuals can undertake the project of abolishing the class structure and the division of labor because it is their own personal powers which have been transformed into material powers. Class and the division of labor are manifestations of those material powers which are the transformation of our personal power. The notion of personal power is placed at the forefront.

Marx amplifies this argument, saying: "Individuals have always built on themselves, but naturally on themselves within their given historical conditions and relationships, not on the 'pure' individual in the sense of the ideologists" (83). This text convinced me that the break between the young Marx and the classical Marx lies not in the abolition of the individual but, on the contrary, in the emergence of the individual from the idealistic concept of consciousness. My main argument against the interpretation of Althusser is that the break between humanism and Marxism is intelligible only if we interpret humanism in terms of a claim of consciousness and not as a claim of the real individual. The break is between consciousness and real individual, not between human being and structures.

If we situate the break in this way, we appreciate better that the division of labor is troublesome because it is a division *within* the individual.

> [I]n the course of historical evolution, and precisely through the inevitable fact that within the division of labour social relationsips take on an independent existence, there appears a division within the life of each individual, insofar as it is personal and insofar as it is determined by some branch of labour and the conditions pertaining to it. (83–84)

The division of labor is problematic only because it divides each of us into two parts, one part being our inner life and the other what we give to the society, to the class, and so on. "The division between the personal and the class individual, the accidental nature of the conditions of life for the individual, appears only with the emergence of the class, which is itself a product of the bourgeoisie" (84). This sentence may be read to agree with both of the interpretative approaches to the text. The division within the individual is engendered by the class, but the class is itself engendered by the cleft within the individual, a cleft between the personal and the class parts of individual existence. The line of division, therefore, passes through each individual.

People's assertion of themselves as individuals is fundamental for understanding the process of liberation, of abolition. Liberation is the claim of the individual against the collective entities. The fundamental motivation of revolution, at least in *The German Ideology,* is the assertion of the individual. It is an individualist claim that may be read *not into* but *in* the text.

Thus, while the refugee serfs only wished to be free to develop and assert those conditions of existence which were already there, and hence, in the end, only arrived at free labour, the proletarians, if they are to assert themselves as individuals, will have to abolish the very condition of their existence hitherto . . . namely, labour [wage labor]. Thus they find themselves directly opposed to the form in which, hitherto, the individuals, of which society consists, have given themselves collective expression, that is, the State. In order, therefore, to assert themselves as individuals, they must overthrow the State. (85)

If the ultimate structure is the class, the ultimate motivating force is the individual. A competition exists in the text between an explanation based on structures and an explanation based on the ultimate motives of the individuals behind these structures.

In question is not only the motivation of the proletarians but also the form of their association. Marx envisages a party that would not be a machine, a bureaucracy, but a free union. The notion of united individuals is a constant in the text. Marx says that even if in the labor process workers are only cogs and act as class individuals, when they meet their comrades in the union, it is as real individuals. They extract themselves from the class relationship when they enter into this other relation. We may say that workers suffer as members of a class but react as individuals.

It follows from all that we have been saying up till now that the communal relationship into which the individuals of a class entered, and which was determined by their common interests over against a third party, was always a community to which these individuals belonged only as average individuals, only insofar as they lived within the conditions of existence of their class—a relationship in which they participated not as individuals but as members of a class. With the community of revolutionary proletarians, on the other hand, who take their conditions of existence and those of all members of society under their control, it's just the reverse; it is as individuals that the individuals participate in it.(85)

The apparent autonomy of the class appears because this mode of relationship is abstract: a worker labors and is paid on the basis of an anonymous, structural relationship. The free association is Marx's answer to the challenge of compulsory association in the class. One of the achievements of communism will be its inclusion of this movement of free association.

Communism differs from all previous movements in that it overturns the basis of all earlier relations of production and intercourse, and for the first time consciously treats all natural premises as the creatures of hitherto existing men, strips them of their natural character and subjugates them to the power of the united individuals. (86)

Attention is drawn to the power of united individuals; the issue is not one of collective entities. Reduction of the Marxist interpretation to a system of forces and forms prohibits any account of the movement that attempts to surpass it, because this movement is rooted in the self-assertion of individuals uniting themselves.

The primacy of the role of individuals is persistent.

> Thus two facts are here revealed. First the productive forces appear as a world for themselves, quite independent of and divorced from the individuals, alongside the individuals: the reason for this is that the individuals, whose forces they are, exist split up and in opposition to one another whilst, on the other hand, these forces are only real forces in the intercourse and association of these individuals. Thus, on the one hand, we have a totality of productive forces, which have, as it were, taken on a material form and are now for the individuals no longer the forces of the individuals but of private property, and hence of the individuals only insofar as they are owners of private property themselves. Never, in any earlier period, have the productive forces taken on a form so indifferent to the intercourse of individuals as individuals, because their intercourse itself was formerly a restricted one. (91–92)

When Marx says that productive forces are real forces only for individuals, the primacy of individuals cannot be asserted more strongly. Even in their most abstract condition (I refrain from saying alienated condition, as this term does not belong to the text), individuals do not disappear but become instead abstract individuals; and "only by this fact [are they] put into a position to enter into relation with one another as individuals" (92). By this fragmentation of all ties, each individual is sent back to himself or herself and then is able to join the others in a union of individuals.

In the prominence granted to the role of individuals, the most important aspect of this role is played by self-activity, *Selbstbetätigung*. Self-activity is a fundamental concept, for me the foundational concept at this point in the text. The emphasis placed on self-activity proves that there is not a complete break between the *Manuscripts* and *The German Ideology*. "The only connection which still links [individuals] with the productive forces and with their own existence—labour—has lost all semblance of self-activity and only sustains life by stunting it" (92). Self-activity has disappeared because of a process of inner destruction. We see that the concept of self-activity preserves from the *Manuscripts* something of the concept of objectification, the self-creation of human being. What confirms the continuity with the *Manuscripts* is that the concept of appropriation is maintained. "Thus things have now come to such a pass that the individual must appropriate the existing totality of productive forces . . ." (92). The word "alienation" may have disappeared, but the term "appropriation" has survived this shift. Marx has abandoned the word "alienation" because it belonged too much to the language of consciousness and self-consciousness, to what now appears an idealistic vocabulary. When replaced, however, by the basic structure of the self-assertion of individuals, then the concept's nonidealistic intent may be recovered. In fact, all the concepts of the *Manuscripts,* previously encapsulated more or less in an ideology of self-consciousness, are now recovered for the sake of an anthropology of self-assertion, of self-activity. "Only the proletarians of the present day, who are completely shut off from all self-activity, are in a position to achieve a complete and no longer restricted self-activity, which consists in the appropriation of a totality of productive forces and in the thus postulated development of a totality of capacities" (92–93). All Marx's arguments are rooted here in this movement of self-activity, loss of self-activity, and appropriation of self-activity. *Selbstbetätigung* is the fundamental concept.

The key concept of individuals living in definite conditions is perhaps now better understood, because this concept is opposed to the notion of the individual as mere individual, of the individual as simply contingent with regard to its condition. Marx characterizes the individual's abstraction from any social conditioning by insisting on its subordination to the division of labor, which plays in *The German Ideology* the role played by alienation in the *Manuscripts.* The division of labor plays the same role as alienation because it has the same structure, except that it is no longer expressed in the language of consciousness but in the language of life. The concept of self-activity has replaced that of consciousness.

If this analysis is correct, it is a complete misunderstanding to conclude from the eviction of such entities as "Man," species, and consciousness the priority of the concepts of class, forces, and forms. It is a misunderstanding because these latter entities are objective precisely in the stage of the division of labor. Thus, to assume that these epistemological abstractions are the real basis is in fact to play the game of estrangement. The state is one example in this text of the self-assertion of an entity which is in fact a product (see 80). Another example is civil society (see 57); civil society is always presented here as a result before becoming in turn a basis. It is a result for a certain genealogy and a basis for a certain kind of explanation. Once again, a difficult problem raised by *The German Ideology* is the correct connection between the two readings, the anthropological reduction or genealogy and the economic explanation; these readings run on two parallel levels without intersecting. It is for the sake of different kinds of explanations that we refer either to the individual or to the class. There are methodological rules for applying this or that language game, the language game of the real individual or the language game of the class, forces, and forms. To eliminate the anthropology for the sake of the economic language, though, is in fact to assume the present state as unsurpassable.

A claim could be raised that I have not quoted the most important passage for our purposes, the one point in the text, as far as I know, where the word "superstructure" is employed. It appears in Marx's discussion of civil society: "Civil society as such only develops with the bourgeoisie; the social organisation evolving directly out of production and commerce, which in all ages forms the basis of the State and of the rest of the idealistic superstructure . . ." (57). I cannot say that this is the first time Marx used the word, I am not enough of an expert in the Marxist texts to assume that, but at least in *The German Ideology* it is the first time that the word occurs and, to my mind, the only time that it appears in part 1 of this text. The idealistic superstructure belongs to what I have called the language game of productive forces in contrast to that of the real, living individuals in certain conditions. My hypothesis in fact is that the great discovery of Marx here is the complex notion of the individual under definite conditions, because the possibility of the second reading is implied in the first one. We may bracket the individual and start from the conditions and contend that the conditions are the causes. In so doing, however, we do not destroy the dialectic between individual and condition, because the individual always exits in a certain condition or under a certain condition.

I recently had the opportunity to read an important work on Marx written by the French philosopher Michel Henry.[2] Henry has also written a big work on the concept of manifestation *(L'Essence de la Manifestation)*, and in his present book he has tried to reorganize Marx's texts around the same notion emphasized there, that of concrete bodily action or effort. He claims that only one other philosopher, Maine de Biran, has anticipated this perspective. For Henry a certain conditionality is implied in the process of effort; an effort is always connected to a resistance. (This connection between effort and resistance is the anthropological kernel of Maine de Biran's work.) On the basis of this relationship, Henry says, we may pass without contradiction to the objective language of the history of the conditions, which now act autonomously as real historical forces and agents. Thus, if we can correctly connect these two levels, then we no longer have two readings but rather a dialectical reading of the concepts of historical forces and real individuals. I am not sure, however, that the connections Henry strives for are so easily attained. In any case, just like Spinoza's and others, Marx's texts are open texts. We need not take a stand for or against communism or any kind of party. Marx's texts are good philosophical texts, and they must be read in the same manner as all others. There is room, therefore, for many interpretations of Marx, and Henry's is one of the plausible ones.

In the lectures that follow, I turn from Marx to Louis Althusser. I shall present first Althusser's reading of the *Manuscripts* and *The German Ideology* and then discuss his own interpretation of the theory of superstructure and his attempt to get rid of the notion of reversal by replacing it with that of epistemological break. Althusser proposes a transformation of Marxism on the basis of an epistemological critique. The concept of reversal, he says, remains inescapably within the framework of idealism. As we shall see, the price Althusser has to pay for this interpretation is high: any kind of humanism must be put on the side of ideology.

If the dividing line, at least in the young Marx, is between praxis and ideology, the dividing line later is between science and ideology. Ideology becomes the contrary of science and not the counterpart of real life. The importance of this stance may be related to the constitution of the Marxist corpus as itself a scientific body, or as at least claiming to be such. It offers a contrary to ideology. For the young Marx, this contrary did not exist and so ideology was opposed to real life. When Marxism itself becomes a corpus, however, then it provides the contrary to ideology. This change will mark the main shift in the history of ideology as a concept.

7

Althusser (1)

The next three lectures may be placed under the title, "Ideology and Science." I shall give an account of the change in the Marxist theory of ideology where ideology is no longer or not only related to reality but to science. I shall say something about the main changes which promoted this move in order to introduce the discussion of Louis Althusser's *For Marx*. I will not follow the historical order of this development, which would have led to theorists like Lukács, but more a logical order, logical at least with reference to what I want to say about the problem. Thus, this order has nothing necessary and still less anything compulsory about it.

I want to emphasize three main changes within the Marxist theory; these will provide us with a leading thread for the next three lectures. First, as I just mentioned, ideology is placed against the background of a different concept, not so much the real practical life-process—the language of *The German Ideology*—but science. For later Marxism the body of Marx's writing itself becomes the paradigm of science. Note that in analyzing the Marxist use of the word "science," we must set aside the positivist sense of the term, particularly dominant in this country, where the word has a much narrower scope than the German *Wissenschaft*. The German *Wissenschaft* preserves something of the Greek *epistēmē*. We should recall, for example, that Hegel called his encyclopedia *Encyclopaedia of the Philosophical Sciences*. In Marxist theory, then, the word "science" is typically not used in the empirical sense of a body of knowledge that can be verified or falsified, as in the Popperian sense of the term. Instead, science is more a fundamental theory. (The word "theory" is in fact preferred by Althusser for that reason.) Science is fundamental knowledge. Therefore, the shift in the concept of ideology must be measured according to the criteria of scientificity as embodied in Marxist "science." Earlier orthodox Marxism expressed this trend by distinguishing proletarian science from bourgeois science, but Althusser despises and rejects this claim. This opposition was extremely harmful to intellectual life within the Communist Party and within countries controlled by the Party; it led to both a certain lag in so-called bourgeois science and a petrification of the so-called proletarian science. Althusser attempts precisely to raise the level of the discussion. Whatever the differences within the Marxist school, though, the first general change in Marxist theory is development of the opposition between ideology and science.

The second important change is linked to the first and concerns the identification of the *real basis* of history. We noticed this concept of the real basis in *The German Ideology* and saw there a certain hesitation between—or at least sufficient room for—two different interpretations of this concept. One interpretation maintains that the real basis is ultimately the real individuals in determinate or definite conditions, while the other argues that the real basis is the interplay of productive forces and productive relations. Orthodox Marxism chooses the latter interpretation, and this too affects the theory of ideology. If we want to continue to oppose ideology to reality, we must recognize that reality is defined here by whatever Marxist science identifies as the real basis. Therefore, Marxist interpretation of the real basis as economic structures is coherent with the emergence of science as the corollary pole, because the object of this so-called Marxist science is precisely correct knowledge of the real basis.

This conjunction between the concept of science and the real basis—that is, economic structures—constitutes the kernel of historical materialism. The word "materialism" does not necessarily imply a cosmology, as in the sense it took on in Engels, a philosophy of nature that is a kind of scholasticism of nature. Engels' position is better described as dialectical materialism. The term "historical materialism," in contrast, is oriented by the connection between science and its object, the real basis. Because ideology is said to be the opposite pole to science and the real basis, it is also placed in opposition to historical materialism. The result is the common opposition in orthodox Marxism between idealism and materialism, as if we can choose only between two colors in order to paint reality. The opposition is implied in the very nature of the contrast allowed: if you are not a historical materialist, you are then an idealist. To be described as an idealist means only that you are not a materialist in the sense endorsed. I recently encountered a contemporary example of this perspective in a book on the philosophy of history written by I. S. Kon, a very good Russian philosopher. In his work *Philosophical Idealism and the Crisis in Bourgeois Historical Thinking,* Kon says that the philosophy of history has two sides only, one of which is the bourgeois philosophy of history; and he includes among this latter group Jean-Paul Sartre. Thus, attribution is a question of elimination; if we are not on one side, we are necessarily on the other.

The third change in Marxist theory, particularly fundamental to our discussion, is that the relation between the real basis and ideology becomes expressed in the language of a fundamental metaphor of an edifice with a base and floors. This topographic metaphor is already implied in the image of a real basis. It is very difficult not to think in terms of this metaphor, to describe cultural phenomena other than in layers. In fact, Marxists are not the only ones to utilize this imagery. It also appears, for example, in Freud; his conceptual structure of the id, ego, and superego is itself topographical. The problem with the topographic model is always to what extent we are deceived by the metaphor when it is taken literally. Classical Marxism develops this metaphor by introducing between the real basis and the superstructure a complex system of relations defined in terms of determination or effectivity, *efficacité*.

To put it in another way, we may say that the relation between infrastructure and superstructure in Marxism is ruled by a complex interaction that has two sides. On the one hand, Marxism argues, there is a causal relation: the superstructure is determined by the infrastructure. On the other hand, though, a second relation exists which more or less qualifies the first one: the superstructure has a relative autonomy, Marxism says, and even has the possibility of reacting back onto its basis. Here we may recognize the classic concept of *Wechselwirkung,* mutual action. This concept has a long history; it stems from Newton's attempt to explain the mutual relationship between forces and appears also in such figures as Kant and Hegel. In Kant's table of categories, *Wechselwirkung* is the third category of relation after substance and causality. In Hegel's *Logic,* quantity is followed by action, reaction, mutual action, and so on. In Marxism, mutual action is encompassed within the notion of a unidirectional relationship; it is a way of qualifying this relationship. For Marxism the cornerstone of the theory of ideology is constituted by the subordination of mutual action to action that proceeds in one direction only.

Many of the scholastic discussions among Marxists are about this paradox or tension between the fundamental claim, coming from *The German Ideology,* that ideology has no history of its own, that the entire thrust of history comes from the basis, and the claim that nevertheless the superstructure has an effect on the basis, the infrastructure. Engels tried to provide a kind of peaceful agreement between different interpretations by introducing the famous concept of determination in the last instance. The elderly Engels addressed the notion against those "economists" within the Marxist school who said that since there is no history of ideology, ideological formations are only shadows, nothing more than ghosts floating in the air. For this position, as I said in the previous lecture, the history of Norway is the history of the herring and nothing more. Engels supplied a moderate way to preserve both the radical determination in the last instance by the infrastructure and the remaining influence of the superstructure on the economic foundation. Engels' comment appeared in his famous letter to Joseph Bloch and is quoted by Althusser in *For Marx:*

> Listen to the old Engels in 1890, taking the young "economists" to task for not having understood that this was a new relationship. Production is the determinant factor, but only "in the last instance": "More than this neither Marx nor I have ever asserted." Anyone who "twists this" so that it says that the economic factor is the only determinant factor "transforms that proposition into a meaningless, abstract, empty phrase." And as explanation: "The economic situation is the basis, but the various elements of the superstructure—the political forms of the class struggle and its results: to wit constitutions established by the victorious class after a successful battle, etc., juridical forms, and then even the reflexes of all these actual struggles in the brains of the participants, political, juristic, philosophical theories, religious views and their further development into systems of dogmas—also exercise their influence upon the course of the historical struggles, and in many cases preponderate in determining their form. . . ." (111–12)

That elements of the superstructure may help to determine the form of historical struggles means that there is a certain plasticity in the possibility of giving shape to the infrastructure. It is within these limits that the theory of ideology has a certain autonomy, but it is a relative autonomy in relation to the final determination by the infrastructure.

My own fundamental contention—I want to say something about where I am headed—is both that this conceptual framework of "effectivity" is inadequate for dealing with such questions as a system of power's claim of legitimacy and that these phenomena are better understood in the framework of motivation than causation. It is in making this claim that I shall want to introduce Max Weber, not as an alternative interpretation but as a better interpretation of the relation between base and superstructure. It is completely meaningless to say that something economic acts on ideas in a causal way. The economic force of something material cannot have effects of another kind unless these effects occur within another conceptual framework, that of motivation. To establish this framework I shall try to use the notions of claim to legitimacy and of belief in legitimacy, an extremely complex interchange between ruling and ruled expressed in terms of the conflict of motives. The question of motivation makes more sense, I think, if we discuss it in terms of our relation to power, to structures of power, and so on. It is for this reason that I shall later pay so much attention to this different kind of vocabulary. My argument is that while Althusser introduces improvements, he never changes the radical structure of effectivity, of determination in the last instance, and I wonder whether that structure finally makes sense.

Thus, my interest in Weber is not only because he saw that there is no ruling power (class, state, or anything else) without a claim to legitimacy and a belief in legitimacy, but because he saw that this relation between claim and belief requires the framework of a comprehensive sociology dealing with agents, goals, motives, and so forth. It is the language game of infrastructure and superstructure that may be both deficient and at the same time also responsible for the unfortunate dispute about what is determination in the last instance or about what is the relative efficacy of the ideological sphere. What may be particularly questionable is the use of effectivity in this context, since it reconfirms the metaphor of an edifice with a base and superstructure. The topographic image leads to endless qualifications of a fundamentally mechanistic model. A certain convergence with the young Marx could have been preserved by arguing that the real basis remains the real individual under definite conditions. But this real basis is compatible only with the conceptual framework of motivation.

In general, therefore, if we keep in mind first that ideology is set against the theoretical claim of Marxism as science, second that ideology is the superstructure of a real basis expressed in terms of economic structures, and third that there is a relation of effectivity between the infrastructure and the superstructure, we have then a framework for the discussion of the changes in the Marxist theory of ideology. If I choose Althusser for the focus of this discussion, it is because he has drawn the most radical consequences of these three changes. We shall read his work as especially the endeavor to draw all the consequences of the first move, whereby he makes science the opposite pole of ideology by reinforcing the theoretical structure of Marxism, claiming that it is not a praxis, a historical movement, but a theory. By means of the second change, Althusser attempts the coherent elimination of all references to real individuals from the real basis of history, since the point of view of the individual does not belong to the structure. The individual is not a structural concept and therefore must be rejected on the side of ideology with all humanisms. Humanism is by definition ideological. Third, Althusser undertakes a more sophisticated interpretation of the relation between infrastructure and superstructure. This is his fundamental contribution, to try to improve the topographic and causalist framework of thought, in both a non-Hegelian and a nonmechanistic sense. Here I think Althusser stands or falls.

We may say in summary that there is a coherent affinity between the three theses of orthodox Marxism and the three I am trying to articulate. The opposition between ideology and science may be contrasted with the opposition between ideology and praxis. The emphasis on productive forces and relationships as the real basis of history may be contrasted with the emphasis on real individuals under definite conditions. And finally, the relation of effectivity between infrastructure and superstructure may be contrasted with the relation of motivation between the claim to and the belief in legitimacy.

As we turn to our discussion of Althusser, I should delineate more fully the particular changes he brings to the Marxist theory of ideology. Our discussion will proceed by following these changes in sequential order. We shall begin by considering Althusser's plea for theory, which defines his position in the Marxist tradition. This theoretical stand describes the opposition between science and ideology already asserted within Marxism in terms of an epistemological break rather than an inversion. If it is true that ideology is the contrary of science, then there can be no relation of inversion between the two. Althusser must give up the concept of inversion, both because it is not epistemological enough and because it causes us to remain in a sense within the framework of what has been inverted. If we invert something, put it upside down, it is still the same; the epistemological break, in contrast, introduces something new. In the second part of this presentation, we shall see how Althusser applies the notion of epistemological break to Marx's writings themselves and therefore draws a dividing line within them between what is and what is not properly Marxist. The decisive fact is that the line is not drawn between the *Manuscripts of*

1844 and *The German Ideology,* as I did for my part, but between *The German Ideology* and *Capital.* While I argued that the shift is between consciousness and the real individual, Althusser maintains that these terms are on the same side. For Althusser the epistemological break in Marx comes between the concern for human being (both as consciousness and as real individual) and the real basis in history expressed in terms of productive forces and relations of production. The real basis lies in objective structures and not in supposed personal powers. The elimination of personal powers from the real basis indicates that any reference to real individuals as the bearers of the process must be considered to be still ideological. As for the third and final part of our discussion of Althusser, we shall see how he refines the Marxist theory of infrastructure and superstructure. Our particular reference point here will be Althusser's theory of ideology proper, its extensions and functions. Thus, the didactic order I propose for the examination of Althusser implies that we start from his plea for theory in order to understand what is meant by the epistemological break.

In the introduction to *For Marx,* Althusser orients his own emphasis on theory by supplying a good account of the situation in recent French Marxism up to 1965, the time of his writing. Althusser summarizes this history as "what, echoing Heine's 'German misery,' we might call our 'French misery': the stubborn, profound absence of any real *theoretical* culture in the history of the French workers' movement" (23; emphasis in the original). In contrast to Germany, Russia, Poland, and Italy, where Marxist theoreticians made important Party contributions, the situation in the French Communist Party was one of theoretical poverty. It is in relation to this theoretical vacuum that Althusser puts forward his own claim. The French Party, says Althusser, had not attracted persons of sufficient philosophical formation to realize that

> Marxism should not be simply a political doctrine, a "method" of analysis and action, but also, over and above the rest, the theoretical domain of a fundamental investigation, indispensable not only to the development of the science of society and of the various "human sciences," but also to that of the natural sciences and philosophy. (26)

This claim is later developed at length in Althusser's lecture on "Lenin and Philosophy," collected in the volume of the same name.

Althusser points out that this claim has several corollaries. The first is that Marxism must resist a certain tendency of the young Marx wherein Marx says that philosophy is dead after Hegel and that what follows is no longer philosophy. Althusser comments that if it is true that political action is philosophy realized, it is precisely philosophy realized. If we must speak of the death of philosophy, it must be a philosophical death (29). This argument derives its importance from the fact that if the theoretical structure of Marxism is not preserved, then all the positivist trends in Marxism will prevail. Principal among these trends is reliance on Marx's eleventh thesis on Feuerbach, that until now philosphers have interpreted the world, while the point is to change it. According to this perspective, the time for interpretation has ended and the time for action has arrived.

A second corollary is that Marxist theory must resist the reduction of itself to mere critique. (This criticism could be expressed in relation to the Frankfurt School, which does not seem to be known by Althusser. I think that he would despise their orientation.) Althusser maintains that the task of Marxist philosophy is not only to criticize illusion, because in doing this work alone, the critique is absorbed into and becomes the mere consciousness of science. Once more this is a return to positivism. Althusser speaks of it as "the living death of a critical consciousness" (30). In contrast, says Althusser, "Marxist philosophy, founded by Marx in the very act of founding his theory of history, has still largely to be constituted . . ." (30–31). Thus, Althusser asserts the vacuum of French Marxist misery as a weakness in theory that has arisen from overemphasis of the practical side.

What is Althusser's claim about Marxist theory, then? He argues that this theory has two levels. First, it is a theory of history—historical materialism—that has as its object the main structures of *Capital:* classes, modes of production, relations of production, and so on. Second, it is a philosophical discipline, a second-order system of concepts ruling the theory itself. It is the theory of the fundamental categories, the categorical structure, in the same way that Freud speaks of metapsychology in relation to the clinical concepts (drives, impulses, cathexes, and so on). At this second level, Marxist theory is dialectical materialism, which Althusser opposes to Engels' philosophy of nature, the latter being a poor Hegelian or, maybe worse, a poor restitution of eighteenth-century French materialism. According to Althusser, it is the distinction between historical and dialectical materialism that has been overlooked in all the positivistic reductions of Marxism. Even *The German Ideology* allows this confusion to persist. "*The German Ideology* sanctions this confusion as it reduces philosophy . . . to a faint shadow of science, if not to the empty generality of positivism. This practical consequence is one of the keys to the remarkable history of Marxist philosophy, from its origins to the present day" (33–34). Althusser resists not only previous schools of Marxism but something found in Marx himself.

This emphasis on theory, not only as a theory of history but also as a theory that reflects upon the categorial structure of the doctrine, rules the concept of the epistemological break. In the *break* between science and ideology, what fundamentally characterizes ideology is its inability to reduplicate itself in its own theory. This is a most significant point of access to the concept of ideology. We shall later return to describe the content of ideology for Althusser, what belongs to ideology, but for now we have at least a criterion. Even if systematic, ideology is systematic in such a way that it cannot give an account of itself. It finds it impossible to provide an account of its own way of thinking.

This critique reminds us more of Spinoza than of Hegel. In Hegel all that has been said in one language may be recuperated in another; we develop the inner content of one mode of thought and preserve it in the next. The notion of a break, on the other hand, is quite anti-Hegelian; here Spinoza is the more appropriate reference. In contrast to the appeal to preservation of one stage in another, Spinoza speaks of a *succession* of modes of knowledge. The first stage, the popular vision that the sun rises, for example, is overcome by a second stage, astronomy, and astronomy has no need for and does not integrate the first view. We shall see later more similarities between Althusser and Spinoza based on this relation between the first and second modes of knowledge: the order of truth is anonymous, rationality is self-supporting, and the first stage has a certain permanence. The last point in particular is relevant to our concern for ideology. Outside his or her work, the astronomer goes on speaking of sunsets and sunrises, so perhaps ideology also has a kind of permanence. This, in fact, will be the last stage of Althusser's doctrine. If we have high requirements for what is scientific, we then relegate a considerable amount of life to the ideological. Althusser's principal allusion to Spinoza appears in a footnote:

> science can by no criteria be regarded as the truth of ideology in the Hegelian sense. If we want a historical predecessor to Marx in this respect we must appeal to Spinoza rather than Hegel. Spinoza established a relation between the first and the second kind of knowledge which, in its immediacy (abstracting from the totality in

God), presupposed precisely a radical discontinuity. Although the second kind makes possible the understanding of the first, it is not its truth. (78 *n.*)

Truth is on the side of the second kind of knowledge; there is no truth in the first. The claim is strong: the second mode of knowledge is self-nourishing and does not borrow from that which it overcomes. This is the anti-Hegelian stand. As we shall see, this kind of radicalism may be finally unsupportable, but for my part at least I greatly admire the intellectual boldness of Althusser's stance.

It is because of the "radical discontinuity" between the two modes of knowledge that the break between ideology and science can no longer be expressed in the language of reversal, of inversion. The process of inversion is something that happens to the content of the first domain; it is the same but upside down. Althusser may push the image of reversal too far here, but this is what the notion implies. Althusser discusses the concept of inversion in yet another footnote. The footnotes are always extremely interesting in Althusser's work, because he uses them to avoid difficulties with the Party. The truth is at the bottom of the page!

[I]t is remarkable that Marx correctly attacked Feuerbach in *The German Ideology* for having remained a prisoner of Hegelian philosophy precisely when he was claiming to have "inverted" it. He attacked him for accepting the presuppositions of Hegel's questions, for giving different answers, but to the same questions. In philosophy only the questions are indiscreet, as opposed to everyday life, where it is the answers. Once the questions have been changed it is no longer possible to talk of an inversion. No doubt a comparison of the new relative rank of questions and answers to the old one still allows us to talk of an inversion. But it has then become an analogy since the questions are no longer the same and the domains they constitute are not comparable, except, as I have suggested, for pedagogic purposes. (72–73 *n.*)

It is difficult to think through this idea of the break, that when the questions are no longer the same, the domains they constitute are no longer comparable. To set Hegel back onto his feet is merely to restore what had been upside down. "A man on his head is the same man when he is finally walking on his feet" (73). I am not sure whether Althusser is himself deceived by the metaphor, but what we must assume here is the idea of the change in problematic. We are now raising new questions. We no longer raise questions about what is human consciousness or about what is the human condition; instead we ask, for example, what is a class. For Althusser there is no connection between these two modes of questioning.

More than that, the Hegelian *Aufhebung* is inadequate. We shall discuss this at greater length in a later lecture, when I shall insist on the radical cleft according to Althusser between the relationship of superstructure and infrastructure and any kind of dialectics. Althusser says:

> [Marx's] "supersession" of Hegel was not at all an *Aufhebung* in the Hegelian sense, that is, an exposition of the truth of what is contained in Hegel; it was not a supersession of error towards its truth, on the contrary, it was a supersession of illusion toward its truth, or better, rather than a "supersession" of illusion towards truth it was a dissipation of illusion and a retreat from the dissipated illusion back towards reality: the term "supersession" is thus robbed of all meaning. (77–78)

What is important in the notion of *Aufhebung* is that in moving from one level to another, we preserve that content of the first through a process of mediation. If we take the master-slave relationship as an example of the Hegelian *Aufhebung,* we know that this relationship is overcome in Stoicism. A moment of *re*cognition occurs between master and slave, and therefore something of the earlier relationship is also preserved. For Althusser, however, we must think something quite different than the preservation of a term through its negation. We must think of the dissipation of an illusion, and this must be expressed in quite another language. An *Aufhebung* implies a substantial continuity; the first term returns as the third through its "negation." Althusser says, on the other hand, that we must think of an emigration of concepts into another terrain of thought. Science is not the truth of what preceded it; it is not the same more true but rather something else. Our problem will be whether such a radical break is thinkable. I leave this question in suspense for the moment, because the possibility of thinking the break must in fact be joined to Althusser's claim that a causal relation, and therefore some unavoidable exchanges, exist between infrastructure and superstructure. We shall discuss later the unthinkable consequences that result from these unavoidable exchanges between the two spheres.

What I would like to move to now is the second major point of our discussion of Althusser, what we might call his hermeneutic principle for reading Marx. This principle is derived from the epistemological break said to occur in Marx. The break is epistemological because it secludes the ideological from the scientific; it separates not the imaginary from the real but the prescientific from the scientific. Since Marxism is said to have the theoretical capabilities to reflect on itself, it is a doctrine that also understands its beginnings and operates on itself its own theoretical or epistemological break. It is through this analysis that Althusser tries to resolve the classical—if perhaps sometimes boring—discussion among Marxists about the problem of periodization, the problem of the succession of works in Marx. Althusser takes this problem and applies it to the notion of the epistemological break. Thus, this concept which was first used to separate Marxism as a whole from its predecessors is now applied within the Marxist corpus itself. Within the history of Marxism there is said to be an epistemological break between what is and what is not truly Marxist in the scientific sense. In the succession of essays forming *For Marx,* Althusser starts from the young Marx and leads up to the mature doctrine. I shall prefer to invert the succession, since the principle according to which we apply the notion of the epistemological break to Marx arises out of the relation between the mature doctrine and the rest of his writings.

I should say a word about the term "epistemological break." The concept comes from Gaston Bachelard, who is better known in this country for his work on aesthetics and poetics but who has also an important epistemological work, *The Philosophy of No.* Bachelard insists that science develops by a succession of negations. There is a leap, perhaps like Kuhn's change of paradigms. A comparison between Kuhn and Bachelard might have been helpful, in fact, for us to grasp better this notion of the epistemological break. We shall restrict ourselves to Althusser, though, and the problem of periodization.

Althusser proposes that Marx's writings may be divided into four stages: the early works (1840–44), the works of the break (1845), the transitional works (1845–57), and the mature works (1857–83) (35). What is particularly interesting for our purposes is that *The German Ideology* is located in the second period precisely because of its ambiguity. What I took to be constitutive of the text becomes here a symptom of the break at work. The break is at work because the old language of the individual and the new language of class struggle both appear. Althusser says that the break remains a negative stage since it is expressed in the old language. I quote Althusser on *The German Ideology,* since I regard this book as the paradigmatic case of the theory of ideology.

> [I]t must be remembered that this mutation [separating the scientific from the ideological] could not produce immediately, in positive and consummated form, the new theoretical problematic which it inaugurated, in the theory of history as well as in that of philosophy. In fact, *The German Ideology* is a commentary, usually a negative and critical one, on the different forms of the ideological problematic Marx had rejected. (34)

Althusser deemphasizes all the positive concepts of the real individual, which form an envelope for the new terminology.

We need, therefore, to become well aware of the kind of reading that is occurring in Althusser, because a book is always read according to some hermeneutical rules. Althusser applies to the Marxist corpus a Marxist hermeneutic, that is to say, he applies the general principles of the theory to itself. Althusser's reading is not with a naked eye and does not claim to be. On the contrary, it is a critical reading; the structure of the mature Marx is applied backwards to its own beginning in order to introduce the cleft with this beginning. Althusser is right, I think, to argue for a critical reading. All reading is a kind of violence; if we do not merely repeat, we interpret. Heidegger and many others assert that all productive reading is recurrent and circular. Althusser's own statement about the recurrence of the principle on its object appears in the following passage:

> That this definition [of the irreducible specificity of Marxist theory] cannot be read directly in Marx's writings, that a complete prior critique is indispensable to an identification of the location of the real concepts of Marx's maturity; that the identification of these concepts is the same thing as the identification of their location; that all this critical effort, the absolute precondition of any interpretation, in itself presupposes activating a minimum of provisional Marxist theoretical concepts bearing on the nature of theoretical formations and their history; that the precondition of a reading of Marx is . . . a theory of epistemological history, which is Marxist philosophy itself; that this operation in itself constitutes an indispensable circle in which the application of Marxist theory to Marx himself appears to be the absolute precondition of an understanding of Marx and at the same time as the precondition even of the constitution and development of Marxist philosophy, so much is clear. But the circle implied by this operation is, like all circles of this kind, simply the dialectical circle of the question asked of an object as to its nature, on the basis of a theoretical problematic which in putting its object to the test puts itself to the test of its object. (38)

Thus, instead of reading Marx's writing forward step by step, we read it backwards, that is, from what we know to be Marxist in order to establish what is not truly Marxist.

Althusser describes his reading as circular; a circularity exists between the principle undergirding a reading and its object. In saying that the operation of interpretation is "like all circles of this kind," Althusser reminds us of Heidegger and the hermeneutic circle, though I doubt he had that at all in mind. (Althusser hardly seems very much Heideggerian; Heidegger must be the worst of all ideologists for someone like Althusser.) In any event, because of Althusser's endorsement of the circularity of reading, he has a ready response for those adversaries who accuse him of reading into the text: this criticism is not an objection since it is assumed by the way of reading. Consequently, it is difficult to use against Althusser's reading of the young Marx the contention that Marx does not actually say what Althusser is arguing. Althusser's reply is that he starts from the stage where the concepts are reflective of their own truth, while the young Marx does not yet know what in fact he is saying. In the case of *The German Ideology,* Althusser notes that his reading does not claim to take the old concepts "at their word" (36). *The German Ideology* is a text that does not provide the key for its own reading; it must be read with a key that does not belong to this work. Althusser speaks of the "still more dangerous false transparency of the apparently familiar concepts of the works of the break" (39).

What we must discuss, though, is whether it is true that the key to *The German Ideology* does not lie in the text. Is there only one way to read the young Marx? Are we obliged to read him according to the concepts of the mature Marx? Have we not a certain freedom before these texts to read them as entities which also speak by themselves and so not only through a further redaction? Can we not distinguish between the epistemological break as a principle internal to the theory and its historical application? This is a most significant problem, critical not only for our interpretation of Althusser but for the theory of ideology we are trying to develop. Does not Althusser overlook the decisive break between a philosophy of consciousness and an anthropological philosophy—for which the subjects of history are " 'real, concrete men' " (37)—because he reads into it a later problematic? For the same reason, does he not deny the importance of the transition from alienation to the division of labor, even though he acknowledges that the latter "commands the whole theory of ideology and the whole theory of science"(37)? Althusser says only of the division of labor that its role is "ambiguous" (37). In the case of the works prior to *The German Ideology,* it is easy to say that the concepts emphasized—consciousness, species being, alienation—are Feuerbachian; Marx is here still involved in the world of the Young Hegelians. I maintain that the test case for the appearance of Marxism is *The German Ideology* and its attention to the concept of real individuals in their conditions. For Althusser, however, this concept no longer speaks by itself. It is an opaque notion made transparent only by a method imported from Marx's later problematic. Althusser's orientation has the fundamental consequence that the differences between the *Manuscripts* and *The German Ideology,* which I have emphasized so much, become unessential. It is unessential that the *Manuscripts* puts consciousness at the forefront and that *The German Ideology* puts real individuals, because both concepts are still anthropological; they are part of an anthropological ideology.

Althusser forges the concept of an anthropological ideology to cover the whole field in which the question is about human being as a whole, either in the language of consciousness or in the language of real life, the language of praxis. This is what I cannot accept. On the contrary, I think that Marx's great discovery in *The German Ideology* in his distinction between real life and consciousness. Althusser, though, believes he is right to say there is no decisive break here because of the necessity for a true theory, as we have seen, to account for itself. The assumption derived from the very notion of theory is that the ideological does not understand itself; Althusser argues against the view that "the world of ideology is its own principle of intelligibility" (57).

The great advantage of Althusser's interpretation is that it provides a principle for reading Marx, a coherent reading that challenges most other Marxist readings' "eclecticism" (57). In his essay "On the Young Marx," Althusser criticizes some Eastern European interpreters who attempt to disentangle in the young Marx materialistic—and therefore truly Marxist—elements from concepts still Hegelian or Feuerbachian. Althusser says that we can no longer speak of elements; we must take an ideology as constituting a whole. The epistemological break is from whole to whole and not between parts or elements; it is between an old mode of thought and a new mode of thought, from one totality to another.

An objection might be raised asking what justification Althusser has to deny his other Marxist opponents the right to read an end into Marx's early writings and to accuse these opponents of discarding certain elements and applying a teleological model to the whole. Does not Althusser himself judge the young Marx according to criteria belonging to the mature Marx? Althusser responds with three points (62–63). We shall spend some time detailing these respones, but let me summarize them briefly. First, says Althusser, the application of the epistemological break to Marx himself preserves the specificity of each phase of his writing; "it is impossible to extract one element without altering its meaning" (62). Second, the work of the early Marx is not explained by that of the mature Marx but by its belonging to the ideological field of it time. Third, the motor principle of development is not in ideology itself but in what underlies it, actual history. (This claim already implies the theory of infrastructure and determination in the last instance.) Only at this level of attention, Althusser maintains, is explanation scientific and no longer ideological. As truth is the measure of error, mature Marxism expresses the truth *about* the young Marx, without needing to be already the truth *of* the young Marx.

I shall return to Althusser's third point later but want to discuss at present his second. That an ideology is a whole means that it is not something individual or personal but is instead a field. To define what works may have in common requires us to identify their common ideological field. The notion of an ideological field is an implication of the epistemological break. What we break with is not this or that individual writing but a whole way of thinking. As a result, the notion of ideology becomes less individual and personal and more an anonymous way of thinking. This raises in turn a great difficulty: how to locate individual works within this field, how to pass from the field to a singularity.

The emphasis on the concept of the field represents one of the infiltrations of structuralist concepts into the work of Althusser. The notion of the field comes from Gestalt psychology and the contrast there between a field and an object. An object—here individual works—is placed against the background of a field. Althusser has many expressions that seem more structuralist than Marxist but which become Marxist in his writings. The structuralist overtones in Althusser are evident in the following quotation; note the allusion to the notion of the text in the sense articulated by Greimas and the French structuralists.

> At this level of the exchanges and conflicts that are the very substance of the *texts* in which his living thoughts have come down to us, it is as if the authors of these thoughts were themselves absent. The concrete individual who expresses himself in his thoughts and his writings is absent, so is the actual history expressed in the existing ideological field. As the author effaces himself in the presence of his published thoughts, reducing himself to their rigour, so concrete history effaces itself in the presence of its ideological themes, reducing itself to their system. This double absence will also have to be put to the test. But for the moment, everything is in play between the rigour of a single thought and the thematic system of an ideological field. (64; emphasis in the original)

The notion of the effacement of the author of a text provides the transition between individual works, which lose their author, and an ideological field, which is anonymous by definition. We are asked to think something that is very difficult to conceive, the notion of a problematic constitutive of a definite ideological field, something that is a problem raised, in a sense, by no one. What we call a question requires some thinker to raise it, but here we must think of a problematic as something expressed by no one. The problematic is "the basic unity of a text, the internal essence of an ideological thought" (66).

My question is whether Althusser's orientation has not dreadful consequences for the theory of meaning, because what is meant in a field if it is meant by nobody? Althusser might reply that he uses the concept of meaning too. Speaking of the typical systematic structure of a field, Althusser says that its determinate content is what "makes it possible both to conceive the meaning *[sens]* of the 'elements' of the ideology concerned—and to relate this ideology to the problems left or posed to every thinker by the historical period in which he lives" (67). Thus, it is not an individual but the historical period which raises questions. This is in agreement with what we earlier saw to be Althusser's third methodological principle: the emphasis on the theory of structure—the relation between infrastructure and superstructure—the emphasis on anonymous entities without subjects. How do we express, though, the suffering of the worker? All the vocabulary of alienation must disappear, since there is no alienation without someone alienated and suffering from this alienation. Althusser's conceptual framework allows us to speak only of fields, structures, and entities of that kind.

We may further clarify Althusser's emphasis on the concept of the field by drawing some of the consequences of his interpretation for the concept of ideology. First, as we have seen, the concept of an ideological field tends to deemphasize the difference between the *Manuscripts* and *The German Ideology*. This is the main consequence of this concept. The *Manuscripts* and *The German Ideology* belong to the same ideological field; they are not individual works with different scopes and different concepts. The notion of an anthropological ideology becomes the ruling concept for the whole range of works which are not Marxist, at least in Althusser's sense of the term. The unity of these anthropological texts of Marx is based on their common problematic. "[T]he problematic of a thought is not limited to the domain of the objects considered by its author, because it is not an abstraction for the thought as a totality, but the concrete determinate structure of a thought and of all the thoughts possible within this thought" (68). As we can see, it is a very difficult notion. We must therefore think of an anthropological ideology as a field which generates several kinds of thoughts, including Feuerbach, the *Manuscripts,* and *The German Ideology.* The identity of the separate works within the field is lost; this is particularly significant for the loss of the fundamental distinction between the idealistic concept of consciousness and the concept of the real individual under definite conditions, that anthropological realism of Marx's which I have praised so highly.

The second major implication of Althusser's reading is that an ideology is not to be discussed as a thought that somebody assumes, because an ideology is not something that is thought, but rather something *within which* we think. This is a striking and perhaps unavoidable finding; it is not necessarily Marxist, either. It has also been emphasized, for example, by Eugen Fink, in a famous article on operative and thematic concepts.[1] The import of this insight is that we cannot think everything that is involved in our thinking. We think *with* some concepts, *by means of* some concepts. This may be why it is impossible to have a radical transparency in what we think; we may thematize something, but in order to do so we use other concepts which are then not thematized, at least during the time that we apply them. In my own language, I would say that absolute reflexivity is impossible; we have available not total reflection but only partial reflection. Thus, it may be an important part of the concept of ideology that we cannot reflect on all our concepts. There are concepts *through which* we think or *with which* we think. Althusser says of a problematic: "in general a philosopher thinks in it rather than thinking of it . . ." (69). This implies that an ideology is unconscious in the sense that it is not mastered by consciousness or self-consciousness. Althusser adds that an ideology's "own problematic is not conscious of itself. . . . [nor] of its 'theoretical presuppositions' . . ." (69). Perhaps there is something fundamental here, and not only in Marxist terms: it is impossible for us to bring everything to the level of consciousness. We rely on heritages, on traditions, on many things which helps us to think and to be, and these rule our approach to thinking. In this sense, ideology is something unsuperable. We must say that even Althusserian Marxists do not have all their thought in front of them. Perhaps this is the best use that we can make of the notion of a field, the fact that our thought is also a field and not only an object. There may also be some Freudian equivalents to this.

For me the objection to this perspective is not the claim that everything is clear, that radical transparency is available; instead the objection emerges by asking what kind of relation exists between a field and a thought if we do not have a motivational framework, a conceptual framework. If we put this relation in terms of causality, everything becomes obscure. If we say on the other hand that all our *motives* are not clear, then the relationship makes sense. The field of motivation, we may say, is behind us or under us. The Freudian concept of the *Es*—id—is quite helpful here; we could say that there is a social *Es* too. For my part I would maintain that the relation between a singular thought and a field requires an individual living under the conditions of his or her own field. A field is part of the condition of an individual's circumstances. Thus, I think it makes more sense to use the language of *The German Ideology* and say that a thinker is within circumstances, in a situation, which he or she does not master, which is not transparent for him or her. In other words, does not the concept of a field belong in a more useful and helpful way to a motivational rather than to a causal relation?

Another text of Althusser's on the relation between a field and a thought seems to open the possibility of an interpretation more similar to the one I have argued here:

> Let me summarize these reflections. Understanding an ideological argument implies, at the level of the ideology itself, simultaneous *[en même temps]*, conjoint knowledge of the ideological field in which a thought emerges and grows; and the exposure of the internal unity of this thought: its problematic. Knowledge of the ideological field itself presupposes knowledge of the problematics compounded or opposed in it. The interrelation of the particular problematic of the thought of the indvidual under consideration with the particular problematics of the thoughts belonging to the ideological field allows of a decision as to its author's specific differences, i.e., whether a new meaning has emerged. (70)

Once more the question of the "specific difference" of *The German Ideology* arises. Has not a "new meaning . . . emerged" there? More generally, this quotation supports the view that if someone brings forth a new idea, this means that a new meaning has emerged in a field. Therefore, we must think of the field not in mechanical terms but as a kind of reserve, a resource, of possible thoughts. The relationship between thought and field makes sense only if we think in terms of meanings and not forces. Further, if we follow Althusser's argument that the anonymous field and an individual thought within this field are strictly contemporaneous, then we must always speak of the field of an individual thought or of this thought within the collective field. Thus, there is a reciprocity between field and indvidual thought, and we need to be able to conceptualize that. Here, once again, we should find useful *The German Ideology*'s language of real individuals in circumstances; the field is one of these circumstances, perhaps the most fundamental circumstance. As you can see, I plead without hiding myself for *The German Ideology* and against the general language of Althusser.

As regards the reference of both individual thoughts and the ideological field to the "real authors of these as yet subjectless thoughts" (71), we are sent back to the question of "the meaning of Marx's evolution and of its 'motor' " (72). The word "motor" is placed in quotation marks but nevertheless used. The claim is that an explanation which finds the "motor" in the history of ideology and not in the real basis of history is itself ideological. What, though, about the epistemological break? The break is itself a problem: who makes the break, is it a break *of* the problematic or *in* the problematic? Althusser must go so far as to question not only the self-consciousness of ideology but that of Marx himself in relation to the break. "[T]o speak of real history . . . is to question 'Marx's path' itself" (74). The meaning of Marx's own break through the crushing layer of ideology is not given by Marx's own consciousness. Is it not already difficult, however, to correlate German ideology with the backwardness of German politics and economics, to correlate its ideological overdevelopment with its historical underdevelopment? It is still more difficult to assign the break itself to such historical conditions. Is not "the rediscovery of real history," the "return to real history" (76) an act of thought? More, if this return is a "retreat" to the pre-Hegelian, a movement back to "the reality of the objects Hegel had stolen by imposing on them the meaning of his own ideology," is not this return to "the objects themselves in their reality" (77) the very definition of thought? The discovery beneath ideology of developed capitalism and class struggle is an act of thinking. Too much is given in Althusser to the concept of the field. The field provides an important way to avoid the ideological problematic of "the deformation of real historical problems into philosophical problems" (80 *n.*), but the notion of the break preserves the capacity for philosophical problems to be raised.

Can we not say, then, that the capacity to put one's self in front of reality, the discovery by Marx of "the reality of the ideological opacity which had blinded him" (82), entails the emergence of a new meaning and the presence of a thinker and of thought? Althusser is even more correct than he thinks when he says that there is more in the discovery of reality than in the Hegelian *Aufhebung,* which disentangles the already present end in the beginning. But what can be "a logic of actual experience and real emergence," "a logic of the irruption of history in ideology itself" (82)? Here there is no place for anything like an ideological field. On the contrary, Althusser says that this logic gives at last some meaning to Marx's "personal style," his "sensitivity to the concrete" revealed in each of his "encounters with reality" (82).

The Marxist account of this "real emergence" is that it is "merely the effect of its own empirical conditions" (83 *n.*). It cannot derive from the ideological, according to this view, because ideology has no history. The conclusion seems to be that this emergence is somehow an absolute beginning. There remains the metaphor of breaking through the gigantic layers of illusion. Marx's relationship with his origins is not one of continuity but of a "prodigious break." Marx's path was one of "freeing himself from the myths" of his time. He had the breakthrough of "the experience of real history" (84). Resorting again to the metaphor of emergence, Althusser says that "the emergence [of Marx's discovery] was analogous to all the great scientific discoveries of history" in that it brought forth "a new horizon of meaning" (85).

Althusser offers at least one qualification to the uncompromising notion of break. He observes that Marx did profit from his contact with Hegel to the extent it offered "practice in abstraction," the "practice in theoretical synthesis and the logic of a process for which the Hegelian dialectic gave him a 'pure,' abstract model" (85). This exception to Marx's break is a tremendous concession by Althusser. He tries to minimize it, however, by arguing that its role is less a "theoretical formation than . . . a formation for theory, a sort of education of the theoretical intelligence via the theoretical formations of ideology itself" (85). This "formation for theory" offered Marx "training . . . in the manipulation of the abstract structure of [the German intellect's] systems, independently of their validity" (85). It seems, then, that the break is not absolute; a continuity in terms of formalism seems to persist. Is this not, however, the claim of Althusser's opponents? Althusser's response is that the change in the objects of analysis in the mature Marx also changes the nature of his method. This question anticipates my discussion in the following lectures. What we must keep in mind, though, is how Althusser speaks of Marx's discovering reality over against the ruling ideology. Althusser says that in Marx there appears "a new horizon of meaning" (85); this seems to imply, despite Althusser's intent, a thinker and a process of thought.

8

Althusser (2)

In the previous lecture on Althusser, I discussed his concept of the ideological break and its epistemological implications. The particular reference was to Althusser's reappraisal and reinterpretation of the early Marx's work as an anthropological ideology. In the present lecture, I shall discuss Althusser's concept of ideology itself. This discussion will proceed in three steps: first, how is the problem of ideology placed in the superstructure-infrastructure framework; second, what can be said about particular ideologies, such as religion or humanism; and third, what is the nature of ideology in general.

As to the first topic, one of Althusser's most important contributions is his attempt to refine and improve the model of infrastructure and superstructure borrowed from Engels. As we recall, the model is summarized both by the efficiency in the last instance of the economic base—this base is the final cause, the prime mover—and by the relative autonomy of the superstructure, a model of the reciprocal action *(Wechselwirkung)* between base and superstructure. For Althusser, the first point we must understand is that whatever the value of Engels' model, it is, contrary to Engels' own beliefs, as far from Hegel's dialectic as possible. We have already emphasized Althusser's critique of the metaphor of inversion; here Althusser's criticism focuses on Engels' commentary on this metaphor. In *For Marx* Althusser introduces the discussion by quoting the statement in Marx, appearing as late as *Capital,* on which Engels relies: " 'With [Hegel, the dialectic] is standing on its head. It must be turned right side up again, if you would discover the rational kernel within the mystical shell' " (89; brackets in original). Althusser maintains that this declaration is not as easily interpreted as first appears. Engels falsely believes that there is a common element between Hegel and Marxism, the "rational kernel," and that there is need to drop only the "mystical shell." This argument appeared frequently among Marxists, the thought being that it was possible to keep Hegel's dialectics and apply it no longer to the Hegelian Spirit but to new objects: to society, classes, and so on. The common use of dialectical argument would imply, so the argument goes, at least a formal continuity between Hegel and Marx.

For Althusser, however, this is still to grant too much, and with good reason. We cannot treat the Hegelian dialectic as an empty or formal procedure since Hegel keeps repeating that the dialectic is the movement of the things themselves. Hegel is against any kind of formalism that would allow us first to establish a method of thinking and then to go on to solve the problem of metaphysics. This is what he discards in Kant. The entire preface of the *Phenomenology of Spirit* is written exactly against the claim that we must first have a method and then do philosophy. For Hegel, philosophy is the method, it is the *Selbstdarstellung,* the self-presentation of its own content. It is not possible to separate method from content in order to retain the method and apply it to new content. Therefore, even the structure of the dialectic in Hegel (negation, negation of negation) must be considered as heterogenous to the structure of the dialectic in Marx. If it is true that we cannot separate method from content, and I am sure that it is, then we must define the Marxist dialectic in terms that leave only the word "dialectic" in common with Hegel. The question then is: why the same word? In fact we should drop the word or say either that there is no dialectic in Hegel or no dialectic in Marx; but this is another problem.

In place of the Hegelian dialectic Althusser substitutes the concept of overdetermination. This concept is obviously borrowed from Freud, although there is also an implication of Lacan. (The influence of Lacan is permanent in all Althusser's work and increasingly evident in his later essays.) To introduce the concept of overdetermination, Althusser starts from a remark by Lenin, when Lenin raises the question: how was it possible that the socialist revolution occurred in Russia, when Russia was not the most advanced industrial country? Lenin's response is that to claim that revolution should occur in the most industrial country implies that the economic basis is not only determinant in the last instance but the sole determinant factor. What we must realize, then, is that the economic basis never works alone; it always acts in combination with other elements:

national character, national history, traditions, international events, and accidents of history—wars, defeats, and so on. An event like a revolution is not the mechanical result of the basis but something involving all the "various levels and instances of the social formation" (101). It is a combination of forces. This nexus is what Althusser calls overdetermination and opposes to the Hegelian contradiction.

It is difficult, though, to locate exactly the difference between Althusser and Hegel on this point. We could say that there is overdetermination in Hegel also. In whatever chapter we read in the *Phenomenology,* each figure has so many conflicting elements that precisely the dialectic must proceed toward another figure. We may say that the instability of the figure is a product of its overdetermination. Althusser's claim, and I am less convinced by this argument, is that there exists in Hegel no real overdetermination involving heterogeneous factors. Instead, Althusser argues, the process is one of cumulative internalization, which is only apparently an overdetermination. In spite of the complexity of a historical form in Hegel, it is actually simple in its principle. Though the *content* of the Hegelian figure may not be simple, its meaning is, because finally it is one figure, whose unity is immanent in its form. In Hegel, says Althusser, an epoch has "an internal spiritual principle, which can never definitely be anything but the most abstract form of that epoch's consciousness of itself: its religious or philosophical consciousness, that is, its own ideology" (103). The "mystical shell" affects and contaminates the supposed rational "kernel." For Althusser, therefore, Hegel's dialectic is typically idealistic: even if a historical period has complex elements, it is ruled by one idea, it has a unity of its own. The point, then, is that if we assume with Althusser the simplicity of the Hegelian form, such that it can be encapsulated in a label like the master-slave relation or Stoicism, the contrast is to the complexity of Marxist contradiction. The complexity of the contradictions spawning the Russian Revolution are not an accident in Marxist theory but rather the rule. The argument is that the contradictions are always this complex.

If we put together this notion of overdetermination with Engels' concept of causality in the last instance by the basis and the reaction back on the basis by the superstructure, we then have a richer concept of causality. We see that in fact the infrastructure is always determined by all the other components. There is a combination of levels and structures. This position was originally developed, we must not forget, to counter the mechanicist trend in Marxism—represented particularly by the German Social Democratic Party. This mechanicism, which endorsed a fatalistic or deterministic view of history, was denounced by Gramsci in an interesting argument reproduced by Althusser. Gramsci says that it is always those with the most active will who believe in determinism; they find in this fatalism of history a confirmation of their own actions. (In a certain sense this is quite similar to the Calvinistic notion of predestination.) Proponents believe that they are the chosen people of history, and therefore there is a certain necessity in history's movement. Althusser quotes Gramsci's strong statement that fatalism has been " 'the ideological "aroma" of the philosophy of praxis' " (105 *n.*). The word "aroma" is an allusion to Marx's early essay on Hegel's *Philosophy of Right*. Just as Marx criticized there the illusions of religion's spiritual aroma, here fatalism is subject to the same censure.

Can we say that Althusser's introduction of the concept of overdetermination in any way displaces the causalist framework of infrastructure and superstructure? In actuality this framework is more reinforced than qualified by this analysis. Althusser repeatedly affirms that the notion of infrastructure and superstructure is what gives meaning to overdetermination, not the contrary. He acknowledges that it is Engels' formula which in fact rules his own concept of overdetermination. Perhaps it is a concession to Marxist orthodoxy, I am not sure, but Althusser is very clear on this point. Speaking of the accumulation of effective determinations (derived from the superstructure) on determination in the last instance by the economic, Althusser says: "It seems to me that this clarifies the expression overdetermined contradiction, which I have put forward, this specifically because the existence of overdetermination is no longer a fact pure and simple, for in its essentials we have related it to its bases . . ." (113). The concept of overdetermination does not help to overcome the weakness of the concept of infrastructure and superstructure, since it is only a commentary on the same argument. The framework of causality is affected not at all.

As a sign that this framework is still troublesome for Althusser—there is a great sincerity and modesty in all his texts—Althusser says that when we put together the determination in the last instance by the economy and the reaction back on the infrastructure by the superstructure, we hold only "the two ends of the chain" (112). This expression is an allusion to Leibniz' description of the problematic relationship between determinations made by God and determinations made by human free will. Thus, Marxism repeats a paradox that was typically theological, the paradox of the ultimate determination; at issue is the relative effectivity of independent actors in a play decided elsewhere and by someone else.

> [I]t has to be said that the theory of the specific effectivity of the superstructure and other "circumstances" largely remains to be elaborated; and before the theory of their effectivity or simultaneously . . . there must be elaboration of the theory of the particular essence of the specific elements of the superstructure. (113–14)

The role of overdetermination remains more than a solution. It is a way of qualifying a concept which itself remains quite opaque.

This is why I wonder whether it would not be more helpful to start from the Freudian-Althusserian concept of overdetermination, to take it for itself, and then try to see whether it does not imply another theoretical framework than that of superstructure and infrastructure. My alternative would be a motivational framework; this structure would allow us to understand that it is in fact in terms of motives and motivation that we may speak of the overdetermination of a meaning. Perhaps without a concept of meaning, we cannot speak adequately about overdetermination. The concept of overdetermination, I think, does not necessarily require a causalist framework. What confirms this attempted change is that, according to Althusser himself, we must grant some meaning to the relative autonomy of the superstructural sphere.

> [A] revolution in the structure [of society] does not ipso facto modify the existing superstructures and particularly the ideologies at one blow (as it would if the economic was the sole determinant factor), for they have sufficient of their own consistency to survive beyond their immediate life context, even to recreate, to "secrete" substitute conditions of existence temporarily. . . . (115–16)

The superstructure is a layer with its own consistency and finally its own history. As the intriguing Marxist theory of "survivals" attempts to take into account, we must come to understand why, for example, bourgeois morality persists even after a period of social transformation. My claim is that such practices may continue to prevail precisely because a certain strain of motives survives the change in the social framework. To my mind at least, the independence, autonomy, and consistency of ideologies presuppose another framework than that of superstructure and infrastructure.

Let me turn, though, away from this theme to what is the most interesting topic for us in Althusser, the theory of ideologies themselves, ideologies considered for their own sake. Althusser undertakes this treatment in two steps, and this is expressed in my own treatment of the problem:

first he speaks of particular ideologies, and then he tries to say something about ideology in general. The distinction between these two themes is not made very clearly in *For Marx* but appears rather in a later, very abstract article called "Ideology and Ideological State Apparatuses." This article, included in *Lenin and Philosophy,* will be at the center of our attention when we discuss Althusser's theory of ideology in general, but let me quote it briefly here to indicate how Althusser introduces the distinction in question. "[I]f I am able to put forward the project of a theory of ideology *in general,* and if this theory really is one of the elements on which theories of ideology in general, and if this theory really is one of the elements on which theories of ideolog*ies* depend, that entails an apparently paradoxical proposition which I shall express in the following way: *ideology has no history*" (159; emphases in original). Mainly under the influence once more of Freud and Lacan, Althusser says that we need to pursue a theory of ideology in general, just as metapsychology is a theory of the unconscious in general, an inquiry separate from specific treatment of the expressions of the unconscious found in such particular areas as mental illness, art, ethics, religion, and so on. As we shall see, the reason ideology in general has no history is because it is a permanent structure. Freud's metapsychology is Althusser's model for the relation between particular ideologies and ideology in general. For our purposes, examination of the nature of ideology in general is the more interesting question, and so I shall treat the problem of particular ideologies fairly quickly.

The approach to a theory of ideology through analysis of particular ideologies is more or less imposed by the Marxist model, where ideologies are always presented in an enumeration. Those familiar with Marxist texts may have noticed that when Marx himself discusses ideology, he continually opens a parenthesis and refers to specific—that is, religious, ethical, aesthetic, and political—ideologies. It is by enumeration of these forms that Marx builds the more general analysis, a method quite similar to Descartes' analysis of the cogito. We should not forget either that Marx also proceeded historically by a similar process: from the critique of religion, to the critique of philosophy, and then to the critique of politics. The dispersion of ideologies is an important aspect of the problem, the fact that there are ideologies, in the plural. We should note, however, that within Marxist texts as a whole the framework of response to this problem is not always the same. In some texts the word "ideology" is used to cover all that is not economic, while in others differentiation is made between economics, politics, and ideologies. In his own comprehensive concept of ideology in his later work, Althusser himself identifies the political structure as a particular ideology.

Let me offer two examples of Althusser's adoption of this enumerative approach: his treatment of humanism and of the state. In *For Marx* the paradigmatic example of a particular ideology is humanism. Humanism is treated as an ideology and as an ideology that has determinant boundaries. It is defined as a specific anthropological field. It is therefore a cultural pattern, something to which some people belong and others do not. A particular ideology may be contrasted to ideology in general, which is not a historical pattern but a permanent structure, just like the Freudian unconscious. Again, the attraction of Freudian concepts is most important. In spite of the narrowness of the concept of ideology when identified with one problematic among others, this concept is nevertheless quite revealing about the structure of ideology in general, since in fact the general structure of ideology in Althusser repeats the structure of humanism, as we shall discover.

The case of humanism is crucial in another respect, since it gives us the right to put *The German Ideology* within the same anthropological field as the earlier texts. What defines humanism, even that which is called socialist humanism, is a common participation in the same ideology. Therefore, Althusser considers the rebirth of humanism in modern Marxism a return to Feuerbach and the early Marx; it belongs to the same anthropological field. Althusser's analysis of humanism is a central illustration of his uncompromising denial of any conceptual blending between ideology and science. "[I]n the couple 'humanism-socialism' there is a striking theoretical unevenness: in the framework of the Marxist conception [Althusser's own, of course], the concept 'socialism' is indeed a scientific concept, but the concept 'humanism' is no more than an ideological one" (223). For Althusser, humanist socialism is a monstrous kind of concept. Unfortunately, this position sometimes has severe political implications. During the 1968 invasion of Czechoslovakia, for example, Althusser kept silent; his stance allowed him to argue that purely theoretically, the reform movement was wrong. The Czechoslovak socialists were attempting something that does not exist—humanistic socialism; they relied on an impure concept.

The argument against linking the concept of humanism to that of socialism is that the former "designates some existents, but it does not give us their essences" (223). The argument is Platonic, an objection that humanism speaks of existence—human beings, life, and so on—and not conceptual structure. Althusser's perspective is a necessary consequence of the epistemological break, which places both the *Manuscripts'* idealism of consciousness and *The German Ideology*'s concrete anthropology on the same—and wrong—side. In his strongest statement about Marx's theoretical antihumanism, Althusser says:

Strictly in respect to theory, therefore, one can and must speak openly of Marx's theoretical anti-humanism, and see in this theoretical anti-humanism the absolute (negative) precondition of the (positive) knowledge of the human world itself, and of its practical transformation. It is impossible to know anything about men except on the absolute precondition that the philosophical (theoretical) myth of man is reduced to ashes. So any thought that appeals to Marx for any kind of restoration of a theoretical anthropology or humanism is no more than ashes, theoretically. (229–30)

Here is perhaps the common side to Althusser, the French structuralist group in general, and others like Michel Foucault: the idea that the "philosophical . . . myth of man" must be reduced to ashes. On the basis of this orientation, I do not see how it would be possible to build, for example, a protest against the betrayal of rights. Someone like Sakharov must be treated as an ideologist, but Althusser would say that Nobel Prizes are both given to ideologists and, even more surely, given by ideologists.

Nevertheless, we have a hint of something else in this analysis, when Althusser says that knowledge of an object does not replace the object or dissipate its existence (230). To say that something is *theoretically* no more than ashes means that we do not change its reality by arguing that it does not really exist. To know that an ideology has no theoretical status is not to abolish it. Here again there is a reminiscence not only of Spinoza—that in the second kind of knowledge the first one survives—but also of Freud, when Freud says that it is not enough in a therapeutic process to understand intellectually, if the balance of forces—of repression and so on—has not changed also. To explain to someone that he or she is caught in an ideology is not sufficient; it does not change the situation. The claim that something is "no more than ashes, theoretically" is only a qualified claim.

We must deal, then, with a strange necessity: we know that humanism has no theoretical status, but yet it has a kind of factual existence. By relating humanism to its condition of existence, Althusser says, we can recognize its necessity as an ideology; it has, in Althusser's strange phrase, a "conditional necessity" (231). Althusser must resort to this term because if Marxism is more than a science, if it is a politics, and if politics is itself based on the assertion that human beings have certain rights, then Marxism must take something from the ideological sphere in order to accomplish something practically. The conjunction between ideology and science is a "conditional necessity" required by action, but this *practical* conjunction does not abolish their *theoretical* break. As we can see, it is very difficult to comprehend that there may be something abolished theoretically but still existent in such a way that we must rely on it in order to act.

A second example in Althusser of a partial or regional ideology—the language is somewhat Husserlian—is the state. Here too Althusser introduces some important changes in Marxist theory. Althusser's main improvement is engendered by his linking ideology to its political function, that is, to the question of the reproduction of the system, the reproduction of the conditions of production. This problem has become quite popular among modern Marxists; their view is that Marx studied the conditions of production, but there must also be reflection on the conditions of the system's *re*production. Examination must be undertaken of all those institutions which have the function of reinforcing and reproducing the system's structure.

To make sense of this concept of reproduction, Althusser has to improve the rigid Marxist concept of the state, which originates in Lenin. In *State and Revolution* Lenin views the state as merely a structure of coercion. The function of the state is repression. Nothing is left from Hegel's idealized concept of the state as the integration of individuals who know themselves as citizens through the constitution. On the contrary, Lenin's view of the state is extremely pessimistic: the state is an instrument of repression, of coercion, for the benefit of the ruling class. The dictatorship of the proletariat will consist in the inversion of this coercive tool and its use against the enemies of this transformed state. Stalin effectively used this notion of inversion to enforce his own position, arguing that he was simply using the bourgeois structure of the state against its enemy. On the day these enemies disappear, he said, then there will no longer be a need for the state.

Althusser's contribution in *Lenin and Philosophy* is to say that we must in fact distinguish two aspects of state power. The first is the repressive and coercive state apparatuses: government, administration, police, courts, prisons, and so on. The second is the ideological state apparatuses: religion, education, the family, the political system, communications, culture, and so forth (143). The structure of the state is both repressive and ideological. To any who might object that introduction of ideology into the theory of the state involves inclusion of something private and not public, Althusser responds that this division between public and private is a bourgeois concept. If we deny the bourgeois concepts, which depend on the concept of private property, then we must consider the state as a system of apparatuses which extend far beyond administrative functions. Only for the bourgeois mentality are there private and public spheres. For Marxist theory these two spheres represent aspects of the same function.

We may connect the importance of the state's ideological apparatuses with the problem of the system's need to reproduce itself by understanding that this reproduction occurs through such ideological state apparatuses as education. I know many leftist educators in Europe—in Germany, Italy, France—who use this notion of reproduction to argue that the function of the school is to reproduce the system, not only by the teaching of technological skills but by the reproduction in students of the rules of the system. The system is maintained by the reproduction of its rule. (Once again there is an intersection with Freud; the ideological state apparatus has its counterpart in the superego.)

> The reproduction of labour power thus reveals as its *sine qua non* not only the reproduction of its "skills" but also the reproduction of its subjection to the ruling ideology or of the "practice" of that ideology, with the proviso that it is not enough to say "not only but also," for it is clear that it is in the forms and under the forms of ideological subjection that provision is made for the reproduction of the skills of labour power. (133)

A system of oppression survives and prevails thanks to this ideological apparatus which both places individuals in subjection and at the very same time maintains and reproduces the system. Reproduction of the system and ideological repression of the individual are one and the same. Althusser's analysis here is quite powerful. We have to join two ideas: a state functions not only by power but also by ideology, and it does so for the sake of its own reproduction.

There are parallels to this analysis outside Marxism. In Plato, for example, the role played by the sophists demonstrates that no master rules by pure force. The ruler must convince, must seduce; a certain distortion of language always accompanies the use of power. Naked power never works; in the use of political power an ideological mediation is unavoidably involved. My question, therefore, is not at all whether Althusser's description is a good one. I did not raise that question with Marx, nor do I do so here. Instead, it is the concepts used which interest me, and in this context particularly the notion of apparatus. This concept belongs to the same anonymous language as superstructure and infrastructure. It is not by chance that Althusser's term is apparatus and not institution, because an apparatus is more mechanical. An apparatus is something which functions, and therefore it has more conceptual kinship with structures and reproduction, with structural language in general. All these functions are anonymous and can exist and go on by themselves. If, however, we raise the question: but how do these functions work, do we not need to introduce, once again, some element like persuasion and therefore a certain capturing of motivation? Once more the problem is one of legitimacy, of the claim to legitimacy and the process of justification, and I do not see how these issues work within the language of apparatus. My difficulty is with the conceptual framework of causality at a place where I think another—motivational—framework would be more helpful. The causal framework has been imposed at the beginning by the notion of the determinant factor in the last instance, and consequently all of the new and quite interesting changes Althusser introduces in Marxist theory have to be put within this imperative framework.

Let us set this point aside, though, and turn to the most interesting part of Althusser's analysis, his attempt to provide a definition of ideology in general. This attempt will be decisive for the rest of the lectures as a whole. Althusser's attempt allows us to move from what we might call a geography of ideologies to a theory of ideology. Althusser's discussion is located in two principal texts, pages 231–36 of *For Marx* and pages 158–83 of *Lenin and Philosophy*. The latter is the section of "Ideology and Ideological State Apparatuses" entitled "On Ideology" and is Althusser's most discussed text. I shall leave this text for the next lecture.

In *For Marx* Althusser puts forward three or four programmatic definitions of ideology, attempts to try, to test, and nothing more than that, since he thinks that this effort has not been undertaken in previous Marxist theory. As we shall see, Althusser's definitions may not be so easy to combine. Althusser's first definition is readily understood, though, because it is an application of the distinction between science and ideology.

> There can be no question of attempting a profound definition of ideology here. It will suffice to know very schematically that an ideology is a system (with its own logic and rigour) of representations (images, myths, ideas or concepts, depending

on the case) endowed with a historical existence and role within a given society. Without embarking on the problem of the relations between a science and its (ideological) past, we can say that ideology, as a system of representations, is distinguished from science in that in it the practico-social function is more important than the theoretical function (function as knowledge). (231)

There are four or five important notions here. First, ideology is a system; this is consistent with what Althusser called a field—an anthropological field, for example—or a problematic. All these concepts overlap. Of what is ideology a system, though? A system of representation. This is its second trait. Althusser uses the vocabulary of the idealistic tradition; the vocabulary of idealism is preserved in the definition of ideology as *Vorstellung,* representation. Third trait, ideology has a historical role. Ideology is not a shadow, as it is in some Marxist texts, since it plays a role in the historical process. It is a part of the process of overdetermination. Thus, we must connect the notion of ideology's historical existence to its contribution to the overdetermination of events. All these traits are very coherent. What is more problematic is ideology's fourth trait, the relative import Althusser ascribes to ideology's practico-social function in contrast to its theoretical function. This trait is more difficult to accept because if, for example, we call humanism an ideology, surely it has some very theoretical claims. To take another case, what work is more theoretical than Hegel's? Althusser's point is quite difficult to comprehend, because nothing is more theoretical than idealism; Feuerbach and the young Marx in fact opposed Hegel's work precisely because it was theory and not praxis. Suddenly in Althusser, however, we discover that praxis is ideological and only science is theoretical. I do not see how Althusser's point here can be maintained.

Althusser's second definition of ideology is more within the framework of the opposition between the illusory and the real. As we recall from earlier lectures, this analysis has some grounds in the young Marx. This second definition of Althusser's will prevail in his later texts. Notice in the following quotation the use of the phrase "lived relation," *vécu;* this is the vocabulary of Husserl and of Merleau-Ponty, the language of existential phenomenology.

So ideology is a matter of the lived relation between men and their world. This relation, that only appears as "conscious" on condition that it is unconscious, in the same way only seems to be simple on condition that it is complex, that it is not a simple relation but a relation between relations, a second degree relation.

This is a torturous way of saying that ideology reflects in the form of an imaginary relation something which is already an existing relation, that is, the relation of human beings to their world. The lived relation is reflected as ideology. The more important part of the text follows:

> In ideology men do indeed express, not the relation between them and their conditions of existence, but the way they live the relation between them and their conditions of existence: this presupposes both a real relation and an "imaginary," "lived" relation. Ideology, then, is the expression of the relation between men and their "world," that is, the (overdetermined) unity of the real relation and the imaginary relation between them and their real conditions of existence. In ideology the real relation is inevitably invested in the imaginary relation, a relation that expresses a will (conservative, conformist, reformist or revolutionary), a hope or a nostalgia, rather than describing a reality. (233–34)

The vocabulary here is quite interesting, not only because we have the notion of the lived relation, but because this relation is lived in an imaginary mode. In an ideology the way of living this relation is imaginary. This definition introduces an important shift from the vocabulary of the young Marx, which it at first sight resembles. While in the young Marx the real and the imaginary are opposed, here the lived and the imaginary are coupled together. An ideology is both lived *and* imaginary, it is the lived *as* imaginary. Therefore, we have a real relation which is distorted in an imaginary relation. Anticipating our later discussion, we may note that it is difficult to adjust this definition to the rest of Althusser's work, since Althusser speaks here of the real relations of real individuals, even though real individuals do not belong to the basic phenomena. More generally, though, it seems that to give an account of ideology we must speak the language of ideology; we must speak of individuals constructing dreams instead of living their real life.

Althusser also introduces at this point the notion of overdetermination as applied no longer to the relation between instances—between elements of the superstructure and infrastructure—but to the relationship between the real and the imaginary. The concept of overdetermination is used in a context that is closer to Freud than to Marx; the mixture of the real and the imaginary is what Freud calls a compromise formation, and it is this notion that rules Althusser's analysis at this point. "It is in this overdetermination of the real by the imaginary and of the imaginary by the real that ideology is active in principle . . ." (234). Thus, ideology is not something bad, it is not something that we attempt to put behind us; instead, it is something that pushes us, a system of motivation. Ideology is a system of motivation that proceeds from the lack of a clear distinction between the real and the unreal.

In his third definition of ideology, Althusser writes of ideology as expressed in the language of layers, of instances. Althusser needs this language to preserve ideology's reality, its real existence in history. As real, ideology must involve real instances, real layers, and not merely imaginary elements; the imaginary has a kind of inexistence. In his later article on "Ideological Apparatuses," Althusser will try to adjust the definition of ideology to include both the terms of illusion and the terms of historical existence, arguing that ideology has its materiality in the famous ideological apparatus. The apparatus will give a certain material existence to these dreams. At the time of *For Marx,* however, Althusser had not yet solved this subtle discrepancy between his definitions. His third definition of ideology moves from the language of the lived to the language of instances.

> So ideology is as such an organic part of every social totality. It is as if human societies could not survive without these specific formations, these systems of representations (at various levels), their ideologies. Human societies secrete ideology as the very element and atmosphere indispensable to their historical respiration and life. Only an ideological world outlook could have imagined societies without ideology and accepted the utopian idea of a world in which ideology (not just one of its historical forms) would disappear without trace, to be replaced by science. (232)

This text is quite positive toward ideology; it is a plea for recognition of ideology's indispensability. Althusser argues against the utopian view of those technocrats who believe that we are now beyond the age of ideologies, that we may now speak of the death of ideologies. In opposition to this theme, famous both in Europe and in this country, Althusser contends that there will always be ideology, because people have to make sense of their lives. This task is not the province of science, which cannot do everything, but rather the function of ideology. Althusser goes far in the direction of a positive appreciation of ideology. It is difficult, though, to think of ideology simultaneously as illusion (Althusser's second definition) and as a real instance essential to the historical life of societies. Perhaps the mediating point is the Nietzschean view that we need illusions to survive the hardness of life, that we would die if we saw the real truth of human existence. Also involved here may be the pessimistic view that people want ideologies because science does not give their lives meaning. Althusser is very antipositivist and again typifies as utopian the positivist view that science will one day replace ideology.

> [T]his utopia is the principle behind the idea that ethics, which is in its essence ideology, could be replaced by science or become scientific through and through; or that religion could be destroyed by science which would in some way take its place; that art could merge with knowledge or become "everyday life," etc. (232)

Against those who maintain that ethics, religion, and art are "survivals," lingering remnants of earlier nonscientific eras, Althusser tends to say that they are necessary ingredients of any society. Ideologies are indispensable; science cannot be everything.

For my part, I interpret this turn of Althusser's in the following way. If we raise the requirements of science so highly, then it is beyond our access. The higher in fact that we raise the concept of science, the broader becomes the field of ideology, because each is defined in relation to the other. If we reinforce the scientific requirement of a theory, then we lose its capacity for making sense of ordinary life. Therefore, the field of ideology is so wide because the field of science is so narrow. At least this is my interpretation of Althusser's discussion here. Althusser's differentiation between science and ideology explains his positive recognition of ideology as something in the indeterminate state of not being true but yet necessarily vital, a vital illusion. This perspective provides a way to interpret Marx's statement that in a class society ruling ideas have to take the form of universality. This necessity is not a lie, it is not a trick, for it is imposed by the unavoidable imaginary structure itself. No one can think without believing that what he or she thinks is in some basic sense true. The illusion is a necessary one.

The persistence of this illusion that is ideology extends even unto the hypothesized classless society. Whatever the classless society may mean—and again I do not discuss it at all in political terms but only according to its own condition of intelligibility—it has about it a quality of the eternal. (In Althusser's "Ideological Apparatuses" article, the word "eternal" returns and is compared to Freud's description of the atemporality of the unconscious.) Similarly, ideology is also atemporal. "[I]t is clear that ideology (as a system of mass representations) is indispensable in any society if men are to be formed, transformed and equipped to respond to the demands of their conditions of existence" (235). The suggestion is that in every society, even in one where by hypothesis class struggle no longer exists, there will always be a situation of inadequation between the demands of reality and our ability to cope. I am reminded of Freud's comments concerning death and the hardness of life, the fact that the price of reality is too high. The requirements of the conditions of reality are high, and our capacity to adjust to reality is limited.

> It is in ideology that the classless society lives the inadequacy/adequacy of the relation between it and the world, it is in it and by it that it transforms men's "consciousness," that is, their attitudes and behaviour so as to raise them to the levels of their tasks and the conditions of their existence. (235)

We have here nearly a fourth definition of ideology as the the system of means by which we try to adjust our capacity to change to the actual conditions of change in society in general. Therefore, ideology has a certain ethical function; it attempts to make sense of the accidents of life, the painful aspects of existence. We must introduce an existential language; when we speak of contradiction, it is not a logical contradiction, a conflict between structures, but a lived contradiction, a contradiction between our capacity to adjust and the demands of reality.

To my mind, Althusser's definitions of ideology in general raise the following questions. My broadest question is: if we assume the value of Althusser's analysis, are we any longer able to speak of ideology simply as nonscience? Under this theme, several more specific questions follow, which I shall return to in later lectures. First, is not the quasi-ethical function of ideology just as valuable as science? Second, how can we understand the notion of the imaginary if the real is not already symbolically mediated? Third, is not the most primitive function of ideology—that which is said to emerge in classless society—not distortive but integrative? And finally, how do we know ideology if not because it belongs to a fundamental anthropology; is it not only within this philosophical anthropology that the vocabulary of Althusser's definitions—"men," "conditions of existence," "demands," "attitudes and behaviour"—makes sense? Is there not, therefore, a primitive connection between the lived and the imaginary that is more radical than any distortion?

The point about Althusser's expressions is that they belong to the vocabulary of humanism. To speak of ideology we must rejuvenate the vocabulary of humanism. Even in the concluding sentence of his discussion—a sentence perhaps, though, a concession to the reader—Althusser resorts to this vocabulary. "In a classless society ideology is the relay whereby, and the element in which, the relation between men and their conditions of existence is lived to the profit of all men" (236). Who would say more than this, that we are all dreaming of the kind of society in which the relations between human beings and their conditions of existence are lived to the profit of all? But this is precisely the discourse of ideology. We must assume at least part of the discourse of ideology in order to speak of ideology. It seems as if we cannot speak of ideology in another language than its own. If we utilize the Althusserian language of science, then we can speak only of apparatuses, instances, structures, and superstructures and infrastructures, but not of "conditions of existence," "attitudes and behaviour," and so on. At least to a certain extent, therefore, only ideology may speak about ideology.

A few more points also need to be made about Althusser's contention that the "disproportion of historical tasks to their conditions" (238) justifies the necessity of ideology. This relationship must be *lived* in order to become a contradiction and to be treated scientifically. The relation of disproportion also reinforces the prestige of the concept of alienation. Althusser maintains, as we have seen, that this concept can be done away with, but are we able to deny it theoretically and preserve it practically? Are not the lived contradictions the conditions for the so-called real relations? Althusser responds that if we return to the language of alienation, it is because we do not yet have a science of ideology. It is a provisory language in the absence of an adequate language. "Within certain limits this recourse to ideology might indeed be envisaged as the substitute for a recourse to theory" (240) or as "a substitute for an insufficient theory" (241). Althusser has accused all Marxist thinkers of theoretical weakness, but he assumes a certain theoretical weakness for himself in order to speak about ideology in positive terms. Because of the present weakness of our theory, he says, we need the language of ideology in order to speak of ideology; one day, however, our theory will be strong enough to cast aside this vocabulary. This argument is for me the most questionable of Althusser's claims. The question is whether this alleged confusion of ideology and scientific theory is not required by the problem itself. Does not this "confusion" in fact express the impossibility of drawing the line between the lived contradiction and the real basis? In order to speak in a meaningful way of ideology, do we not have to speak of the motives of people, of individuals in certain circumstances, of the adequate or inadequate relation between human behavior and its conditions? We cannot eliminate as a problem the status of a philosophical anthropology if we want to speak about these issues.

The next lecture turns to Althusser's article on "Ideological Apparatuses" and analyzes the theory of ideology in general that is articulated there. This analysis will conclude our discussion of Althusser.

9

Althusser (3)

In the lectures on Althusser, we have taken as a leading thread the contrast between ideology and science. In emphasizing the *break* between ideology and science, the trend of Marxism represented by Althusser reinforces the scientific nature of its own theoretical claims. Anything that cannot be expressed scientifically is said to be ideological. What defines this Marxist science is its turn away from concepts with an anthropological basis to concepts of a rather different kind: forces of production, modes of production, relations of productions, classes, and so on. The language is distinctly nonanthropological. This epistemological break between the two sets of concepts provides the main framework for the theory of ideology. Within this framework Althusser attempts to refine and improve Engels' model concerning superstructure and infrastructure, since the notion of ideology is identified as superstructural. Althusser endeavors to give the correlation between superstructure and infrastructure a non-Hegelian cast, because the Hegelian mode of thought—one of *Aufhebung,* overcoming contradiction—is still linked to a philosophy of the subject and must be itself placed on the side of ideology. Althusser attempts to provide a certain content to ideology itself, the assumption being that ideology is not a world of shadows but has a reality of its own. It is with this notion of the reality of something which is illusory that Althusser's later writings deal. In the last lecture we reached the stage where Althusser moves from speaking about particular ideologies to a concept of ideology in general. We interrupted our inquiry following the examination of Althusser's remarks on this theme in *For Marx;* I want to end our inquiry into Althusser by considering his later proposals in *Lenin and Philosophy*.

Althusser's most advanced attempt to provide an inclusive concept of ideology appears in the *Lenin and Philosophy* essay titled "Ideology and

Ideological State Apparatuses." The purpose of this essay, we should recall, is to argue that the fundamental function of ideology is reproduction of the system, training of individuals in the rules governing the system. To the problem of production raised by Marx we must add the problem of *re*production. On the basis of this reconceptualization, we must then reformulate the Leninist concept of the state—defined only in terms of coercion—by adding the notion of what Althusser calls ideological state apparatuses. Ideology is institutionalized and so appears as a dimension of the state. There is a dimension of the state which is not merely administrative or political but specifically ideological. The superstructure is related to reproduction through specific institutional apparatuses, and the problem of a general theory of ideology is proposed in conjunction with this reformulation.

In this text, Althusser goes so far as to ascribe to ideology all positive functions which are not science. At the same time, he emphasizes more strongly than ever the illusory character of imagination. Here Althusser borrows from Spinoza the theme that the first kind of knowledge is merely a distorted conception of our relation to the world. He also and more importantly borrows from the distinction made by the French psychoanalyst Jacques Lacan between the imaginary and the symbolic. Significantly, Althusser drops the notion of the symbolic to retain the notion of the imaginary understood on the model of the mirror relationship. The imaginary is a mirror relation at a narcissistic stage, an image of oneself that one has in a physical mirror and also in all the situations of life in which one's image is reflected by others.

In turning to the text, we shall focus particularly on the section of Althusser's essay called "On Ideology." Althusser begins by contrasting his position to that of Marx in *The German Ideology*. Here, Althusser claims, Marx did not take seriously the paradox of a reality of the imaginary.

> In *The German Ideology* . . . [i]deology is conceived as a pure illusion, a pure dream, i.e. as nothingness. All its reality is external to it. Ideology is thus thought as an imaginary construction whose status is exactly like the theoretical status of the dream among writers before Freud. For these writers, the dream was the purely imaginary, i.e. null, result of "day's residues," presented in an arbitrary arrangement and order, sometimes even "inverted," in other words, in "disorder." For them the dream was the imaginary, it was empty, null and arbitrarily "stuck together" *(bricolé)*. (159–60)

Against this purely negative text Althusser maintains that ideology has a reality of its own: the reality of the illusory. This statement seems to challenge another assertion of *The German Ideology,* that ideology has no history. (The argument, we remember, was that only economic history really exists. This became the framework for all orthodox Marxist approaches to history.) Althusser in fact agrees that ideology is nonhistorical but in a very different sense than that argued by *The German Ideology.* Ideology is nonhistorical not, as the orthodox approach would have it, because its history is external to it but because it is omnihistorical, just like Freud's unconscious. Once more the influence of Freud is strongly reinforced. In his essay, "The Unconscious," Freud said that the unconscious is timeless *(zeitlos),* not in the sense that it is supernatural but because it is prior to any temporal order or connections, being prior to the level of language, of culture, and so on. (An earlier, similar assertion appeared in the seventh chapter of Freud's *The Interpretation of Dreams.*) Althusser's explicit parallel between ideology and the unconscious draws on this basis and takes a step further by rendering timelessness as the eternal: "ideology is eternal, exactly like the unconscious" (161). Althusser suggests that in the same way that Freud attempted to provide a theory of the unconscious in general—as the underlying structure of all the cultural figures of the unconscious, which appear at the level of symptoms—similarly, he himself proposes a theory of ideology in general that would underlie the particular ideologies.

On this basis the imaginary features of ideology must be qualified and improved. Here I raise two points. First, what is distorted is not reality as such, not the real conditions of existence, but our relation to these conditions of existence. We are not far from a concept of being-in-the-world; it is our relation to reality which is distorted. "Now I can return to a thesis which I have already advanced: it is not their real conditions of existence, their real world, that 'men' 'represent to themselves' in ideology, but above all it is their relation to those conditions of existence which is represented to them there" (164). This leads to a most important insight, because what is a relation to the conditions of existence if not already an interpretation, something symbolically mediated. To speak of our relation to the world requires a symbolic structure. My main argument, therefore, is that if we do not have from the start a symbolic structure to our existence, then nothing can be distorted. As Althusser himself observes: "it is the imaginary nature of this relation which underlies all the imaginary distortion that we can observe . . . in all ideology" (164). We are not far from a complete reversal in our approach to the problem of the imaginary. We could not understand that there are distorted images if there were not first a primary imaginary structure of our being in the world underlying even the distortions. The imaginary appears not only in the distorted forms of existence, because it is already present in the relation which is distorted. The imaginary is constitutive of our relation to the world. One of my main questions, then, is whether this does not imply before the distorting function of imagination a constitutive function of imagination. Or, to use the language of Lacan, is there not a symbolic role of imagination distinct from the narcissistic component of imagination, that is to say, distinct from the imaginary taken in the sense of the mirror relationship.

My second remark is that this relation to our conditions of existence no longer falls very easily within the framework of causality. This relation is not causal or naturalistic but rather an interplay between motives, between symbols; it is a relation of belonging to the whole of our experience and of being related to it in a motivational way. Althusser himself hints that this relationship destroys the general framework of superstructure and infrastructure expressed in terms of causation; he says that here we need "to leave aside the language of causality" (164).

Thus, we must introduce two levels of imagination, one which is the distorting, and another which is the distorted and therefore the primary.

> [A]ll ideology represents in its necessarily imaginary distortion not the existing relationships of production (and the other relationships that derive from them), but above all the (imaginary) relationship of individuals to the relations of production and the relations that derive from them. What is represented in ideology is therefore not the system of the real relations which govern the existence of individuals, but the imaginary relation of those individuals to the real relations in which they live. (164–65)

Expressed more simply, this means that in fact we are never related directly to what are called the conditions of existence, classes and so on. These conditions must be represented in one way or another; they must have their imprint in the motivational field, in our system of images, and so in our representation of the world. The so-called real causes never appear as such in human existence but always under a symbolic mode. It is this symbolic mode which is secondarily distorted. Therefore, the notion of a primitive and basic distortion becomes questionable and perhaps completely incomprehensible. If everything were distorted, that is the same as if nothing were distorted. We must dig in under the notion of distortion. In so doing, we rediscover a layer not far finally from what *The German*

Ideology described as real life or real individuals placed under certain circumstances. Althusser denies this anthropological approach, however, claiming that it is itself ideological. As a result, this discourse remains *en l'air,* floating without a basis, because we must use the so-called language of ideology, the anthropological language, in order to speak of this primitive, ineluctably symbolically mediated relation to our conditions of existence.

Perhaps anticipating this difficulty, the text suddenly takes a quite different approach. Althusser relinquishes the language of representation and substitutes for it that of apparatus. He turns away from the questions he has just raised to consider the material criteria of ideology. Althusser's thesis here is that ideology has a material existence. The claim is that while no Marxist can say anything that is not ideological concerning the roots of distortion in some more imaginary layer, he or she may still speak scientifically of the ideological apparatus within which the distortion works. The only Marxist language about the imaginary bears not upon its ontological, anthropological rooting but upon its incorporation in the state apparatus, in an institution. Therefore, we have a theory about imagination as institutionalized but not about imagination as a symbolic structure.

> While discussing the ideological State apparatuses and their practices, I said that each of them was the realization of an ideology. . . . I now return to this thesis: an ideology always exists in an apparatus, and its practice, or practices. This existence is material. (166)

The materialist approach asks in which apparatus does ideology work and not how is it possible according to the fundamental structure of human being; the latter question belongs to an ideological language. Questions about the underlying imaginary—the nondistorted or predistorted imaginary—must be canceled for the sake of questions about the apparatus. The apparatus is a public entity and so no longer implies a reference to individuals. Althusser talks about individual beliefs as belonging to an "ideological 'conceptual' device *(dispositif)*" (167). In French *dispositif* expresses the idea of something which functions by itself, something which shapes behavior.

It is difficult, though, to speak of the practice of a believer, for example, merely in terms of an apparatus unless the apparatus is reflected in the rules governing the behavior. The ideological device which shapes the behavior of the believer—the example is Althusser's (167)—must be such that it speaks to the attitudes and therefore to the motives of the individual involved. We must link the apparatus with what is meaningful for the individual. The apparatus is an anonymous and external entity, however, so it is difficult to connect and to have intersect the notion of apparatus with the notion of a practice, which is always the practice of someone. It is always some individual who is bowing, praying, doing what is supposed to be induced in him or her by the apparatus.

In order not to speak the language of ideology about ideology, Althusser must put the notion of practice itself into a behaviorist framework, the latter being something more appropriately connected with the Marxist concept of apparatus. The language of ideology, says Althusser, "talks of actions: I shall talk of action inserted into practices. And I shall point out that these practices are governed by the rituals in which these practices are inscribed, within the material existence of an ideological apparatus . . ." (168). For Althusser the concept of action is too anthropological; practice is the more objective term. Finally it is only the material existence of an ideological apparatus which makes sense of practice. The apparatus is a material framework, within which people do some specific things.

The behaviorist overtone in Althusser is evident in the following quotation:

> I shall therefore say that, where only a single subject . . . is concerned, the existence of the ideas of his belief is material in that his ideas are his material actions inserted into material practices governed by material rituals which are themselves defined by the material ideological apparatus from which derive the ideas of that subject. (169)

The word "material" is used in four ways: material actions, kneeling, for example; material practices, kneeling as religious behavior; material rituals, kneeling as part of a service of worship; and the material ideological apparatus, the church as an institution. Just as Aristotle said that "being" has several meanings, so Althusser gives several meanings to matter, a comparison he explicitly acknowledges with some humor (166). While admitting that the four inscriptions of the word "material" are affected by different modalities, though, Althusser provides no rule for their differentiation. "I shall leave on one side," he says, "the problem of a theory of the differences between the modalities of materiality" (169). In fact, then, we must qualify our concept of what is material in order to apply it properly to something that is not material in the way, for instance, that a chair is.

We must rely on a polysemy of the word "matter" to make sense of these differences, and this is hardly forbidden, because in ordinary language we use the word in so many divergent contexts. We rely on a common sense concept of matter or on the rules of everyday language, in the Wittgensteinian sense, to extend and stretch the notion of materiality in order that it covers the notion of practice.

The remaining part of Althusser's essay is devoted to the functioning of the category of the subject in ideology. Althusser says that the function of ideology and of the subject is for each to give content to the other.

> I say: the category of the subject is constitutive of all ideology, but at the same time and immediately I add that the category of the subject is only constitutive of all ideology insofar as all ideology has the function (which defines it) of "constituting" concrete individuals as subjects. (171)

Althusser puts "constituting" within quotation marks because this is the language of Husserl. The phenomenology of the ego falls under the concept of ideology to the extent that it defines ideology; ideology is humanism, humanism relies on the concept of the subject, and it is ideology which constitutes the subject. Ideology and the subject are mutually constitutive. Whereas someone like Erik Erikson argues that ideology is a factor of identity and so maintains that the relationship between ideology and the subject should be taken in a positive sense, the language of Althusser is much more negative. We are forced to put on the side of ideology what in a sense is the most interesting philosophical problem: how do we become subjects? It is a bold attempt to give so much to ideology in order to deny it so much also. This is why I have said that if we give too much to science, we have to give still more to ideology. It becomes more and more difficult to treat ideology merely as a word of illusions, of superstructures, because it becomes so constitutive of what we are that what we might be when separated from ideology is completely unknown; we are what we are precisely thanks to ideology. The burden of ideology is to make subjects of us. It is a strange philosophical situation, since all our concrete existence is put on the side of ideology.

Althusser's interesting analysis of what he calls "interpellation" demonstrates more specifically the relationship between ideology and the subject. "As a first formulation, I shall say: all ideology hails or interpellates concrete individuals as concrete subjects, by the functioning of the category of the subject" (173). We are constituted as subjects through a process of recognition. The use of the term "interpellation" is an allusion to the theological concept of call, of being called by God. In its ability to interpellate subjects, ideology also constitutes them. To be hailed is to become a subject. "The existence of ideology and the hailing or interpellation of individuals as subjects are one and the same thing" (175). The idea is that ideology is eternal and so does not belong to the history of classes and so on, and it acts to constitute and be constituted by the category of the subject. The theory of ideology in general rebuilds the framework of a complete anthropology, but it does so with a negative cast. This anthropology is the world of illusion.

Althusser's claim about the illusory nature of what constitutes us as subjects is based on the Lacanian notion of the mirror-structure of the imagination. "We observe that the structure of all ideology, interpellating individuals as subjects in the name of a Unique and Absolute Subject is speculary, i.e. has a mirror-structure, and doubly speculary: this mirror duplication is constitutive of ideology and ensures its functioning" (180). When emphasis is placed on the primacy of illusion in the symbolic process, all ideology must be illusory. Here there is a complete merging of the concept of the mirror—the narcissistic structure—with ideology. Ideology is established at the level of narcissism, the subject looking at itself indefinitely. Althusser takes as an illustrative example religious ideology. He says that the function of Christian theology is to reduplicate the subject by an absolute subject; they are in a mirror relation. "The dogma of the Trinity is precisely the theory of the duplication of the Subject (the Father) into a subject (the Son) and of their mirror-connexion (the Holy Spirit)" (180 *n.*). Althusser's treatment here is not a good piece of work; I do not think it makes much sense. It is expeditive; Althusser summarizes Trinitarian theology in a footnote. We perhaps could say that the mirror relation would be more interesting as an expression of a neurotic way of life. If we took, for example, the Schreber case analyzed by Freud, and in particular what Freud called Schreber's theology, we would see this reduplicative process, there being in fact no god to worship but only a projection and reinjection indefinitely of oneself, a projection and assimilation of one's own image.

It is most difficult, therefore, to construct the whole concept of the subject on the narrow basis of the narcissistic relation of mirroring. We can more easily understand this relation as distortive, the distortion of a constitution, but it is difficult to understand it as constitutive itself. The only way to maintain that this relation is constitutive—and this is Althusser's stance—is to argue the radical position that the constitution is the distortion, that all constitution of a subject is a distortion. If ideology is eternal, though, if there are always already interpellated individuals as subjects, if the formal structure of ideology is continuingly the same, then what happens to the epistemological break? The problem of the epistemological break has to be removed from the sphere of particular ideologies to that of ideology in general. The break with religious ideology, with humanism, and so on is nothing compared to the break with this mutual constitution of primary ideology and subjectivity. I would agree that a break must occur, but not where Althusser places it. Instead, we may break and we have to break with the "miscognition" *(méconnaissance)* that adheres to recognition *(reconnaissance)*. What point would there be in a critique of miscognition if it were not for the sake of a more faithful recognition? We must make sense of true recognition in a way that does not reduce it to ideology, in the narrow and pejorative sense of that term. Althusser, however, rejects this possibility. He talks of "the reality which is necessarily ignored *(méconnue)* [so "miscognized," not ignored] in the very forms of recognition . . ." (182). All recognition is miscognition; it is a very pessimistic assertion. If ideology must have no value in itself, then it must be the world of miscognition, *méconnaissance*. The whole dialectic of recognition is broken by Althusser's ideological reduction of the problematic of the subject.

Instead of there being a relation of recognition, Althusser correlates the mirror relation with a relation of subsumption. "There are no subjects except by and for their subjection" (182), he says. Althusser uses the play on words to indicate that the subject means both subjectivity and subjection. The two meanings are in fact reduced to one: to be a subject means to be submitted to. Yet is there not a history of the individual's growth beyond the "speculary" stage? What about the dialectic of the speculary and the symbolic within imagination itself? For Althusser, however, to be a subject means to be subjected, to be submitted to an apparatus, the ideological apparatus of the state. To my mind, if ideology must be tied to the mirror stage of the imagination, to the submitted subject, I do not see how it would ever be possible to have as citizens authentic subjects who could resist the apparatus of the state. I do not see from where we could borrow the forces to resist the apparatus if not from the depths of a subject having claims that are not infected by this supposed submissive constitution. How else will someone produce a break in the seemingly closed shell of ideology?

The task, then, is to disentangle recognition *(reconnaissance)* from miscognition *(méconnaissance)*. I shall later connect my analysis of Habermas precisely at this point. The problematic for Habermas is the need to start from a project of recognition. Ideology is troublesome because it makes impossible the true recognition of one human being by another. Further, if this situation is placed entirely on the side of ideology, then no weapons exist against ideology, because the weapons themselves are ideological. Therefore, we need a concept of recognition, what Habermas' more recent work speaks of as a concept of communication. We need a utopia of total recognition, of total communication, communication without boundaries or obstacles. This supposes that we have an interest in communication which is not, we might say, ideology-stricken from the beginning. In order to connect, as does Habermas, the critique of ideology to an interest in liberation, we must have a concept of recognition, a concept of the mutual task of communication, that is not ideological in the distortive sense of that word.

Before we reach our examination of Habermas, however, we shall spend some time discussing Mannheim and Weber, and we have some final questions of Althusser as well. To prepare for the transit from Althusser, I would like to present a general framework of the questions arising from our readings of his work. I shall consider five main problems. First is the question of the scientific claim of Marxism: in what sense is it a science? While Althusser speaks in some more recent writings of the discovery of a continent, the continent of history, even here the subject matter is to be raised to the level of a systematic science. The focus of this history is not empirical historiography but the systematic concatenation of stages in the development of economic relationships (from primitive communism to feudalism to capitalism and so forth). If we speak of science in a positivist sense, then a theory must be submitted to verification and therefore to the whole community of, we might say, intellectual workers. It is hard, though, to identify this science with the science of a class. To put the notion of scientific verification within the framework of class struggle introduces a practical concept within the theoretical framework. My question, then, is in what sense can Marxism be a science if it is not verifiable or falsifiable in the Popperian sense? Perhaps it can be scientific in another fashion, that of a critique. But what motivates a critique if not an interest, an interest in emancipation, an interest in liberation, something which pulls a critique necessarily into the ideological sphere? It is quite difficult to think of a nonpositivist science that is not supported by a human interest, a practical interest. It is also difficult to think of a science that is not understandable for all, even for members of other classes. As we shall discover, the problem of Mannheim's paradox in fact starts from the generalization of the concept of ideology at the point where ideological analysis is raised to the level of a science, that of the sociology of knowledge.

Our second problem, a corollary of the first, concerns the notion of the epistemological break. Is a complete break understandable without some kind of intellectual miracle, a sense of someone emerging from the dark? In Althusser's more recent *Essays in Self-Criticism,* even while subjecting himself to reproach (saying that he has been too theoretical and needs to return to the class struggle in a more militant way), he still reinforces his concept of the epistemological break. He says that it is an unprecedented event. Althusser even speaks of Marx as a son without a father, a kind of absolute orphan. He argues that it is the idealists who are always seeking continuity. Possibly a certain providentialism does imply continuity, but I do not know why historical continuity alone should be considered necessarily ideological and, perhaps, even theological. The concept of discontinuity gives rise to difficulty itself. It does so principally if we consider, once more, the motivation of this break. The epistemological break appears to be motivated, and if we want to connect this break to the emergence of a certain interest, then we have to borrow this motivation from the ideological sphere. The motivation belongs to the anthropological sphere, to the interest in being more fully human. We cannot completely separate the idea of the break from a certain human project which is to be improved, possibly even disclosed, by this science.

For my part Althusser's representation of the epistemological break does great damage not only to the theory of ideology but to the reading of Marx. It causes us to overlook an important break in Marx; it causes us to place the break at a different point from where it should be. Though I am not a Marxist scholar, my reading of Marx reinforces a conviction that the more important change at the philosophical level comes not after *The German Ideology* but between the *Manuscripts of 1844* and *The German Ideology,* that is to say, in the emergence of the concept of the real human being, real praxis, individuals acting in certain given conditions. Seen in this light, the destiny of anthropology is not sealed by that of idealism. The great damage done to Marx by Althusser is that he forces us to put under one heading—anthropological ideology—two different notions. The first is an ideology of consciousness, which Marx and Freud have rightly broken. The second, though, is the ideology of real, concrete, human being, a being composed of drives, labor, and so on. This latter notion, I believe, can be expressed in nonidealist terms. Ideology and idealism, therefore, are not identified in such a way that no place any longer exists for an anthropology. For me, a nonidealistic anthropology is the only way to make sense of all the other problems that we shall consider during the rest of the lectures. Marx's breakthrough must make sense at the level of this deep-rooted interest in the plenitude of indvidual existence.

The issues here lead us to a third question arising from our reading of Althusser, the problem of his conceptual framework. The conceptual framework of infrastructure and superstructure is a metaphor of a base with stories, an edifice with a base. This metaphor is quite seducing at first sight, but it becomes very dangerous when taken literally to mean something prior to something secondary or derived. One of the signs that this metaphor is misleading when frozen and taken literally is the difficulty of reconnecting the action of the basis and the reaction back on the basis by the superstructure. We are caught in a scholasticism of determinant factors and real but nondeterminant factors. This scholasticism, I believe, leads nowhere, but the metaphor is harmful for even more important reasons. It is not that the metaphor creates paradoxes, for all doctrines in fact proceed by solving their own paradoxes. Rather, the conceptual framework here prevents us from making sense of some very interesting contributions of Althusser himself to Marxist doctrine. In particular I think of the concept of overdetermination, that is, recognition of the simultaneous action of infrastructure and superstructure, the fact that in history the basis never acts alone but is always intertwined with actions, specific historical events, and so on. I wonder whether we could not make more sense of the concept of overdetermination if we placed it in another conceptual framework than that of infrastructure and superstructure. This might cause us, in fact, to reconsider what finally is really the basis.

If we raise this radical question about what is basic for human beings, we may come to realize that a great deal of what is placed in the superstructure is basic from another point of view. Take into consideration any culture, and we find that its symbolic framework—its main assumptions, the way in which it considers itself and projects its identity through symbols and myths—is basic. It seems that we can call basic exactly what is usually called the superstructure. The possibility of this juxtaposition is always present with a metaphor. We must destroy a metaphor by the use of a contrary metaphor; we therefore proceed from metaphor to metaphor. The opposing metaphor here is the notion of what is basic for human beings: what is basic for human beings is not necessarily what is the basis in Marxist structure. Indeed, I wonder whether the notion of overdetermination does not imply that we must in fact give up the distinction between infrastructure and superstructure.

This point is made even more evident when we realize that the very action of the superstructure implies some intermediary concepts which break the infrastructure/superstructure framework. Once again let me refer to the concept of authority. A system of authority never works only by force, by sheer violence; instead, as we have discussed, it works through ideology, through some meaningful procedures. These procedures call for the comprehension of individuals. Althusser's schema of "effectivity" must be improved or perhaps completely recast in order to make room for the claim to legitimacy, which is characteristic of a ruling authority whether a group or class. I shall later turn to Max Weber to deal with this problem further, because his fundamental problem was how does a system of authority work. For Weber the problem of domination implied a system of motives wherein the claims to legitimacy of an authority attempt to meet the capacity of belief in this legitimacy. We are forced to deal, therefore, with beliefs and claims, and it is difficult to put these psychological factors within a framework of infrastructure and superstructure.

Another reason we should question this conceptual framework is if we want to make sense of another of Althusser's claims, that ideologies have a reality of their own. I think that Althusser is right to assert the relative autonomy and self-consistency of ideologies; in this he opposes the classical Marxists, with the possible exception of the Italians, Gramsci above all. The relative autonomy of the superstructure, though, requires that ideologies have a content of their own. In turn, this requires before an understanding of these ideologies' use a phenomenology of their specific mode. We cannot define these ideologies' structure only by their role in the reproduction of the system. We must make sense of their meaning before considering their use. The assumption that ideologies' content is exhausted by their use is without justification; their use does not exhaust their meaning. We can take as an example the problem raised by Habermas, that in modern societies—and particularly in the military-industrial structure of the capitalist world—science and technology function ideologically. This does not mean that they are constitutively ideological but rather that they are being used ideologically. The present capture of science and technology by a certain interest—in Habermas' terms, an interest in control—is not constitutive of the inner meaning of their field. We must distinguish between the inner constitution of a given ideological field (granting, for the moment, that we still want to call it an ideology) and its function. The problem of distortion does not exhaust the constitution of a certain sociological force or structure.

As an example here, we may return to Lenin's definition of the state. In determining that the state is defined only by its coercive funciton, Lenin neglected its many other functions; he did not see that the coercive function is a distortion of these other functions. Lenin's approach, however, typifies the orthodox Marxist model. Religion is said to have no other constitution than its distorting function, and some now say the same of science and technology. Again I wonder, though, is not the only way to give meaning to the relative autonomy of the superstructural spheres to distinguish between the rules of their constitution and the distortive modes of their use? If we cannot make this distinction, then we have to say that the procedure of unmasking is constitutive of its object. The content of an ideology becomes uniquely what we have unmasked and nothing more than that, a very reductive procedure.

The failure to recognize the specificity of each superstructural sphere—the juridical, political, religious, cultural—has not only dangerous theoretical consequences but dangerous practical and political consequences also. Once it is assumed that these spheres have no autonomy, then the Stalinist state is possible. The argument is that since the economic basis is sound and since all the other spheres are merely reflexes, shadows, or echoes, then we are allowed to manipulate the latter spheres in order to improve the economic basis. There is no respect for the autonomy of the juridical, the political, or the religious, because they are said to have no existence in themselves.

Do we not want, then, a quite different theoretical framework in which the process of distortion would have as its condition of possibility a constitution which would not be defined by the distorting function? This would entail that the juridical sphere, for example, retain a certain constitutive specificity even though it may be true that is has been captured by the bourgeoisie for the latter's benefit. If we take the relation between work and capital expressed in the notion of the wage, the wage is presented as a contract, and the contract is represented as a juridical act. The juridical form of the exchange suggests no one is a slave, since people hire out their work and receive a wage in return. This is clearly a grave distortion, because the juridical concept of contract is applied to a situation of domination. Here the real situation of exploitation is concealed in an exchange of work and salary that is only apparently reciprocal. My claim is that while the juridical function is greatly harmed by the way this juridical framework in the capitalist system serves to conceal the real structure of exploitation, it is not exhausted, as the orthodox Marxists maintain, by this distortive function. I insist on the possibility of disconnecting and reconnecting the distortive and constitutive functions; this presupposes, once again, a motivational framework.

The fourth problem arising from our reading is that of particular ideologies. We may start here from the previous problem and ask what makes these particular ideologies specific. Let us take the example of humanism. In the United States the argument for humanism may be too easy, because humanism is a positive term, which is not always the case in Europe. We must reconsider the concept of humanism in order to disentangle what about it is ideological in the bad sense of that word, that is, a mere way to cover up real situations. We must look for a strong concept of humanism, which would not be ideological in a pejorative sense. Here I think that a theory of the system of interests, like Habermas', could help to show that there exists a hierarchy of interests that is not reducible to the mere interest in domination or control. This would imply construction of a complete anthropology and not a mere assertion of humanism, the latter being merely a claim if not a pretense. This strong concept of humanism must be linked to three or four other concepts within the same conceptual framework. First is the concept of the real individual under definite conditions, which has been elaborated in *The German Ideology*. This notion provides a strong philosophical basis for a humanism that would not be merely a claim. A strong concept of humanism is implied, second, in the entire problematics of legitimacy, because of the individual's relation to a system of order and domination. Perhaps here is the individual's major fight to achieve his or her identity over against a structure of authority. We need to stress, then, the important dialectic between individual and authority within the polarity between belief and claim. Third, I would say that the epistemological break relies on the emergence of this humanistic interest. We can make no sense of the sudden outburst of truth in the midst of obscurity and darkness if it is not the emergence of something which was distorted in ideology but now finds its truth. In a sense, the break must be also at the same time a recovery of what was covered up by ideology. I wonder whether a notion of radical break can be thought.

The fifth and final problem to arise from our reading is that of ideology in general. This raises the most radical question: what is distorted if not praxis as something symbolically mediated? The discourse on distortion is itself neither ideological nor scientific but anthropological.[1] This is in agreement with all the previous suggestions concerning a philosophical anthropology that includes motives and symbols. The parallelism between the discourse on ideology in general and Freud's discourse on the unconscious in general reinforces the argument. Thus, we must have a theory of symbolic action. Recourse to the material existence of ideology does not suffice, for how can an imaginary relation be an apparatus? The functioning of the category of the subject in ideology becomes a warrant for ideology. We cannot speak of miscognition *(méconnaissance)* without the background of recognition *(reconnaissance)*, a background that is not ideological but anthropological.

These central issues, derived from our reading of Althusser, provide the main directions in which the remaining lectures shall proceed. I shall propose to advance in four steps. First, we shall turn to Karl Mannheim. Mannheim asks whether a complete break between ideology and science is possible. Are not in fact all theoretical claims in some sense ideological? If so, Mannheim points out, then generalization of the concept of ideology leads to a paradox. If everything is ideological, then how is it possible to have other than an ideological discourse on ideology? This is Mannheim's paradox. I shall then consider the problem of domination in another framework of thought than that of superstructure and infrastructure, one considering the legitimation of a system of authority, and I shall introduce Max Weber for that purpose. We shall ask how in a motivational framework there are conflicts about power. The third step will be to raise the connection between interests and science, more specifically, a critical science carried out and supported by an interest. Here I shall use Habermas. Finally, I shall consider the fundamental symbolic structure of action as itself the precondition for any kind of distortion. At this point I shall turn to Clifford Geertz and to some of my own personal approaches to this problem. I shall attempt to show that it is the structure of symbolic action which is distorted by ideology, in the more narrow sense of this term. When reappropriated in a broader sense, one that gives full weight to the structure of symbolic action, we shall see that ideology—a primitive, positive ideology—acts for both groups and individuals as the constitution of their identity. This will be the turning point to the problem of utopia, since at this level it is the imagination which is both ideological and utopian.

10

Mannheim

Our discussion of Karl Mannheim's *Ideology and Utopia* concentrates on the two chapters entitled "Ideology and Utopia" and "The Utopian Mentality." Mannheim is of interest for our purposes for two major reasons. First, he was perhaps the initial person to link ideology and utopia together under the general problematic of noncongruence. He observed that there are two ways in which a system of thought may be noncongruent with the general trend of a group or society: either by sticking to the past, thus a certain resistance to change, or by leaping ahead, and thus a type of encouragement of change. In some sense a polarity exists, therefore, between the two modalities of discrepancy. I shall reserve our major discussion of Mannheim's correlation between ideology and utopia for the final stages of the lectures as a whole, but want to make a few anticipatory remarks on this topic at the end of the present lecture.

Mannheim's second merit, which is no less great, is that he tried to enlarge the Marxist concept of ideology to the point where it becomes a perplexing concept, because it includes the one who asserts it. Mannheim pushes quite far the notion of the author's self-involvement in his or her own concept of ideology. This interplay leads to what has been called Mannheim's paradox. The paradox is similar in form to Zeno's paradox about movement; both strike at the foundations of knowledge. Mannheim pushes the concept and the critique of ideology to the point where the concept becomes self-defeating, a stage reached when the concept is extended and universalized such that it involves anyone who claims its use. Mannheim's argument is that this condition of universalization is one in which we are now unavoidably caught. To put it in the language of Clifford Geertz, ideology has become a part of its own referent (*The Interpretation of Cultures,* p. 194). We speak about ideology, but our speech is itself caught up in ideology. My own claim is that we must struggle with this paradox in order to proceed any further. To formulate and assume this paradox will be the turning point of our entire study, and it will compel us to look for a better description of ideology itself. We must question whether the polarity between ideology and science can be maintained or whether another perspective must instead be substituted.

In discussing Mannheim's contribution to this topic, we shall consider three points: first, the process of generalization which generates the paradox; second, the transfer of the paradox into the field of the sociology of knowledge; and third, Mannheim's attempt to overcome the paradox at this level. As to the first point, when we view the historical development of ideology as a theme, the Marxist concept of the term appears as only one stage in the process of generalization. Says Mannheim: "It is therefore first necessary to state that although Marxism contributed a great deal to the original statement of the problem, both the word and its meaning go farther back in history than Marxism, and ever since its time new meanings of the word have emerged, which have taken shape independently of it" (55). Mannheim maintains that there is a long history of the suspicion of false consciousness and that Marxism is only a link in this long chain. Following Mannheim, we shall discuss the developing historical status of the problem of ideology before considering his own contribution.

Mannheim takes the problem of false consciousness so far back historically as to invoke the Old Testament concept of the false prophet (the prophet Baal and so on). The religious origin of suspicion arises in the question of who is the true and who the false prophet. For Mannheim, this was the first problematic of ideology in our culture (70). In modern culture, Mannheim cites principally Bacon and Machiavelli as forerunners of the conception of ideology. In Bacon's theory of idols, the idols of the tribe, cave, market, and theater were all sources of error (61). Machiavelli started the process of systematic suspicion toward public utterances in contrasting the thought of the palace and that of the public square (63). I also think of the sixth chapter of Hegel's *Phenomenology of Spirit,* where Hegel discusses the language of flattery and the language of the court, the distortions of language for political use. Surely the Enlightenment concepts of superstition and prejudice are also an important link in this chain.

I would also insist, as does Mannheim (71 ff.), on the role of Napoleon in these pre-Marxist stages. More and more I think that Napoleon's role is an important factor. It is sometimes forgotten that French philosophers at the end of the eighteenth century were called *idéologues*. *Idéologie* was the name for their theory of ideas. *Idéologie* was the name for both a school of thought and a theoretical domain. Napoleon created the derogatory meaning of the term, labeling these adversaries to his political ambitions ideologists in a defamatory sense. Perhaps it is part of the concept now that it is defamatory and something expressed, finally, by the hero of action. The hero of action labels as ideological a mode of thought that claims only to be a theory of ideas; the theory is said to be unrealistic with reference to political practice. Ideology is first a polemical concept and second a concept which disparages the adversary, and it undertakes this disparagement from the point of view of the hero of action looking at, to use Hegel's expression, the "beautiful soul."

Thus, the concept of ideology in philosophical discourse perhaps always includes the specific experience of the politician with reality. Though alerting us to this situation, Mannheim does not pursue it himself, since his own outlook is that of the sociology of knowledge, the point of view of the onlooker or observer. Nevertheless, it is most important that we be aware that a "political criterion of reality" (73) is introduced into the discussion of ideology. I do not make this observation in order to conclude that we can make no use of the concept of ideology but rather to locate it. There is room in philosophic discourse for polemical concepts and for concepts which proceed from a certain stratum—here the political stratum–of human experience. In this regard, I think that it is stronger to take this stance than to say with Althusser that theory—science—provides the concept of ideology. No, the concept is provided by a practical experience, in particular, the experience of the ruler. Perhaps when we denounce something as ideological, we are ourselves caught in a certain process of power, a claim to power, a claim to be powerful. Because of ideology's origin in the disparaging labeling used by Napoleon against his adversaries, we must keep in mind the possibility that it is never a purely descriptive concept. I remember, for instance, the accusations made against critics by those in power when France lost Algeria and when the United States lost China.

What is specific to Marx's contribution to the development of the concept of ideology, says Mannheim, is that he fused a more comprehensive conception to the existing psychological orientation toward the term (74). No longer is ideology only a psychological phenomenon concerning individuals, a distortion either merely a lie, in a moral sense, or an error, in an epistemological sense. Instead, an ideology is the total structure of the mind characteristic of a concrete historical formation, including a class. An ideology is total in the sense that it expresses an opponent's basic *Weltanschauung,* including his or her conceptual apparatus. This, for Marx, was ideology's essential aspect. To express the psychological and comprehensive approaches to ideology, Mannheim resorts to the unfortunate vocabulary of "particular" and "total" conceptions (see 55 ff.), and this has created many misunderstandings. What he means is not so much that one approach is particular, but that it is located in the individual. It is particular in the sense that it is particular to the individual. The total conception, on the other hand, includes a whole world view and is supported by a collective structure.

Marx's second contribution, Mannheim claims, is that he saw that if ideology is not merely a psychological phenomenon—an individual distortion—then to unmask it requires a specific method of analysis: an interpretation in terms of the life-situation of the one who expresses it. This indirect method is typical of the critique of ideology. Mannheim's contention, though, is that this discovery has escaped, has exploded the Marxist framework, because suspicion is now applied not to one specific group or class but to the entire theoretical frame of reference in a chain reaction that cannot be stopped. For me, the dramatic honesty of Mannheim lies in his courage to face this challenge, a challenge which is not complete even when we have a "total" conception of ideology, that is, one encompassing the intellectual foundations upon which rest the specific beliefs of one's opponent. What forces us to push the process beyond Marx's fusion of particular and total is essentially the collapse of a common criterion of validity. In a situation of intellectual collapse, we are caught in a reciprocal process of suspicion.

In fact this predicament is the main intuition lying behind Mannheim's book. There are no common criteria of validity in our culture. It is as if we belong to a spiritual world with fundamentally divergent thought systems. Mannheim has many strong expressions of this crisis. He speaks of "the intellectual twilight which dominates our epoch" (85). "[T]he unanimity is broken" (103). We are in a process of "inevitable disintegration" (103). "Only this socially disorganized intellectual situation makes possible the insight, hidden until now by a generally stable social structure and the practicability of certain traditional norms, that *every* point of view is particular to a social situation" (84–85; emphasis added). This process of generalization goes much further than a mere theory of interests, which remains psychological in its core and still belongs to the "particular" meaning of ideology. It is not so much that we have opposing interests, but that we have no longer the same presuppositions with which to grasp reality. The problem is not an economic phenomenon, it is not because there is class struggle, but because our spiritual unity has been broken.

The problem is raised, then, at the level of the spiritual and intellectual framework of thought, that which makes possible our grasping of reality. Thus, the post-Marxist concept of ideology expresses a crisis occurring at the level of the spirit itself. This post-Marxist concept is mature when we acknowledge that "the objective ontological unity of the world" has collapsed (66). We live spiritually in a polemical situation of conflicting world views which are, for one another, ideologies. We face a process of mutual labeling; an ideology is always the ideology of the other. There is an other here, though, when there are *only* others. I am an other among others when there is no longer a common ground. We must recognize that these differences are not merely "particular"—individual—but a "grasp in its totality [of] the structure of the intellectual world" (58). We are no longer dwellers of the same world. "This profound disintegration of intellectual unity is possible only when the basic values of the contending groups are worlds apart" (65). The word "basic" is applied to values and not to economic entities. A certain spiritual disease is the starting point.

Mannheim calls this conception of ideology post-Marxist because we can no longer assume, he says, that there is a class consciousness which is not ideological itself, as was the claim of Marx and Lukács. I regret not having had time to speak of Lukács, because Lukács tried to save the concept of class consciousness by resorting to the Hegelian concept of totality. Lukács spoke of the proletariat as a universal class, because it expresses a universal interest; its world view is the only one not ideological, because it is the only one able to assume the interests of the totality. For Mannheim, however, the process of disintegration has proceeded so far that all class consciousnesses are caught in the destructive process of collapse. There is a lack of a center in the evolution of human society. Because there is no true universality anywhere, no group may claim to be the bearer of universality. No passage in the book states this position explicitly; rather, it is a question of omission. The notion of a class that would be the bearer of a universal consciousness, and so overcome relativism, is absent; it is silently denied. Instead, Mannheim lists class ideology among other modes of historical relativity—historic periods, nations, and so on—and does so without assigning to one kind of class a function that would exempt it from the process. This tacit skepticism concerning the concept of class consciousness is a decisive component in *Ideology and Utopia,* and surely it is on this point that Marxists would reject the book. For Mannheim, we are now too far from the classical Marxist conception. Marxism does not provide a new center. It is one part of the picture and a stage in the disintegrative process. The disintegrative process has swallowed class consciousness. False consciousness is no longer a Marxist question but a question which Marxism has made more acute. Marxism is unable to stop the process which it has advanced because its insight into the socioeconomic origin of intellectual frameworks is a weapon that cannot in the long run remain the exclusive privilege of one class.

On the merit of Marxism as an acceleration—though not the generation or closure—of the process, Mannheim has several important texts. "It was Marxist theory which first achieved a fusion of the particular and total conceptions of ideology." A particular conception, we remember, is a local error, while a total conception occurs when ideology is conceived not as one doctrine among others but as the whole conceptual structure itself. Mannheim continues:

> It was this theory which first gave due emphasis to the role of class position and class interests in thought. Due largely to the fact that it originated in Hegelianism, Marxism was able to go beyond the mere psychological level of analysis and to posit the problem in a more comprehensive, philosophical setting. The notion of a "false consciousness" hereby acquired a new meaning. (74)

I do not know the exact history of the expression "false consciousness," but it seems that Mannheim borrowed it from Lukács. I do not think that the term is in Marx himself, but I am not sure. Mannheim ascribes to Marxism not only the generalization of the concept of ideology, in the sense that what is affected is a world view, but the conjunction of two criteria, a theoretical criterion—the critique of illusions—and a practical criterion—the fight of one class against another. Here we reintroduce the origins of the concept in Napoleon. It is the point of view of the man or woman of action. Thus, we may recall, it is important in the discussion of Althusser to see that in his *Essays in Self-Criticism* he can accuse himself of being too theoretical if he severs the Marxist concept from a certain position in the class struggle. Marxism does not provide a theoretical concept of ideology but a theoretico-practical concept. Mannheim says:

> Marxist thought attached such decisive significance to political practice conjointly with the economic interpretation of events, that these two became the ultimate criteria for disentangling what is mere ideology from those elements in thought which are more immediately relevant to reality. Consequently it is no wonder that the conception of ideology is usually regarded as integral to, and even identified with, the Marxist proletarian movement. (75)

This is a most important statement. To call something ideological is never merely a theoretical judgment, but rather implies a certain practice and a view on reality that this practice gives to us. The characterization derives from a point of view, a certain movement, not so much that of class consciousness as the praxis of a certain political movement. Ideology is a political concept in that sense. Mannheim's most important text on Marxism follows the paragraph just quoted:

> But in the course of more recent intellectual and social developments . . . this stage [that is, the Marxist concept of ideology] has already been passed. It is no longer the exclusive privilege of socialist thinkers to trace bourgeois thought to ideological foundations and thereby to discredit it. Nowadays groups of every standpoint use this weapon against all the rest. As a result we are entering upon a new epoch in social and intellectual development. (75)

This is a good summary of Mannheim's position both about what we owe to Marxism and about why we must go further and so find ourselves engulfed in this pervasively ideological process. The merit of Marxism is unique, but its concept of ideology has been superseded by the very process of ideology's expansion and diffusion that it has hastened.

Now I shall try to show how Mannheim attempted to master this paradox and to escape its circularity, the destructive recurrent effects of ideological denunciation, a kind of *machine infernale,* infernal machine. It is necessary first to say something about the frame of reference within which Mannheim deals with this paradox. The framework is a sociology of knowledge. Mannheim was one of those like Max Scheler who thought that a sociology of knowledge could overcome the paradoxes of action and in fact play the role of a Hegelian system, if in a more empirical way. The idea is that if we can create a survey and exact description of all the forces in society, then we will be able to locate every ideology in its right place. Understanding the whole saves us from the implications of the concept. Perhaps here is the failure of Mannheim, because this sociology of knowledge never really succeeded in becoming a science and achieving its full development. The liabilities of the sociology of knowledge may be even more fundamental than that, however. It requires that the position of the sociologist be a kind of null point, a zero degree point; the sociologist does not belong to the play but is rather an observer and therefore has no place in the picture. This stance is paradoxical, though, because how can it be possible to look on the whole process if everything is in the process of mutual accusation? I consider Mannheim's attempt to overcome this paradox one of the most honest and perhaps *the* most honest failure in theory. The problematic here is a battlefield with many dead on it, and Mannheim is the most noble of them all. Mannheim's intention is that the sociology of knowledge must overcome the theory of ideology to the extent that this theory is caught in the circularity of its argument. Let us turn to how he proceeds.

At the beginning of this discussion, Mannheim seems to claim for himself a nonevaluative standpoint. "With the emergence of the general formulation of the total conception of ideology, the simple theory of ideology develops into the sociology of knowledge" (77–78). What had been the weapon of a party is transformed into a method of research, and the sociologist is the absolute observer who undertakes this research. The impossibility of the absolute observer, however, becomes the strain of the argument. The recourse to a nonevaluative judgment attempts to duplicate the approach of earlier German sociologists, especially Max Weber, regarding the possibility of value-free judgments. "The task of a study of ideology, which tries to be free from value-judgments, is to understand the narrowness of each individual point of view and the interplay between these distinctive attitudes in the total social process" (81). The sociologist looks at the map of ideologies and observes that each ideology is narrow, each represents a certain form of experience. The sociologist's judgment is value-free because it is said to make no use of norms belonging to one of these systems. This is the problem, of course, because to judge is to use a system of norms, and each system of norms is in some sense ideological. In any event, in this first stage of the investigation of a field, the sociologist notes the presence of this ideology, that ideology, and so on, and does not go further than stating correlations between thoughts and situations. The process is one of enumeration and correlation.

This nonevaluative stage must be traversed, it must be assumed to a certain degree, because unmasking the social conditions of all norms laying claim to formal validity represents the intellectual honesty of the modern intellectual. We have here in Mannheim the notion of the German scientist and his or her intellectual integrity, what Nietzsche has defined precisely as intellectual honesty, the famous *Redlichkeit*.[1] Therefore the nonevaluative must be assumed as a first stage. Mannheim says: "in all of these investigations use will be made of the total and general conception of ideology in its nonevaluative sense" (83). A total conception refers not simply to this idea and that idea, but to a whole framework of thought; the conception is general because it involves everyone, including oneself. The nonevaluative is a skeptical moment, the stage at which we look at things. Mannheim also maintains, dramatically, that the nonevaluative claim implies that the concept of truth must be dropped, at least in its atemporal sense (84). Our intellectual honesty, our skeptical *Redlichkeit*, entails the loss of the concept of truth that was supposed to rule the conceptual process itself. The problem will be to recover another concept of truth that is more historical, no longer an atemporal judgment about reality but one congruent with the spirit of the times or harmonious with the stage of history.

Mannheim's attempt to develop a nonevaluative concept of ideology situates his well-known distinction between relationism and relativism. This distinction did not in fact make the breakthrough that Mannheim thought it would, but was his own desperate attempt to prove that he was not a relativist.

> This first non-evaluative insight into history does not inevitably lead to relativism, but rather to relationism. Knowledge, as seen in the light of the total conception of ideology, is by no means an illusory experience, for ideology in its relational concept is not at all identical with illusion. . . . Relationism signifies merely that all of the elements of meaning in a given situation have reference to one another and derive their significance from this reciprocal interrelationship in a given frame of thought. (85–86)

Mannheim's attempt is to say that if we can see how systems of thought are related to social strata, and if we can also correlate the relations between different groups in competition, between situation and situation, system of thought and system of thought, then the whole picture is no longer relativist but relationist. To be a relativist, he says, is to keep an old, atemporal model of truth. If we have given up this model of truth, though, then we are directed toward a new concept of truth which is the sense of the correlation of changes that are in mutual relationship. This desperate attempt is in fact a reconstruction of the Hegelian Spirit in an empirical system. (This often occurred in German, a hidden return of Hegelianism under neo-Kantian cover.) The claim to have a total system of relationships is precisely the Hegelian system. The Hegelian system made sense, at least for Hegel, because he presumed the existence of something like Absolute Knowledge. The sociologist of knowledge repeats the claim of absolute knowledge but in an empirical situation, where perhaps if anyplace it is impossible. The sociologist assumes the role of the Hegelian *Geist*.

What, according to Mannheim, is then the new kind of truth that may emerge? We may take the first steps toward this new path when we recognize that if, as we have just seen, relationism entails that "all the elements of meaning in a given situation have reference to one another" (86), then the situation is one not simply of correlation but of congruence. "Such a system of meanings is possible and valid only in a given type of historical existence, to which, for a time, it furnishes appropriate expression" (86). At any time in history, certain positions are congruent, compatible, appropriate. Realization of the difference between correlation and congruence provides us with the transition from a nonevaluative to an evaluative concept of ideology (88), and hence also the basis for a new concept of truth. The nonevaluative stage of analysis is only provisory, a stage that trains us to think in dynamic and relational terms, rather than in terms of atemporal essences. It is a way of drawing all the consequences from the collapse of absolute, eternal norms and from the state of ideological war.

The transition to an evaluative concept is implied in the nonevaluative to the extent that the latter is already a weapon against intellectual dogmatism. The notion of relativism itself supposes an opposition to and fight against dogmatism. Mannheim knows that neither he nor anyone else can stay in a position above or outside the total game; everyone is inextricably part of the game. This recurrence of the analysis on the analyst provides what Mannheim calls an "evaluative-epistemological" presupposition (88), something that runs not only against dogmatism but also against positivism. It is impossible for anyone to be merely a descriptive thinker.

> In fact, the more aware one becomes of the presuppositions underlying his thinking, in the interest of truly empirical research, the more it is apparent that this empirical procedure (in the social sciences, at least) can be carried on only on the basis of certain meta-empirical, ontological, and metaphysical judgments and the expectations and hypothesis that follow from them. He who makes no decisions has no questions to raise and is not even able to formulate a tentative hypothesis which enables him to set a problem and to search history for its answer. Fortunately

positivism did commit itself to certain metaphysical and ontological judgments, despite its anti-metaphysical prejudices and its pretensions to the contrary. Its faith in progress and its naive realism in specific cases are examples of such ontological judgments. (89)

This is a most courageous statement. To be a strict empiricist is in fact impossible, because if one has no questions, then one searches for nothing and will in turn receive no answers. One cannot claim to be a mere empirical observer of ideologies, because even this supposedly nonevaluative standpoint falls under the ideology of objectivity, which is itself part of a certain concept of truth.

The question once more arises, what kind of new criterion for an evaluative standpoint can emerge after the collapse of all the objective, transcendent, empirical criteria? This question is capable of solution only for the one who no longer opposes ultimate and transcendent truths to history but tries to find meaning in the historical process itself. Here lies Mannheim's desperate attempt to see history furnish the criteria which can no longer be provided by either a transcendental or an empirical method. "[T]he circumstance that we do not find absolute situations in history indicates that history is mute and meaningless only to him who expects to learn nothing from it . . ." (93). It seems that it is from a kind of crypto-Hegelianism that Mannheim expects an answer: the study of intellectual history seeks "to discover in the totality of the historical complex the role, significance, and meaning of each component element" (93). We must give up the position of the absolute observer and merge in the movements of history itself. Then a new diagnosis will be possible—the point of view of congruence, the sense of what is congruent in a certain situation.

The transition to an evaluative point of view is necessitated from the very beginning by the fact that history as history is unintelligible unless certain of its aspects are emphasized in contrast to others. This selection and accentuation of certain aspects of historical totality may be regarded as the first step in the direction which ultimately leads to an evaluative procedure and to ontological judgments. (93–94)

Why are these judgments called ontological? Recourse to the word "ontological" is strange, since Mannheim has in principle given up a transcendent standpoint. But decisions have to be made about what is real; we must distinguish the true from the untrue, says Mannheim, in order to fight against false consciousness, a concept to which the text now turns.

In Mannheim's discussion of false consciousness, the key concept is that of the inadequate, the inappropriate, the noncongruent. The danger of false consciousness must be faced by determining "which of all the ideas current are really valid in a given situation" (94), and the noncongruent are those which are not valid. The concept of the noncongruent provides us with the correlation between ideology and utopia, as will become evident in our discussion of the utopian mentality. By way of anticipation we may repeat a point made at the outset of this lecture, that a mode of thought is noncongruent in one of two ways. It either lags behind or stands ahead of a given situation. These two modalities of noncongruence are continually fighting against one another. In either case, says Mannheim, "the reality to be comprehended is distorted and concealed. . . ." (97). Mannheim will leave discussion of the utopian mode of noncongruence until later and focuses here on the problem of ideological noncongruence. "Antiquated and inapplicable norms, modes of thought, and theories," he says, "are likely to degenerate into ideologies whose function it is to conceal the actual meaning of conduct rather than to reveal it" (95).

Mannheim provides three well-chosen examples of this inadequation between the trend of society and a system of thought. First is the late medieval church's condemnation of interest on loans (95–96). This interdiction failed because it was inadequate to the economic situation, particularly with the rise of capitalism at the beginning of the Renaissance. The prohibition failed not as an absolute judgment about lending money but because of its inadequacy to the historical situation. Mannheim's second example of noncongruence is the following:

> As examples of "false consciousness" taking the form of an incorrect interpretation of one's own self and one's role, we may cite those cases in which persons try to cover up their "real" relations to themselves and to the world, and falsify to themselves the elementary facts of human existence by deifying, romanticizing, or idealizing them, in short, by resorting to the device of escape from themselves and the world, and thereby conjuring up false interpretations of experience. (96).

Mannheim calls this an attempt "to resolve conflicts and anxieties by having recourse to absolutes" (96). The example has some overtones of the Hegelian beautiful soul; it is an escape into an absolute position but an escape which cannot be applied, which has no possibility of being realized. Mannheim's third example of inadequacy is perhaps less striking. It is the case of a landed proprietor "whose estate has already become a capitalistic undertaking" (96) and yet who tries to preserve a paternalistic relation with his employees. The owner's system of thought, that of the patriarchal age, is inadequate to the situation in which he is in fact a capitalist.

The noncongruence is a discordance between what we say and what in fact we do. What, though, are the criteria for determining this lack of congruence? Who is the good judge who determines the truth regarding this congruence? This is the enigma, because once again we seem to need an independent observer of noncongruence, and this distant observer may only claim that "every idea must be tested by its congruence with reality" (98). What is reality, though, and for whom? Reality ineluctably includes all sorts of appreciations and judgments of values. Reality is not only objects but involves human beings and their thought. No one knows reality outside the multiplicity of ways it is conceptualized, since reality is always caught in a framework of thought that is itself an ideology. Mannheim seems to want to return to a nonevaluative concept of both reality and ideology precisely in order to judge what is and what is not congruent. Mannheim is always quite self-conscious about what he is doing, and he is aware at this stage of the difficulty in which he is entangling himself. Each step in advance seems to reintroduce the contradiction. We want to evaluate the congruence between a thought and a situation, but the judgment of congruence requires a nonevaluative act. Mannheim refers to his problem here in an embarrassed footnote:

> The careful reader will perhaps note that from this point on the evaluative conception of ideology tends once more to take on the form of the non-evaluative, but this, of course, is due to our intention to discover an evaluative solution. This instability in the definition of the concept is part of the technique of research, which might be said to have arrived at maturity and which therefore refuses to enslave itself to any one particular standpoint which would restrict its view. This dynamic relationism offers the only possible way out of a world-situation in which we are presented with a multiplicity of conflicting viewpoints. . . . (98 *n.*)

Our thought must be flexible and dialectical, and once again we have a Hegelian element, if without Absolute Knowledge. While it may appear that we have escaped the pitfalls of a quasi-Hegelian survey of the whole, the concept of reality assumed by Mannheim's exposition in fact reintroduces the Hegelian thematic.

What we find, therefore, is that the claimed judgment of congruence or noncongruence between an alleged "traditional mode of thought and the novel objects of experience" (101) raises as many questions as it solves. The problem at issue here will return in our discussion of Habermas and his analysis of self-reflection, because the critique of ideology always presupposes a reflective act that is itself not part of the ideological process.

This is the great difficulty of the problem of ideology. We are caught in a kind of tornado, we are literally engulfed in a process which is self-defeating, which seems to allow only ideological judgment, but we are also supposed to be able at one point or another to assume a position outside this whirlwind in order to go on speaking about the process.

In Mannheim what preserves the thinker from being completely destroyed by this tornado, by the ruins of the temple falling in on him or her, is precisely the claim that one may have total reflection, may see the whole. Mannheim resorts to the category of totality. He has several references to the concept of a "total situation" (102, 104). We want, he says, "a more inclusive knowledge of the object" (103). He argues against positivism, which exalts philosophy while exiling it from the fruits of empirical investigation and thereby avoids "the problem of the 'whole' " (104). He says we must "find a more fundamental axiomatic point of departure, a position from which it will be possible to synthesize the total situation" (105). "Only when we are thoroughly aware of the limited scope of every point of view are we on the road to the sought-for comprehension of the whole" (105). We are caught in an ever enlargening process. Mannheim speaks of "the striving towards a total view" (106). To see oneself in the context of the whole represents in miniature "the ever-widening drive towards a total conception" (107). Mannheim's concept of totality is not the transcendent absolute, but it plays the same role of transcending the particular point of view. Again, it is the assumption of Hegelianism without Absolute Knowledge.

I do not want to insist too much on Mannheim's failure to admit that we cannot get out of the circle between reflection and ideology, to admit that total reflection is not finally a human possibility, because his discussion has its reward elsewhere, in the fourth chapter of his book. In turning to that chapter, "The Utopian Mentality," I shall be more brief, because I shall reserve its description of concrete utopias for presentation in the last part of the lectures. At this point, I shall consider only the chapter's first two sections, since they provide a partial answer to the problems we have just raised. I immediately anticipate this answer by saying that what we must assume is that the judgment on an ideology is always the judgment from a utopia. This is my conviction: the only way to get out of the circularity in which ideologies engulf us is to assume a utopia, declare it, and judge an ideology on this basis. Because the absolute onlooker is impossible, then it is someone within the process itself who takes the responsibility for judgment. It may also be more modest to say that the judgment is always a point of view—a polemical point of view though one which claims to assume a better future for humanity—and a point of view which declares itself as such. It is to the extent finally that the correlation ideology-utopia replaces the impossible correlation ideology-science that a certain solution to the problem of judgment may be found, a solution, I should add, itself congruent with the claim that no point of view exists outside the game. Therefore, if there can be no transcendent onlooker, then a *practical* concept is what must be assumed. In this fourth chapter of Mannheim's, which I find a more positive treatment of our problem, ideology and utopia make sense together as a significant pair of opposite terms.

In the first pages of the chapter, Mannheim provides formal criteria for utopia, criteria to which his later description of concrete utopias will supply some content. For Mannheim there are two formal criteria of utopia, and these provide by contrast the laws of ideology. The first criterion, which it shares in *common* with ideology, is a certain noncongruence, a noncoincidence, with the state of reality in which it occurs. There are many synonyms of this expression in Karl Mannheim; the emphasis is on ideas and interests that are "situationally transcendent" (193). These ideas are transcendent not in the sense of a philosophy of transcendence but with respect to the present state of reality. Again the difficulty is determining what is in fact reality. To measure noncongruence we must have a concept of reality, but this concept of reality is itself part of the evaluative framework, and once more a circularity returns.

The second criterion of utopia is more decisive. A utopia tends "to shatter, either partially or wholly, the order of things prevailing at the time" (192). Here ideology may be defined by *opposition* to utopia; it is what preserves a certain order. This criterion of ideology is a better one than the first. It is more limited and is also not necessarily pejorative, although Mannheim himself does not go this far. Ideology is not necessarily pejorative because, as I shall try to show in the last ideology lecture, we need a certain concept of the self-identity of a group. Even a historical force that works to shatter the present order also presupposes something else that preserves the identity of a certain group, a certain class, a certain historical situation, and so on.

Let us consider at greater length these two criteria of ideology and utopia, where the first is common and the second differential. The interest of

Mannheim's chapter is the interplay between these two criteria. Mannheim is aware that even his first criterion, noncongruence, implies a stand concerning what is reality. Attention to the nature of "existence as such," he says, is a philosophical matter, and of no concern here. Instead, what is important is that which is regarded as the "real" historically or sociologically.

> Inasmuch as man is a creature living primarily in history and society, the "existence" that surrounds him is never "existence as such," but is always a concrete historical form of social existence. For the sociologist, "existence" is that which is "concretely effective," i.e. a functioning social order, which does not exist only in the imagination of certain individuals but according to which people really act. (193–94)

We must assume that there exists something like a collective body functioning according to certain rules and so an " 'operating order of life' " (194). (In the next lecture we shall see some similar concepts in Max Weber.) Just as in Marx, Mannheim permanently returns to oppose ideology not to science but to what is really operative, and therefore to a concrete criterion of praxis. It may be difficult to assume that we know what is in fact the operative in society, but it is this criterion to which we oppose the illusory as the important fancy. In contrast to someone like Geertz, Mannheim has no notion of a symbolically constituted operating order; hence an ideology is necessarily the noncongruent, something transcendent in the sense of the discordant or that which is not implied in humanity's genetic code.

The definition of reality as an operating order of life has difficulties even on Mannheim's own terms, because we must include in it, he says, more than simply economic and political structures:

> Every concretely "operating order of life" is to be conceived and characterized most clearly by means of the particular economical and political structure on which it is based. But it embraces also all those forms of human "living-together" (specific forms of love, sociability, conflict, etc.) which the structure makes possible or requires. . . . (194)

The operating order of life is both infrastructural and superstructural. This creates problems, because the elements of noncongruence must be placed in the same sphere as forms of human living-together; both imply cultural roles, norms, and so on. It is difficult to determine what makes some social modes of thought and experience congruous with the actual operating order of life and others not. Once more it is a practical decision to claim that certain modes of thought belong to the operating order of life and others do not. Mannheim tries to define as situationally transcendent and therefore unreal conceptions whose content cannot be realized in the actual order (194). These conceptions are said not to fit into the current order. But what about the case of ideologies, which do not shatter the existing order but rather preserve it? Mannheim wants to say that conceptions are not part of the operating order of life if they cannot be realized without shattering the given order. Ideologies, though, are situationally transcendent yet can be actualized without upsetting the order that exists. Mannheim's definition of noncongruence is a criterion very difficult to apply.

As an illustration of his argument about the situationally transcendent nature of ideologies, Mannheim offers the idea of Christian brotherly love touted during the medieval period.

> Ideologies are the situationally transcendent ideas which never succeed *de facto* in the realization of their projected contents. Though they often become the good-intentioned motives for the subjective conduct of the individual, when they are actually embodied in practice their meanings are most frequently distorted. The idea of Christian brotherly love, for instance, in a society founded on serfdom remains an unrealizable and, in this sense, ideological idea. . . . (194–95)

What we actually have here is characterization of ideology's noncongruence at a second level. Ideology's noncongruence is of a certain sort: the transcending ideas espoused are invalid or incapable of changing the existing order; they do not affect the status quo. With ideology the unreal is the impossible. The ideological mentality assumes the impossibility of change either because it accepts the systems of justification explaining the noncongruence or because the noncongruence has been concealed, by factors ranging from unconscious deception to conscious lie (195).

The criterion of utopia, on the other hand, seems to be success.

> Utopias too transcend the social situation, for they too orient conduct towards elements which the situation, in so far as it is realized at the time, does not contain. But they are not ideologies, i.e. they are not ideologies in the measure and in so far as they succeed through counteractivity in transforming the existing historical reality into one more in accord with their own conceptions. (195–96)

The sterility of ideology is opposed to the fruitfulness of utopia; the latter is able to change things. The capacity to change provides the criterion. This formal distinction between ideology and utopia has the advantage of offering a common kernel and a difference. As we have seen, though, the common kernel—noncongruence—is difficult to ascertain in any formal, nonevaluative manner, and as we now turn to discuss, the difference—realizability—is questionable also. The allocation of realizability to utopia gives it a univocal efficiency which does not allow us to derive its pathology as wishful thinking. On the other hand, because ideology is viewed as the unrealizable, its possible congruence with existing society is dismissed, and we are led to overlook ideology's conservative function, in the several senses of that word.

We can pursue these questions about Mannheim's formal criteria of ideology and utopia by examining in greater detail the supposed realizability of utopia. This criterion is odd, because when we attempt to apply it in society, it is often reversed. When it is representatives of the ruling class who pass judgment, a utopia is precisely the *un*realizable. Application of the formal criterion raises a problem, because "What in a given case *appears* as utopian . . ." (196; emphasis added) depends on who in society is speaking. To give this formal criterion some content, to transform it into the concrete, we must consult those who assume these concepts. We have a strange exchange in meaning, because what appears as utopian or ideological depends not only "on the stage and degree of reality to which one applies this standard" (196) but also on which group is doing the labeling. Thus it is both a question of something being labeled *as* ideological or utopian and of the label being ascribed or assigned *by* someone. For the representatives of a given order, the utopian means the unrealizable. This contradicts, however, the formal criterion advocated by the sociologist. Further, it is a self-deception for the representatives of order to call unrealizable what is not realizable according to their order. Because they take the given order as the measure of everything, then a utopia appears as the unrealizable, whereas it is defined formally precisely by its capacity for change. The formal definition is defeated by those who use the label, and this is one more paradox of the discussion. We are caught in so many paradoxes, and Mannheim may be viewed exactly as the exponent of this self-defeating process of thought about utopia and ideology. The formal definition of utopia should be without perspective, but this very possibility seems to be denied by the perspectival constitution of social existence. As Mannheim himself puts it:

> The very attempt to determine the meaning of the concept "utopia" shows to what extent every definition in historical thinking depends necessarily upon one's perspective, i.e. it contains within itself the whole system of thought representing the

position of the thinker in question and especially the political evaluations which lie behind this system of thought. (196–97)

Those protecting the status quo call utopian everything that goes beyond the present existing order, no matter whether it may be an absolute utopia, unrealizable in any circumstance, or a relative utopia, unrealizable only within the given order. By obscuring this distinction, the present order can "suppress the validity of the claims of the relative utopia" (197). What is realizable in another order is the criterion of utopia proposed by the sociology of knowledge and defeated by those who use the criterion of realizability for their own purposes.

We may attempt to defend the formal conception of utopia by claiming that it is distorted by ideology. Ideology typifies utopia as what cannot be realized, whereas formally it is precisely what can be realized. Yet this does not remove the formal conception from taint, because as Mannheim himself suggests, the criteria for determining what is realizable are in actuality always provided by the representatives of dominant or ascendant groups and not by the sociology of knowledge. We find here the positive aspect of Mannheim's analysis, an effort to relate the labels advocated to the social positions of those doing the labeling. At this point Mannheim is perhaps more Marxist than anywhere else in his book.

Whenever an idea is labelled utopian it is usually by a representative of an epoch that has already passed. On the other hand, the exposure of ideologies as illusory ideas, adapted to the present order, is the work generally of representatives of an order of existence which is still in process of emergence. It is always the dominant group which is in full accord with the existing order that determines what is to be regarded as utopian, while the ascendant group which is in conflict with things as they are is the one that determines what is regarded as ideological. (203)

As an illustration of this labeling process Mannheim offers the changing views about the concept of freedom (203–4). From the beginning of the sixteenth century until the end of the eighteenth, the concept of freedom was a utopian concept. As soon, though, as the ruling class discovered that the concept had implications concerning the notion of equality, extensions which they refused, then their own advocacy of freedom became a way to preserve the social order against those in fact pressing for these extensions. The same concept was alternatively utopian, conservative, and utopian once more. Characterization depends on which group is advocating the concept.

We have to deal, then, with both what is actually regarded *as* utopian and what is said to be utopian from a more distant point of view. Mannheim's whole work is an attempt to change this distance, to make us look at the concept both from within the groups advocating or denying it and from the sociologist's point of view. The problem, though, is that the two definitions do not coincide. For the sociologist the utopia is the realizable, whereas for those in power the utopia is precisely what they refuse, what they find to be incompatible with their order. A contradiction exists within the criteria according to who uses the criteria.

What may we conclude from these difficulties in applying the formal criterion? Mannheim concedes that in the midst of a conflict of ideas the criterion of realizability, which is the criterion of what is truly utopian, is of little use (204). It is only for past utopias that we may apply Mannheim's criterion. Realizability is a nearly useless criterion for present controversies, because we are always caught in the conflict not only between ideologies but also between rising and dominant groups. The conflict between dominant and ascendant involves the polemics, the dialectics, of utopia and ideology.

From this discussion of utopia we may derive three consequences for ideology. First, the connection between utopia and an ascending group provides the fundamental contrast for the connection between ideology and the ruling group. The criterion for what is ideological seems to depend on the critique proffered by the utopian mind. The capacity to unconceal something as ideological seems to be an effect of the utopian potentialities of the rising group or at least of those who think with or for this group. If this is true, if ideology is recognized only in the process of unmasking it, then the so-called epistemological break becomes more concrete when coupled with these utopian possibilities. It is always the product of a utopia.

I submit, therefore, that there is no mind which liberates itself suddenly without the support of something else. Is it not always the utopian possibilities of individuals or groups which nourish our capacity to distanciate ourselves from ideologies? We cannot get out of the polarity between utopia and ideology. It is always a utopia which defines what is ideological, and so characterization is always relative to the assumptions of the conflicting groups. To know this is also to know that utopia and ideology are not theoretical concepts. We cannot expect too much from these concepts since they constitute a practical circle. Consequently, any claim to a scientific view of ideology is merely and only a claim. The insight here may be another way of saying with Aristotle that in human matters we cannot expect the same kind of accuracy as in scientific matters. Politics is not a science, it is an art of orienting oneself among conflicting groups. The concept of politics must remain polemical; there is a place for polemics in life, and to acknowledge this is the honest import of the problem. Politics is not a descriptive concept but a polemical concept provided by the dialectics between utopia and ideology.

The second insight of our discussion is that if utopia is what shatters a given order, by contrast ideology is what preserves order. This means that the problematic of domination and the place of power in the structure of human existence become a central issue. The question is not only who has power but how is a system of power legitimized. Utopia also operates at the level of the legitimation process; it shatters a given order by offering alternative ways to deal with authority and power. Legitimacy is what is at stake in the conflict between ideology and utopia, and in the next lecture I shall address myself to Max Weber to inquire into this critical issue. I think also of Hannah Arendt's main work. Arendt keeps returning to the question of the relation in human existence between power and labor, work, and action, and she formulates this problematic in terms of existential categories and not merely sociological structures.

A third consequence of our discussion is that once we situate the conflict between ideology and utopia in terms of legitimation or the questioning of the system of power, then the opposition stressed by Mannheim between ideology as the harmless and utopia as the historically realizable seems less decisive. If we now emphasize that utopia is what shatters order and ideology what preserves order (sometimes by distortion but sometimes also by a legitimate process), then the criterion of realizability is not a good way to distinguish the two. To begin with, the criterion may be applied only to the past, as we have already noted. Second, it also sacralizes success, and it is not simply because an idea succeeds that it is either good or for the good. Who knows whether what has been condemned by history will not return in more favorable circumstances? Realizability is also not a good criterion because ideologies are in a sense already realized. They confirm what exists. The "unreal" element in the dialectic is not defined by the unrealizable but by the ideal, in its legitimizing function. The transcendent is the "ought" which the "is" conceals.

Further, utopias themselves are never realized to the extent that they create the *distance* between what is and what ought to be. Mannheim's own typology of utopias confirms this and also indicates that Mannheim himself did not apply the criterion of realizability to the end. As we shall discuss at greater length in the lectures specifically on utopia, Mannheim claims that the first form of the utopian mentality occurred at the point when Chiliasm—a millenarian movement—"joined forces with the active demands of the oppressed strata of society" under Thomas Münzer and the Anabaptists (211). This conjunction provided the original moment of utopian distance. At the other end of the typology—the contemporary period—Mannheim envisages the actual *loss* of utopia in the "gradual descent" and the "closer aproximation to real life" of the utopian forces (248). The decisive trait of utopia is then not realizability but the preservation of *opposition.* The entropy of utopia in the present situation, the threatened loss of total perspective resulting from the disappearance of utopia, is leading to a situation where scattered events no longer have meaning. "The frame of reference according to which we evaluate facts vanishes and we are left with a series of events all equal as far as their inner significance is concerned" (253). If we could imagine a society where everything is realized, there congruence would exist. This society, however, would also be dead, because there would be no distance, no ideals, no project at all. Mannheim fights against those who claim—and herald—that we are now living in the time of the death of ideology and utopia. The suppression of noncongruence, the suppression of the disconnection between ideals and reality, would be the death of society. It would be the time of a prosaic attitude, a "matter-of-factness" *(Sachlichkeit)* (262); we would have precisely a nonideological and nonutopian society, and this would be a dead society. The critical mark of utopia is then not realizability but the preservation of distance between itself and reality.

It may appear that Mannheim's analysis in many ways has circular and self-defeating results. What we have also discovered, though, is that he provides us with the grounds for a new theoretical framework. We have had to learn that we cannot get out of the circle between ideology and utopia, but we have also taken the first steps toward demonstrating that this circle is in fact a practical one and so not vicious and self-defeating.

II

Weber (1)

Before entering my discussion of Max Weber, I would like to say a few words about the general framework within which my approach to Weber is located. In examining first Marx and then Althusser, the lectures began with the Marxist concept of ideology as distortion. The rest of the ideology lectures are a response to the problem raised by the Marxist orientation: within what conceptual framework does the concept of ideology as distortion best make sense? My intention is not at all to refute Marxism but to resituate and strengthen some of its statements concerning the distorting function.

To respond to the Marxist orientation on ideology, we must raise four questions. The first, which we have discussed with Mannheim, is where do we stand when we speak of ideology? If the claim is that we may approach ideology scientifically, then we are supposedly outside the social game in the position of the onlooker. We attempt to elaborate a nonevaluative concept of ideology. This is impossible, however, since sociology itself belongs to the social game. Therefore, my argument was that we must preserve and do justice to the polemical element of ideology, something which can be accomplished principally by relating ideology to utopia. It is always from the point of view of a nascent utopia that we may speak of a dying ideology. It is the conflict and intersection of ideology and utopia that makes sense of each.

My second question concerns the relation between ideology and domination. One of Marxism's strongest points and most important insights is that the ruling ideas of an epoch are the ideas of a ruling class. This correlation between domination and ideology is what I shall try to elucidate with the help of Max Weber. I shall then ask, third, whether it is possible to have a critique of ideology without a certain project, a certain interest, such as an interest in the extension of communication, an interest in emancipation, and so on. I shall address myself to Habermas for this connection between a critique of ideology and a specific kind of interest, an interest which cannot be put, as in Althusser, simply on the side of ideology, because if there is no interest to support the critique, then the critique collapses.

My fourth and final question asks whether there can be distortion in society unless society has a fundamental symbolic structure. The hypothesis is that at the most basic level what is distorted is the symbolic structure of action. Logically if not temporally the constitutive function of ideology must precede its distortive function. We could not understand what distortion meant if there were not something to be distorted, something that was of the same symbolic nature. I shall introduce Geertz as the best author to make this demonstration. I myself published something on this topic in France before knowing Geertz,[1] but I shall use Geertz since I think he develops the issue better than I did. Geertz says that we may identify the constitutive function of ideology at the level of what he calls symbolic action.

As a whole, therefore, the lectures on ideology start from the surface level of ideology as distortion and proceed to a second-level correlation of ideology with domination, then to the crucial transitional connection between interest and critique, and finally to what I call the constitutive function of ideology. The movement is a regressive analysis of ideology from its distortive function to its legitimative function and then to its constitutive function.

This depiction of ideology will allow us, at the end of the lectures, to establish by contrast the character of utopia. Whether distorting, legitimating, or constituting, ideology always has the function of preserving an identity, whether of a group or individual. As we shall see, utopia has the opposite function: to open the possible. Even when an ideology is constitutive, when it returns us, for example, to the founding deeds of a community—religious, political, etc.—it acts to make us repeat our identity. Here the imagination has a mirroring or staging function. Utopia, on the other hand, is always the exterior, the nowhere, the possible. The contrast between ideology and utopia permits us to see the two sides of the imaginative function in social life.

In turning now to Weber, I am interested in one aspect of his theory, his concept of *Herrschaft*. Two of the principal ways this concept has been translated into English are as authority and domination, and for our purposes the relationship between authority and domination is precisely the issue. Weber's approach to *Herrschaft* is important to our discussion for two reasons. First, he provides us a better conceptual framework to deal with the problem of domination than the orthodox Marxists. (Note that the comparison is to the orthodox Marxists, not to Marx himself. As I have argued, Marx's own work seems to allow a reading congruent with the framework that I am attempting to promote.) The orthodox Marxist model is mechanicist and based on the relation between infrastructure and superstructure. It involves the impossible scholasticism concerning the efficiency in the last instance of the base and the relative autonomy of the superstructure and its capacity of reacting back on the base. Because dependent on the notion of efficiency, classical Marxism has been caught in an impossible and finally nondialectical model; its concept of causality is pre-Kantian, precritical. The alternative Weber proposes to this mechanicist perspective is a motivational model. I shall first discuss this model of Weber's in order to situate the applicability of some of his other concepts for our discussion of ideology.

Weber is important, second, because he provides within this motivational framework a complementary analysis on the relation between the ruling group and ruling ideas. He introduces the critical concept of legitimacy and discusses the conjunction between claims to legitimacy and beliefs in legitimacy, a nexus that supports a system of authority. The question of legitimacy belongs to a motivational model, because the interaction of claim and belief must be placed within an appropriate conceptual framework, and, as we shall see, this framework can only be motivational. My argument is that ideology occurs in the gap between a system of authority's claim to legitimacy and our response in terms of belief. This interpretation is my own and not available in Weber, so it is a footnote to Weber, but perhaps a footnote that makes its own contribution to Weber's model. Ideology functions to add a certain surplus-value to our belief in order that our belief may meet the requirements of the authority's claim. The Marxist notion of distortion makes more sense if we say that it is always the function of ideology to legitimate a claim of legitimacy by adding a supplement to our spontaneous belief. The function of ideology at this stage is to fill the credibility gap in all systems of authority. This argument is coherent, though, only in a motivational and not in a mechanistic model. For this reason I shall devote the first part of the lecture to clarifying the motivational model itself. Our text is Weber's major work, *Economy and Society (Wirtschaft und Gesellschaft)*.

Let us begin with Weber's definition of the task of sociology. Sociology is defined as an interpretive understanding; the notion of interpretation is included in the task of sociology. From Weber to Geertz there will be no important change in this philosophical background. "Sociology (in the sense in which this highly ambiguous word is used here) is a science concerning itself with the interpretive understanding *[deutend verstehen]* of social action and thereby with a causal explanation of its course and consequences" (4). The causal element is included within the interpretive element. It is because sociology is interpretive that it can offer causal explanation. What must be both interpreted and explained is action, precisely action *(Handeln)* and not behavior, because behavior is a set of movements in space, whereas action makes sense for the human agent. "We shall speak of 'action' insofar as the acting individual attaches a subjective meaning to his behavior . . ." (4). It is critically important that the definition of action include the meaning of action for the agent. (We may foresee that the possibility of distortion is included within this dimension of *meaning*.) There is not action first and only then representation, because meaning is an integral component of the definition of action. An essential aspect of the constitution of action is that it must be meaningful for the agent.

Action depends not only on its making sense for the subject, however, because it must also make sense in correlation with other subjects. Action is both subjective and intersubjective. "Action is 'social' insofar as its subjective meaning takes account of the behavior of others and is thereby oriented in its course" (4). The intersubjective element is incorporated from the beginning. Sociology is interpretive to the extent that its object implies, on the one hand, a dimension of subjective meaning and, on the other hand, an account of the motives of others. From the start we have a conceptual network involving the notion of action, meaning, orientation to others, and understanding *(Verstehen)*. This network constitutes the motivational model. What is particularly significant for our discussion is that orientation to the other is a component of subjective meaning.

This notion of being oriented to or of taking into account the other is described more thoroughly when Weber returns several pages later to the concept of social action. "Social action, which includes both failure to act and passive acquiescence, may be oriented to the past, present, or expected future behavior of others. Thus it may be motivated by revenge for a past attack, defence against present, or measures of defence against future aggression" (22). Within this framework of orientation to the other, several factors stand out. We must recognize that passive acquiescence is part of social action, as it is a component of the belief in authority; to obey, to submit oneself to, to assume the validity of an authority, is part of an action. Not doing is part of doing. Further, social action's orientation to "past, present, or expected future behavior of others" introduces an element of time. As Alfred Schutz develops this notion, we are oriented not only to our contemporaries but to our predecessors and to our successors; this temporal sequence constitutes the historical dimension of action. Finally, the motivation of action by past, present, or future events—whether external aggression or not—alerts us that one of the functions of an ideology is to preserve identity through time. This will be a major point in our discussion of Geertz. Erik Erikson has a similar theory about the individual's integration of stages. What remains the most significant factor in the definition of social action, though, is its orientation to the behavior of others. This orientation to others is the key component of the motivational model. "[T]he actor's behavior is *meaningfully* oriented to that of others . . ." (23; emphasis added).

If I insist on this definition of social action, it is to argue against a position like Althusser's. If we place all references to the subject on the distortive side of ideology, we separate ourselves from the definition of social science to the extent that its object of study is action. If no agent is available to make sense of his or her action, we have not action but behavior. We are then condemned either to social behaviorism or to an examination of social forces, such as collective entities, classes, and so on, and no one will be oriented to or attempting to make sense of these factors. Meaningful action is contrasted with causal determination. As an example of this difference, Weber offers the case of imitation, an influential subject at the beginning of this century. The question was whether social reality is derived by one individual imitating another. Weber discards the concept of imitation as foundational, precisely because it is too causal; it does not imply a meaningful orientation. "[M]ere 'imitation' of the action of others . . . will not be considered a case of specifically social action if it is purely reactive so that there is no meaningful orientation to the actor imitated." This action is "*causally* determined by the action of others, but not meaningfully" (23–24; emphasis in original). If causality is not included within the meaningful, that is, if the connection is only causal, then it is not part of action.

The first point about the motivational model, then, is that it is interpretive understanding oriented to the action of others. A second point is that Weber develops this model through ideal types, and we must understand the role these ideal types play. For Weber, the concept of meaning becomes a pitfall for science if science can relate to what is meaningful for the individual only by a form of intuition. This leaves us lost in the immense variety of individual motivations. Weber's alternative is that we must handle individual cases by placing them under types, ideal types, which are only methodological constructs. What is real is always the individual orienting himself or herself toward other individuals, but we need some modes of orientation, modes of motivation, to classify the fundamental types of this orientation. Sociology, as the understanding of meaningful action, is possible only if meaningful action may be classified according to some significant types.

Social action, like all action, may be oriented in four ways. It may be:
(1) instrumentally rational *(zweckrational),* that is, determined by expectations as to the behavior of objects in the environment and of other human beings . . . ;
(2) value-rational *(wertrational),* that is, determined by a conscious belief in the value for its own sake of some ethical, aesthetic, religious, or other form of behavior, independently of its prospect of success;
(3) affectual (especially emotional), that is, determined by the actor's specific affects and feeling states;
(4) traditional, that is, determined by ingrained habituation. (24–25)

As we shall see in more detail in the following lecture, this typology of orientation is fundamental for Weber's typology of legitimacy. The first type of social action that Weber defines is a rationality of ends. In the system of legitimacy it will have more affinity with the bureaucratic type of legal authority, which is supported by rules. The second type's expectation of meaning will find support in the system of legitimacy provided by the charismatic leader, who is believed to be the voice of God, sent by God. The charismatic leader also relies on the third type, the emotional link between leader and followers. The fourth type, the appeal to tradition, will play a significant role in the system of legitimacy to the extent that leaders are obeyed because of their traditional status.

The methodological import of ideal types is that they allow us to grasp the complexity of singular cases by a combinatory system based on a limited set of fundamental types. By proceeding on the basis of combinatory types, sociology can cope with the manifoldness of reality. The ideal types are intermediary structures which are neither a priori nor merely inductive but in between. They are not a priori since they have to be supported by experience, but in another sense they also precede experience since they provide a leading thread that orients us. There are many discussions concerning the status of ideal types, and I shall not enter into them here, but we should be aware that we cannot discuss the types of legitimacy if we do not keep in mind the epistemological difficulties surrounding the concept of the ideal type in general.

Weber's typology of the orientations or motivations of action foreshadows his analysis of legitimacy, because his examples precisely involve the tension between claims to and beliefs in legitmacy. We may take the second classification, orientation to an absolute, as an example.

> Examples of pure value-rational orientation would be the actions of persons who, regardless of possible cost to themselves, act to put into practice their convictions of what seems to them to be required by duty, honor, the pursuit of beauty, a religious call, personal loyalty, or the importance of some "cause" no matter in what it consists. In our terminology, value-rational action always involves "commands" or "demands" which, in the actor's opinion, are binding on him. It is only in cases where human action is motivated by the fulfillment of such unconditional demands that it will be called value-rational. (25)

Commands and demands bring into play the relation between beliefs and claims. The function of a political ideology, for example, may be to capture the individual's capacity for loyalty for the sake of an actual system of power embodied in authoritative institutions. The system of power is then able to reap benefits from this human aptitude for loyalty to a cause, a willingness to sacrifice oneself to a cause. Politics draws heavily on this disposition to loyalty.

I have anticipated somewhat the discussion about legitimacy, but we must be aware of the importance of the order of notions in Weber. Weber proceeds step by step, starting from the most fundamental notions toward the derived notions. The concepts of belief and claim will not yield their potential meaning for ideology before the development of Weber's other notions is complete. Of greatest significance in the development of Weber's notions, we must observe that the concept of power comes at the end and not at the beginning. Weber starts from what makes action human and then turns to what makes the social link meaningful; before introducing the notion of power, he says we must introduce another intermediary notion, that of order.

Introduction of the concept of order is a decisive turn in Weber's analysis. The word has taken on many negative connotations in English, but we must approach the term in its most original sense, as the constitution of a meaningful whole comprised of individuals. The German word is *Ordnung,* an ordering of human beings that precedes orders in the sense of imperatives. We must not put the notion of an imperative too early in the concept of order; instead, we must think more in terms of the organization of an organism, an organism which introduces relations between parts and wholes within human being. To underline the distinction between order and imperatives, Weber's discussion emphasizes the notion of legitimate order, an important move despite the possible inconveniences caused by referring to the concept of legitimacy too early in the analysis. We must not define order merely in terms of force. As Geertz will see, this differentiation alerts us that ideology already plays a role at this level. I would argue that Geertz introduces his concept of constitutive ideology exactly at the level of legitimate order. We cannot speak of an order which is merely enforced and which does not at all claim legitimacy. The claim of legitimacy is constitutive of order.

> The legitimacy of an order may be guaranteed in two principal ways:
>
> I. The guarantee may be purely subjective, being either
>   1. affectual: resulting from emotional surrender; or
>   2. value-rational: determined by the belief in the absolute validity of the order as the expression of ultimate values of an ethical, esthetic or of any other type; or
>   3. religious: determined by the belief that salvation depends upon obedience to the order.
>
> II. The legitimacy of an order may, however, be guaranteed also (or merely) by the expectation of specific external effects, that is, by interest situations. (33)

Again we find the partial parallelism between the modes of orientation previously described and the types of legitimacy. More significantly, it is not by chance that to speak of order we must speak of legitimacy and that to speak of legitimacy we must speak of motives. It is only within a system of motives that the legitimacy of an order may be guaranteed. Weber's expressions make sense only within the conceptual framework of meaningful action.

As we have just seen, it is important that the problem of legitimacy is introduced by that of order. It is no less important that legitimacy can be ascribed to an order only by reference to the beliefs and representations held by those acting subject to it. The point of view is the agent's or actor's.

> The actors may ascribe legitimacy to a social order by virtue of:
> (a) tradition: valid is that which has always been;
> (b) affectual, especially emotional, faith: valid is that which is newly revealed or exemplary;
> (c) value-rational faith: valid is that which has been deduced as an absolute;
> (d) positive enactment which is believed to be legal. (36)

We are not interested in the typology for itself; there are many overlapping classifications in Weber, and these have embarrassed the commentators. Sometimes there are four types—and not always exactly the same four—and in other places, like in the system of legitimacy, there are three types. Our concern is not with these possible conflicts in Weber's description but rather with the general level of his concepts. We must recognize that this level is always motivational as soon as the concept of legitimacy is introduced.

Weber leaves little doubt that the legitimacy of order is the central clue for the problem of authority. A few lines after the previous quotation Weber comments: "All further details, except for a few other concepts to be defined below, belong in the Sociology of Law and the Sociology of Domination *[Herrschaftssoziologie]*" (36). The concept in question, we remember, is *Herrschaft;* it is the basic concept toward which our discussion is directed and headed. The concept of authority or domination is introduced at the point when order and legitimacy are considered together. We have the first hints of what Weber develops in the third chapter of *Economy and Society,* a discussion to which we shall turn in the next lecture.

In order to make sense of the sociology of authority or domination, though, we need to present first a few other intermediary concepts. We shall consider only those four that are important for our further discussion. The first intermediary concept after that of order concerns the type of the social connection or bond (40 ff.). This type does not concern us directly, and yet it is not irrelevant to the process of legitimacy whether the link is deeply integrative or merely associative. The difference is whether people have the feeling of belonging together *(Gemeinschaft)* or whether they see their ties with others more as a contractual link, something more exterior and less involving *(Gesellschaft)*. This distinction is a classical one in German sociology and unfortunately has had some dreadful consequences. Though not at all Weber's intention, the plea for the integrative against the associative became one of the arguments of Nazi sociologists. The emphasis was on promotion of common life with its emotional links and on denial of conflict; the argument was that the unity of the race or the nation is greater than the conflict of classes. Hidden was the fact that often lying behind *Gemeinschaft* is coercion.

In contrast, even though Weber's sociology is generally nonevaluative, he puts more stress on the associative relationship. In the title of his book it is *Gesellschaft* which prevails and not *Gemeinschaft*. Attention to the associative link proceeds from the juridical tradition of the contract from Hobbes through Rousseau and so on. (Rousseau, we might note, can actually be read to support both types of the social bond, since the general will is more integrative than aggregative.) Weber is as much interested in the problems of the economy and the structure of the market as in the structure of power, and he emphasizes the associative tie throughout as the more rational. For Weber the associative link predominates, at least in those economic relations based on the market of the capitalistic system. The world here is a realm of conflict, and individuals and organizations relate to one another by shaping contracts. The bureaucratic state—which Weber generally regards quite positively—is another example of associative relationships. In their relationship to the system of administration, workers have no feeling of emotional belonging, and for Weber this is good. Workers have social roles, and these roles are connected one to another without an entaglement of feelings. Weber finds that the role of feelings is dangerous, because it leads precisely to the search for a *Führer* or leader. Between the notions of integration and *Führer* there are many hidden links.

In today's society we often resent the bureaucratic system, and with more right than Weber. What Weber may still teach us, though, is that any dream of a return to the communal instead of the associative may be quite ambiguous. Any effort to reconstruct society as a big commune may have either ultra-leftist or ultra-rightist consequences: anarchism or fascism. The oscillation of the concept of *Gemeinschaft* between these two poles may be typical of its character and requires at the very least some vigilance. This does not mean that nothing is needed and nothing is lost in the mere associative link—for example, the sense of participation in a common work. The kind of analysis of ideology initiated by Geertz might, in fact, be one way to reestablish the positive dimensions of *Gemeinschaft*. The constitutive character of ideology may play a significant role, because as Weber acknowledges, the "existence of common qualities"—race, even language—is alone not enough to generate "a *communal* social relationship" (42; emphasis added).

A second intermediary concept after the types of social connection is the degree of a group's closure (43 ff.). This concept is also important for a possible theory of ideology based on Weber, because the problem of a group's identity is linked to the existence of limits—territorial or other—regarding who does and who does not belong. The rules of affiliation and therefore of exclusion are significant for the constitution of a group's identity. Once again Geertz may offer a contribution here, because his notion of ideology as a cultural system may be related to the preservation of social identity. Since I am interested more in Weber's conceptual framework than in his content, what is noteworthy at this point is that we cannot define even the concept of closure in mechanical terms. While it may seem that the closure of a figure is something material, the concept is also motivational: "The principal *motives* for closure of a relationship are: (a) The maintenance of quality . . . ; (b) the contraction of advantages in relation to consumption needs . . . ; (c) the growing scarcity of opportunities for acquisition" (46; emphasis added). Even the concept of closure must be defined within a motivational system.

The next concept introduces the distinction within some closed groups between those who are the rulers and those who are the ruled; order is enforced by a specific segment of these groups. This type is decisive for Weber because it inserts into the analysis of order the concept of power. We may conceive of an order which has no hierarchy; many utopias have the notion of an ordered common life in which all roles are equal. Once we introduce, however, a distinction between the one who rules and the rest of the group, a polarization between ruler and ruled, we also introduce a certain kind of political structure. Weber calls this type an organization *(Verband)*. This type does not coincide with the distinction between *Gemeinschaft* and *Gesellschaft,* since the latter involve the nature of the link—internal or exterior—between individuals, while here the important concept is hierarchy. A hierarchical structure is introduced into the collective body. "A social relationship which is either closed or limits the admission of outsiders will be called an organization *(Verband)* when its regulations are enforced by specific individuals: a chief and, possibly, an administrative staff, which normally also has representative powers" (48). We are able to distinguish the governing body as a distinctive layer within the group.

With this concept of the ruling body, we have the notion of an order which is now enforced. (In Weber the concept of the ruling body comes before that of the ruling class, although for our purposes it is the very notion of ruling which is significant.) It is not the group as a whole which provides for its organization; instead, there are those in the position of enforcing order and those who are submitted to this order. The concrete problems of legitimacy proceed from this division of labor between ruler and ruled; a possible concept of ideology is prepared by the necessity of legitimating enforcement of the governing body's rules. Weber insists strongly on the concept of enforcement, which is contemporaneous with this polarization between ruler and ruled. "This criterion is decisive because it is not merely a matter of action which is *oriented* to an order, but which is specifically directed to its *enforcement*" (48; emphasis in original). A specific kind of action now exists which is oriented not to the action of others but to the system of enforcement: to obey, to follow the rules, even if the requirements of this system may sometimes be mild—stopping our car at a red light, for example. We have not established the rule, but we are oriented to the system that enforces it. Some might argue that it is in our own interest to accept the rule—we feel safer if there are regulations on the road—but we must recognize that this becomes one of the motives for legitimating the order and its enforcement powers.

Not every form of a closed communal or associative relationship is an organization. As Weber points out, we do not call an organization either an erotic relationship or a kinship group without a leader (48–49). The key notion, then, is the formalized system of authority. For me, this reinforces the idea that in fact the conflict between ideology and utopia is always displayed at this level. What is at stake in all ideology is finally the legitimation of a certain system of authority; what is at stake in all utopia is the imagining of an alternate way to use power. A utopia, for example, may want the group to be ruled without hierarchy or by giving power to the wisest (as in Plato's solution, the philosopher-king). Whatever the utopia's definition of authority, it attempts to provide alternate solutions to the existing system of power. The function of ideology, on the other hand, is always to legitimate the given, the actual system of rule or authority.

In his consideration of the concept of enforcement, Weber's contention is that we have no example of a society without some element of enforced rules. It is implausible that any form of governance will satisfy everyone. There are differences not only in interest but in age (those who are more directed toward the values of the past) and so on. The presumption that the minority will submit to the majority reintroduces the element of coercion. Only in a unanimous group would there seem to be noncoercion, but actually this could be the most coercive group. The law of unanimity is always more dangerous than the law of majority, because at least in the latter we may identify the minority and define its rights. If we claim to work on the basis of unanimity, then those who are not as unanimous as the others lose all their rights, since their rights are not defined. To use Orwell's imagery, we might say that in 1791 all the French were equal, except some were more equal than others; and these others were sent to the guillotine. As for Weber himself, he discusses the imposition of order in relation not to unanimity but majority rule.

> [A]n order is always "imposed" to the extent that it does not originate from a voluntary personal agreement of all the individuals concerned. The concept of imposition hence includes "majority rule," in that the minority must submit. For that reason there have been long periods when the legitimacy of majority rule has either not been recognized at all, or been held doubtful. (51)

Weber credits those who have some reservations about majority rule, because they recognize that it is another kind of violence, more subtle perhaps but still violence, especially since there are no rules for establishing the rule of the majority. Even "voluntary" agreement implies an amount of imposition. We see that in all electoral systems, because some trick is always available to gain the desired response from the electorate, either by dividing it or by establishing some procedure that allows the system to prevail over its critics. At this stage of his presentation, though, Weber does not take the question of the imposition of order as far as I have here. Rather, he says once again, "This will be further discussed in the Sociology of Law and of Domination" (51). What I have attempted to do is pick out most of the passages where the problem of authority is constituted in its basic condition.

In his discussion of the nature of order, the main concepts Weber has introduced are those of the associative or integrative link, the group's closure, and the group's hierarchy. In turn, the concept of hierarchy has included a relation of imperative structure. Only at this point does Weber introduce *Herrschaft* as a full-fledged concept; it is the relation between command and obedience. While some translators, Parsons in particular, translate *Herrschaft* by authority or imperative control, I prefer the present edition's translation of *Herrschaft* as "domination." The issues are clearer if we say "domination." " 'Domination' *(Herrschaft)* is the probability that a command with a given specific content will be obeyed by a given group of persons" (53). *Herrschaft* is defined by the expectation of others' obedience. The system of power has a certain credibility, and this allows it to count on the behavior of its members. When police officers go into the street, they expect that everyone will submit their behavior to them. Obedience is a result not only of the officers' power—their ability to carry out their will, even to kill—it is also a result of people's belief in their function. The problem to which Weber addresses himself is how some people are in a position of successfully issuing orders to others. The probability that we will follow the rules itself constitutes the domination. This situation is not so far from Hegel's master/slave relation; the slave believes that the master is the real figure of human being not only because he or she as slave is the weaker but because he or she believes in the humanity of the master.

The last stage in Weber's development of the concept of order is reached when he introduces the possibility of physical force. Weber maintains that by adding to the concepts previously enumerated the threat of the legitimate use of force, we arrive at the definition of the state. The state's structure of power depends on its upholding "the claim to the *monopoly* of the *legitimate* use of physical force in the enforcement of its order" (54; emphasis in original). (Note the concept of claim, "the *claim* to the monopoly . . . ," introduced here.) This is a pessimistic concept of the state, but Weber was not at all a romanticist. In a sense, this definition is not so far from Lenin's. In *State and Revolution,* Lenin said that the state is not defined by its goals but by its means, and its means is coercion. Weber speaks similarly:

> It is not possible to define a political organization, including the state, in terms of the end to which its action is devoted. . . . Thus it is possible to define the "political" character of an organization only in terms of the *means* peculiar to it, the use of force. This means is, however, in the above sense specific, and is indispensable to its character. It is even, under certain circumstances, elevated into an end in itself. (55; emphasis in original)

Examples of the use of force becoming an end in itself include situations of emergency and war. Whatever the resemblance between Weber's and

Lenin's definition of the state, though, the remaining difference is that for Weber the coercion of the state is finally sustained not by its physical power but by our response of belief to its claim of legitimacy. To put this in the language of Plato, we might say that what enables the state's domination is more its sophistic or rhetorical structure than its sheer force. Nevertheless, we must still insist on the fact that the state is defined by the recourse to force. The state has the last word in terms of force. It can put us in jail, while no other group legally can. It is legal for the state finally to use violence. Only with the introduction of the role of force is the concept of domination complete. Only then is the concept of claim, the claim to legitimacy, also complete. We must understand the concept of claim not only when there is an order but when there are rulers, rulers who may use force as a last resort.

The troublesome nature of the claim to legitimacy demonstrates why the scope of the question of legitimacy is so easily maneuvered down to the level of politics. It is true, by and large, that the question of claim is a political one. Yet this question is not simply political, in the narrow sense of the term, for two reasons. First, we must recognize the problematic of legitimate order which rules that of political domination through the intermediary notion of the organization, the compulsory association, the differentiation between ruler and ruled. If by chance the state should die, it is not certain that the problem of legitimate order would disappear. The role of ideology persists. The second reason why legitimacy is not simply a matter of politics, of force, is that we cannot get rid of the motivational framework, because it is only within this framework that the question of the *claim* to legitimacy makes sense.

Our analysis of Weber's categories of political order has laid the groundwork for our discussion in the next lecture of the ideological structure of the system of legitimacy. To conclude I would like to spend a bit more time analyzing the nature of Weber's interpretive structure. Marxists would object to Weber's schema because not only is class not a leading concept, it does not even belong to the fundamental concepts. The imposition of order is a structural trait which is not necessarily linked to class struggle. Here is the anti-Marxist tendency of Weber. His definitions are intended to encompass any group, whether in a class or in a potentially classless society. Weber advances an atemporal analysis of some fundamental questions; his typology attempts to be transhistorical. His framework is supposedly valid for any society, from the pre-Columbian to the modern. The

Marxist response would be precisely that history is excluded from Weber's approach; this is particularly indicated by Weber's exclusion of the concept of class, because history, the Marxists would say, came about with the history of classes. I think Weber would defend his orientation by arguing that history is not essential for defining the fundamental structure of society. He would agree with Marxists that we are now in a society in which the class structure is decisive, but he would maintain that this historical circumstance does not affect the main structure of society. The proof of this is that if classes are eliminated or if the ruling role of the bourgeoisie disappears, the same problems of norms, regulations, and so on will arise in a classless society.

I see two possible attacks on Weber by those who would argue that his ideal types are too ahistorical. The first claim is that the variety of historical situations is so great that we must proceed at a more grassroots level. For example, American sociologists typically proceed in a more localized and descriptive manner. They are reluctant to deal with the concept of order as a global entity. They would call Weber's concepts too Platonistic. A rather different kind of criticism would come from those who see sociological analysis as a critical tool. Post-Marxists like Habermas argue that the task is not so much to describe as to unmask. In Weber's defense, though, I wonder whether we can either describe concretely or criticize without a certain conceptual network with which to handle the phenomena we are studying. Our definitions may be partly conventional—"I call an organization this and that"—but they also allow us to identify situations in such a way that we may have discussions about notions like power that are meaningful in different historical and cultural circumstances. We must first understand the structures in which we live.

My conviction, finally, is that historicity may have been emphasized too much; for there may be societal structures just as there are linguistic structures. Chomsky has shown that there is more permanence in semantic structures than Benjamin Lee Whorf and others allowed. There may be a certain permanence in social structures also. The political problematic may have a greater permanence than something like economic structures, which are more historically bound. A certain universality in the problematic of power allows us to identify a problem when we read political authors of the past. Aristotle's biology may be completely obsolete, but when he speaks of democracy and oligarchy we are still able to identify the same figures. When we read Plato on the tyrant, we understand. In politics we always make the same mistakes, and this may be because we have to do with questions that are very repetitious: the use of power, the use of lies by those in power, and so on. Marxists are right when they argue that we exclude history when we exclude classes. Weber's response is that class structure, historical as it may be, does not change fundamentally the problem of how human groups should be ruled. The Egyptians, the Incas, and the Chinese all confront the same problems. Perhaps it is a bias on my part, but to justify the lack of a historical dimension in Max Weber, I would say that he addresses himself to what is the less historical in the structure of human societies because he relies on a certain identity of motives.

It is true that Weber's ideal types take on a certain perspective. What speaks through his types is the ideal of the German liberal intellectual before Nazism. The types are culturally situated; as we shall see, they express a strong confidence in the legal-bureaucratic state. Our objection, through, cannot be that the kind of state favored by these types is in fact what failed in Germany. We must distinguish between a failure that is a fault of the structure and one that arises because people stopped believing in the structure. The structure's claim to legitimacy requires a corresponding belief on the part of the citizenry. Where this response to the state is lacking, where people want instead a leader, a *Führer,* then a democracy is dead no matter what the extent of its own structural problems. Evident is a kind of disease in the belief supporting the claim. This would be Weber's argument, I think. Nevertheless, it is still the case that Weber's ideal types are characterized by a certain ranking. As we shall discuss, Weber proceeds from what he calls the most rational toward the less rational, from the legal form of legitimacy to the traditional form and then to the charismatic. The charismatic is defined by its lack of rationality. Therefore, there is in Weber a prejudice toward rationality. Perhaps we can reconcile Weber's perspectival orientation with his notion of permanent societal structures by arguing that the structures are indeed permanent but their formulation, description, and interpretation remain the product of more situated points of view.

12

Weber (2)

At the beginning of the last lecture, I mentioned that we address ourselves to Max Weber at this stage of our inquiry in order to meet two main difficulties in the Marxist theory of ideology. The first concerns the general conceptual framework of the Marxist approach, which is structured in more or less causal terms through the notions of infrastructure and superstructure. My claim was that an alternate, motivational model could be derived from Weber's work, and this is what we unfolded in the last session. The second strength of Weber is that within his motivational framework we can make more sense of the notion of ruling ideas being expressed by a ruling class. To defend this claim is the task now at hand. I approach Weber, therefore, not to treat him as an anti-Marxist but as one who provides a better conceptual framework for integrating some important Marxist ideas. We must consider Marx's ideas with the same critical attention that we give any other thinker; in so doing, we resist the intellectual blackmail imposed on us either by Marxists or by anti-Marxists. No one asks us whether we are Cartesian when we speak of Descartes or Spinozist when we speak of Spinoza. We take the good where we find it, and this has been my own aim. The motivational model I have presented is an alternate model to Marxism, but it is presented in order to deal with a Marxist problem.

The current lecture's discussion of Weber's concept and typology of legitimacy should make this orientation even more apparent. Our focus is the third chapter of *Economy and Society,* "The Types of Legitimate Domination." This section of the work was anticipated several times in the previous lecture, at each point that Weber presented the notion of a claim. As we saw, Weber's concept of claim develops in three main stages. A claim is implied first in the very concept of *Ordnung*. This notion does not mean compulsory order but an ordering that gives a shape, a gestalt, a pattern to a group. This order already involves a question of belief, because it consists of individuals orienting themselves to the behavior of others. Everything must be expressed in terms of the mutual orientation of individuals, and the inscription of this claim in the motivational field of each individual is a belief. In Weber's vocabulary the word usually used to describe this notion is *Vorstellung*. Translation of *Vorstellung* by "belief" is limited, particularly since the emotional aspect of belief predominates. *Vorstellung* is not so much belief as representation. A *Vorstellung* is each individual's representation of the order. The order exists more as an intellectual representation than as an emotional belief.

The notion of claim takes on a more radical and more cogent meaning when we shift from the general concept of *Ordnung* to the notion of an order which implies a differentation between rulers and ruled. Here, as we observed, we are on the way to the definition of the state, since the state is precisely one of those structures in which we may identify and distinguish formally the decision-making layer of the organization. This hierarchy need not belong only to the state, however; it can be found within a school system, a church, a sports organization, or wherever certain specified people are in charge of making decisions and implementing them. Present is not only an order but an implemented or imposed order. The concept of imposition injects an element of conflict between wills. The notion of claim must then incorporate not only recognition of who we are but obedience to the one who rules.

The third step taken in the development of the concept of claim introduces the notion of the threat of the use of force. For Weber this is the distinctive trait of the state among all other institutions. The state, Weber says, has a claim to the monopoly of the ultimate legitimate use of violent force against the recalcitrant individual or group. In the criminal and penal laws of a given society it is finally the state which enforces the decision of the judge; the state ensures both the decision's finality and its implementation. The distinctive character of the state may be recognized exactly here. Thus to summarize, we have three stages in the concept of claim: the claim of an order in general, the claim of a ruling group within an organization, and the claim of those in power to have the capacity to implement order by the use of force.

In approaching the texts for the present lecture, my hypothesis is that the problem of ideology is raised at least in principle when we confront the claim to legitimacy with the belief in legitimacy. Weber provides us a more meaningful conceptual framework for examining this problem than Marxist theory, but unfortunately he does not treat the problem of ideology himself. It is puzzling why we have in Weber a good conceptual framework and yet the question of ideology is absent. He provides the tools for dealing with ideology and yet makes no allusions to this issue. One reason for this lacuna may be suggested by what we need to add to Weber's framework, something fundamental that is available only in Marxism, the notion of a ruling class. Weber speaks only of the notion of a ruling group in general. Perhaps Weber's systematic avoidance of class in his list of basic concepts explains his strange silence on the problem of ideology as such.[1] We shall return to this question at the end of the lecture.

What particularly strikes me in Weber's presentation of the concept and typology of legitimacy is that the question of belief is introduced as something supplementary, something not founded. For me the place of ideology lies in the empty space of this concept. When Weber speaks of claim, its construction is coherent, but when he speaks of belief, it is only supplemental. There is a discrepancy between the status granted to claim and that granted to belief. Evidence of this disparity appears on the first pages of the chapter on legitimacy. Weber discusses the many motives for obedience. "[C]ustom, personal advantage, purely affectual or ideal motives of solidarity," he says, "do not form a sufficiently reliable basis for a given dominaton. *In addition* there is normally a further element, the belief in legitimacy" (213; emphasis added). It is the phrase "in addition" which attracted my attention. The belief in legitimacy is not the result of the factors mentioned but something more. This something more is what intrigues me. The nature of this "addition" receives no specific treatment in Weber, since as we shall see, he returns to the typology of the claim. Weber assumes that the typology of the claim is reflected in the typology of the belief, in spite of the fact that the belief is an addition, something more.

Some might argue that Weber's use of the phrase "in addition" was said by chance. Yet Weber returns to the phrase in the next paragraph. "Experience shows that in no instance does domination voluntarily limit itself to the appeal to material or affectual or ideal motives as a basis for its continuance. *In addition* every such system attempts to establish and to cultivate the belief in its legitimacy" (213; emphasis added). Here is the empty place of a theory of ideology in Max Weber. Weber indicates in the quotation that the knowledge expressed about the belief in legitimacy is based on *experience,* as though we cannot derive this factor from the basic concepts which have been elaborated so accurately. The belief in legitimacy is a supplement which must be treated as a mere fact, since it is derived from experience. We have no other way, he thinks, of comprehending how systems of authority work. Beliefs contribute something beyond what sociologists understand to be the role of motivation.

I wonder whether it is not because this supplement of belief is opaque that Max Weber chooses to "classify the types of domination according to the kind of *claim* to legitimacy typically made by each" (213; emphasis added). The typology is provided by the claim, not by the belief. The belief adds something more, which allows the claim to be accepted, assumed, or taken for granted by those submitted to its order. It is here that I graft my own hypothesis concerning the whole problem of the role of belief in relation to claim. I state my hypothesis in three points. First, can we not say that the problem of ideology concerns precisely this supplement, this gap between claim and belief, the fact that there must be something more in the belief than can be rationally understood in terms of interests, whether emotional, customary, or rational? Second, is it not the function of ideology to fill in this credibility gap? If this is the case, then third do we not need to elaborate a concept of surplus-value, now linked not so much to work as to power? Marx elaborated a theory of surplus-value to explain why a good in the market has more value than the amount paid to the worker who made it. The difference between what the worker is paid and what the good is worth is the surplus-value (the *Mehrwert*) produced by the worker and stolen by the employer in order to provide capital with the appearance of productivity. All Marxism relies on the fact that capital has an appearance of productivity which is in fact derived from the worker's productivity but is no longer recognized as such. Marx calls this transfer of productivity from work to capital the fetishism of commodities. We have the impression that money produces something, that there exists a productivity of things, whereas what really exists is only the productivity of people. My question is whether we do not need to elaborate a parallel theory of surplus-value no longer in relation to work but to power.

If this third part of my hypothesis is correct, it can explain what happens in socialist societies, where the Marxist surplus-value is more or less suppressed but the surplus-value in terms of power is not. Systems of authority are superimposed on a socialist system of production, but the system of power stays exactly the same. Perhaps, then, there are several sources of surplus-value, not only an economic source of surplus-value but also one related to the source of authority or power. At least this is the hypothesis that I propose. We can formulate this hypothesis in general by saying that there is always more in the claim of a given system of authority than the normal course of motivation can satisfy, and therefore there is always a supplement of belief provided by an ideological system. This framework allows us to make sense of a position like Althusser's, when he says that the state is not only, as Lenin claimed, a system of coercion but is also an ideological apparatus. Although Althusser's own terms for this are mechanistic, the ideological apparatus is the supplement to the coercive functon of the state and more generally the supplement to the functioning of institutions in civil society as a whole.

We must therefore read Weber's chapter on the types of legitimacy with a certain reservation. We shall try to see what is lacking in his typology of claims that prevents its transposition into a typology of beliefs. By this difference we shall obtain the concept of ideology missing in the text itself. Our reading is oriented, which I do not deny. We are looking for something that is not in the text, and so must read between the lines. We shall see that the problem of belief keeps returning in a system which starts as a classification of claims and not a classification of beliefs. The question of belief persists because we cannot speak of legitimacy without speaking of grounds and grounds refer to beliefs. A ground is both a ground and a motive. It is a motive, to use the language of Elizabeth Anscombe, functioning as a reason for.

The most auspicious place to look for Weber's view of the role of belief is in his famous typology of the three kinds of claims to legitimacy. While Weber has already stated that he classifies the types of domination according to their claims, in fact the classification proceeds on the basis of beliefs. Note that Weber presents the typology not in terms of the claims themselves but in terms of the validity of these claims. Validity is a question addressed to those submitted to these claims and therefore rests on the belief in the claims.

There are three pure types of legitimate domination. The *validity* of the claims to legitimacy may be based on:

1. Rational *grounds*—resting on a *belief* in the legality of patterns of enacted

rules and the right of those elevated to authority under such rules to issue commands (legal authority).

2. Traditional *grounds*—resting on an established *belief* in the sanctity of immemorial traditions and the legitimacy of those exercising authority under them (traditional authority); or finally,

3. Charismatic *grounds*—resting on *devotion* to the exceptional sanctity, heroism or exemplary character of an individual person, and of the normative patterns or order revealed or ordained by him (charismatic authority). (215; emphases added)

In his typology the notion of ground returns three times and three times with it the notion of belief. The word is not uttered in the third case, but when we speak of devotion, this is typically belief. In order to elaborate a system of claims, then, we have to look at the counterpart system of belief, whether a belief in an impersonal order according to rules, a belief based on personal loyalty, or a belief in the leadership of the prophet or chief.

The phenomenon of belief is the most prominent in the third type, because we immediately recognize its religious origin. The concept of charisma means the gift of grace and is taken, says Weber, from the vocabulary of early Christianity (216). As the typology alerts us, though, it would be wrong to assume that the problem of belief exists only in the cases of charismatic authority or traditional authority. For even legality relies on belief. We shall spend the rest of the lecture tracing the surplus-value of belief to claim in each of the three types of domination, and we shall begin with legal authority.

The last lecture already indicated one reason why legality rests on belief. If we assume the existence of an honest system of representation—some electoral system, for example—the rule of the majority is the rule of the whole, and the problem for the minority is to accept this rule. The minority must have some confidence, some trust, in the rule of the majority. Even the majority must trust that majority rule and not a false, pretended, or claimed unanimity is the best way to govern. An element of agreement is present of the kind expressed in classical contract theory. Ideology has a role here as the necessary supplement to the contract. "Legal authority rests on the *acceptance* of the validity of the following mutually interdependent ideas" (217; emphasis added). Acceptance is the belief on which legality lies. Acceptance is a form of recognition; once again "belief" is too narrow to cover the *Vorstellung* of the German.

Weber presents a series of five criteria on which legal authority depends.

I shall cite only part of the first criterion and summarize the other four. "1. That any given legal norm may be established by agreement or by imposition, on grounds of expedience of value-rationality or both, with a *claim* to obedience at least on the part of the members of the organization" (217; emphasis added). The notion of claim must be introduced in relation to legal authority, because we cannot grant legality to a system simply on account of its formal structure. The legality of a structure cannot be assumed, for its legality is what is in question. A legal norm must make appeal to interests or personal commitments, and a commitment to the system has the nature of a belief corresponding to a claim. Weber's other criteria for legal authority concern the fact that the rules must be consistent, usually intentionally established, and the product of an impersonal order. Persons in authority are themselves subject to the impersonal order and govern according to its rules, not their own inclinations; people do not owe obedience to authorities as individuals but as representatives of the impersonal order. All relationships are depersonalized. What we must recognize for our purposes is that the system is formalized, but the system also requires our belief in this formalization.

If asked to consider at greater length what is ideological in this system of rules, I would raise three points. First, the fact that even legal authority requires its subjects' belief confirms that authority is best understood within a motivational model. This alerts us that there may be a positive meaning of ideology which we must retrieve if we are to comprehend adequately the nature of legitimacy. Discussion of this nonpejorative meaning of ideology will be the focus of the lecture on Geertz.

A second, more negative ideological aspect of a system of rules is that any system of formalization may be pretended, and this may serve to cover for an organization's real practice. We must measure an authority's real practice over against its alleged system of rules, but Weber says nothing about this problem. We cannot take for granted the declaration of a system of power that it relies on a particular set of rules. The problem is the discrepancy between its practice and the alleged rules. A given form of authority may comply in appearance with Weber's criteria, precisely to use in a more efficient way another kind of power. An example of this which Marx unmasked is the use of the contractual relation to cover the real wage relationship between capital and labor. The contract model maintains that the relationship between worker and employer is no longer one of slave and master, because both parties are juridically equal: one provides work, the other provides money. Because the participation of each party in the wage relationship is said to be free and equal, the relationship is thus said to be a contract. The formal structure of the wage hides the real nature of the relation of forces underlying it. We must take seriously, then, the accusation by Marxists against what they call with some contempt—and surely too much contempt—formal freedom. Marxists argue that they are interested in real freedom and not the formal freedom of capitalistic systems. This contempt of formality can itself be a justification for violence, though, so both sides may be in some sense hypocritical. Nevertheless, the important point here is the possibility of an ideological use of a formal system by the pretense of a legal course that in fact covers a different kind of course altogether.

The third source of ideology in a system of rules may be not so much the hypocritical use of formalism but the advocacy of formalism itself. The belief in formalism has become a much greater issue since Weber's day. We have less confidence than Weber in bureaucratic procedures. For Weber the bureaucracy's depersonalization of all relations acted to protect the individual's rights. There is something to that, and some critiques of bureaucracy fail to recognize the advantages of an abstract system of role relations. Where all relations are personal, the system is one of hatred and love. In his attention to a system's means, though, Weber loses sight of its goals and the underlying beliefs which suport it. Note the following characterization: "The purest type of exercise of legal authority is that which employs a bureaucratic administrative staff' (220). Legal authority is identified merely by the means that it "employs." My hypothesis is that this shift of interest from the underlying belief to the technical means prevents Weber from developing a theory of ideology about how belief supports the bureaucratic system. Weber's question is how does an administrative staff work, what are the rules of its employment by a legal authority? I do not consider it unfair to Weber to say that because he identifies with the most rational type of authority, he looks to what is the most rational in its support, and that may be found not in beliefs but in bureaucratic tools. A theory of means takes the place of an investigation into motivation, despite the fact that Weber begins his investigation with a system of motivations. The system of motivations is dropped in order to look at the most abstract functioning of an administrative staff.

Weber is the first to discuss the nature of bureaucracy in this analytical manner, the first to introduce a sociology of bureaucratic institutions. A bureaucracy has a clearly defined hierarchy of officers, the sphere of competence is defined, the system of selection and promotion is public, and so on. None of these rules has anything to do with belief. Weber does not take into account that his depiction of bureaucracy as the most rational and therefore the best form of organization is itself a belief; his enterprise is attuned rather to description alone. As a result, Weber does not reflect on the diseases of the bureaucratic state, problems so important for Marcuse and others. The repressive implications of a rationalist system are not considered. For me, Weber's lack of reflection on this point betrays the failure to elaborate the problem of ideology, which affects all systems from the most rational to the least. Rules too may hide some less laudable practices: arbitrariness, hidden cooptation, autonomization of the administrative body, and irresponsibility in the name of obedience to the system. Here we must read Hannah Arendt on the authoritarian state. All those like Eichmann who were accused of killing Jews in Germany defended themselves by saying that they obeyed orders, that they were good officers. The administrative system, then, may not only deprive the individual of personal responsibility, it may even cover up crimes committed in the name of the administrative good. Also troublesome are the size of present administrative bodies and the anonymity of organizational relationships. The latter in particular has led to the diffusion of anonymity in society at large. Something in the human texture is harmed.

In Weber there are only two or three allusions to these problems, and they are all the more precious because they are so few. Here the repressed side of the problematic briefly appears.

> The question is always who controls the existing bureaucratic machinery. And such control is possible only in a very limited degree to persons who are not technical specialists. Generally speaking, the highest-ranking career official is more likely to get his way in the long run than his nominal superior, the cabinet minister, who is not a specialist. (224)

Yes, the question is who controls the bureaucratic machinery; the average citizen is said not to be competent to discuss these matters. The specialists supposedly know better than we do. The citizen is placed into a kind of exterritoriality by the technicality of the bureaucratic machinery. The technocrats may take hold of the political machine because of the incompetence of politicians. Sometimes this may be good, because the specialists may be more rational about matters than the politicians, but no one knows who finally controls these technocrats.

The rise of bureaucracy also creates other difficulties. Weber notes the connection between bureaucracy and the capitalist system. The development of bureaucracy, he says,

> largely under capitalistic auspices, has created an urgent need for stable, strict, intensive, and calculable administration. It is this need which is so fateful to any kind of large-scale administration. Only by reversion in every field—political, religious, economic, etc.—to small-scale organization would it be possible to any considerable extent to escape its influence. (224)

The attempt to lower the level of bureaucracy, to put it closer to the citizenry, is a central issue in modern utopias. The growing distance between the bureaucratic machinery and the individual is a problem itself. Weber adds that this problem is not attributable to capitalism alone. A socialist system does not by definition solve the issue any better. After seeing the experience of centralized socialism, we know that the need to decentralize the bureaucracy is present there too. A socialist form of organization, says Weber, does not alter the need for effective bureaucratic administration. Weber's question is only "whether in a socialistic system it would be possible to provide conditions for carrying out as stringent a bureaucratic organization as has been possible in a capitalistic order." We now know the answer: the possibility is actually more likely.

> For socialism would, in fact, require a still higher degree of formal bureaucratization than capitalism. If this should prove not to be possible, it would demonstrate the existence of another of those fundamental elements of irrationality in social systems—a conflict between formal and substantive rationality of the sort which sociology so often encounters. (225)

Not only does bureaucratization have repressive aspects, but the most rational system has an irrationality of its own. This is a most important observation. Any attempt to perpetuate the claim of rationality in the midst of the bureaucracy's repressive and irrational qualities requires the presence of belief. Weber interprets irrationality here as the conflict between formal and substantive rationality. A formalized system is independent of individuals, whereas substantive rationality has a more Hegelian tone; it is the *Geist,* the substance of the group or community, which wants to understand itself. Formalized systems, on the other hand, are opaque in terms of the roles they allow to and the meaning they offer for individual and collective life. This is the place where belief does not correspond to claim, because the claim to rationality is overshadowed by a cloud of irrationality which the belief has to get through.

Most of the examples I have just cited about the diseases of bureaucracy are merely alluded to in Weber's work. He more explicitly describes the limit of his analysis in the case of one particular criterion of bureaucracy, that of free selection. In the pure type of legal authority, Weber says, "The office is filled by a free contractual relationship. Thus, in principle, there is free selection" (220). Yet Weber recognizes that in the capitalistic system there is something fundamental which escapes free selection: the selection of the owners of capital. The owners of capital are not selected by the system based on their technical qualifications; instead, they achieve their positions on their own. The economic body of a capitalist system escapes the rationality of the bureaucratic state and relies instead on another form of rationality, that of profit. To the extent that the capitalistic entrepeneur is not freely selected and also has the power to lobby and influence political decisions, this top of the administrative staff is not so much administrative as political. Since the owners of capital influence political leaders, the capitalistic hierarchy also becomes entangled with the political hierarchy. "There is no question but that the 'position' of the capitalistic entrepreneur is a definitively appropriated as is that of a monarch." The capitalist enterprise has a monarchic structure at the top, which is quite discordant with the claim of democracy in the political sphere. "Thus at the top of a bureaucratic organization, there is necessarily an element which is at least not purely bureaucratic. The category of bureaucracy is one applying only to the exercise of control by means of a particular kind of administrative staff" (222). Instead of being the organizational structure of the whole, bureaucratic rationality is a limited rationality functioning within a system that follows quite different rules. These problems will be picked up by Habermas and other post-Marxists. They will discuss the fact that technology itself may function ideologically; we see only the empty place for that discussion in Weber.

I wonder whether the weak point in Weber's analysis of the legal type is that the issue of domination is reduced to the problem of the employment of a bureaucratic administrative staff. The persisting role of domination is then not scrutinized with the same accuracy as the system's rules. Weber fails to appreciate sufficiently that the nature of domination is not exhausted by the bureaucracy's privileged means. As we have just seen, Weber neglects to incorporate into his analysis the political dimension, which tends to be absorbed into a question of administration. Marxists would say that

Weber has systematically bracketed the capitalistic aspects of political democracy and reduced them simply to issues concerning the techniques of power. The legal type is ideological to the extent that it uses formal bureaucratic efficiency to mask the real nature of the power at work.

My own hypothesis is that the legal type remains a form of domination to the extent that it preserves something of the two other structures of claims and that legality serves to hide this residue of the traditional and the charismatic. It may be that the three types cannot be independently juxtaposed because they are always more or less intertwined with one another. This is not contrary to what Max Weber says in general about ideal types. Though he proposes three types, the distinctions are supposed to be only a way to disentangle significant connections. Nothing functions on the basis of one type alone; all real systems of power imply, if in different proportions, elements of legality, traditionality, and the charismatic. In fact it may be that the legal type functions only on the basis of what remains from the traditional and charismatic types. This is one way of reading Max Weber. I do not claim that it is the best way, since Weber presents the three types and describes them separately according to different criteria. If my hypothesis deserves at least to be discussed, however, then it can be asked whether legal power does not hold on to some features of the traditional and the charismatic in order to be power and not only legal. We have described what makes it legal, but what makes it a power may be finally borrowed always from the two other kinds of power. This is why we have to look carefully to the definition of the two other types. If it is true that they implicitly provide a certain opaqueness, they preserve this opaqueness even in the legal type.

Let us turn, then, to Weber's definitions of the traditional and charismatic types in order to ascertain their sources of power, elements which depend on our belief. As for the traditional type, "Authority will be called traditional if legitimacy is claimed for it and believed in by virtue of the sanctity of age-old rules and powers." The word "sanctity" is most important; it indicates that a quasi-religious element appears not only in the charismatic type but in the traditional type as well. In broad terms we may call it an ideological element. People believe that this order has a kind of sanctity; even if it does not deserve to be obeyed, even if it is not loved, at least it is revered.

> The masters are designated according to traditional rules and are obeyed because of their traditional status. This type of organized rule is, in the simplest case, primarily based on personal loyalty which results from a common upbringing. The

person exercising authority is not a "superior," but a personal master. . . . (226–27)

A network of more personalized relationships exists based on the belief that what comes from the past has more dignity than what is instituted in the present. There is a prejudice in favor of tradition, our ancestors, the weight of the past.

What suggests my hypothesis that any kind of authority implies at least an element of traditionality is that a political body is governed not only by technical rules of efficiency but also by the way it identifies itself among other groups. As we shall see with Geertz, this may be the first function of an ideological system: to preserve the group's identity through time. A political community is a historical phenomenon. It is a cumulative process which reclaims something of its past and anticipates something of its future. A political body exists not only in the present but in the past and in the future, and its function is to connect past, present, and future. In a political community several generations exist at the same time; the political choice is always an arbitration between the claims of these different generations, whereas a technical decision occurs only in the present and only according to the present system of tools. The political body has more memory and more expectations or hope than a technological system. The kind of rationality implied by politics is thus more integrative in terms of the temporal dimension. The French philosopher Eric Weil has developed this contrast between technological and political rationality in his book *Philosophie Politique* (The Philosophy of Politics). Weil distinguishes between what in French is the *rationnel* and the *raisonnable*. Technology and economics have to be "rational," the technical connection between means and ends, whereas in politics rationality is the "reasonable," the capacity to integrate a whole. It is something other than to add one means to another. A strategy of means can be technological, but a political decision always implies something else, and this is more opaque.

Unfortunately, though, when Weber discusses the functioning of a traditional authority, he attends merely to its means, and only by comparison to the means of the legal state. Because of his emphasis on the bureaucratic instrument in the legal type, Weber analyzes the traditional type in terms of its technique in implementing order, rather than in terms of the motivation for belief in its rationality. Weber does not do what he claims—treat each type on its own basis—because he considers the traditional and the charismatic only by comparison to the legal and bureaucratic. Weber's biases are evident in the strategy of his text, because he starts with the legal system, then proceeds to the traditional, and finally to the charismatic. He analyzes the rational first and then treats the others in order to uncover what by comparison they are lacking. He proceeds from the most rational to the less rational. The succession is not at all historical; on the contrary, there is no doubt that the charismatic always precedes the traditional and the traditional the rational. The analysis proceeds in reverse historical order, which is the order of decreasing rationality. Weber puts into this description all his expectations about the nature of rationality in society.

Evidence of this bias is patent in Weber's discussion of the traditional type. We see such phrases as: "In the pure type of traditional rule, the following features of a bureaucratic administrative staff are absent. . . ." "In place of a well-defined functional jurisdiction, there is a conflicting series of tasks and powers. . . ." "The absence of distinct spheres of competence is evident . . ." (229). Weber treats traditionality by negative contrast. The problem of the underlying ideology of tradition escapes, because bureaucracy is the measure of comparison and it is itself analyzed in the least ideological way possible. Even within these narrow limitations, though, we may ask whether it is not the case that the more substantive qualities Weber observes in the traditional type—gerontocracy, patriarchalism, patrimonialism, the personal appropriation of authority—always persist, even in a legal state.

As for the charismatic type, our question is whether it is a type that has been overcome, or is it instead the hidden kernel of all power. Weber defines the charismatic authority in the following way:

> The term "charisma" will be applied to a certain quality of an individual personality by virtue of which he is considered extraordinary and treated as endowed with supernatural, superhuman, or at least specifically exceptional powers or qualities. These are such as are not accessible to the ordinary person, but are regarded as of divine origin or as exemplary, and on the basis of them the individual concerned is treated as a "leader." (241)

Because of its more supernatural qualities, it may seem that the charismatic authority has been superseded in today's world by the two other types of authority. As Hegel argues in the *Philosophy of Right,* however, there is always an element of decision-making in a system of power and this element is always personal to a certain degree (paragraph 273). Hegel expresses this within the framework of a monarchy, which exemplifies more clearly than any other system that the problem of the leader can never be completely excluded. Even in a democratic system like the British form of government, people vote for three things at the same time: a program, a party, and a leader. Therefore, we can never bracket completely the element of leadership, because politics is the place where decisions are made for the whole. The necessity of decision-making preserves, at least as a residual element, the charismatic.

If the notion of charismatic authority is not dispensable, we must then consider the leader's credentials. Here the problem of belief comes to the forefront, because there is no leader, no prophet, who does not claim to be the true prophet and therefore seek our belief. "It is recognition on the part of those subject to authority which is decisive for the validity of charisma" (242). In this sentence is the place for a problematic of ideology. Belief is required and yet, Weber goes on, the leader does not rely on belief. On the contrary, it is because the leader raises a claim that others must believe.

> No prophet has ever regarded his quality as dependent on the attitudes of the masses toward him. No elective king or military leader has ever treated those who have resisted him or tried to ignore him otherwise than as delinquent in duty. Failure to take part in a military expedition under such leader, even though recruitment is formally voluntary, has universally met with disdain. (242)

This speaks for today as well as for the past. "Recognition is a duty" (244). The relation between belief and claim is replaced simply by a belief in the sign. In the sign is the proof given by the leader. This is the validity of charisma. "[R]ecognition is freely given and guaranteed by what is held to be a proof, originally always a miracle, and consists in devotion to the corresponding revelation, hero worship, or absolute trust in the leader" (242). The religious value of charisma is captured for the sake of the political structure. This may be finally the first ideology of power: the belief that the power is divine, that it does not come from us but from above. The origin of power in the people is stolen to the same extent that, in Marxist terms, the surplus-value of their labor seems to belong to capital; both power and capital are said to function on their own basis. In both cases we have the same capture of meaning. The decisive trait of charismatic authority, then, is the lack of reciprocity between claim and belief. The claim does not rely on the belief, but the belief is extorted by the claim. My question is whether this disjuncture between claim and belief in charismatic authority is not the basis for all issues of power and domination in general.

In concluding this lecture, I would like to return to the question of why even though Weber's conceptual framework is a good one for the study of ideology, he does not analyze this topic. We may summarize the importance of Weber's framework by considering one example of its application. In his book *The Protestant Ethic and the Spirit of Capitalism,* Weber deals with a problem that is similar to Marx's; Weber shows that there is a certain reciprocity between the ethics of Protestantism and the ideology of the entrepeneur. A certain circularity exists between the class structure and the religious ideology. Much of the controversy about Weber's thesis concentrates on this relation between the Protestant ethic and capitalism and whether one gave rise to the other. Because of our analysis of Weber's conceptual framework, though, I think we can now see that raising the question of the initial cause is not a good question. To ask whether the ethics produced the capitalist mind or vice versa is to remain in an inappropriate framework. Instead, I would rather say that the ethics provide the symbolic structure within which some economic forces work. It is more an issue of the relation between a framework of reference and a system of forces. The same problem arises in Freud, the question, for example, of how infantile drives work within a cultural framework provided by the structure of parenthood and the family. If we attempt to deal with this problem in causal terms, we are lost. It is not possible to ask which comes first, because a force works within a certain framework of meaningfulness, and this framework cannot be put in terms of infrastructure and superstructure.

This is the point where Weber does not provide so much an alternate solution to the Marxists as a better framework to deal with the same problem. Weber eludes this result, though, perhaps because he did not consider what was so important for *The German Ideology,* the fact that our relationships are frozen and no longer appear to us as what they are; there is a reification of human relationships. It may be that the anti-Marxist element in Weber prevented him from dealing with the problem of the reification of his own categories. Perhaps for the same reason he did not emphasize the notion of class, which is one of the structures within which this distortion takes place. I think Weber's conceptual framework can be reappropriated, though, to show that the process of reification occurs within a symbolic system. Only a symbolic system may be altered in such a way that it looks like a deterministic system. There is a kind of simulation of determinism by frozen symbolic relationships. This, in any case, is the kind of solution which I am now preparing to introduce through discussion of Habermas and Geertz. Weber always thought that he was dealing with transparent structures, whereas we know they are not transparent.

It may be that one reason Weber had to resort to ideal types is because no transparency exists. The argument then advanced is that the only way to recapture meaning is to stand outside the distorting process and proceed by the abstractions of ideal types. The supposed noninvolvement of the sociologist is said to allow him or her not to be caught in the distorting process. Even if we grant this possibility, though, Weber does not describe the distortive subject matter through which his own analysis moves. It may be true that the existence of a system of power rests on our belief, but we do not recognize that immediately. We have to break through the structure's appearance of objectivity, but Weber never really alerts us to this fact. When Weber says, for example, that a state depends on the probability that people obey its rules, this notion of probability is put forth for a particular reason: to account for the fascination of the group's member with the system of rules. To transpose the member's response into terms of probability presupposes that we have unfrozen the frozen relationships, that we have reconstrued the system of motivation as a transparent system. In contrast to someone like Habermas, the subject of the next two lectures, Weber does not indicate that this transparency occurs only at the end of a critical process. Only at the end of a process of critique do we recover as our own work what appears to be the productivity of capital, recover as our own motivating beliefs what appears to be the power of the state. Weber's conceptual framework allows us to see the gap between claim and belief, but the reasons for and the significance of this discrepancy are factors Weber himself does not attend.

Some may claim that my reading of Weber, just as my reading of Marx, does violence to his text. By doing apparent violence to Marx, though, I think that I actually succeeded in reading *The German Ideology* better. Marx does say that the class is not a given but a result of action, of interaction, a result that we do not recognize to be a consequence of our action. While orthodox Marxists may contend that my reading does violence to *The German Ideology,* my own stance is that this reading recognizes a dimension of the text. In fact, I would claim to have done more violence to Weber than to Marx. I forced Weber, I compelled him to say what he did not want to say: that it is through some ideological process that we take hold of our own motivation in relation to power. In Weber we never have the idea that something is repressed in this experience, that our communicative competence, to use Habermas' vocabulary, is lost. Weber does not see that it is because this competence is lost that we can only describe types or structures.

13

Habermas (1)

For our analysis of ideology, Habermas offers a point of transition between Weber's discussion of legitimation and Geertz's on ideology as identification. Habermas shows that the significance of the gap Weber reveals between claim and belief can only be fully understood at the end of a process of critique, and he lays the groundwork for Geertz in suggesting that ideology at bottom concerns communication and the symbolic mediation of action. In the two lectures on Habermas, I shall follow the same path as the lectures on Weber. I first build Habermas' conceptual framework, which should be placed at the same level as Weber's motivational framework, and then turn in more detail to the concept of ideology that Habermas develops on this basis. Our text is Habermas' book *Knowledge and Human Interests*.

Habermas' conceptual framework is metacritical. Metacritique, says Habermas, "subjects the critique of knowledge to unyielding self-reflection" (3). What Habermas wants to show is that metacritique is still critique to the extent that the central issue of the latter, as we learn in Kant's *Critique of Pure Reason,* is the question of the synthesis of the object. The problem is how does a subject have an object in front of him or her, or, in more Freudian terms, how do we construe the principle of reality? In Kant the synthesis is secured by the categorial network which he named the understanding; lying behind this categorial framework is the principle of unity called the transcendental ego. The transcendental ego is the principle of the synthesis of the object through categories, schematism, time, and so on. The notion of philosophy as itself a critique originated in Horkheimer, and Habermas follows his predecessors in the Frankfurt School by placing the concept of critique at the forefront of his own conceptual framework.

In the development of his own methodological perspective, Habermas wants to show how Marx fits in the tradition of a critical philosophy deriving from Kant. For Habermas, Marxism is neither an empirical science nor a speculative science but a critique.

In his attempt to read Marx against the background of critique, Habermas claims that the materialist solution to the problem of synthesis is to put labor in the place of Kant's schematism. To speak of labor or work as the bearer of synthesis admittedly does violence to Marx, but it is a creative violence. One tradition lying behind this approach to Marx is the master-slave relation in Hegel, where the role of the object is central. The master consumes the object and the slave produces it, and each recognizes the other through what the other does. Each also recognizes itself according to what the other does to it. In this exchange of positions, the master sees the meaning of its consumption in the labor of the other, and the slave sees the meaning of its work in the consumption of the master. Expressed in Kantian terms, we have the constitution of the object through work and consumption. The following passage clarifies how Habermas arrives at his notion of synthesis and the extent to which it is a reconstruction and not a mere reading of Marx:

> Marx did not arrive at an explicit concept of this synthesis. He had only a more or less vague conception of it. He would have found the very concept of synthesis suspect, although the first thesis on Feuerbach directly contains an injunction to learn from idealism insofar as it grasps the "active side" of the cognitive process. Nevertheless, from various indications we can extrapolate the way in which social labor is to be conceived as the synthesis of man and nature. We must clearly articulate this materialist concept of synthesis if we wish to understand how all the elements of a critique of knowledge radicalized by Hegel's critique of Kant are present in Marx and yet are not combined to construct a materialist epistemology. (30–31)

Based on his reconstruction of Marxism, Habermas gives a most interesting meaning to materialism. He contrasts it to the intellectual operations of idealism—the categories, schematisms, and so on—and replaces the transcendental ego as bearer of the synthesis of the object by the productivity of a working subject as materialized in his or her work.

Habermas' interpretation is post-Marxist; it apprehends both its boldness and its expansion beyond its source in Marx. Because Habermas believes he has taken a stance beyond Marx, he is able, he thinks, to proceed both to recognition of Marx's accomplishments—his greatness—

and to criticism of Marx's limits—his weaknesses. Habermas therefore has a principle for the assessment and appreciation of Marx; his effort is not a mere repetition of Marx but, we might say, a critical repetition. We shall follow Habermas as he moves through discussion of Marx's merits to discussion of Marx's limitations.

For Habermas the greatness of Marx is that he did in fact provide the solution to the problem of synthesis. In Marx, says Habermas, "The subject of world constitution is not transcendental consciousness in general but the concrete human species, which reproduces its life under natural conditions" (27). Habermas grafts his interpretation onto Marx at the point where the vocabulary is that of *The German Ideology,* the work I chose myself as the most interesting for an anthropological approach. Habermas seems to agree that the dividing line in Marx is not between *The German Ideology* and *Capital* but between *The German Ideology* and the *Manuscripts of 1844*. The synthesis, for Habermas, is not the synthesis of a consciousness but that of an activity. Praxis is the bearer of the synthesis. As the lines just cited indicate, Habermas uses the concept of the "concrete human species," which is a residue, we may remember, of Feuerbach's *Gattungswesen.* A practical humankind takes the place of the transcendental consciousness. This concept of the "concrete human species" may be taken in a phenomenological sense as the definition of materialism. Use of the term "materialism" is awkward, because we always have to defend it from misunderstanding. Habermas' definition is not a thesis about matter. Unlike in general usage, where materialism is more a provocative word, a differentiation from idealism, here it means more a realistic anthropology.

Characterization of the concrete human species as the bearer of the synthesis has several advantages. The first is that we have at the same time an anthropological category and an epistemological category. To state that labor produces the synthesis of the object is not simply to observe the economic role of human activity, it is also to understand the nature of our knowledge, the way we apprehend the world.

> That is why labor, or work, is not only a fundamental category of human existence but also an epistemological category. The system of objective activities creates the factual conditions of the possible reproduction of social life *and at the same time* the transcendental conditions of the possible objectivity of the objects of experience. (28; emphasis in original)

This conjunction between epistemological and anthropological categories is critical to the relationship we shall discuss in the following lecture between an interest and a field of experience. As we shall see, Habermas maintains that certain sciences correspond to certain interests. The interest in control and manipulation corresponds with the empirical sciences, the interest in communication with the historical and interpretive sciences, and the interest in emancipation with the critical social sciences such as psychoanalysis. To lay the groundwork for these correlations, Habermas must introduce at the outset the connection that the title of his work suggests: the connection between an anthropological concept—an interest—and an epistemological concept—a categorial system for dealing with certain fields of knowledge. This relationship between the two sets of categories originates in the notion of labor taken as a synthesis. Articulation of the correlation between the epistemological and the anthropological, between knowledge and interest, is the general problematic of our current focus of attention, the second chapter of Habermas' volume.

A second advantage of the framework Habermas develops from Marx is that discussion of synthesis provides an improved interpretation of the concept of *Lebenswelt,* of "life-world," a concept originally formulated in the last work of Husserl, *The Crisis of European Sciences.* Understanding social labor as synthesis allows us to eliminate "a transcendental-logical misunderstanding" (28); we can avoid taking the concept of "life-world" ahistorically. Habermas argues that Husserl never rid himself of a Kantian transcendental approach; even when he speaks of the *Lebenswelt* it remains an invariant, like the Kantian categories. Husserl has an anthropology, but it is expressed in the language of Kant's atemporal categories. What Marx teaches us, says Habermas, is that we must speak of humanity in historical terms. "[T]he human species is not characterized by any invariant natural or transcendental structure, but only by a mechanism of humanization *(Menschwerdung)*" (29). The *Manuscripts,* we remember, speak of nature becoming more human and of humanity becoming more natural. Humanity and nature are promoted together, and together they become both more natural and more human.

According to Habermas, this historicization of the transcendental is possible because Marx linked history to productive forces. Habermas stresses the historical nature of praxis—evident in the accumulation of tools, a technological history—and shows how Marx linked this history to the concept of productive forces. The historical dimension is introduced by productive forces; they are the bearer of history. Thus, the synthesis undertaken by labor is distinct from the fixed essence ascribed by Kant to the categories. In a sense, it is only because there is a history of industry that history exists at all. In making this claim, it appears that Habermas does not subscribe to Marx's prejudice that ideologies have no history. Understanding has a history of its own, which may be exemplified by the history of science. Industry is not the only factor that gives a historical dimension to human existence; ideas have a history also. It is difficult to deny that an anti-idealistic stand like Habermas' against Husserl leads in this direction.

A third implication of Habermas' starting point, and another objection to idealism, is that we should put the economic dimension of humanity in the place granted by Hegel to logic. If the key to synthesis is not transcendental logic, in either the Kantian or the Hegelian sense of that term, then we may say that an economics takes the place of a logic. This is an extreme claim, and one that I am not sure I would assume myself, but there is no doubt about Habermas' assertion:

> The point of departure for a reconstruction of synthetic accomplishments is not logic but the economy. Consequently what provides the material that reflection is to deal with in order to make conscious basic synthetic accomplishments is not the correct combination of symbols according to rules, but social life processes, the material production and appropriation of products. Synthesis no longer appears as an activity of thought but as one of material production. . . . That is why for Marx the critique of political economy takes the place held by the critique of formal logic in idealism. (31)

Habermas adds, a few pages later: "The synthesis of the material of labor by labor power receives its actual unity through categories of man's manipulations" (35). This reading of Marx puts him more or less within the same category as Peirce and Dewey. In a later chapter Marx appears as a forerunner of an enlightened pragmatism. I know that American philosophers will be pleased with that!

A fourth advantage of treating labor as the synthesis of the object is that it extends an important analysis begun by Fichte. In the tradition of German idealism, Fichte is the other figure besides Kant who is an ancestor to Marx's elaboration of the problem of synthesis, and Habermas returns to Fichte throughout his book. Fichte is the one who made the decisive step from a philosophy of theory to a theory of praxis, because his fundamental concept is the self-positing activity of human being. Fichte connected the synthesis in imagination to the active subject. The fundamental ego in Fichtean thought is the active subject. The ego that must be able to accompany all my representations—to use the Kantian language—is not an ultimate representation, it is not a representation of a higher order but *die Tathandlung,* an action, the self-positing ego. As we may remember, there are many texts in *The German Ideology* where the concept of self-activity, *Selbstbetätigung,* is central. Habermas is right to trace back this concept of *Selbstbetätigung* to Fichte's notion that humanity posits itself by the process of praxis and the intercourse with nature. The mutual generation of human being and nature is at the same time a *self*-generation of human being.

> The identity of consciousness, which Kant understood as the unity of transcendental consciousness, is identity *achieved through labor.* It is not an immediate faculty of synthesis, or pure apperception, but an act of self-consciousness in Fichte's sense. That is why a social subject attains consciousness of itself in the strict sense only if it becomes aware of itself in its production or labor as the self-generative act of the species in general and knows itself to have been produced by the "labor of the entire previous course of world history." (40; emphasis in original; no reference cited to quotation)

Thus we have Habermas' recognition, in Kantian and Fichtean terms, of Marx's merits. The concept of labor as synthesis takes the place of a synthesis through Kantian understanding or a synthesis through Fichtean self-apperception of the ego.

The same interpretation which retrieves Marx's merits, though, also starts the critique. Habermas' objection, to which he continually returns, is that Marx reduced the concept of activity to production. The scope of the concept was collapsed. While Marx solved the problem of synthesis by labor, he reduced the compass of his discovery by identifying work merely with instrumental action. The concept of instrumental action is the permanent point of reference in Habermas' discussion; the critique is that Marx's analysis is not a good tool for resisting the reduction Marcuse has described as the "one-dimensional" character of human being. An element of one-dimensionality is already present in the concept of instrumental action, and this infects Marx's analysis as a whole. Just like bourgeois ideology, Marxist ideology also leads to a technological reduction.

If we admit this critique of Marx, if we acknowledge the flattening of the Fichtean concept of production to economic or technological production, this has dreadful consequences for Marx's theory itself, because it cannot then legitimate its own critical function. If human beings only synthesize reality by labor, and no critical distance from this labor is available, then we cannot give an account of Marx's own work in terms of his categories. We have a theory which cannot make sense of its own achievement. What is lacking is the self-reflective element abolished by the reduction of the self-generative capacity of human action to mere instrumental action. "[T]he philosophical foundation of this materialism proves itself insufficient to establish an unconditional phenomenological self-reflection of knowledge and thus prevent the positivist atrophy of epistemology" (42).

In a certain sense, then, Habermas' stance here is anti-Marxist, and yet his attempt is to find support for his objection in Marx himself. This is the most interesting part of Habermas' discussion at this point, an effort to show that there exist within Marx himself hints of the duality within the concept of the self-generation and self-production of human being. The basis for Habermas' analysis is the important distinction that we spoke of several times in our own discussion of Marx, the difference between forces of production *(Produktivkräften)* and relations of production *(Produktionsverhältnisse)*. Habermas' principal argument is that while this distinction is denied by Marx's theory, it is recognized in all his concrete inquiries. Therefore, he contends, we must look at what Marx actually does and not at what he says that he does. The theory that Marx elaborates concerning his work is narrower than what is implied by his concrete work itself.

What does it mean to say that production has two sides, forces and relationships? By relations of production, we must understand the institutional framework of labor, the fact that labor exists within a system of free enterprise or within a state-run enterprise and so on. The relations of production are constituted by the institutional system within which we shall find precisely the kind of symbolic mediations that Geertz will discuss. An institutional framework is not only the legal rules, the juridical framework, but what Habermas calls the structure of symbolic interaction and the cultural tradition through which a people apprehends its own work. If we look, for example, at the present state of socialism in eastern Europe, the Soviet Union, and China, the traditions of the people in each setting influence the content of the socialism developed. The structure of symbolic interaction and the cultural tradition are components of the institutional framework. We must take the word "institutional" in a broader sense than a merely juridical or legal concept.

Alongside the forces of production in which instrumental action is sedimented, Marx's social theory also incorporates into its approach the institutional framework, the relations of production. It does not eliminate from practice the structure of symbolic interaction and the role of cultural tradition, which are the only basis on which power *(Herrschaft)* and ideology can be comprehended. (42)

Habermas' statement here is central to our inquiry, because only within a conceptual framework that distinguishes between relations and forces may we speak of ideology. Ideology intervenes only at the level of the relations of production, not the forces of production.

If we want a Marxist theory of ideology, therefore, we must first make sense of the distinction between relations and forces. This means that we need a concept of praxis. In the vocabulary of Habermas, praxis includes both instrumental action and the structure of symbolic interaction. Ideology will appear as a distortion affecting one of the components of praxis. For Habermas, the concept of praxis is an attempt to recover the density of the Fichtean concept of action *(Tathandlung)* within a Marxist vocabulary. Labor is the source of synthesis, but human labor is always more than instrumental action because we cannot work without bringing in our traditions and our symbolic interpretation of the world. Our work also includes the institutional framework of society, because our work is defined by contracts and other stipulations. When we work, we work within a system of conventions. We cannot define praxis only in terms of the labor techniques that we apply. Our praxis itself incorporates a certain institutional framework. Once again we see that the distinction between superstructure and infrastructure is not appropriate, because we include something of the so-called superstructure within the concept of praxis. We have then a complete reshaping of the vocabulary ordinarily used to describe praxis. We can no longer say that people first have a praxis and then have some ideas about this praxis, which is their ideology. Instead, we see that praxis incorporates an ideological layer; this layer may become distorted, but it is a component of praxis itself.

According to Habermas, recognition of this duality in the constitution of praxis is what Marx presupposes in his own practice of inquiry but excludes from his theoretical frame of reference. We must therefore follow the practice of Marx's inquiry and not the reductive framework of his philosophical self-understanding. Marx's practice implies that the history of humankind is comprehended "under categories of material activity and the critical abolition of ideologies. . . ." The critical abolition of ideologies is included in the process of action. Habermas expresses this relation in several different ways, but they all rely on this dual functioning of the concept of praxis:

> Thus in Marx's works a peculiar disproportion arises between the practice of inquiry and the limited philosophical self-understanding of this inquiry. In his empirical analyses Marx comprehends the history of the species under categories of material activity *and* the critical abolition of ideologies, of instrumental action *and* revolutionary practice, of labor *and* reflection at once. But Marx interprets what he does in the more restricted conception of the species' self-reflection through work alone. The materialist concept of synthesis is not conceived broadly enough in order to explicate the way in which Marx contributes to realizing the intention of a really radicalized critique of knowledge. In fact, it even prevented Marx from understanding his own mode of procedure from this point of view. (42; emphases in original)

My own response here is to ask whether we can preserve what was said earlier about the synthesis as labor if we substitute for the concept of labor that of praxis, which implies both labor and something else. Between labor, praxis, and also action there is a certain vacillation, which I find a recurring problem in Habermas. These concepts overlap. Sometimes labor is the all-encompassing concept which does the synthesis, and it is then equal to praxis; at other times, though, labor is identified with instrumental action. It is not easy to locate the concept of labor.

Habermas properly relocates this problem by redefining the distinction between labor and praxis as one between instrumental action and interaction or communicative action. In the third chapter of *Knowledge and Human Interests,* to which we now turn, Habermas draws the epistemological implications of this division. Habermas' question is what is the status of a science about praxis? Marx never discussed systematically "the specific meaning of a science of man elaborated as a critique of ideology and distinct from the instrumentalist meaning of natural science" (45). What Marx did was critique and not natural science, but he offered no epistemological justification for this social theory. Instead, he continually described his work analogously to the natural sciences. The fact that Marx's work was a critique of political economy should have directed his attention to the reflective component of this critique, but it did not. Habermas argues therefore that to the extent we reduce praxis to material production, to instrumental action, then the model is that of the natural sciences. We simply treat the science of praxis as an extension of the natural sciences. On the other hand, if we elaborate the dialectics between the instrumental and interactive poles of praxis, then we have a science which is not an extension or a transposition of natural sciences but a different kind of science, and this is critique. The status of a social science as a critique is linked to the critical dimension available in the symbolic system of interaction, the possibility of taking distance from and reacting back on the level of instrumental action. The epistemological discussion of the third chapter must be linked to the anthropological topic of the preceding chapter.

What characterizes a natural science, says Habermas, is that it can be unreflective. It can be unreflective because it deals with objects distinct from the knower, the scientist. As a result, the scientist is not implied in his or her science. We need not discuss whether Habermas' characterization here is necessarily correct. We may accept for the purpose of discussion that the natural sciences may be unreflective; the important point is that the social sciences surely are reflective. This is the positive part of Habermas' argument, which does not necessarily imply its counterpart. When the social sciences are viewed erroneously as analogous to the natural sciences, then the control of productive forces is itself understood under the category of what Habermas calls "knowledge for control" (47). In German the term is *Verfügungswissen,* which relates to having something at one's disposal. Behind the term there seems to be the Heideggerian notion of having something at hand. When the model of the natural sciences rules, says Habermas, reflective knowledge *(Reflexionswissen)* is swallowed up within *Verfügungswissen,* this knowledge for control. The power of technical control encompasses everything.

> According to this construction the history of transcendental consciousness would be no more than the residue of the history of technology. The latter is left exclusively to the cumulative evolution of feedback-controlled action and follows the tendency to augment the productivity of labor and to replace human labor power—"the realization of this tendency is the transformation of the means of labor into machinery." (48)

The quotation is taken from Marx's *Grundrisse;* it is therefore a comment not by the early Marx but by the mature Marx.

The assumption that all science is patterned on natural science reduces the Fichtean notion of human self-activity into an industrialist mentality. For Habermas this reduction is the modern ideology. Ideology proceeds from the reduction of action to labor, of labor to instrumental action, and instrumental action to the technology which swallows our work. The science investigating human being becomes nothing more than a province of the natural sciences. For Habermas, something is repressed in this interpretation. The industrialist reading of human activity conceals "the dimension of self-reflection in which it must move regardless" (50). Even for Marx in the *Grundrisse,* says Habermas, "the transformation of science into machinery does not by any means lead of itself to the liberation of a self-conscious general subject that masters the process of production" (51). Something more is needed than mere instrumental action: the power relations that regulate human beings' interactions among themselves. "Marx very precisely distinguishes the *self-conscious control* of the social life process by the combined producers from an *automatic regulation* of the process of production that has become independent of these individuals" (51; emphases in original). This "self-conscious control of the social life process" is what Habermas calls the system of interaction.

Habermas' distinction between a theory of interaction and a theory of instrumental action is his response to the tension in Marx between the technical and the practical. We must understand by the practical not simply the matter-of-fact but all the dimensions of action ruled by norms and ideals; it covers the whole field of ethics and applied ethics. The practical includes all areas of action that have a symbolic structure, a structure that both interprets and regulates action. The technical and the practical represent a twofold division in the field of human action. For our inquiry into ideology this differentiation is fundamental, because ideology affects the individual's action at the basic stage of its organization.

> At the level of his material investigations . . . Marx always takes account of social practice that encompasses both work and interaction. The processes of natural history are mediated by the productive activity of individuals and the organization of their interrelations. These relations are subject to norms that decide, with the force of institutions, how responsibilities and rewards, obligations and charges to the social budget are distributed among members. The medium in which these relations of subjects and of groups are normatively regulated is cultural tradition. It forms the linguistic communication structure on the basis of which subjects interpret both nature and themselves in their environment. (53)

The reference to cultural tradition, norms, institutions, the linguistic structure of communication, and interpretation confirms our hypothesis that distortive processes make sense only if action is conceived as symbolically mediated. The concept of interpretation belongs to this primitive layer and represents the activity individuals undertake with respect both to nature and to themselves in their environment.

Without the distinction between instrumental and communicative action, there is no room for critique and even no room for ideology itself. It is only within an institutional framework that social dependency and political power may display their repressive effects. Also only within this framework does "communication free from domination" (53) make sense. (We shall return to the utopian overtones of this phrase later.) The "self-generative act of the species" (53) must therefore encompass both productive activity (labor) and revolutionary activity. Emancipation is twofold: from natural constraints and from human oppression. The development of new technologies and of ideological struggle is "interdependent" (55). (As the vocabulary itself suggests, ideological delusion and its critique both belong to the same sphere of self-reflection, which must be as primitive as productive action itself. Again this implies that we must give up the distinction between infrastructure and superstructure.) Marx was unable to elaborate this dialectic between the two developments because the distinction between forces and relations of production remained submitted to the categorical framework of production. Habermas, on the other hand, claims that the "self-constitution of the human species in natural history" must combine both "self-generation through productive activity and self-formation through critical-revolutionary activity" (55).

In some ways Habermas' distinction between the practical and the technical seems to be based more in Hegel than in Marx. Habermas relies on an early phase of Hegel's reflection, the lectures at Jena, the *Jenenser Realphilosophie* (56). (Habermas discusses these lectures in more detail in his essay on "Labor and Interaction" in *Theory and Practice.*) Hegel's Jena philosophy was self-sufficient and was not completely absorbed into his *Phenomenology of the Spirit.* In these early writings Hegel elaborates for the first time the problem of recognition, which is the main moral issue. We may remark that traces of this discussion do reappear at various points in the *Phenomenology of the Spirit;* what is at stake in the master-slave relation, for example, is a struggle not for power but for recognition. Habermas discovers within this framework of recognition a model for the relation between subjects. It is important for Habermas, therefore, that the problem finally is not to suppress our enemy but to come to an agreement which is beyond our differences. As we shall see, Habermas finds the model of the psychoanalytical situation most relevant on this topic. For Habermas the class struggle is not a problem of suppressing one class but of overcoming struggle so that there may be a state where recognition between human beings occurs. To be sure, institutions like capitalism have to be crushed in order for this possibility to be actualized. The important point, though, is that it is not individuals who have to be suppressed but a certain structure.

Another place in the *Phenomenology of the Spirit* where this problem of recognition returns, one closer to the Jena philosophy, is in the recognition between the culprit and the judge. The judge must both judge and recognize the culprit and must also be judged by the culprit in order to be recognized himself or herself. There is an exchange of places between the judging consciousness and the guilty consciousness. As the Jena philosophy discusses more fully, the framework of recognition between the criminal and the judge indicates that the estrangement of each party has been overcome. The judge has been as much estranged as the culprit. Between the judged and the judging there is a situation of mutual excommunication, and recognition is the victory over this situation of estrangement. The master-slave, the judge-culprit, and so on constitute a framework of struggle; the issue is not supremacy, which would remain bound to the same structure of power, but recognition. We shall return to this emphasis on recognition instead of power when we discuss the problem of whether a utopia rules the critique of ideology.

This framework of recognition is important for Habermas because it situates his theory of interaction as a "dialogic relation" (56). The situation of excommunication, which recognition must overcome, is a disease of communication. Ideology is therefore itself a disease of communication. Ideology is not the accidental but the systematic distortion of the dialogic relation. We cannot speak of the dialogic relation except through the process of recognition, and ideology is the system of resistances to the restoration of the dialogic relation. Only with this frame of reference can we understand such otherwise strange if striking statements as the following: "Unlike synthesis through social labor, the dialectic of class antagonism is a movement of reflection" (58). This does not sound very Marxist. If we interpret reflection on the basis of recognition, however, then we may say that finally the class struggle is a problem of recognition between the members of the society.

> Thus it is not unconstrained intersubjectivity itself that we call dialectic, but the history of its repression and re-establishment. The distortion of the dialogic relation is subject to the causality of split-off symbols and reified grammatical relations: that is, relations that are removed from public communication, prevail only behind the backs of subjects, and are thus also empirically coercive. (59)

The word "ideology" is not uttered, but this statement is in fact a definition of ideology.

When Habermas says here that "the dialogic relation is subject to the causality of split-off symbols," he purposely introduces the notion of causality. As Habermas' recourse to the Freudian model will further illuminate, we must speak in terms of causality even within a situation of motivation, because when the motives have been frozen they look like things. We must apply a causal model within an interpretive model. Causal relationships are fragments of explanation within a process of interpretation. Arguing a position similar, if for different reasons, to my own writings on the theory of the text, Habermas denies the opposition between interpretation and explanation. In reified relationships we must treat motives as causes. An example of this is Habermas' notion of the "causality of fate" (56), another borrowing from Hegel. Fate is something which happens to freedom, but it simulates the regularity of nature. In the state of reification, human reality simulates natural reality, and this is why we must speak of causality.

We may amplify that the reified situation still exists within a motivational framework by noting that motivation does not require consciousness. Meaning and consciousness are separable; something may be meaningful without being recognized. Reference to the interpretation of Freud is pertinent, because we must fight against a mechanistic interpretation of the so-called unconscious. In a mechanistic framework, the unconscious is a place where there are forces. The impossible task is then to show how a force has meaning if it is not already meaningful at the unconscious level. As I claimed in my book on *Freud and Philosophy,* we should say instead that the topographical representation of the unconscious has a certain phenomenological value because it expresses the fact that we are no longer the author. The system of repression implies that our motivation appears to be like a thing.

The topography of the unconscious in Freud has its counterpart in the Marxist concept of infrastructure. The concept of infrastructure is not inapposite if we are not deceived by it and think we can analyze it only as an object of the natural sciences. In fact, the infrastructure belongs to the field of the human sciences but under the condition of alienation which transforms motivations into things. This implies that we have to deal with concepts which have a kind of physical appearance, and in a sense this is the case. Some Marxists say that materialism is the truth of a society which has lost the sense of its creativity, a society which has become buried under its own products. Materialism is then not a philosophical truth but a truth proper to the historical situation. Similarly, we can say that the language of superstructure and infrastructure is the appropriate language for speaking of a system of motivations which have been reified. Borrowing from the German theorist on Freud Alfred Lorenzer, Habermas speaks of a desymbolized process which has to be resymbolized (256 f.). In his attempt to link Marx and Freud, Habermas argues that the notion of alienation in Marx has its correlative concept in desymbolization, and he follows Lorenzer in affirming that psychoanalysis is the process by which we go from desymbolization toward resymbolization through the intermediate stage of transference. As we shall see, Habermas maintains that critical social science parallels psychoanalysis in this regard and is itself a process incorporating explanation within a larger interpretive model.

At the end of the third chapter of *Knowledge and Human Interests,* Habermas again claims that his differentiation between instrumental and communicative action is supported not simply by Hegel but by the inquiry of Marx himself. Habermas looks for this support in Marx's famous text in *Capital* on the fetishism of commodities. Here Marx uses the Feuerbachian model of inversion not as a form of explanation but as a metaphor. Just as religion transformed human activity into the power of the divine, so capitalism has reified human labor in the form of the commodity. Those fascinated by the reifications of our work are in exactly the same situation as those who project our freedom onto a supernatural being and then worship it. There is a relation of worship in both, and this is a strong argument against Althusser, because worship should have no place after the so-called epistemological break. Habermas quotes Marx: " 'Here it is only the specific social relation of men themselves that assumes for them the phantasmagoric form of a relation of things' " (60). A human relation " 'assumes . . . the phantasmagoric form of a relation of things.' "

Marx's text on the fetishism of commodities is crucial for a theory of ideology, because it shows that in bourgeois society ideology does not function merely or even mainly as a social form which institutionalizes political domination. Instead, its most important function is to stabilize class antagonism through the legal institution of the free labor contract. By concealing productive activity in a commodity form, ideology operates at the level of the market. For my own part, I draw the conclusion that in the capitalistic era the major ideology is no longer a religious ideology but precisely a market ideology. To speak like Bacon, we may say that ideology now takes the form of a market idol. Habermas himself comments:

Thus, according to Marx, the distinguishing feature of capitalism is that it has brought ideologies from the heights of mythological or religious legitimations of

> tangible domination and power down into the system of social labor. In liberal bourgeois society the legitimation of power is derived from the legitimation of the market, that is from the "justice" of the exchange of equivalents inherent in exchange relations. It is unmasked by the critique of commodity fetishism. (60)

There is an emigration of ideology from the religious sphere to the economic sphere.

Moving beyond Habermas to my own interpretation here, may we not say that because religion is now less involved in the production of ideologies—since the fetishism of commodities can work by itself—then perhaps a utopian use of religion may be part of the critique of ideology. Religion may act not only as an ideology but as a critical tool to the extent that ideology has emigrated from the religious sphere to the marketplace and to science and technology. If the market and science and technology are the modern ideologies, then the present ideological role of religion may be less a burning issue. Religion still has an ideological role but this function has been superseded by the ideological role of the market and technology. We may then place religion in a dialectical position between ideology and utopia. Religion functions as an ideology when it justifies the existing system of power, but it also functions as a utopia to the extent that it is a motivation nourishing the critique. Religion may help to unmask the idol of the market.[1]

In any event, the main interest of the second and third chapters of *Knowledge and Human Interests* is to place the concept of class struggle within the framework of communicative action and so not limit it to the system of production. For Habermas the concept of class struggle is homogeneous not with the concept of production but with the institutional framework within which productive forces work. It is therefore part of the process of self-consciousness. To be aware of the situation of class struggle is to be raised to a new dimension of consciousness, class consciousness. This process makes sense, however, only to the extent that it is already the beginning of a critique and of a movement toward recognition. Class struggle is part of the movement from alienation to recognition within the symbolization process; it is a moment of desymbolization. Class struggle is then a process distinct from mere social labor because it confronts subjectivities; one way that we identify ourselves as subjects is by our class identification. We now understand that the critique of ideology, to which the next lecture turns, is itself part of the communicative process; it is the critical moment within this process.

14

Habermas (2)

In this lecture I shall discuss Habermas' theory of ideology, which is presented in terms of a critique, a critique of ideology. I shall focus mainly on the parallelism claimed between psychoanalysis and the critique of ideology, since Habermas bases his theory of ideology on the transfer of some psychoanalytic insights into the field of the critical social sciences.

Before turning to this discussion, however, we need to situate the character of psychoanalysis and ideology-critique as critical social sciences. In establishing the distinctiveness of critical social sciences, Habermas moves from a twofold division between instrumental and practical sciences to a threefold division between instrumental, historical-hermeneutic, and critical social sciences. This change in Habermas' framework is set out in the appendix to *Knowledge and Human Interests.* The appendix does not belong to the German edition of *Knowledge and Human Interests;* it was added to the English translation. This essay is the inaugural address Habermas delivered upon assuming his chair at Frankfurt in 1965, a chair he left only a few years later after receiving condemnation for his support of German student protests in the late 1960s. The appendix is addressed not to Marx but rather to the tradition of phenomenology in Husserl and its offshoot, the hermeneutics of Gadamer. While never named, Gadamer is clearly the major person the address is directed against. Habermas' threefold division of both knowledge-constitutive interests and their corresponding sciences is central to his response to Gadamer, who maintains a twofold division. A second reason for Habermas' formulation may be that this division comes from his friend and colleague Karl-Otto Apel. Apel is a much more systematic thinker, even an architectonic thinker. Apel is interested more in epistemology, whereas Habermas' focus is the sociology of knowledge. When Habermas shifts from a sociology of knowledge to an epistemology, the discrepancy in framework may therefore be the change from his own portrayal of the former's duality between the instrumental and the practical to acceptance of Apel's tripartite characterization of the latter.

I shall not examine in any detail the first four sections of the appendix, because the critique of Husserl presented there is not very good. The sections are directed against the theoretical claims of philosophy, but it is a weak argument to oppose praxis to theory and to say that everything is theory which is not post-Marxist thought. Husserl is accused of committing the Platonic sin, because he remains under the spell of theory. Positivism is also treated as an heir of this theoretical illusion, and as a result the fight between Husserl and positivism becomes meaningless. I question even more whether this opposition between praxis and theory does not weaken Habermas' own position, because how can there be a critical position that does not participate in the theoretical trend of philosophy? The critical moment within praxis is surely a theoretical moment; the capacity for distanciation is always a part of theory.

The interesting part of the appendix is the fifth section, and I shall restrict myself to that because it gives us a good summary of Habermas' project here as a whole. There are two main ideas. The first is that an interest, which is an anthropological concept, is at the same time a transcendental concept in the Kantian sense of the word. A transcendental concept is the condition of possibility of a certain type of experience. Each interest then rules a certain domain of experience and provides this domain with its major categories. We have already discussed this in considering labor as a synthesis; in acting as a synthesis, labor is both an anthropological and an epistemological concept. The concept offers a principle of classification, and it also provides the major rules of a given science. A type of science corresponds to an interest because an interest supplies the expectations for what can be accepted, identified, and recognized in a given field.

Habermas' second idea delimits this relationship by suggesting that there are three interests which rule three type of sciences. The first interest is one we have already discussed, the instrumental. An equivalence is drawn between the technical-instrumental, which rules the domain of the empirical sciences, and what can be put under control by empirical knowledge. "This is the cognitive interest in technical control over objectified processes" (309). Habermas owes more than he claims to Husserl's critique in

The Crisis of European Sciences, since Husserl there tried to show that we have natural sciences because we have objectified and expressed in mathematical law the domain of nature within which we live. What is post-Marxist is Habermas' identification of objectification with the notion of control and manipulation. As we have briefly noted before, for Habermas the modern ideology may be defined as the reduction of all other interests to this interest. This is the Marcusean component of Habermas, an argument that the hierarchies of interests and sciences have been flattened to one dimension only. When a cognitive interest supersedes and rules a communicative interest, there arises the situation of modern ideology in which science and technology function ideologically, because they justify the reduction of human being to this one-dimensional figure.

The second interest is called a historical-hermeneutic interest, and it too has methodological implications. What is striking here is that this interest is defined in Gadamerian terms.

> Access to the facts is provided by the understanding of meaning, not observation. The verification of lawlike hypotheses in the empirical-analytic sciences has its counterpart here in the interpretation of texts. Thus the rules of hermeneutics determine the possible meaning of the validity of statements of the cultural sciences. (309)

Each interest is transcendental, that is, a space for a particular kind of validation. We do not validate all statements in the same way; the kind of validation we resort to depends on the nature of our interest. We do not want to verify or falsify historical propositions; instead, we validate them by their capacity to enlarge our communication. As Habermas puts it in some more recent essays, historical-hermeneutic validation centers on the possibility of building a narrative of our own life. One way Habermas attempts to interpret psychoanalysis is in terms of its ability to construct a consistent narrative. The notion of a text is then decisive, and the rule of hermeneutics concern this text.

The third kind of interest, that found in the critical social sciences, is not hermeneutic. Pursuit of Habermas' argument about the distinctiveness of the critical social sciences will orient our examination of his portrayal of psychoanalysis, which Habermas finds the prototypical example of this science. The appendix lays the groundwork for and provides the transition to this discussion. Habermas distinguishes between systematic and critical social sciences; not all social sciences are critical. "The systematic sciences of social action, that is economics, sociology, and political science, have the goal, as do the empirical-analytic sciences, of producing nomological knowledge" (310). Nomological knowledge means that individual cases are put under more general regulative laws; explanation takes the form, as Hempel expresses it, of a covering law. (It seems that any social science that is not critical belongs to the first, instrumental kind of interest, and this is one reason why Habermas' division is not so satisfying.) A critical social science, on the other hand, is not content with producing nomological knowledge. "It is concerned with going beyond this goal to determine when theoretical statements grasp invariant regularities of social action as such and when they express ideologically frozen relations of dependence that can in principle be transformed" (310). The task of the critical social sciences is therefore to draw a line between cases where theoretical statements grasp the real human situation and cases where the laws developed describe in actuality the situation of reification. As we may remember, this is an argument Marx used at the beginning of the *Manuscripts* against the British political economists, claiming that they correctly described the character of capitalism but did not see that its underlying principle was alienation. What they took as a regularity was in fact the disguise of a situation of alienation. According to Habermas, then, the more standard social sciences are unable to differentiate between what is really human in what they describe and what is already reified and so has the appearance of a fact. The factuality of the social sciences is ambiguous because it includes two elements which are not distinguished: that which belongs to the fundamental possibilities of communciation, symbolization, institutionalization, and so on, and that which is already reified and appears as a thing. The critique of ideology takes on a central role, because its function is to distinguish between these two kinds of social facts.

The final point about the third kind of interest, says Habermas, is that to the extent that it makes a distinction between the two kinds of facts, "the critique of ideology, as well, moreover, as psychoanalysis, take into account that information about lawlike connections sets off a process of reflection in the consciousness of those whom the laws are about" (310). The critique is a process of understanding that advances by means of a detour through a process of scientific explanation. This detour encompasses explanation not only of what has been repressed but of the system of repression, explanation not only of distorted content but of the system of distortion. It is because of this emphasis on systemic analysis, Habermas claims, that critical social science cannot be regarded as an extension of hermeneutics. According to Habermas, hermeneutics tries to extend the spontaneous capacity of communication without having to dismantle a system of distortion. Its concern is only local mistakes, misunderstanding, not the distortion of understanding. The model for hermeneutics is biography and philology. In biography we understand the continuity of a life on the basis of both its self-understanding and the direct understanding of others and not by digging under appearances. In philology we rely on the universal capacity of understanding based on the similarity between minds. The critical social sciences are distinctive because they allow us to make the detour required to explain the principle of distortion, a detour necessary so that we may recapture for understanding and self-understanding what in fact has been distorted.

I do not want to press too far, however, this opposition between hermeneutics and critique. I take this position for two reasons. First, I cannot conceive of a hermeneutics without a critical stage itself. This critical stage is exemplified in the development out of philology of modern structuralism and other objective approaches. Second, the critical sciences are themselves hermeneutical, in the sense that besides tending to enlarge communication they presuppose that the distortions of which they speak are not natural events but processes of desymbolization. The distortions belong to the sphere of communicative action. I try to minimize the discrepancy between a twofold and threefold division of the sciences, then, by saying that a division *within* the practical introduces the distinction between hermeneutic and critical social sciences. As the argument developed in the last lecture maintains, the element of critique is itself the key to the process of reestablishing communication; excommunication and the reestablishment of communciation therefore belong to the practical. I do not agree with the threefold division, which tends to identify the practical with the third kind of science and isolates the second as a distinct sphere. I am therefore more and more inclined to take the conflict between Habermas and Gadamer as a secondary one. There is, of course, the difference of their generations and also of their political stands. For Habermas, Gadamer is an old gentleman who must vote on the right, and so hermeneutics represents the conservation of the past in a kind of museum. Gadamer, on the other hand, sees Habermas as the radical who made concessions to the students and was punished for it. I no longer find interesting this opposition between the two figures, because I do not see how we can have a critique without also having an experience of communication. And this experience is provided by the understanding of texts. We learn to communicate by understanding texts. Hermeneutics without a project of liberation is blind, but a project of emancipation without historical experience is empty.

In order to recover a conceptual framework of two stages and not three, I turn back from the appendix of *Knowledge and Human Interests* to the main part of the text. Recognition of Habermas' tripartite analysis helps us to understand why he depicts psychoanalysis and the critique of ideology as critical social sciences, but the two-part conceptual framework allows us to comprehend more adequately the topic to which we now turn, the transfer of concepts from psychoanalysis to the critique of ideology. This topic is Habermas' most interesting contribution. For this part of our discussion, I rely mainly on chapters ten through twelve of Habermas' text, and I shall raise two questions. The first asks what is paradigmatic for the critique of ideology in psychoanalysis. At issue is the nature of psychoanalysis as a model. The second question concerns the adequacy of this model; we must consider whether there are any significant differences between the psychoanalytic situation and the position of critique in the social sciences. In concluding the lecture, I shall link this second issue to one of the main questions that generates my reading of Habermas: is it not on the basis of a utopia that we can do critique?

To anticipate this conclusion, I might note that there is little in Habermas concerning the question of the differences between psychoanalysis and critique, because he is more interested in finding a certain support in psychoanalysis than in identifying divergences. It may be that the principal difference has precisely to do with the absence in critique of something comparable to the experience of communication in the transference situation. The absence of transference in social critique makes more obvious the utopian status of its claim to cure the diseases of communication. The psychoanalyst does not need to be utopian, because he or she has the experience, even if a limited one, of the successful reestablishment of communication. The sociologist, on the other hand, does not have this experience, since he or she remains at the level of the class struggle, and so without this miniature of recognition that is the situation of the psychoanalyst.

The fundamental thesis of chapters ten through twelve is that psychoanalysis is distinctive because it incorporates a phase of explanation in a process that is fundamentally self-reflective. Psychoanalysis is self-reflection mediated by an explanatory phase. Explanation is not an alternative to understanding but a segment of the process as a whole. In exploring the nature of the psychoanalytic model, Habermas proceeds in three steps. The first examines the paradoxical structure of psychoanalysis, paradoxical because it encompasses both understanding and explanation. This paradoxical structure explains why there are so many misunderstandings of psychoanalysis, misunderstandings which are not entirely unfounded. Freud and his followers did not themselves maintain the relation between understanding and explanation but instead attempted to reduce the process to an explanatory, even merely causal, framework of thought. In the eleventh chapter Habermas calls this an "energy-distribution model" (247). Habermas, though, insists that the paradoxical structure of psychoanalysis must be upheld, because psychoanalysis deals with both linguistic analysis and causal connection. Freud's genius is that he preserved the balance between these two factors, even though he did not maintain this balance in his metapsychology. The paradoxical structure of psychoanalysis is a consequence of the psychoanalytic situation itself, since it involves not only a distorted text but a systematically distorted text. We must insist that the distortions are systematic. Philology, in comparison, is an instance of mere linguistic analysis. It examines distortions—mutilated texts, errors in copying a text, and so on—and requires us to establish the text through the critique, but it does not encompass systematic distortions. We must not only interpret what is distorted; we must explain the distortions themselves. Thus we have the conjunction of "linguistic analysis with the psychological investigation of causal connections" (217). This conjunction is also the fundamental reason for the epistemological ambiguity of psychoanalysis.

> Psychoanalytic interpretation is concerned with those connections of symbols in which a subject deceives itself about itself. The *depth hermeneutics* that Freud contraposes to Dilthey's philological hermeneutics deals with texts indicating *self-deceptions of the author.* Beside the manifest content . . . , such texts document the latent content of a portion of the author's orientations that has become inaccessible to him and alienated from him and yet belongs to him nevertheless. Freud coins the phrase "internal foreign territory" to capture the character of the alienation of something that is still the subject's very own. (218; emphases in original; quoting *New Introductory Lectures on Psychoanalysis*)

Because the latent content is inaccessible to the author, a detour through an explanatory method is required. Note also in this passage that Habermas calls Freud's method "depth hermeneutics." Again this reinforces that a dividing line between hermeneutics and critical science cannot be maintained.

A good example of the duality of language in psychoanalysis may be found in analysis of the dream. On the one hand, a certain linguistic analysis is required. The dream needs hermeneutic decoding, it is a text to decipher. Here the language of the method is philological. On the other hand, however, the need to explain the distortion of the dream calls for a theory of dream work and a technique addressed to the resistances opposed to interpretation. Here the language is quasi-physical. All the terms in the sixth chapter of Freud's *The Interpretation of Dreams* involve mechanisms of distortion: condensation, displacement, representability, and secondary revision. This vocabulary of censorship and repression belongs to an energetics and not to a hermeneutics. Yet this does not prevent us from saying that the distorted meaning is still a question of communication. The dreamer is excommunicated from the linguistic community, but excommunication is a distortion of communication. Habermas has several phrases that circle this paradox. To excommunicate is to "exclude from public communication." Relations are "delinguisticized"; language is "privatized." We have "the degrammaticized language of the dream" (224). Present is the Wittgensteinian notion of language games; the excommunication of the dream is a disease in the language games that make up communication.

> The object domain of depth hermeneutics comprises all the places where, owing to internal disturbances, the text[s] of our everyday language games are interrupted by incomprehensible symbols. These symbols cannot be understood because they do not obey the grammatical rules of ordinary language, norms of action, and culturally learned patterns of expression. (226)

"Because the symbols that interpret suppressed needs are excluded from public communication, the speaking and acting subject's communication with himself is interrupted" (227). The first point about the psychoanalytic model, then, is that it treats symptoms, dreams, and all pathological or quasi-pathological phenomena as cases of excommunication based on systematic distortion, and these systematic distortions all require explanation in order to be dissolved.

Habermas' second point is that in psychoanalysis the analytic situation is paradigmatic. This theme will be central to our discussion of the relationship between psychoanalysis and the critique of ideology. For Habermas, the most interesting philosophic contribution of Freud is his papers on analytic technique, that is, his papers on the situation of transference. Here an artificial circumstance of communication is created in which the basic situation of excommunication is transposed and dealt with. Habermas' claim is that we must construe a metapsychology upon the paradigm supplied by these papers on technique and not the reverse. In his metapsychology Freud elaborated two different models, first the topological model for the mental apparatus—the unconscious, preconscious, and conscious—and second the model of superego, ego, and id. Habermas argues that these models are diagrammatic representations of something which happens in the situation of transference. Therefore, the analytic technique must rule the metapsychological model and not the contrary. Unfortunately, says Habermas, the stance that evolved in both Freud and the Freudian school was to start from the model and to interpret what happens in the analytical situation according to this model; Freud and his followers forgot that the model was in fact derived from the analytical experience.

Habermas' assessment of Freud here has an interesting parallelism with his approach to Marx. As we have seen, Habermas argues that what Marx's inquiry actually does is more important than what Marx says that it does. Marx's inquiry maintains the distinction between relations of production and forces of production, even while this dialectic is abolished in a unidimensional model involving only the structures of production. In order to rescue Marx we have to rescue Freud, for Freud's insights into the situation of transference help to revitalize understanding of the import of the relations of production. In a sense our task is the same in both Marx and Freud: we must appeal to their real, concrete contribution to technical inquiry and must plead on the basis of these inquiries' real indications against Marx's and Freud's explanatory models. Their actual inquiries must rule their models and not the reverse.

Before saying something about the transcription of Freud's inquiry into the psychoanalytic model, we should say something about the analytic experience itself. This common experience between patient and analyst is the experience of a genesis of self-consciousness (228). This, for Habermas, is a central perception of psychoanalysis and a key to the critique of ideology. The aim of class struggle is recognition, but we know what recognition means on the basis of the psychoanalytical situation. Freud's important formula summarizes the analytic insight: "Wo Es war, soll Ich werden"; where the id was, the ego must become. The first reason why the analytic situation is paradigmatic for psychoanalysis, then, is because self-recognition rules its whole process.

The second reason why the analytic situation is paradigmatic is because self-recognition is an aim achieved by dissolving resistances. The concept of resistance in psychoanalysis will become the model for ideology. An ideology is a system of resistance; it resists recognition of where we are, who we are, and so on. The crucial insight of psychoanalysis here is that intellectual understanding of the system of resistance is not sufficient. Even if a patient understands his or her situation intellectually, this information is useless as long as it has not led to a restructuration of the libidinal economy. For a parallel in the social world, we might look to the role of the mass media. To whatever extent that media inform us about the real nature of power in society, this knowledge is useless in itself because it has no impact on the distribution of power. The liberal system of information is neutralized by the real system of power. This is my own example and not in the text. In fact, Habermas himself does not offer explicit comparisons between Freud and Marx on this question of the proper model for the critical sciences. We are the ones who have to make this effort. Habermas draws a connection between Freud and Marx only later, when speaking in the twelfth chapter of Marx's theory of culture. At the present stage, Habermas' focus is on Freud alone. The analytic situation is an exemplary model for the critical social sciences because it is based on a theory of resistance. The task of analysis is to dissolve resistances by a kind of work, what Freud called *Durcharbeitung,* a working-through. "Working-through designates the dynamic component of a cognitive activity that leads to recognition only against resistances" (231). This is a good definition, because it integrates three concepts: a cognitive activity that leads to recognition through dealing with resistances.

I shall only allude to the fact that Habermas incorporates into this process the reconstruction of a life history (233). For those of us interested in the constitution of narratives—as story, as history—there is much available in Habermas' discussion of the narrative structure of the analytic experience. Because it involves a life history, its criteria are not those of verification. Its concern is not with facts but with the capacity to make a significant whole of our life story. The reconstruction of one's life history reverses the process of splitting-off that typifies excommunication.

If cognitive activity, the overcoming of resistance, and recognition are the implications of the psychoanalytic situation, this kernel experience is transformed by Freud into a structural model (237). This transformation is Habermas' third general point about psychoanalysis. Habermas thinks of this development as applicable particularly to *The Ego and the Id,* written in 1923, but the transformation is apparent in all Freud's successive models, as in the writings of 1895 and in the model of the seventh chapter of *The Interpretation of Dreams,* written in 1900. Habermas argues that the structural model is legitimate because we have to introduce casual connections within a process that is more generally interpretive. The process is interpretive but includes causal episodes. As long as we remain aware of the derivation of the structural model from the analytic situation, there is no danger of its abuse. When this model is isolated from the situation that it describes, however, then it becomes an ideology. (Use of the term "ideology" at this point is not Habermas' vocabulary but my own.) When separated from the analytic experience, the structural model becomes an objectification by which psychoanalysis denies its affiliation with depth hermeneutics and claims to imitate the natural sciences.

Indeed, many texts in Freud do maintain that psychoanalysis is a natural science. There are several reasons, I think, why Freud takes this step. First, Freud had to fight so hard for recognition that he had to claim to be a scientist. The only way for him to be recognized was as a scientist. Second, his own training in physiology led him to think that psychoanalysis was only a provisory stage and that one day it would be replaced by pharmacology. Psychoanalysis is necessary only because we ignore or do not understand some of the workings of the brain. This point is odd, because his emphasis throughout on self-understanding is incompatible with a science like pharmacology.

In any event, we may reappropriate the structural model if we keep in mind its derivation from the experience of analysis. Within this framework a term like the id makes sense because we may take it as literally the neutral. Because some parts of ourselves are no longer recognized, are excommunicated not only from others but from ourselves, they then must appear as a thing. The id describes well the existence of a part of our experience that we no longer understand, something to which we no longer have access and so is like a thing. The id is the name of what has been excommunicated.

The concept of excommunication rules the structural model. Because excommunication itself belongs to the system of the concepts of communicative action, a species of communicative action provides the key for a model that is quasi-naturalistic.

It seems to me more plausible to conceive the act of repression as a banishment of need interpretations themelves. The degrammaticized and imagistically compressed language of the dream provides some clues to an excommunication model of this sort. This process would be the intrapsychic imitation of a specific category of punishment, whose efficacy was striking especially in archaic times: the expulsion, ostracism, and isolation of the criminal from the social group whose language he shares. The splitting-off of individual symbols from public communication would mean at the same time the privatization of their semantic content. (241–42)

I like very much this part of Habermas' analysis. Only by a process of internal banishment is there something like an id. The id is not a given but a product of expulsion. I think that this is an orthodox interpretation of Freud; repression is produced not by natural forces but by forces under certain cultural circumstances. Repression is not a mechanical phenomenon, it is the expression in causal language of what happens when we do not recognize ourselves, when we banish ourselves from our own company.

In concluding our discussion of Habermas' characterization of psychoanalysis, we may say that his general argument is: "The language of [psychoanalytic] theory is narrower than the language in which the technique was described" (245). For Habermas this comment is just as important as when he said that an interpretation of Marx in mechanistic terms cannot give an account of Marx's critique, since the critique is not a part of the mechanistic system. Similarly in Freud, if we deal with a mechanistic model of psychoanalysis, we cannot give an account of the process of self-reflection that the analytic experience requires. "Strangely enough, the structural model denies the origins of its own categories in a process of enlightenment" (245). This statement provides us with the transition to the last topic in our analysis of Habermas. We must discuss how the process of enlightenment—*Aufklärung,* the name of the eighteenth-century philosophy—orients Habermas' critique, a critique whose interest is in emancipation. To what extent is enlightenment, understood as emancipation, a utopian element at the center of the critique of ideology?

Two problems merit our attention here. First, we must consider to what extent the psychoanalytic model helps us to construe the concept of a critique of ideology. We must ascertain the principle of this parallelism and the range of its extension. We must consider, second, to what extent there is a utopian component in the concept of self-reflection and in the concept of critique in general. I shall link these two questions, because I think that the difference finally between psychoanalysis and ideology-critique is that the element of utopia in the latter is irreducible. This conclusion is more a personal interpretation than a strict reading of Habermas' text.

As I have mentioned previously, in *Knowledge and Human Interests* Habermas strangely says only very little about the possibility of transferring to the critique of ideology some of his conclusions about psychoanalysis. The reader is the one who generally has to extract these consequences. On the basis of our reading, I shall try to draw these comparisons between psychoanalysis and ideology-critique, and I shall proceed in a certain order, from what is the most similar to what is the least similar. We shall end by raising the question of these two enterprises' fundamental difference.

There are four main points where the psychoanalytic model is transferable to the critique of ideology. The detour through psychoanalysis illustrates first that self-reflection is the principal motive of the critical social sciences as a whole. Psychoanalysis is exemplary because it is a process of self-recovery, of self-understanding. A second transferable aspect is that in both psychoanalysis and ideology-critique, distortions belong to the same level of experience as emancipation. Distortions occur within the process of communication. Thus, we are compelled to speak even of class struggle in terms of communication. Class struggle involves not only conflicting forces but a disruption of a process of communication between human beings. People become strangers; in different classes people do not speak the same language. Excommunication extends even to the level of style, grammar, the amplitude of the lexicon, and so on. The difference is not only between groups' linguistic tools, though, but between the symbolic systems through which they look at one another.

> [J]ust as in the clinical situation, so in society, pathological compulsion itself is accompanied by the interest in its abolition. Both the pathology of social institutions and that of individual consciousness reside in the medium of language and of communicative action and assume the form of a structural deformation of communication. (288)

Freud helps us to reread Marx in terms of processes of communication not just when Marx speaks of forces but throughout.

The third point of commonality between psychoanalysis and the critique of ideology is that because their distortions are systematic, we cannot expect dissolution of these distortions by mere extension of our ordinary capacity to communicate. The ordinary means of interpretation which constitute conversation are useless, because we are faced not with misunderstanding but systematic distortion. This requires us to apply an intermediary technique, the detour of causal explanation. In both psychoanalysis and ideology-critique, then, the movement from excommunication to the reestablishment of communication has an explanatory phase which implies that we construe a theoretical model for dealing with this segment of concealed and reified processes.

This leads us to the fourth and final parallelism: the structural model in which we deal with the casual connections must always be derived from the situation of communication, but the model can become abstracted from this situation and so reified. For Habermas there is a complete parallelism here between what happened in Marxism and in psychoanalysis; the model of each was abstracted from the original situation for which it was conceived and became a reified structural model. The energy-distribution model in Freud has the same ambiguous status as superstructure and infrastructure in the orthodox Marxist model.

Turning to a second group of statements, we can see where the comparison between psychoanalysis and ideology-critique begins to fail. Discrepancy starts to arise when we attempt to identify what Marx and Freud each emphasize in the human fabric of culture. "[W]hat interests [Marx] as the natural basis of history is the physical organization specific to the human species under the category of possible labor: the tool-making animal. Freud's focus, in contrast, was not the system of social labor but the family" (282). A human being is described by Marx as a tool user and by Freud as someone who remains a child even after having moved beyond the age of childhood. With Freud the fundamental problem is not labor but the instinctual renunciations by which a cultural system may function. In Freud's three great texts on culture—*The Future of an Illusion, Civilization and Its Discontents,* and *Moses and Monotheism*—everything is measured in terms of libidinal loss, the libidinal pleasures that must be sacrificed in order that one may be a member of society. Freud's view of culture is a pessimistic one, because he thinks society functions only on the basis of the compensations, prohibitions, and sublimations that protect the social system. Freud "concentrates on the origins of the motivational foundation of communicative action" (283).

This divergence between Marx and Freud begins to appear in chapter twelve of the text, the only place where there is a direct comparison between both figures. Habermas writes of "the psychoanalytic key to a social theory that converges in a surprising manner with Marx's reconstruction of the history of the species while in another regard advancing specifically new perspectives" (276). The parallelism does not extend all that far because Freud's concern is limited to the fact that a human being is more than an animal only because of the renunciation of instinct. Habermas quotes a striking and in many ways terrifying assertion from Freud's *The Future of an Illusion:* "every individual is virtually an enemy of civilization . . ." (277). Society must take measures against this destructive dimension, a dimension linked by Freud to sadism and to the death instinct. The latter in particular seems to have no parallel in Marx. For Freud guilt is the guardian of the city against disruption by the individual. Habermas comments:

> The last assertion, that *everyone* is virtually an enemy of civilization, already points up the difference between Freud and Marx. Marx conceives the institutional framework as an ordering of interests that are immediate functions of the system of social labor according to the relation of social rewards and imposed obligations. Institutions derive their force from perpetuating a distribution of rewards and obligations that is rooted in force and distorted according to class structure. Freud, on the contrary, conceives the institutional framework in connection with the repression of instinctual impulses. (277; emphasis in original)

Repression is fundamental for Freud, whereas in Marx it is a supplement, a distortion introduced by the division of labor and by the class structure. For some time Freud had a certain sympathy for the Bolshevik enterprise, but he also viewed it with caution, because he perceived that a political experiment which did not fundamentally change the balance of instincts was not a real revolution.

In spite of these differences between Freud and Marx, however, Freud may still be helpful at this second level of comparison. At this second stage, there is a balance of difference and similarities between psychoanalysis and ideology-critique, whereas in the first part there were only similarities. What remains paradigmatic in Freud is the kind of hope that he proposes. This may be more difficult to find in Marx, because as long as the class structure has not been overcome, then the rationality of human existence cannot be established. In contrast, we may observe in the process of psychoanalysis something of the emergence of self-understanding and self-reflection.

To discuss this dimension of psychoanalysis, which affects not only the second stage of its comparison with the critique of ideology but the third, where the lack of parallelism comes to the fore, I shall concentrate on pages 284–90 of the text. As far as I know, these are the only pages outside the appendix where the word "utopia" occurs. Habermas views Freud as a man of the eighteenth century, a man of the Enlightenment, and this is surely correct. Habermas understands the aim of the Enlightenment to be advocacy of the rationality of utopia, promotion of a rational hope. "The ideas of the Enlightenment stem from the store of historically transmitted illusions. Hence we must comprehend the actions of the Enlightenment as the attempt to test the limit of the realizability of the utopian content of cultural tradition under given conditions" (284). This statement is linked to an idea developed in the late writings of Freud, when Freud differentiates between illusion and delusion. A delusion is an irrational belief, whereas an illusion represents the possibilities of rational human being. Habermas quotes Freud's *New Introductory Lectures:* " 'My illusions are not, like religious ones, incapable of correction. They have not the character of a delusion. If experience should show . . . that we have been mistaken, we will give up our expectations' " (284). Freud advances the notion of a tempered utopian mind, a mind tempered by the spirit of the Enlightenment, by the spirit of rationality. Why is this notion present in Freud? "Freud encounters this unity of reason and interest in the situation in which the physician's Socratic questioning can aid a sick person's self-reflection only under pathological compulsion and the corresponding interest in abolishing this compulsion" (287). There is an identity of interest and reason which gives to hope a rational content. This quality may be what is lacking in any suggested parallelism between ideology-critique and psychoanalysis.

We now reach the point where emphasis should be placed on the lack of parallelism between psychoanalysis and the critique of ideology. To my mind, the fundamental difference is that there is nothing in the critique of ideology comparable to the psychoanalytic relation between patient and physician. It is not by chance that Habermas never speaks of the parallelism between ideology-critique and psychoanalysis when developing the notion that the patient-physician relation is paradigmatic in psychoanalysis and that the structural model is derived from this situation. We must inquire ourselves whether there is anything similar in the critique of ideology. The important text here is the one just cited for the stage of transition. Let me begin several lines earlier than before:

> The analytic situation makes real the unity of intuition and emancipation, of insight and liberation from dogmatic dependence, and of reason and the interested em-

ployment of reason developed by Fichte in the concept of self-reflection. . . . Freud encounters this unity of reason and interest in the situation in which the physician's Socratic questioning can aid a sick person's self-reflection . . ." (287).

The analytic situation makes real *(wirklich)* the unity of intuition and emancipation, and the physician's Socratic questioning supplies the aid for this to occur. This relationship between patient and physician is unique to the psychoanalytic situation. It is sometimes presented, at least in this country, even as a contractual relationship. Someone calls himself or herself the patient, and someone else is trained as a physician and recognized as the physician by the patient. There is recognition of the situation that I am ill, I call for help, and you are the one who can help me. The situation is, in Habermas' definition of the term, dialogic, not in the sense of shared experience—the analyst is abstinent and shares nothing—but in the sense that the analyst is present to the patient and offers aid.

This initial situation of the doctor-patient relationship has no parallel in ideology-critique. In ideology-critique no one identifies himself or herself as the ill, as the patient, and no one is entitled to be the physician. Some might argue that to a certain extent the sociologist or the writer is able to take on the role of physician, but this raises the problem of whether there can really be a value-free thinker. In a way the psychoanalyst in the analytic situation may be a value-free thinker, because he or she is the object of transference. I do not see, however, what would be a similar position in ideology-critique, because even the thinker is part of the polemical situation. The thinker does not transcend the polemical situation, and so the notion of ideology remains a polemical concept for the thinker also. The psychoanalyst, on the other hand, does not use the concept of neurosis as a polemical tool against the patient. The lack of parallelism here between psychoanalysis and ideology-critique has dreadful consequences for the status of the latter, since it becomes a member of its own referent. The status of ideology-critique itself belongs to the polemical situation of ideology. This is the first point where the parallelism between psychoanalysis and the critique of ideology fails.

The second point where the parallelism fails is that there is nothing in ideology-critique comparable to the psychoanalytic situation of transference. Transference is the decisive procedure where what happened on the neurotic scene is transposed onto the miniature and artificial scene of the patient-physician relation. It constitutes an intermediary scene between the neurotic scene and the original infantile scene. The art of creating this intermediary and artificial situation gives the psychoanalytic experience its efficiency. Once again I wonder whether, for example, an ideology-critique's examination of class affiliation can play the same role as this transference situation.

The third and final point where parallelism fails is in the lack of recognition intrinsic to ideology-critique. The relation between physician and patient is not only a situation of contract and not only a procedure of transference; it is also an occasion where mutual recognition is finally implied. We cannot say, however, that recognition is at work in *Ideologiekritik*. In *Lenin and Philosophy,* for example, Althusser radically denies the possibility of recognition. We must draw the party line, he says, between the Marxist intellectual and the bourgeois intellectual. At least for the orthodox Marxists the situation is one of war, and we must take this perspective as exemplary rather than that of those other Marxists who are more tamed and humanized. In the orthodox claim, the notion of recognition is a projection only about the classless society. In the classless society there will be recognition, but we cannot say that recognition gives its thrust to the current enterprise.

My criticism is not so much an argument against Habermas as an analysis for the sake of the problem itself, that psychoanalysis and ideology-critique have different criteria of success. We may agree that there are certain therapeutic moments in ideology-critique. Even if we are not Marxists, when we read Marx it is a personal event, and one that transforms our outlook on society. We are less deceived by the appearances of democracy and so on. So this change has both direct and indirect political implications. Dissident voices are fundamental to the democratic process itself. We must preserve this margin of dissidence for the sake of inner critique. We may also say that ideology-critique can lead to conscientization, a theme developed by Latin American thinkers such as Paulo Freire. This too is a form of political therapy. In general, though, ideology-critique lacks an immediate, experiential component. It functions much more at the level of analysis of the wheels of the social machinery. Though ideology-critique may have some therapeutic results, its purpose is still critique. Psychoanalysis, on the other hand, includes both critique and cure. The function of therapy is to cure, but virtually no one is cured by the process of ideology-critique. Many are wounded but very few are cured.

Ideology-critique is part of a process of struggle and not one of recognition. The idea of free communication remains an unfulfilled ideal, a regulative idea, an "illusion" in the sense the Freud distinguishes the term from delusion. Perhaps here a utopian element fills the gap that the experience of recognition satisfies in the psychoanalytic situation. The utopian element is linked to the absent counterpart of the psychoanalytic situation. What suggests this relationship is Habermas' appeal to the utopian thematic at this point in his discussion of Freud.

> That is why for the social system, too, the interest inherent in the pressure of suffering is also immediately an interest in enlightenment; and reflection is the only possible dynamic through which it realizes itself. The interest of reason inclines toward the progressive, critical-revolutionary, but tentative realization of the major illusions of humanity, in which repressed motives have been elaborated into *fantasies* of hope. (288; emphasis added)

Habermas adds, several lines later: "The 'good' is neither a convention nor an essence, but rather the result of fantasy. But it must be fantasied so exactly that it corresponds to and articulates a fundamental interest: the interest in that measure of emancipation that historically is objectively possible under given and manipulable conditions." The German for fantasy is *Phantasie,* and it means not fancy but imagination. So Habermas' discussion, I was pleased to see, is about the social imagination.

In more recent work, Habermas tries to respond to criticisms about the lack of parallelism between psychoanalysis and ideology-critique by advancing the notion of communicative competence. Communicative competence is a utopian construction, an ideal speech situation, the possibility of undistorted communication. Recourse to this concept, however, raises questions about the nature of the utopian element that are similar to those arising from our reading of *Knowledge and Human Interests.* The word "competence" is used ambigously. On the one hand, a competence is something at our disposal, a potentiality that we can either use or not use. It is the correlate of performance in Chomsky. Because I am competent to speak French, I can perform a sentence in French. Communicative competence, however, is not something at our disposal but rather something that must appear as a Kantian Idea, a regulative idea. My question is whether we can have this idea without a certain anthropology or an ontology in which it makes sense for dialogue to succeed. This is the permanent argument of Gadamer in his discussion with Habermas. If we do not understand the poet Hölderlin when he speaks of *das Gespräch das wir sind,* the dialogue that we are, then we cannot make sense of the dialogue that we ought to be. If we have no ontology in which dialogue is constitutive of who we are, then can we have this communicative ideal? Perhaps it is merely a matter of emphasis, though, and Habermas' question is how can we understand the dialogue that we are if not through the utopia of a communication without boundary and constraint.

As for myself, I assume completely the inextricable role of this utopian element, because I think that it is ultimately constitutive of any theory of ideology. It is always from the depth of a utopia that we may speak of an ideology. This was the case with the young Marx when he spoke of the whole human being, the famous person who went fishing in the morning, hunting in the afternoon, and in the evening did critique. This reconstruction of a totality lying beyond the division of labor, this vision of an integral human being, is the utopia which allows us to say that the British economists did not dig beneath the surface of the economic relations between wage, capital, and work.

I want to conclude by saying a few words about the structure of utopia. For my part, I see utopia as itself a complex network of elements with different origins. It is not something simple but a cluster of forces working together. Utopia is supported first by the notion of self-reflection. This is the main notion of utopia, and it is the teleological component of all critique, of all analysis, of all restoration of communication. I call it the transcendental component. This factor preserves the unity between ideology-critique and German idealism and also finally the unity between ideology-critique and the whole tradition of philosophy in spite of Habermas' claim that we have broken with theory for the sake of praxis. What remains common to theory and praxis is this element of self-reflection, something which is not historical but transcendental, in the sense that it has no date, no point of historical origin, but is instead the fundamental possibility of being human. When the young Marx speaks of the difference between animal and human being, he draws a line; the difference is an element of transcendence available only to human being. I prefer to say this factor is transcendental, because it is the condition of possibility for doing something else.

The second component of the utopian structure is cultural. This attribute is modern and comes from the tradition of the Enlightenment; it adds to the element of fantasy the possibility of correction, of testing the limits of realizability. To repeat a quotation already cited: "The ideas of the Enlightenment stem from the store of historically transmitted illusions. Hence we must comprehend the actions of the Enlightenment as the attempt to test the limit of the realizability of the utopian content of cultural tradition under given conditions" (284). The ideas are transmitted historically. The utopia is then not merely a transcendental element without history, for it is part of our history. This allows me to say that perhaps the great difference between Gadamer and Habermas is that they do not have the same traditions. Gadamer relies more on the tradition of German idealism plus Romanticism, whereas for Habermas it is more the Enlightenment plus German idealism. That Habermas and Gadamer are both situated historically is inevitable; no one is outside all tradition. Even emphasis on self-reflection has a certain tradition. Self-reflection has both an ahistorical factor, what I have called its transcendental component, and a cultural component, a history. When Habermas speaks of the unity of interests and reason (287, 289), this is typically a theme of the Enlightenment.

The third element of the utopian structure is fantasy. Fantasy is Habermas' term for what Freud calls illusion. Illusion is differentiated, we remember, from delusion, where delusion is both the unverifiable and the unrealizable. Illusion or fantasy is the element of hope, a rational hope. Habermas develops this theme not only in his discussion of Freud but also in his systematic theses in the appendix. In the latter, Habermas says that humanity is rooted in fundamental structures like work, language, and power. He adds, though, that there is also something in us which transcends this conditionality, and this is the utopian. Habermas specifically uses the word "utopian" in this context. "[S]ociety is not only a system of self-preservation. An enticing natural force, present in the individual as libido, has detached itself from the behavioral system of self-preservation and urges toward utopian fulfillment" (312). Fantasy is that which "urges toward utopian fulfillment." Habermas' opposition between utopia and self-preservation is a good insight into the relation between ideology and utopia in their best senses. As we shall see with Geertz, the fundamental function of an ideology is to establish identity, whether the identity of a group or of an individual. Utopia, on the other hand, breaks with the "system of self-preservation and urges toward utopian fulfillment." For Habermas, realization of this utopian element's role leads to the thesis that "knowledge equally serves as an instrument and transcends mere self-preservation" (313). Utopia is precisely what preserves the three knowledge-constitutive interests—the instrumental, the practical, and the critical—from being reduced to one. The utopian opens the spectrum of interests and prevents it from being closed or collapsed to the instrumental.

It may be, then, that utopia, in the positive sense of the term, extends to the boundary line between the possible and the impossible which perhaps cannot be rationalized finally even in the form of rational hope. May we not say therefore that this utopian factor is irreducible, that ideology-critique cannot rely on an experience similar to that of transference in psychoanalysis, where the process of liberation may lead to self-recognition under the guidance of an actual, mutual recognition? It may even be that full mutual recognition is a utopian element in all therapy itself. The utopian fantasy is that of an ideal speech act, an ideal communicative situation, the notion of communication without boundary and without constraint. It may be that this ideal constitutes our very notion of humankind. We speak of humanity not only as a species but as in fact a task, since humanity is given nowhere. The utopian element may be the notion of humanity that we are directed toward and that we unceasingly attempt to bring to life.

Before turning to the more detailed discussion of utopia in the final three lectures, we shall close our analysis of ideology with the following lecture on Clifford Geertz. Habermas has been a figure of transition. He establishes the possibility of a social critique that avoids Mannheim's paradox, the division between ideology and science, he builds on Weber and shows that only at the end of the process of critique can we recover as our own work what are the claims of authority, and he alerts us that this recovery moves from excommunication and desymbolization to recognition and communication. On the last point he anticipates Geertz, who demonstrates that ideology must be understood on the basis of the symbolic structure of action, a conclusion that moves us beyond distortion and legitimation to the third and final level of ideology, a nonpejorative concept of ideology as integration.

15

Geertz

We end our regressive analysis of ideology[1] by discussion of Clifford Geertz. Discussion of Geertz is the last step in an analysis that covers three main stages. We started from the surface concept of ideology as distortion. When we read *The German Ideology,* we asked how can we make sense of Marx's assertion that a ruling class is expressed by ruling ideas, ideas which become the ruling ideas of an epoch. We recognized that at this stage the concept of ideology was systematic distortion, and we saw that in order to approach this first concept, we had to take into account a concept of interest—class interest—apply an attitude of suspicion, and proceed to a causal dismantlement of these distortions. Here the paradigmatic model was the relation between superstructure and infrastructure.

We then raised the question, how does it make sense to have a distorting thought caused by such structures as class structures? We were led to ask what is implied in the notions of ruling class and ruling idea. Our answer was the problem of authority. This uncovered the second concept of ideology, ideology as legitimation. Here we introduced discussion of Max Weber, since the paradigmatic case was no longer a class interest but the claim to legitimacy made by all forms of authority. Our focus was the gap within a group between the leader's claim to authority and the members' belief in this authority. The attitude of analysis at this second stage was not suspicion but the value-free attitude of the sociologist. Further, the conceptual framework was not causality but motivation, and we spoke of this framework not in terms of structures and forces but in terms of the ideal types of the authority's claims. In this second stage the ideal types of claims played the same role as the superstructure in the first stage.

It is to build a third concept of ideology as integration or identity that we finally resort to Geertz. At this stage, we reach the level of symbolization, something that can be distorted and something within which lies the process of legitimation. Here the main attitude is not at all suspicion nor even the value-free but conversation. Geertz himself comes to this attitude as an anthropologist. In *The Interpretation of Cultures,* Geertz says of his ethnographic research: "We are seeking, in the widened sense of the term in which it encompasses very much more than talk, to converse with [people of another culture], a matter a great deal more difficult, and not only with strangers, than is commonly recognized" (13). "Looked at in this way," Geertz continues,

> the aim of anthropology is the enlargement of the universe of human discourse. . . . [I]t is an aim to which a semiotic concept of culture is peculiarly well adapted. As interworked systems of construable signs (what, ignoring provincial usages, I would call symbols), culture is not a power, something to which social events, behaviors, institutions, or processes can be causally attributed; it is a context, something within which they can be intelligibly—that is, thickly—described. (14)

In conversation we have an interpretive attitude. If we speak of ideology in negative terms as distortion, then we use the tool or weapon of suspicion. If, however, we want to recognize a group's values on the basis of its self-understanding of these values, then we must welcome these values in a positive way, and this is to converse.

This attitude is linked to a conceptual framework which is not causal or structural or even motivational but rather semiotic. What particularly interests me in Geertz is that he tries to deal with the concept of ideology by the instruments of modern semiotics. Geertz declares early in the text, "The concept of culture I espouse . . . is essentially a semiotic one." What he means by this is that analysis of culture is "not an experimental science in search of law but an interpretive one in search of meaning." Geertz is thus not far from Max Weber, since he follows Weber in believing that "man is an animal suspended in webs of significance he himself has spun" (5). At this level we address ourselves to motives not as motivational but as expressed in signs. The signitive systems of the motives constitute the level of reference.

Because culture is understood as a semiotic process, the concept of symbolic action is central for Geertz. This theme is most present in his article, "Ideology as a Cultural System," which is included in *The Interpretation of Cultures.* This article will be our focus for the rest of the discussion in this lecture. Geertz borrows the concept or at least the term "symbolic action" from Kenneth Burke (208). It seems that what Geertz borrows is more the term than the actual concept, because in the book of Burke's that Geertz cites for this notion, *The Philosophy of Literary Form: Studies in Symbolic Action,* symbolic action appears to have a different meaning than it does for Geertz. Burke says that language in fact is symbolic action. Geertz's point, though, is that action is symbolic just like language. The notion of symbolic action may therefore be deceiving in the context that Geertz intends. I prefer to speak of action as symbolically mediated. This seems less ambiguous than the term "symbolic action," because symbolic action is not an action which we undertake but one which we replace by signs. This is Burke's concept, that in literature we have symbolic action. Literature is symbolic action, whereas here we want to say that action itself is symbolic in the sense that it is construed on the basis of fundamental symbols.

Geertz also utilizes the doubtful concept of an extrinsic symbol, in the sense of an extrinsic theory of symbolic systems (214 ff.). If I am correct in my understanding of Geertz on this point, I think that the expression is unfortunate. Geertz wants to show that action is ruled from within by symbols, and he calls these symbols extrinsic, in contrast to another set of symbols provided by genetics, where the codes are incorporated in the living organism. This differentiation between extrinsic and intrinsic models is an attempt to draw the line between models that we find in biology and those developed in cultural life. In the latter, all the symbols are imported instead of being homogeneous to life. There is a heterogeneity between the cultural model and the biological potentiality of life. Geertz's point is that the biological plasticity or flexibility of human life does not give us guidance for dealing with various cultural situations—scarcity, labor, and so on. Therefore, we need a secondary system of symbols and models which are no longer natural but cultural models. The salient consideration, then, is not so much the fact that these symbols and models are extrinsic to the organism as that they function exactly in the same way as the intrinsic models.

The defining proposition of the extrinsic theory is that symbol systems are matched with other systems. "[T]hought consists of the construction and manipulation of symbol systems, which are employed as models of other systems, physical, organic, social, psychological, and so forth, in such a way that the structure of these other systems . . . is, as we say, 'understood.' " We think and understand by matching "the states and processes of symbolic models against the states and processes of the wider world" (214). If we enter into a ceremony but do not know the rules of the ritual, then all the movements are senseless. To understand is to pair what we see with the rules of the ritual. "[A]n object (or an event, an act, an emotion) is identified by placing it against the background of an appropriate symbol" (215). We *see* the movement *as* performing a mass, *as* performing a sacrifice, and so on. The notion of pairing or matching is the central theme. Cultural patterns are therefore programs. They provide, says Geertz, "a template or blueprint for the organization of social and psychological processes, much as genetic systems provide such a template for the organization of organic processes" (216). The semiotic process provides a plan.

There is a further implication of Geertz's analysis which is I think the most significant part of his article, and that is the possibility of comparing an ideology with the rhetorical devices of discourse. This may be the point where Geertz goes the farthest. In the earlier part of his article, Geertz criticizes the more usual theories of ideology—ideology as the representation of certain interests, ideology as the product of certain sociopsychological strains—for always assuming something that they do not understand: how the release of a strain becomes a symbol or how an interest is expressed in an idea. He claims that most sociologists take for granted what it means to say that an interest is "expressed by" something else. How do interests become expressed, though? Geertz argues that we can provide an answer only by analyzing "how symbols symbolize, how they function to mediate meanings" (208). "With no notion of how metaphor, analogy, irony, ambiguity, pun, paradox, hyperbole, rhythm, and all the other elements of what we lamely call 'style' operate . . . in casting personal attitudes into public form," we cannot construe "the import of ideological assertions" (209). Geertz takes as an example an attack by organized labor on the Taft-Hartley Act, where labor assailed the act as being a " 'slave labor law' " (209). This metaphor should not be reduced to its literal meaning, Geertz says, because it derives its informative value from being a metaphor. Its language is not merely distortion, because it says what it wants to say by the comparison to and the metaphor of slave labor. The phrase is not a literal label but a metaphoric trope (210).

What is especially intriguing here is Geertz's attempt to connect analysis not only to semiology in the broad sense of the word but to the part of semiology that deals with figures of speech, with tropology, with rhetorical devices that are not necessarily intended to deceive either oneself or others. The possibility that rhetoric can be integrative and not necessarily distortive leads us to a nonpejorative concept of ideology. If we follow this path, we may then say that there is something irreducible in the concept of ideology. Even if we separate off the other two layers of ideology—ideology as distortion and as the legitimation of a system of order or power—the integrative function of ideology, the function of preserving an identity, remains. It may be that our regressive analysis can go no further, because no group and no individual are possible without this integrative function.

Here I find a provocative similarity between Geertz and Erik Erikson. Let me draw the connection briefly. In Erikson's *Identity: Youth and Crisis,* there are several statements about ideology that are very close to Geertz. These statements are completely independent of Geertz's influence, we may note, since they were written many years before Geertz's article. (Geertz himself makes no reference to Erikson.) Erikson calls ideology the guardian of identity. "For the social institution which is the guardian of identity is what we have called ideology" (133). A number of pages later, he writes: "More generally . . . an ideological system is a coherent body of shared image, ideas, and ideals which . . . provides for the participants a coherent, if systematically simplified, over-all orientation in space and time, in means and ends" (189–90). Because Erikson raises the problem of the condition of identity, he says that we must go beyond the propagandist concept of ideology, where ideology is "a systematic form of collective pseudologia" (190).

On the basis of this analysis of ideology as integrative, I would like to emphasize three points. First, by transforming how the concept of ideology is construed, we stress the symbolic mediation of action, the fact that there is no social action which is not already symbolically mediated. Therefore, we can no longer say that ideology is merely a kind of superstructure. The distinction between superstructure and infrastructure completely disappears, because symbolic systems belong already to the infrastructure, to the basic constitution of human being. The only aspect of the notion of superstructure that we can say possibly remains is the fact that the symbolic is "extrinsic," in the sense that it does not belong to organic life. This is perhaps more a problem in the term "extrinsic," however, for what is called extrinsic is still constitutive of human being.

A second point is the correlation established between ideology and rhetoric. In some ways Habermas prepared us for this connection, since he discussed the problem of ideology in terms of communication or excommunication. Now the correlation is more positive, though, because ideology is not the distortion of communication but the rhetoric of basic communication. There is a rhetoric of basic communication because we cannot exclude rhetorical devices from language; they are an intrinsic part of ordinary language. In its function as integration, ideology is similarly basic and ineluctable.

My third point questions whether we are allowed to speak of ideologies outside the situation of distortion and so with reference only to the basic function of integration. Can we speak of the ideologies of nonmodern cultures, cultures which have not entered into the process that Mannheim describes as the collapse of universal agreement, if that ever existed? Is there ideology where there is no conflict of ideologies? If we look only at the integrative function of a culture, and if this function is not challenged by an alternative form for providing integration, may we have ideology? My doubt is whether we can project ideology on cultures outside the post-Enlightenment situation in which all modern cultures are now involved in a process not only of secularization but of fundamental confrontation about basic ideals. I think that integration without confrontation is pre-ideological. Nevertheless, it is still most important to find among the conditions for the possibility of having a distorted function a legitimating function and under this legitimating function an integrative function.

We may also note that the process of deriving the three forms of ideology can proceed in the reverse direction. As Geertz observes quite accurately, ideology is finally always about power. "[I]t is through the construction of ideologies, schematic images of social order, that man makes himself for better or worse a political animal." "The function of ideology," he continues, "is to make an autonomous politics possible by providing the authoritative concepts that render it meaningful, the suasive images by means of which it can be sensibly grasped" (218). The notion of the authoritative is a kernel concept, because when the problem of integration leads to the problem of a system of authority, the third concept of ideology sends us back to the second. It is not by chance that a specific place for ideology exists in politics, because politics is the location where the basic images of a group finally provide rules for using power. Questions of integration lead to questions of legitimation, and these in turn lead to questions of distortion. We are therefore forced to proceed backwards and upwards in this hierarchy of concepts.

A question might be raised asking why I take Geertz's notion that ideology provides the "authoritative concepts" that "make an autonomous politics possible" as necessarily a statement that ideology is finally about political power. Could not the "authoritative concepts" be provided by religion, for example? In response, I would say that consistent with themes running throughout the lectures, I understand the concept of the authoritative as the transition from the integrative function to the legitimation of hierarchy. Geertz comes to my aid here, observing in a footnote to the text just cited:

> Of course, there are moral, economic, and even aesthetic ideologies, as well as specifically political ones, but as very few ideologies of any social prominence lack political implications, it is perhaps permissible to view the problem here in this somewhat narrowed focus. In any case, the arguments developed for political ideologies apply with equal force to nonpolitical ones. (281 *n.*)

I am tempted to say that ideology has a broader function than politics to the extent that it is integrative. When integration comes to the problem of the authoritative function of models, however, then politics becomes the focus and the question of identity becomes the frame. What is at stake finally in the process of integration—as we have learned from Weber—is how we can make the transition from the general notion of a social relationship to the notion of rulers and ruled.

The problem of religion is yet a significant one. We may compare Geertz's analysis of ideology with his analysis of religion in "Religion as a Cultural System," an article also included in *The Interpretation of Cultures*. It is not the case that ideology replaces religion in modern life; Geertz does not relegate religion simply to past societies. I see three basic points on which Geertz establishes the continuing role of religion. First, religion is the attempt to articulate an ethos and a world view. He never says that about ideology. Geertz makes a long analysis about the problem of suffering and death and says that the function of a religious system with regard to this issue is not to elude suffering but to teach us how to endure suffering. It is difficult to say that this is a function only of past societies, because at the point when we learn how to suffer, the difference between the ethical and the cosmic collapses; we are taught both a way of looking at life and a way of behaving. Religion is beyond the opposition between the traditional and the modern in a second sense, because its dispositional function allows it to establish a mood. Religion provides a fundamental stability at the level of our most basic feelings. It is a theory of feelings, and as such it again deals with both the ethical and the cosmic. The third point about religion is that it stages these feelings through rituals, and we have some residues and perhaps even some permanent traditions representing that in modern society. Ideology arises not on the collapse of the ritual dimension but from the open conflictual situation of modernity. Systems—even religious ones—are confronted with other systems which raise similar claims of authenticity and legitimacy. We are caught in a situation of ideologies, in the plural.

We may say that Geertz's purpose is not so much to eliminate current theories about ideology—ideology as interests or strains—as to found them at a deeper level. Finally, though, Geertz is more on the side of a strain theory of ideology. The concept of integration precisely has to do with the threat of the lack of identity, what is discussed by Erikson in psychological terms as crisis and confusion. What a group fears most is no longer being able to identify itself because of crises and confusions creating strain; the task is to cope with this strain. Once again the comparison with religion is relevant, because suffering and death play exactly the same role in personal life as crisis and confusion in the social sphere. The two analyses tend to overlap.

I would add that another positive element about ideology as integration is that it supports the integration of a group not simply in space but in time. Ideology functions not only in the synchronic dimension but also in the diachronic dimension. In the latter case, the memory of the group's founding events is extremely significant; reenactment of the founding events is a fundamental ideological act. There is an element of a repetition of the origin. With this repetition begin all the ideological processes in the pathological sense, because a second celebration already has the character of reification. The celebration becomes a device for the system of power to preserve its power, so it is a defensive and protective act on the part of the rulers. Can we imagine, though, a community without the celebration of its own birth in more or less mythical terms? France celebrates the fall of the Bastille, and the United States celebrates the Fourth of July. In Moscow a whole political system is based on a tomb, Lenin's tomb, perhaps one of the only cases in history after the Egyptians where a tomb is the source of a political system. This permanent memory of the group's founders and founding events, then, is an ideological structure that can function positively as an integrative structure.

It may be that Geertz's point of view as an anthropologist is the decisive reason for his emphasis on integration and thus on strain theory. As an anthropologist, Geertz has a different perspective from someone like Habermas, who is a sociologist of modern industrial society. In the kind of societies with which Geertz deals—the main sources of his fieldwork are Indonesia and Morocco—the problematic is not that of industrial or postindustrial society but that of societies which are developing, in every sense of that word. For these societies the critique of ideology is premature; their focus is more the constitutive nature of ideology. When intellectuals or other dissidents in these societies use the tools of ideology-critique, whether in the sense of Habermas or, more typically, in the sense of Althusser, they are usually sent to prison if not killed. Dissidents become marginal when they apply the critical tools of an advanced society to the birth of a new society. The methodological point, then, is to consider to what extent Geertz's viewpoint as an anthropologist commits him to an analysis which cannot be that of a Habermas.

It may be too simple, though, to say that developing countries have only to deal with the constitutive character of ideology, because their arduous task is to find their own identity in a world already marked by the crisis of industrial societies. Not only have the advanced industrial societies accumulated and confiscated most of the means and the tools for development; they have engendered a crisis of advanced society which is now a public and world phenomenon. Societies are entering into the process of industrialization at the same time as nations at the top of this development are raising questions about the process. Countries have to incorporate technology at the same time that the critique and trial of technology has begun. For intellectuals in these countries, the task is an especially difficult one, because they live in two ages at the same time. They live at the beginning of the industrial period, let us say the eighteenth century, but they are also part of the twentieth century, because they are raised in a culture which has already entered into the crisis of the relation between its goals and the critique of technology. The concept of ideology has now become universal, therefore, because the crisis of the industrial societies is a universal crisis; it is part of the education of any intellectual at any place on the world. I remember traveling a number of years ago in Syria, Lebanon, and other parts of the Middle East, and in their libraries one finds the works of Simone de Beauvoir, Sartre, and so on. Everyone is now the contemporary of everyone else. People in developing countries are educated at the same time with the intellectual tools of their own culture and the tools of the crisis of the developed countries.

If ideology is now a universal issue, the Marxist claim is that the concept of ideology came into being with the development of social classes. The argument is that ideology did not exist prior to the rise of class structures. Althusser goes so far as to say that before the bourgeoisie there was no ideology. There are creeds and beliefs, but only the class structure created the situation that an important part of the population did not share the values of the whole. As we have seen, the Marxist perspective emphasizes the distortive aspects of ideology rather than its integrative function. In response to this emphasis, I would claim that the primitive concept of ideology as integration cannot be used in political practice except for the purpose of preserving even in the situation of struggle the problematic of recognition. If I understand that the distorting function could not appear if there were not a symbolic structure of action, then at least I know that it is because an integrative process is under way that there may be some class conflicts. Class conflicts are therefore never exactly situations of total war. Realization of the integrative character of ideology helps to preserve the appropriate level of class struggle, which is not to destroy the adversary but to achieve recognition. To put it in Hegelian terms, the struggle is for recognition and not for power. The underlying integrative function of ideology prevents us from pushing the polemical element to its destructive point—the point of civil war. What prevents us from making a plea for civil war is that we have to preserve the life of our adversary; an element of belonging together persists. Even the class enemy is not a radical enemy. In some sense he or she is still a neighbor. The concept of ideology as integrative puts a limit on social war and prevents it from becoming a civil war. Some of the European communist parties—particularly in Italy and now in France and Spain—have formulated the idea that the problem is to develop a society better integrated than in the class structure. The point, then, is really to integrate and not to suppress or destroy one's enemy.

The grounds for this transformation may already exist in class society. Even in class society integrative processes are at work: the sense of a common language, a common culture, and a common nation. People share at least the linguistic tools and all the communicative means that are linked to language, so we have to locate the role of language in a class structure. Resolution of this question was an important battle among Marxists earlier this century. At least for a time Stalin was on the correct side against those

Marxists who said that even grammar has a class structure. Stalin argued instead that the language belongs to the nation as a whole. The status of the nation in Marxist theory is difficult to elaborate because it cuts across class lines. We may say that Geertz's concept of ideology is more appropriate for an issue like this, since the status of the nation is not radically affected by the class structure. In attempting to define the nature of the nation, the question is as problematic as the definition of sex roles: it is difficult to say what is really fundamental and what is merely cultural. Only by changing traits or roles do we discover what cannot be changed. It is by questioning class affiliations that we may be able to identify what is constitutive of a community beyond or above its class structure. Many Marxists now say in fact that Marxism must be realized according to the different cultural situations in which it finds itself. These situations are then defined precisely by what Geertz calls an ideological system. We have to deal with the norms and the images that project a group's identity in the same way as some psychologists speak of the body image. There is a social group image, and this image of identity is particular to each group.

We may take the ideology of the United States as an example. The first point about this ideology is that it cannot be defined in isolation from its relations with other countries and their own ideological patterns. The United States is hardly in the position of isolation that would shield it from confrontation with other national ideologies. As Lenin was quite conscious, the stage is now the world. We should note that this situation is of rather recent origin. Before the First World War, the inner conflicts of Europe ruled the world situation. Now that Europe has collapsed by its inner wars, though, the conflict is more global. The relation, for example, between the Third World and the industrial world is currently a fundamental battle. Thus, the ideology of the United States is defined in part by its external relations.

As for judging the internal determinants of this ideology, we have more difficulty responding if we no longer rely solely on the Marxist concept of class, where one group is the dominant class and sets forth the ruling ideas—the ideology—of the nation. Someone like Mannheim is both quite clever and quite cautious on this issue, because he always speaks of a social stratum. He leaves us the task of identifying which groups are at work in society and in what way. In fact, the task is precisely to consider all the various social groupings and not to preclude other determinants than the notion of class. Perhaps class is only one structure among many. Consider, for instance, the question of racial and ethnic minorities, a most prominent issue in this country. In what category do we put minorities? They are not a class nor a nation. We must be flexible with the concept of social stratum; perhaps the connection between a stratum and an ideology or utopia is what gives unity to both. It may be, as some argue, that the United States is shifting from a melting pot to a mosaic. This means that many groups and consequently many ideologies make up whatever is the whole. Ethnic consciousness is now a collective component of a broader national ideological mixture.

It is still true, though, that the United States does have a common ideology. As a foreigner, I am quite conscious of the unity of the ideology in this country, and I take the term "ideology" here in a neutral sense. Consider the question of unemployment. For me, this is a typical difference between Europe and the United States. In Europe, to be unemployed is an injustice; one has a right to work. Here unemployment is seen as an individual failure. It is not an accusation directed against the system but a personal problem. The unemployed must rely on welfare and food stamps, which makes them still more dependent on the system. The failure of being unemployed is accentuated by this dependence. Although the concept of free enterprise may be an object of criticism, it is finally taken for granted. Everyone is competing against everyone else. Even the way students work in this country—individual against individual—is quite different from Europe. This pervasive individualism has some healthy implications but also implies that while everything run by private enterprise is in good condition, public enterprises like the railroad suffer. There is no sense of the common property. The United States does have something like a collective ideology, then, though I know that those who live within it are more aware of its subideologies or subcultures.

To conclude this last lecture on ideology, let me say that the concept of integration is a presupposition of the two other main concepts of ideology—legitimation and distortion—but actually functions ideologically by means of these two other factors. Further, the nexus between these three functions may be situated by relating the role of ideology to the larger role of the imagination in social life. My presupposition at this more general level, which I shall develop further in the lectures on utopia, is that imagination works in two different ways. On the one hand, imagination may function to preserve an order. In this case the function of the imagination is to stage a process of identification that mirrors the order. Imagination has the appearance here of a picture. On the other hand, though, imagination may have a disruptive function; it may work as a breakthrough. Its image in this case is productive, an imagining of something else, the elsewhere. In each of its three roles, ideology represents the first kind of imagination; it has a function of preservation, of conservation. Utopia, in contrast, represents the second kind of imagination; it is always the glance from nowhere. As Habermas has suggested, perhaps it is a dimension of the libido itself to project itself *aus*—outside, nowhere—in this movement of transcendence, whereas ideology is always on the brink of becoming pathological because it has a conservative function in both the good and the bad senses of that word. Ideology preserves identity, but it also wants to conserve what exists and is therefore already a resistance. Something becomes ideological—in the more negative meaning of the term—when the integrative function becomes frozen, when it becomes rhetorical in the bad sense, when schematization and rationalization prevail. Ideology operates at the turning point between the integrative function and resistance. In the next lecture we turn to the concept of utopia and start to determine how its functions compare.

Part II

UTOPIA

16

Mannheim

We finally begin the lectures on utopia. The lack of proportion between the number of lectures devoted to ideology and those devoted to utopia reflects something of the situation in the secondary literature. There is an enormous literature on ideology—perhaps because of Marxism and post-Marxist thought—and much less on utopia. I shall address myself first precisely to the question of the obstacles that make so difficult the recognition of utopia both as an autonomous problem and as a concept related to ideology.

This inquiry may best proceed by discussion of several points where a lack of parallelism between ideology and utopia is evident. The first difficulty is that both phenomena differ in their appearance. We are tempted to acknowledge only utopias as a written genre. Specific to the field of utopia is the fact that it constitutes from the outset a literary genre. There are works which are called utopias, the first being Thomas More's *Utopia* (1516), which coined the term. Nothing similar exists in ideology. No one has written a work called *Ideology* and said that he or she was explicitly writing an ideology. This creates a dissimilarity and lack of connection between ideology and utopia. Utopia is a declared genre, not only declared but written, whereas ideology by definition is not declared. It is always the other who says that we are victims of our ideology. The ideology is therefore more naturally denied, while the utopia is more easily claimed. The problem is one of authorship. We may speak of the utopias of Saint-Simon, Owen, and so on, but no proper names are linked to ideology.

The second lack of parallelism appears in the attitudes with which we approach the two phenomena. We approach ideology by means of a critique; out attempt is to unmask. As I tried to argue in the last lecture, perhaps it is only at the end of a very difficult and cumbersome process that we may approach ideology with a more friendly attitude, as we saw in Geertz. Only at this stage has ideology lost its sting as a process of justification. Our general attitude toward utopia is rather different. In some cases utopia does have a negative connotation, particularly when labeled by the representatives of ruling groups who feel threatened. For them the utopia is something impossible and unrealizable, at least within their own order. Nevertheless, the utopia in its literary form engenders a kind of complicity or connivance on the part of a well-disposed reader. The reader is inclined to assume the utopia as a plausible hypothesis. It may be part of the literary strategy of utopia to aim at persuading the reader by the rhetorical means of fiction. A literary fiction is an imaginative variation whose premises the reader assumes for a while. In the utopian work we are not faced with a polemical attitude that must be disarmed by the cleverness of the reader's redactional act.

A third lack of parallelism and still greater obstacle both for comparison of ideology and utopia and for discussion of utopia as a specific genre is the fact that utopias (in the plural) do not easily yield a central meaning for utopia (in the singular). This result is a consequence of the utopias' authorship: specific utopias are written by specific authors. It was difficult enough to try to isolate a kernel of ideology as a unique problem; it is still more difficult to try to isolate a kernel of utopia. We may approach ideologies according to their themes, but a content analysis of utopias finally scatters completely; it dismantles the field to the point where it seems that we have before us dreams or social fictions that are unconnected. There are, of course, some limits to this dispersion. A certain permanence of concerns does obtain, a recurrence of themes about the family, property, consumption, social and political organization, institutionalized religion, and so on. I shall return to this point in the next lecture, where I discuss a utopia—Saint-Simon's—that belongs to the tradition of socialist utopias; comparison of the persisting themes seen there may provide an opportunity for a new discussion with Marxism and a renovation of French utopian socialism. If we look more generally at each utopian theme, though, each one explodes in contradictory directions. Further, utopias are scattered not only in terms of their projects and contents but in terms of their intentions. In Lewis Mumford's *The Story of Utopias,* he attempts to show that there are at least two families of utopias which are very difficult to connect together, what he calls utopias of escape and utopias of reconstruction.

Perhaps we need to find a link between the different utopias in the structure of the imagination. For the purposes of a surface semantics, though, we are faced with a plurality of individual utopias that are very difficult to gather under the utopian name.

This problem is also reflected in the method of approach. Ideology-critique is sociological, whereas utopias are historical. The major utopian literature is composed of histories of particular utopias. There is, in fact, some kinship between the literary genre and the historical approach. In history we tell the story of the stories, a reduplication of the history. When we speak of the utopias of Saint-Simon, Fourier, Owen, Wells, Huxley, and Skinner, we have a list of authors who tend to substitute historical monographs for sociology. The difficulty of subsuming this diversity under one concept is exemplified by one of the best books written on utopia. Raymond Ruyer's *L'Utopie et les Utopies.* Ruyer divides his text into two parts, one part on "Utopia" and the other on "Utopias." He finds it problematic to overcome the structure of a series of monographs with a summary and general introduction to the genre as a whole.

A fourth and even more formidable difficulty for our analysis is that in Marxist thought the distinction between utopia and ideology tends to disappear. To reinstate this distinction is to counter if not Marxism in general then at least orthodox Marxism. In the final two lectures I shall address this question more directly by examining two alternatives to Marxist socialism, the utopian socialisms of Saint-Simon and Fourier. On the basis of our previous study of Marx, we can understand why the distinction between ideology and utopia tends to disappear in Marxism. As we have seen, Marxism has two differing criteria for ideology. First, it opposes ideology to praxis, and what is opposed to praxis is fancy or the imagination. This is the stance we saw in *The German Ideology.* At this stage both ideology and utopia can be put within the same grouping of what is not real. The unreal covers both. We reach the same conclusion, though, if we follow the second Marxist criterion of ideology and oppose ideology to science. In this case, the unscientific covers both ideology and utopia. This latter emphasis started with Engels, when he wrote "Socialism: Utopian and Scientific." Utopian socialism is considered to belong to the realm of ideologies. Marxism tends to reduce utopias to a subclass of ideologies by applying to them the same analysis as for ideologies. Utopias are said to be the efflux of a certain social stratum. The explanation for both ideologies and utopias is the same. The monotony of explanation reduces the specificity of the analysis. The same is true in Althusser, because for him all that is prescientific is ideological; the status of ideology as the imaginary can as well be applied to utopia. Even the prophetic appears as a mere disguise of interest. Both ideology and utopia are "echoes," "reflections."

The merit of Karl Mannheim, to whom we now return, is that he both connected ideology and utopia and at the same time reserved their differences. We shall begin our discussion of Mannheim where we left off, in the chapter of *Ideology and Utopia* on "The Utopian Mentality." I shall indicate my differences with Mannheim, but he provides us at the very least a good sociological tool for approaching the methodological difficulties I have summarized.

Mannheim's study of utopia is presented in three steps. In the previous lecture on Mannheim, I spoke only of the first, a criteriology of utopia, and I shall repeat Mannheim's analysis of this stage briefly. The second step is a typology, and here Mannheim tries to apply a method fairly similar to Max Weber's on ideal types, though we shall see one important difference. Third, Mannheim attempts to interpret the direction of the changes in utopia, that is, its temporal dynamics. Thus, the three main contributions of Mannheim to the problem of utopia are first, an attempt to provide a concept, a working hypothesis covering the inquiry; second, an attempt to orient us within the variety of utopias by overcoming this dispersion, this scattered multiplicity, with a typology; and third, an attempt to say something about the irreducible movement of this typology. Mannheim's main idea is that the process is leading to a decline of utopias and therefore to the progressive disappearance of any noncongruence with reality. People are more adjusted to reality, and this adjustment kills utopia. This situation is finally the major issue in Mannheim's text.

On the first step of Mannheim's analysis, his criteriology, let me simply summarize the points made in our earlier lecture. For Mannheim, ideology and utopia have both a common feature and a differential feature. The common feature is what he calls noncongruence, a kind of deviation or split. It is difficult to say what the noncongruence is a deviation from; we might say it is a deviation from the state of action and reality within which it occurs. The differential feature of ideology and utopia is that utopia is situationally transcendent while ideology is not. As I suggested earlier, criteria for determining who knows the "reality" of a situation and so can decide whether something is transcendent is yet another problem. The second aspect of utopia's transcendent character is that a utopia is fundamentally realizable. This is significant, because it runs against a prejudice that a utopia is merely a dream. On the contrary, says Mannheim, a utopia shatters a given order; and it is only when it starts shattering order that it is a utopia. A utopia is then always in the process of being realized. Ideology, in contrast, does not have the problem of being realized, because it is the legitimation of what is. If there is noncongruence between ideology and reality, it is because reality changes whereas ideology has a certain inertia. The inertia of ideology creates the discrepancy. The differential criterion of ideology and utopia is manifested in two ways, and these are corollaries of the common criterion of noncongruence. First, ideologies relate mainly to dominant groups; they comfort the collective ego of these dominant groups. Utopias, on the other hand, are more naturally supported by ascending groups and therefore more usually by the lower strata of the society. Second, ideologies are directed more toward the past and so are stricken by obsolescence, whereas utopias have a futuristic element.

The second step in Mannheim's analysis is a typology. Mannheim's typology is sociological, and what is interesting methodologically is the difference here between a sociological approach and a historical one. This is an important topic for a philosophy of the human sciences. It is precisely the historian who emphasizes the singularity of works. The basic trend in historical research is to address oneself not to generalization but to the uniqueness of events. The trend is less true now than when Mannheim's book was written, because there has been a shift in history toward sociology, but nevertheless, history is not absorbed into sociology to the extent that it preserves the notion of the event, a theme of great interest to my own reflections. This attention to the notion of the event explains why those who write a history of utopias take as their model Thomas More's *Utopia;* his work exemplifies the affinity that exists between the historical method and the literary genre. The literary genre deposits individual works into the course of history. This implies that the historian cannot overcome descriptive concepts, and the latter, says Mannheim, obstruct systematic innovation.

> Such an historically "naive" concept [of historical uniqueness] would be, for example, that of "utopia" in so far as in its technical historical use it comprised structures which in the concrete are similar to the *Utopia* of Thomas More, or which in a somewhat broader historical sense refer to "ideal commonwealths." It is not our intention to deny the utility of such individually descriptive concepts as

long as the objective is the comprehension of the individual elements in history. (201)

In contrast, Mannheim's own effort is dedicated toward establishment of a sociology of utopia. A sociology of utopia, says Mannheim, follows three methodological rules. First, it must construct its concept, not in the sense of an individually descriptive concept but in the sense of a generalization, a working concept. An example would be "whether there are not ideas as yet unrealized in reality which transcend a given reality . . ." (201). This is how Mannheim constructs the concept of utopia. We are not passive in relation to experience but try to reconstruct it structurally. "Constructive abstraction is a prerequisite for empirical investigation . . ." (202). If the first methodological rule is to construe an overarching concept, the second is to differentiate utopias according to social strata. The problem is to connect each form of utopia with a social stratum, and we shall see that this is not always easy to do. "[T]he key to the intelligibility of utopias is the structural situation of that social stratum which at any given time espouses them" (208). A utopia is the discourse of a group and not a kind of literary work floating in the air. This rule entails that the individuality of authors significantly disappears; while individuality is not completely canceled, it is greatly deemphasized. The third methodological rule is that a utopia is not only a set of ideas but a mentality, a *Geist,* a configuration of factors which permeates the whole range of ideas and feelings. The utopian element is infused into all sectors of life. It is not something that can be identified and expressed in propositional form but is rather, to use the language of Geertz, an overarching symbolic system. Mannheim speaks here of the "dominant wish" (209), something which can be retained as a methodological concept if we understand by it an organizing principle that is more felt than thought. The utopian mentality gives "an immediately preceptible picture" to experience, or at least "a directly intelligible set of meanings" (209). This concept will be most significant when we consider what Mannheim calls the death of utopia; the death of utopia may also be the death of a global picture of reality, and this leaves viable nothing but a piecemeal approach to events and situations.

These three methodological criteria—utopia as a construed concept, a correlation with a corresponding social stratum, and a dominant wish—are not that far from the ideal types of Max Weber. The typology differs from Weber's in one fundamental respect, however, and that will be decisive for the following part of Mannheim's analysis. Mannheim considers the *antagonism* between utopias to be fundamental. We have already said this of ideology, that ideology perhaps does not exist as long as a common culture is not broken. There must be the notion of an antinomy, of an antagonism. This antagonism is easier to acknowledge in the case of utopias because for Mannheim each utopia is defined by the nature of its antagonism to the others. It is not by chance that the section of Mannheim to which we now move speaks of changes in the *configuration* of the utopian mentality. There is a configuration of the utopian mentality because it is the system of utopia as a whole that makes sense of the opposition between one specific utopia and another. Utopias have come "into existence and maintained themselves as mutually antagonistic counter-utopias" (208). Mannheim opens room here for the concept of counterutopias; some utopias may be typically anti-utopian only because there is an element of counterutopia in each utopia. The notion of the counterutopia allows Mannheim to list conservatism as a utopia, which ordinarily is rather questionable. According to his own three criteria, though, as long as we have present in conservatism a form which structures life, appears noncongruent, and includes a dominant wish, then it is a utopia. Even if conservatism is a project for the future to restore the past, it is still a utopia because it counters another utopia. It is essential that one utopia orients itself to another. "[T]he sociologist can really understand these utopias only as parts of a constantly shifting total constellation" (208).

This emphasis on the configuration of utopia prepares the transition from what I termed Mannheim's typology to a dynamics. This difference is already present in the title of the section to which we turn: "*Changes* in the Configuration of the Utopian Mentality . . ." (211; emphasis added). The global shift of the system, the general evolutionary trend of the whole constellation, is the object of this section. We shall bracket for the moment, though, the problem of the general trend which displaces the whole configuration to see first in a more static way how the configuration of utopia is built. The temporal order cannot be discarded, but we shall bracket the direction of this change. Because the section is a long one, I shall retain one point of view to give us a leading thread throughout: the way in which each utopia deals with the sense of time. The recurrent argument in Mannheim's analysis is that each utopia has a particular sense of historical time: "Just because of this central significance of the historical time-sense, we will emphasize particularly the connections which exist between each utopia and the corresponding historical time-perspective" (210).

The first utopia that Mannheim names is not Thomas More's. Instead, Mannheim starts with Thomas Münzer, the Anabaptist (211–19). (It is interesting to see Mannheim's conjunction here with Ernst Bloch, who wrote eight years before Mannheim on *Thomas Münzer als Theologe der Revolution* [1921].) Why does Mannheim choose Münzer and not Thomas More? First, because Münzer's Anabaptism represents both the largest gap between idea and reality—the most stark example of the criterion of non-congruence—and at the same time the prototypical case where the utopian dream is in the process of being fulfilled. For Mannheim the criterion of utopia is not satisfied by the fact that something starts to shatter the existing order. Münzer's movement is chiliastic; it has the idea of a millennial kingdom coming from heaven. The transcendent element manifests itself in the descent of heaven to earth. Chiliasm assumes a transcendent point of departure for a social revolution based on religious motives. The descent of the transcendent overcomes the distance between the utopian idea and reality. We may note that the chiliastic utopia is a limit to Marx's claim that religion is by necessity only on the side of ideology. This fundamental exception to Marx's claim perhaps provides the model for all utopias, since all utopias will represent a reduction of the initial gap between idea and reality.

The second reason for Mannheim's choice of the chiliastic utopia is that it conjoins the ideal with the demands of an oppressed stratum. It is the conjunction between the preacher and the revolt of the peasants that is decisive here. "Longings which up to that time had been either unattached to a specific goal or concentrated upon other-worldly objectives suddenly took on a mundane complexion. They were now felt to be realizable—here and now—and infused social conduct with a singular zeal" (212). Notice again the criterion of realizability. For Mannheim this movement represented the first break in a fatalistic acceptance of power as it is. This is the reason why Mannheim does not consider Plato's *Laws* or even less the *Republic* as utopian. Can we even speak of a utopia before the Renaissance, or does the utopia depend precisely on this unique conjunction between a transcendent ideal and the rebellion of an oppressed class? For Mannheim this is the birth of at least the modern utopia. And that excludes Thomas More as a first stage. What confirms the choice of this point of departure is its continual influence, and this includes its persisting threat to the other utopia forms. The chiliastic utopia arouses counterutopias, which are more or less directed against the threat of the resurgence of this fundamental utopia. Conservative, liberal, and even socialist revolutionary utopias all find the anarchism of the chiliastic utopia a common enemy. For Mannheim there is a line that can be drawn from Münzer to Bakunin where the same energies are launched by this shortcut between an ideal and an earthly demand coming from below. Mannheim insists precisely that the dynamics of this utopia are "ecstatic-orgiastic energies" (213). We may question whether the term is well-chosen, but Mannheim means by it an emotional impulse yielded by the conjunction of ideal and demand that is in opposition to all the ideals of culture of classical Eruope, the latter culminating in the German concept of *Bildung*—culture, education—and typifying the liberal model of utopia. In the chiliastic utopia there is a certain antiliberal energy, since it is not ideas that lead history but the energies liberated by the breaching of the millennium.

As for our touchstone, a utopia's sense of time, what is specific to the sense of time in this utopia and perhaps all utopias that proceed from it is the sudden shortcut between the absolute and the immediate here and now. There is no delay, no postponement between the immediate and the absolute. "For the real Chiliast, the present becomes the breach through which what was previously inward bursts out suddenly, takes hold of the outer world and transforms it" (215). The sense is that the kingdom of God is now. There is one time, and that is the present. The chiliastic experience is the opposite of the mystic's *departure* from space and time. Chiliasm avows the instaneity of the promise against the slow preparation that a didactic concept of culture develops or the sense of opportunity linked to real conditions advanced by Marxist thought. For Mannheim, the disregard for preparation and opportunity is characteristic of the chiliastic utopia.

The second form that Mannheim considers is the liberal-humanitarian utopia (219–29). It is based mainly on a trust in the power of thought as an educative, informative process. The utopia is in conflict with an existing order, but in the name of an idea. It is not Platonism, though, because Platonism remains a model and not a potentiality for change. In a sense we may say that the university proceeds from this utopia, because the notion is that we may change reality by better knowledge, by higher education, and so on. This form is utopian to the extent that it denies, and sometimes very naively, the real sources of power in property, money, violence, and all kinds of nonintellectual forces. It overemphasizes the power of intelligence to form and to shape. In this regard it is antichiliastic, because it does not speak of energies but of ideas. For Mannheim the liberal utopia culminates in German idealism, which reflects this philosophy of education, of *Bildung.* This utopia is typified by the permanent fight in Europe from the beginning of the Renaissance through at least the French Revolution between an intellectualistic world view and a theocratic or clerical world view. The first group is represented by the bourgeoisie—the most "enlightened"—who fought against the theocracies and the monarchies and, particularly after the French Revolution, against the return of monarchies to theocratic legitimation. The main notion of this utopia is the idea of humanity as a formative ideal, despite the lack of this notion's concreteness. This utopia was present in both the French and German Enlightenment (the French Enlightenment was more political and immediate, the German more a theory of culture), and perhaps something similar was at work in the secularization of pietism in England.

As for the sense of time in the liberal utopia, the notion is that history is like individual life with childhood and maturity but without old age and death. The idea is that there is a growth toward maturity. To become mature is the main concept. There is a sense of unilinear progress, and this philosophy of progress is directed exactly against the time sense of the chiliastic utopia. Change does not occur at any moment but as the culmination of historical evolution. Instead of a focus on the outburst of the *kairos,* the emphasis is on growth and becoming. This myth of human education is always anti-anarchist. The symbols and metaphors that belong to this utopia center around the notion of light: an enlightenment, a theme also common in some sense to the Reformation and the Renaissance. The idea is, *post tenebras lux,* after darkness, light; in the end, light wins.

The third utopia Mannheim discusses is conservatism (229–39). At first sight it seems quite strange to call this utopian. Conservatism is more a counterutopia, but as a counterutopia that is compelled to legitimate itself under the attack of the others, it then becomes a utopia of a certain kind. Conservatism discovers its "idea" after the fact; it is like Hegel's owl of Minerva that takes to flight only at the end of the day. As a utopia, conservatism develops some fundamental symbols like that of the *Volksgeist,* the spirit of a people. Its imagery is morphological. The people of a community, folk, nation, or state are like an organism, parts making up a whole. Growth cannot be hastened; people must be patient; things take time to change. There is a sense of historical determinateness like the growth of a plant, and this is opposed to ideas, which simply float. Evident is an anti-abstract turn of mind. As for the time sense of conservatism, priority is given to the past, not the past as abolished but one that nourishes the present by giving it roots. There is a notion of tradition, an assertion that something is transmitted and still living and that the present without this subterranean efflux of the past would be empty. Against the *kairos* of the first utopia and the progress of the second, a sense of duration is affirmed.

Mannheim's fourth form is the socialist-communist utopia (239–47). Here too we may have many reservations about Mannheim's categorization. Most particularly, how can we name the socialist-communist movement utopian when it claims precisely to be anti-utopian? Mannheim has two responses. This movement is utopian first because of its relation to the three other utopias, a relation that is not only competitive but synthetic. Mannheim claims that this fourth mode is "based upon an inner synthesis of the various forms of utopia which have arisen hitherto . . ." (240). It preserves from the chiliastic utopia the sense of a break in history, this leap from the era of necessity to the era of freedom. It also preserves the best of the tradition of progress, that there are temporal preparations, historical stages. The transition, for example, from ownership based on land to that based on capital constitutes a rational development which makes possible at a certain time a break in the main social structure. Even the conservative utopia provides an element: the sense of necessity, the sense that we cannot do anything at any time, the deterministic element that is so strangely linked with the notion of a leap. (In his dialectic of nature, Engels tried to connect the different models of the break, progress, and necessity by arguing that quantitative changes produce at a certain point a qualitative leap.) After the revolution, the conservative trend plays another important role in the socialist utopia to the extent that the Party tries to preserve all its gains. When the Party is in power, it uses all the strategies of a conservative utopia. A yet more fundamental relation of the socialist-communist utopia to the other utopias is that it attempts to reduce them all to ideologies (241). Althusser's notion of an epistemological break can therefore be applied to the relation between this utopia and the other three.

The intertwining of the three previous utopias with this fourth mode is especially recognizable in the socialist-communist utopia's sense of time. Mannheim thinks that the decisive contribution of this utopia is the way it articulates the relation between the near and the remote. Achievement of communism is the remote; it will be the end of class struggle, the end of oppression, and so on. The near implies the steps taken to achieve this goal, steps that must be very rational. Socialism must occur first, for example, before the stage is ready for communism. Mannheim calls this the socialist-communist utopia's strategic appreciation of time. "Time is experienced here as a series of strategical points" (244). Those who have worked with communists know this well, their patience to say this is not the right time, a capacity to endure the present and preserve their ideal for the right moment. In a most interesting line, Mannheim says of this utopia: "only through the union of a sense of determinateness and a living vision of the future was it possible to create an historical time-sense of more than one dimension" (245). The future is prepared in the present, but at the same time there will be more in the future than in the present. "The socialist 'idea,' in its interaction with 'actual' events, operates not as a purely formal and transcendent principle which regulates the event from the outside, but rather as a 'tendency' within the matrix of this reality which continuously corrects itself with reference to this context" (246). This utopia refines the idea of progress by introducing the notion of crisis, which was more or less absent from the liberal utopia except in the case of Condorcet (223). In the socialist-communist utopia, "Historical experience becomes . . . a truly strategic plan" (247).

The main problem Mannheim has now prepared is the direction of change of the utopian configuration. The four forms of utopia are not merely antagonistic, for their constellation is oriented: the nature of their antagonism affects the general trend of the changes. The forms constitute a temporal sequence. (We could make an interesting comparison on this point with the types of legitimacy claims in Max Weber and the general trend from the charismatic to the traditional and then to the rational-bureaucratic.) Mannheim's basic idea here is that the history of utopia constitutes a gradual "approximation to real life" and therefore to the decay of utopia. I must say that I have grave doubts about this, and Mannheim will qualify this statement, as we shall see. Nevertheless, he writes at the beginning of the section on "Utopia in the Contemporary Situation": "The historical process itself shows us a gradual descent and a closer approximation to real life of a utopia that at one time completely transcended history" (248). It is as if the utopian distance is being progressively reduced. After this supposedly descriptive characterization, Mannheim moves, exactly as he did with ideology, from a nonevaluative to an evaluative position about the merits of this change. It is difficult to avoid deciding whether the trend in utopia is a good or bad one. Because Mannheim has defined ideology and utopia as what is *noncongruous* to reality, his conclusion may be preordained. He must take the elimination of noncongruence as a positive gain. The idea is that this "approximation to real life" is wholesome since it expresses an attempt to cope more closely with social reality; it is a progressive "mastery of the concrete conditions of existence" (248).

> The general subsidence of utopian intensity occurs in still another important direction, namely that each utopia, as it is formed at a later stage of development, manifests a closer approximation to the historical-social process. In this sense, the liberal, the socialist, and the conservative ideas are merely different stages, and indeed counter-forms in the process which moves continually farther away from Chiliasm and approximates more closely to the events transpiring in this world. (249)

Modern history is a movement taking increasing distance from Chiliasm. I never know what Mannheim means finally by the "events transpiring in this world," though, because who knows these events other than the utopia? This is a stumbling block in our reading.

However wholesome the attempt to cope more closely with social reality, this process in another sense quite disquieting. Mannheim thinks that radical anarchism has disappeared from the political scene. (I doubt that we could say that today; Mannheim obviously wrote before 1968.) He sees very clearly the conservative trend of socialism, the bureaucratization of liberal utopia, the growing tolerance and skepticism, and above all, the reduction of all utopias to ideologies; the last, we remember, was his own argument in the earlier chapter on ideology. Now everyone knows that he or she is caught in an ideology. Marxism has reduced all utopias to ideology, but Mannheim points out that Marxism itself undergoes the same erosion.

Near the end of the chapter on utopia, Mannheim suddenly is afraid of what he has discovered. There is a visceral protest, a cry. It is not by accident that Mannheim quotes the words of a poet, Gottfried Keller: " 'The ultimate triumph of freedom will be barren' " (250). Mannheim suggests the symptoms of this barrenness: the general disintegration of world views, the reduction of philosophy to sociology. Philosophy is less and less the matrix of global perspectives, and sociology itself, without a philosophical perspective to ground it, is reduced to endless piecemeal inquiry. "At this mature and advanced stage of development, the total perspective tends to disappear in proportion to the disappearance of the utopia. Only the extreme left and right groups in modern life believe that there is a unity in the developmental process" (252).

The sense of historical time is deeply affected by this decay of utopia. "Whenever the utopia disappears, history ceases to be a process leading to an ultimate end" (253). Mannheim believes that the category of totality has been effaced, and he thinks that this is the main character of our epoch. We might compare this perspective, though, with other contemporary approaches. On the present theological scene, for example, an emphasis on the theology of the word is now being followed by an attempt to reenact theologies of history. Theologies of history are surely an attempt to react against the disintegration of perspectives and to maintain that once more the task is to speak of history in terms of totality. This is another argument for rereading Lukács. Lukács is the kind of Marxist who had this sense of totality, as did Sartre in his *Critique of Dialectical Reason,* where he borrowed the concept of totality from Lukács. For Lukács in *History and Class Consciousness,* totality means not so much the necessity of determinism as the capacity to put all conflicts within a picture of the whole. It is this sense of general orientation that disappears in Mannheim, and disappearing with it is the notion of a goal. Mannheim thinks that the result of this effacement is the reduction of all events, all human actions, to functions of human drives. He credits Pareto and Freud with this notion (255), though I would not say that Freud is responsible, because his concept of the drive is always related to the superego, to cultural life. In any case, Mannheim sees the victory of a certain matter-of-factness *(Sachlichkeit).* It is the empty victory of congruence: people are adapted, and because they are adapted they have no illusions; but with the loss of illusions people also lose any sense of direction. Mannheim sees all the diseases of modern sociology here. There is no longer the impulse to draw general pictures.

Is this view of a world without utopias true, though? Are we not witnessing a renewal of utopias because of the failure of matter-of-factness? Acknowledgement that science and technology may themselves be ideological reopens the door to utopia. Mannheim anticipates this response at least to some degree. He makes two qualifications to the apparent lack of tension in the world of his day. On the one hand he says that there are still strata "whose aspirations are not yet fulfilled" (257). Of course! Today the problems of the Third World would completely shatter this image. Nothing is less true than Mannheim's claim that we are "in a world which is no longer in the making" (257). It is also very strange that someone could write that in 1929, so few years before the triumph of Hitler. There is something frightening in this blindness to events. Perhaps it is the triumph of the liberal utopia that inspired his sociology, if we may say that there is a utopia behind this science. The idea that *Bildung* was culminating was soon cruelly denied. The second qualification Mannheim makes to his thesis is that he sees another group which is unsatisfied, and that is the intellectuals. Mannheim here anticipates Marcuse and others in the Frankfurt School. "[S]ince the intellectuals by no means find themselves in accord with the existing situation and so completely congruent with it that it no longer presents a problem to them, they aim also to reach out beyond that tensionless situation" (259).

I would like to conclude our discussion of Mannheim by quoting a very strong statement. In the last paragraph of the utopia chapter, Mannheim identifies where the parallelism between ideology and utopia ends:

> [T]he complete elimination of reality-transcending elements from our world would lead us to a "matter-of-factness" *[Sachlichkeit]* which ultimately would mean the decay of the human will. Herein lies the most essential difference between these two types of reality-transcendence: whereas the decline of ideology represents a crisis only for certain strata, and the objectivity which comes from the unmasking of ideologies always takes the form of self-clarification for society as a whole, the complete disappearance of the utopian element from human thought and action would mean that human nature and human development would take on a totally new character. (262)

If we call ideology false consciousness of our real situation, we can imagine a society without ideology. We cannot imagine, however, a society without utopia, because this would be a society without goals. Our distance from our goals is different from the ideological distortion of the image of who we are. "[W]ith the relinquishment of utopias, man would lose his will to shape history and therewith his ability to understand it" (263).

As I have briefly started to suggest, Mannheim may be criticized at several points. We can put in question his method, his choice of sociology versus history, and the construction of his typology of utopia, its affiliation with and listing of this and that particular utopia. Is Mannheim's typology too schematic? Is his list complete? Why four utopias and not seven or ten? What is the principle for construing his typology? The dynamics of Mannheim's typology seems to be linked with the utopia of progress. There is also an apparent tie to Hegel, because Mannheim's conservative type comes after the liberal, exactly as in Hegel. After the Enlightenment comes the beautiful soul and the regret for the past. Mannheim seems to share the Romantic idealization of the past, which was so strong in Germany. Although Romanticism in France was more lyrical, in Germany it was more political, in the sense of the restoration of the blood and the earth. Nazism surely had some roots in this tradition of the people as a body.

I was particularly surprised that Mannheim's typology allows no room for socialist utopias. Mannheim does consider as a utopia the form of socialism framed by Marxism, but this form is utopian only in terms of the traits it borrows from the other utopias. In its constitution I would say that Marxist socialism is not utopian, except in its development in the young Marx, where it is the utopia of the whole person, the integrity of the whole person. Once again, this is the category of totality promoted by Lukács. By turning in the final two lectures precisely to true examples of socialist utopias, we may find that alternatives exist to the conclusions drawn by Mannheim. We shall see that it may be possible to resolve the tension with which his chapter on utopia ends. Mannheim's final plea for utopia may be coherent, but we shall have to establish it on new grounds. Mannheim's text is finally more cryptic than it seems at first glance, but reappropriation of the notion of utopia may unravel some of the problems his text brings to light.

17

Saint-Simon

In the remaining two lectures I shall discuss two examples of nineteenth-century utopian socialism. I have selected these examples for three reasons. First, I want to test Mannheim's typology of utopia. I am not sure that it is correct in its basic definition of utopia as noncongruence. Because utopian communities may attempt to and do actually exist, utopia is perhaps better defined by its claim to shatter the existing order than by noncongruence. Mannheim's typology is also incomplete, because he in fact neglects the role played by non-Marxist socialist utopias. The second reason I have chosen to discuss the utopian socialists is that I want to pursue Mannheim's investigation of the relation between individual utopias and the general utopian mentality. Mannheim claims that he can reduce the individual element, which is the object of history, to social structure. My question is to what extent does this reduction work? Third, I want to inquire whether the Marxist characterization of utopia adequately represents specific utopias. Engels coined the concept of utopian socialism, and I shall focus on his delineation of this utopian type and contrast it to the two specific examples of utopian socialism that we shall discuss. In Engels' analysis we see that utopias are not always acknowledged as utopian by their proponents but may instead be labeled as such by their adversaries. Mannheim said something on this point when he noted that rising groups promote utopias while ruling groups defend ideologies. As we shall discover, it may be quite difficult to identify the rising group behind certain utopias. This too is a good test for my theory of utopia.

I shall start from Engels' ascription of utopia to this group of nineteenth-century socialists in order to take his characterization as a leading thread and to see how well it works. The expression "utopian socialism" was used by Engels in a brochure published in 1880 under the title, "Socialism: Utopian and Scientific." The English translation to which we shall refer appears in *Marx and Engels: Basic Writings on Politics and Philosophy,* edited by Lewis S. Feuer. Engels' essay is not an independent piece but a three-chapter excerpt from Engels' large work *Anti-Dühring.* Engels saw quite correctly that these socialist utopias were offshoots of the French Enlightenment. An initial question for us, therefore, is how did the Enlightenment produce utopias? The rise of utopias from the Enlightenment accords well with Mannheim's typology, because the second type of utopia, we recall, was the rationalist utopia. In the Enlightenment reason alone is the bearer of radical protest against political and ecclesiastical domination. Reason becomes utopian when this protest against the ruling power has no historical issue. This in fact was the historical situation, because most of these utopias appeared after the failure of the French Revolution, that is, when it became a bourgeois revolution and no longer a popular revolution.

In the development of utopian socialism, individual genius replaces rising groups. This substitution of genius for class is what interested Engels; he, of course, speaks against the utopian socialists but not with the brutality and bitterness he reserved for bourgeois thought. Engels assumes that reason is merely, in a very simplistic way, the idealization of the interests of the bourgeoisie (69). For Marxist thought very early on, then, there was a shortcut between reason and interests. Engels believes that reason is the idealized form of the bourgeoisie's domination. In this process of idealization, however, there is not only the development of an ideology—that is, justification of the position of the dominant class—but also a by-product, the utopia. Individual geniuses then have the ability to do something other than merely represent the ruling interest.

For Engels the utopian illusion is the expectation that truth will be recognized simply because it is the truth, independent of all combinations of power and historical forces (71). We recognize here what Mannheim said about the chiliastic utopias, their indifference to circumstances. The sense is that it is always a good time to undertake a revolution. There are no necessary historical preparations and no conditions for success. This indifference to historical circumstances is a counterpart of the outburst of genius (71), which finds little support for its positions in the present historical forces. Engels suggests that at the time of the utopian socialists, the lack of maturity of capitalistic production and the class situation was met by a lack of maturity in theory (70). Theory was not mature because the classes that could support a revolutionary program were not yet mature. This theoretical immaturity was exemplified in the utopian belief that society could change on the basis of reason alone. Marxists have always said that capitalism must reach a certain level in order for a revolutionary situation to develop; promotion of utopia corresponds to the stage of immaturity. Yet even in being described negatively as a lack of maturity, the utopia is recognized as something specific that cannot be merely discarded and denied as ideological. Even Engels' rationalistic Marxism had to deal with a specific mode of thought that could not be called ideology. Engels does not say precisely that these alternative socialist models are utopias but rather that they are "foredoomed as utopian" (74). Engels uses this phrase because he has in mind a certain model of utopia—the utopias of the Renaissance: More's *Utopia,* Campanella's *The City of the Sun,* and so on. The model is a literary one; it is a regressive model, because it is a fantasy and a fantasy of the past. This thought which claimed to be an advance was in fact a return backwards to some great literary social fantasies (74). Elsewhere, Engels calls at least one form of this utopian thought social poetry.[1] Engels' characterization was intended to be negative, but we may regard it, on the contrary, as a good description of utopian thought as a whole, because there may indeed be a place in our lives for social poetry.[2] In fact, my question at the end of this lecture will be whether we are not ready now to read these utopias in a more favorable way, because we know what Marx and Engels have produced historically at least in terms of state socialism. After this failure, it may again be time for utopia.

Engels gives three examples of utopian socialists—Saint-Simon, Fourier, and Owen—and we shall discuss the first two. Saint-Simon will be our topic in the present lecture and Fourier in the next. It is interesting to note that these two thinkers wrote between 1801 and 1836, that is, during a period of restoration. Utopias appear during a time of restoration, and this perhaps makes sense for our time too. Saint-Simon was prudently revolutionary during the French Revolution, though as we shall see, he hated violence. This negative attitude toward violence is also a part of the utopian mentality; the effort is to convince others, because imagination and not violence must make the break with the past. Saint-Simon and Fourier represent the two poles of the socialist utopia; Saint-Simon is the radically rationalist while Fourier is a romanticist. Discussion of the two is a good approach to the inner dialectic of utopia, its rational and emotional sides.

In my analysis of these two figures, I follow mainly the French sociologist of utopias, Henri Desroche, and his book *Les Dieux Rêvés* (Dreamt Gods). The title itself is interesting for our purposes, because it is about the imagination. Imagination has the function of a social dream. Desroche argues that Saint-Simon's thought developed in three stages. Saint-Simon's rationalistic utopia started by being close to the Enlightenment but changed over time into one attempting to reenact the chiliastic dream of a new religion. It is a striking trait of utopias that they often begin with a radical anticlerical and even antireligious stand and end up by claiming to recreate religion. We shall leave for later discussion to what extent this change may be a criterion of utopia.

Saint-Simon's first utopian project is expressed in his work *The Letters of an Inhabitant of Geneva to His Contemporaries,* written in 1803. This work represents a purely rationalist orientation. Its form is that of a revelation, but its content shows that it is a project of social science. The prophetic form is typical of utopias, as is the use of the future tense to indicate what *will* occur. This utopia shifts power to intellectuals and scientists. The kernel of the utopia is the power of knowledge. This focus confirms a hypothesis I presented in the introductory lecture, that all kinds of utopian projects want to replace the state as a political power by an administration that would have no charismatic aura and and whose only role would be to recruit and support financially a high council of learned persons, a lay priesthood. Saint-Simon speaks in this regard of a government under the shadow of Newton. Saint-Simon confirms my hypothesis that both ideologies and utopias deal with power; ideology is always an attempt to legitimate power, while utopia is always an attempt to replace power by something else. At the same time, this transfer of power in utopia is merely asserted; no practical means for implementation of the dream is set forth. Saint-Simon says always that the learned people, the scientists, *will do* such and such. The future represents the picture of the dream, but not the program for its attainment. As we shall see, Saint-Simon's last form of utopia attempts to fill this gap between the dream and the present state of things.

Nell Eurich points out in her book *Science in Utopia: A Mighty Design* that the idea of replacing political power by the power of scientists has a long lineage. The background for this kind of utopia comes principally from Francis Bacon and his *New Atlantis.* (Condorcet, the French Encyclopedist, was the intermediary link for the French utopian socialists.) Bacon's utopia was essentially a conjunction between the resources of an enlightened nation and the power of scientists, a coalition between an enlightened nation and individual genius. The idea was to replace a political democracy by a scientific democracy; the charismatic element would belong to the scientists and the state would be the bureaucracy supporting this body of scientists.

The scientists do not have power for their own sake, however; this is the important point. They have power for the sake of liberating creativity by a kind of chain reaction. This emphasis, which persists from Bacon to Saint-Simon, corroborates the claim of Mannheim's which at first sight seemed paradoxical, that a utopia is not only a dream but a dream that wants to be realized. It directs itself toward reality; it shatters reality. The utopia's intention is surely to change things, and therefore we cannot say with Marx's eleventh thesis on Feuerbach that it is a way only of interpreting the world and not changing it. On the contrary, the thrust of utopia is to change reality. The claim of the rationalist utopia is that what I have called the "chain reaction" of change —the expression is taken from Desroche (37)—starts from knowledge. Further, this utopia is anti-elitist, in spite of the fact that we give power to those who know. The scientists do not exercise power for the sake of their own comfort.

The great difference between Bacon and Saint-Simon is that while Bacon stressed the physical sciences—a mastery of the earth by good knowledge and therefore a kind of industrialist ideology proceeding from the natural sciences—Saint-Simon emphasized the social sciences. The reason Saint-Simon was able to transfer the concept of science from the natural to the social sciences is that he maintained that the Newtonian law of universal gravitation was the single principle governing all phenomena, both physical and moral. For nature to have order, all sciences had to have the same underlying principle.

In this first stage, where science is the basis for the utopia, we can verify an idea presented by Mumford that finally there are two kinds of utopias: those which are escapes and those which are programs and want to be realized. Speaking of the latter, Eurich shows how these utopias may generate counterutopias—Orwell's *1984,* Huxley's *Brave New World.* The counterutopias proceed from a reversal of the Baconian utopia. If we take the Baconian utopia far enough, it leads to an absurd world. The utopia becomes self-defeating.

It is precisely to prevent the scientific utopia from becoming self-defeating that Saint-Simon takes a second step. He promotes an alliance between scientists and the industrious. A practical basis for the utopia can be provided by *les industriels,* the industrious. We may note that Saint-Simon develops this argument at the beginning of industrialization in France, which was lagging in comparison to Great Britain, where industrialization had begun at least fifty years earlier. For a comparison with Marxism, it is also important to observe that Saint-Simon writes thirty years before the *Manuscripts of 1844* and in quite a different situation. In the Germany of Marx's time there was no political economy and indeed no politics. For his part, Saint-Simon does not take the concept of industry (or, in the more usual terminology today, the concept of work) as a class concept that opposes the bourgeoisie and the working class, but on the contrary as a concept that encompasses all forms of work and opposes itself only to idleness. The main opposition in Saint-Simon is between industry and idleness. Idle people—priests, nobles—are contrasted to industrious people. Saint-Simon does not have the concept of work that Marx opposes to capital. Engels says that it is because the class struggle is not mature that the distinction between work and capital has not been produced (73).[3] What is interesting, though, is precisely that while this distinction is not produced, another one is, the opposition between industry and laziness.

Saint-Simon's larger concept of production encompasses all those who are not idle. In the language of Desroche, Saint-Simon's second stage establishes a conjunction between *homo sapiens,* represented by the scientist, and *homo faber,* represented by the industrialist. Saint-Simon's interests here are evident in the actual projects he promoted during his lifetime. He was enthusiastic about the development of the railroads and the building of canals. He even participated in a project attempting to build a canal linking Madrid to the ocean! Saint-Simon was also impressed by America, where he had been a soldier under Washington and Lafayette. He saw the United States as a prefiguration of industrialist society; it was a land of workers and producers. Saint-Simon's disciples were influential in the building of Suez Canal. The period as a whole had a special interest in communication, in physical communication by all means. While the image of the island, an island protected by the ocean from exterior interferences, was so important for the Renaissance utopias, for Saint-Simon's time the globe was the place for the utopia. Today we respond to this glorification of industry with more mistrust and doubt. Saint-Simon's period, though, spoke of the glory of human being as producer. (Note that the emphasis was not on human being as consumer.) Perhaps the time shared the very old idea of completing creation, of completing the world in this case by the mobilization of the working nation against the idle. Saint-Simon and his followers did succeed in establishing a conjunction between scientists, bankers, and industrialists at the beginning of industry in France.

In Saint-Simon's view, the utopia substitutes industrial power for an ecclesiastical feudalism. We find in Saint-Simon a certain denial of religion that is in a sense similar to Marx's. The common idea is that religion is a kind of surplus. It is interesting to speculate whether the more contemporary emphasis on play might change this perspective. Perhaps because we are fed up with industry, a utopia is said to be more utopian if based on the idea of play rather than on the idea of industry. It may be that a concept of religion linked to play could make sense now, whereas for Saint-Simon religion was on the side of idleness and laziness.

Since I am also interested in the semantics of Saint-Simon's utopia, I should point out that while he spoke of a dream in the first stage, he presents the second stage in the form of a parable, what he calls the industrial parable. He says, let us suppose that France loses the fifty best physicists, chemists, poets, bankers, carpenters, and so on down a long list. The result he suggests, is that the nation would become a soulless body. Let us suppose on the other hand, he continues, that France loses its princes, dukes and duchesses, councillors of state, chief magistrates, its cardinals, bishops, and so on. In this case, he concludes, "This mischance would certainly distress the French, because they are kind-hearted, . . . [b]ut this loss . . . would only grieve them for purely sentimental reasons and would result in no political evil for the State" (73).[4] The idle class can be suppressed, but the industrial class cannot. This hypothesis of Saint-Simon's is both attractive and frightening, because the poetic function must be reintroduced somewhere. As we shall see, it is the third stage of Saint-Simon's utopia which recovers the poetic function.

Another interesting aspect of the development of this utopia that conjoins administration by the learned, by scientists, with the activity of the industrialists is that it makes the present state of the society appear to be upside down. "These suppositions," says Saint-Simon, "show that society is a world which is upside down" (Saint-Simon, 74). I was surprised to see that Saint-Simon, like Marx, had the idea of a countersociety which would be society right side up. It seems that the image was a common one. Engels remarks that this notion of reversal or inversion was in fact already used by Hegel. Hegel said that when reason governs the world—and this for Hegel is the task of philosophy—then the world properly stands on its head. Engels quotes Hegel's *Philosophy of History:* " 'Since the sun had been in the firmament, and the planets circled around him, the sight had never been seen of man standing upon its head—i.e., on the Idea—and building reality after this image' " (Engels, 69 *n.*). Humanity is supposed to stand on its head according to the idea. The reign of the idea is humanity standing on its head instead of on its feet. Marx could make a joke of that and say that his own argument was that humanity should walk on its feet and not on its head. Hegel's stance is intelligible, though, in the sense that because the idea or *Begriff* is now said to govern reality, then people do walk with their head instead of with their feet. We would lose sight of Saint-Simon's effort, though, by suggesting that he simply reverses this reversal.

In the second stage of Saint-Simon's utopia, the goal is still the good of the people. Industry is not undertaken for the sake of power, for the utopia denies the value of power as an end in itself. Instead, industry is supposed to serve all classes of society. The parasitic class of society is not the industrialists but the idle. Saint-Simon has complete confidence that the linkage of industry with scientism is for "the improvement of the moral and physical condition of the most numerous class," that is, the poor (Saint-Simon, 100). In his short summary of Saint-Simon, Engels gives Saint-Simon credit precisely for having spoken of a government—or, we might say, an antigovernment—that exists for the sake of "the class that is the most numerous and the poorest" (Engels, 75). As we can see, the word "class" has a meaning distinct from its usage in orthodox Marxism. Differentiation between the class of the scientist and the class of the poor is only a logical division, a subdivision; it is not the concept of class that exists in relation to capital and work. Marxists would say that the opposition between capital and work was not yet formed, but the utopian claim is that the historical rise of the Marxist concept of class does not necessarily eliminate the possible perpetuation of this different notion of class. The utopian notion looks to some future society governed, for instance, by a middle class. Saint-Simon sees no contradiction between the interests of the industrialists and the needs of the poorest. On the contrary, he thinks that only this conjunction will improve society and so make revolution unnecessary.

This is an important component of Saint-Simon's thought; he believes that revolution occurs because of bad government. Because revolution is the punishment for the stupidity of government, it would be unnecessary if the leaders of industrial and scientific progress had power. Saint-Simon had a strong distaste for revolution; in his memoirs he writes of his aversion for destruction. This is not far from what Hegel says about terror in the sixth chapter of the *Phenomenology of the Spirit.* It seems that the problem of terror was very important for this generation, perhaps as for the Spaniards now, who do not want at any cost to repeat their civil war. The Europe of Hegel and Saint-Simon had a deep disgust with terror, since the best political heads had been cut off.

It is also part of Saint-Simon's utopia to say that a certain isomorphism exists between scientists and industrialists. Ideas originate with the scientists, and the bankers—whom Saint Simon views as the general industrialists—circulate the ideas through their circulation of money. There is a utopia of universal circulation. Industry is to be improved through ideas. Utopias are always in search of the universal class. While Hegel thought that the bureaucracy would be the universal class, for Saint-Simon at this point it was the conjunction of scientists and industrialists.

The third stage of Saint-Simon's utopian project is interesting because it is repesented by a new Christianity. The title of the book Saint-Simon wrote to set forth this stage was exactly *Nouveau Christianisme* (New Christianity). Here Saint-Simon develops not only the religious overtones already present in the two first stages but adds something new. When I speak of religious overtones, I mean that what is retained from the traditions of organized religion is the necessity of an institutionalized administration of salvation. People need to administrate salvation, and this is the job of the industrialists and the scientists. Another religious overtone in Saint-Simon's notion of the emancipation of humankind, which provides science and industry with an eschatological goal.

The decisive step in the third stage is the introduction of artists into the forefront of the framework. Some industrialists became afraid of Saint-Simon's project when they saw it was leading them toward a kind of state capitalism, or at least not to a free enterprise system. Saint-Simon became despondent over the lack of support for his ideas and even reached the point where he shot himself. (The bullets grazed his skull and caused the loss of one eye.) He finally discovered the importance of the artists, though, and decided that because of their power of intuition they had to assume a leadership role in society. Saint-Simon's hierarchy, then, was first the artists, then the scientists, and finally the industrialists. As he recounts (and as ever, the form is confident, declarative sentences):

> "I had addressed myself first to the industrialists. I had engaged them to take the head of endeavors necessary for establishing the social organization that the present state of enlightenment requires.
>
> New meditations have proved to me that the order in which classes must march is: the artists first *[en tête],* then the scientists, and the industrialists only after these two first classes."[5]

Why do artists take the lead? Because they bring with them the power of imagination. Saint-Simon expects that the artists will solve the problems of motivation and efficiency, which are obviously lacking in a utopia composed of merely scientists and industrialists. What is missing, says Saint-Simon, is a general passion.

It is striking that both Saint-Simon and Fourier emphasize the role of the passions. As we shall see, Fourier grafts his entire utopia onto a search about passions; he returns to an old reflection that is present in Hobbes and even in Hume, the notion that a social order is built on passions more than on mere ideas. Saint-Simon writes of his own view: " 'artists, men of imagination, will open the march. They will proclaim the future of the human species. . . . [I]n a word, they will develop the *poetic* part of the new system. . . . Let the artists bring about earthly paradise in the future . . . and then this system will constitute itself quickly' " (quoted in Desroche, 72; emphasis added). Present is the idea of a shortcut in time; if there is suddenly this kind of fire, this explosion of emotion created by the artists, then what I have called the chain reaction will occur. The artists will open the way and develop "the poetic part of the new system."

It is at this point that Saint-Simon's ambiguous relation to religion comes to a point of rupture. On the one hand Saint-Simon preserves his strong antipathy for all kinds of clergy, but on the other hand he expresses a nostalgia for early Christianity. Saint-Simon thought that the utopia he intended had actually been realized in the early church. The church of Jerusalem was the model because it had the gift of the holy spirit. For Saint-Simon the artist represented the holy spirit of the utopia. Saint-Simon was in search of an equivalent to or substitute for religion, in which the cults and the dogmatic elements would be superseded by what he called the spiritual or ethical element. This, to him, was the kernel of early Christianity. Saint-Simon's view was common to his time, at least among dissident personalities and groups; Strauss in Germany is another example.

Christianity was first merely an ethics, and only later did it become a cult, a form of organized worship, and a dogmatic system. Christianity was first the enthusiasm of its founders and had only an ethical purpose. The paradox is that no one can invent a religion, and this is always a problem for utopia. Saint-Simon had to imagine a new clergy, one reduced to didactic tasks in order that it not become once more the idle, eating the bread of the people. The clergy would be reduced to teaching the new doctrine; they would be functionaries of the system but not the center of gravity. They would be merely propagandists of the truth. At the top of the utopia is the triumvirate of artists, scientists, and industrialists; as the true creators of values they reign above the administrators. In Desroche's schema, as we have seen, he describes the movement from *homo sapiens*—the scientist—to *homo faber*—the industrialists. The artist, he adds, has the role of *homo ludens,* a term Desroche borrows from Huizinga. The artists introduce an element of play absent in the idea of industry. Nothing is more serious than industry, as everyone knows. The new Christianity provides the room for festivity—for play and also organized festivity.

Here we reach the moment where the utopia becomes a kind of frozen fantasy. This is the problem Ruyer addresses in his book, *L'Utopie et les Utopies*. All utopias start with creative activity but end with a frozen picture of the last stage (70 ff.). As I shall discuss at greater length in the next lecture, it may be that the specific disease of utopia is its perpetual shift from fiction to picture. The utopia ends up by giving a picture of the fiction through models. Saint-Simon, for example, proposed that there be three houses of parliament, and he diagramed the hierarchy of their rule. One chamber would be the house of invention, another the house of reflection or review, and the third the house of realization or execution. Each house was composed of specific numbers of specific groups. The house of invention, for example, had three hundred members: two hundred engineers, fifty poets or other literary inventors, twenty-five painters, fifteen sculptors or architects, and ten musicians. This accuracy and this obsessive relation to special configurations and symmetries is a common trait of written utopias. The utopia becomes a picture; time has stopped. The utopia has not started but rather has stopped before starting. Everything must comply with the model; there is no history after the institution of the model.

If we try to go beyond this sense of utopia as picture, we face the critical problem raised by the very idea of a new Christianity: how to give flesh and blood to a rationalist skeleton. This requires that we ascribe not only a will to the system but a motive—a motive, motion, and emotions. To have motive and motion the utopia must have emotions. The question, then, is the incantation of the utopia, how the word of the writer may become the incantation that replaces the historical forces which Marxism will put precisely in the place of a new Christianity. At issue is the need for a political aesthetics, where the artistic imagination will be a motivating force politically.

What interests me here in relation to Mannheim's analysis is that when a rationalist utopia is developed to this stage, it finally reinstates the chiliastic element of utopia, what Mannheim always considered the germinal cell of utopia. It is not by chance that a certain messianic vocabulary always comes with this factor. Christianity is dead as a dogmatic body but must be resuscitated as a general passion. Saint-Simon even speaks of an ecumenical passion generated by people of imagination.

> "I work to the formation of a free society whose goal would be to propagate the development of principles which must serve as the basis of a new system. The founders will be the artists, who will employ their talents to impassionate the general society for the improvement of the fate of mankind." (quoted in Descroche, 76)

We have here the role of the social imagination. To impassionate society is to move and motivate it. " 'This enterprise,' " Saint-Simon observes, " 'is of the same nature as the foundation of Christianity' " (Ibid.).

We must also note that Saint-Simon affirms the chiliastic utopia in yet another way: the logic of action is denied. In his characteristically emphatic tone Saint Simon declares: " 'The true doctrine of Christianity, that is, the most general doctrine which can be deduced from the fundamental principle of divine morals, will be produced, and immediately the differences which exist between religious opinions will disappear' " (quoted in Desroche, 77). Present is the magic of the word, a shortcut between the outburst of passion and the revelation of truth. The logic of action takes time, and it requires us to choose between incompatible goals and to recognize that any means we choose brings with it some unexpected and surely unwanted evils. In utopia, however, everything is compatible with everything else. There is no conflict between goals. All goals are compatible; none has any opposing counterpart. Thus, utopia represents the dissolution of obstacles. This magic of thought is the pathological side of utopia and another part of the structure of imagination.

On the basis of this presentation of Saint-Simon, I would like to raise several points. We should consider first the implications of promoting a utopia of knowledge, of science. There seem to be two different ways of interpreting this utopia. On the one hand it can be interpreted as a religion of productivity and technocracy and therefore the foundation for a bureaucratic society, even a bureaucratic socialism. On the other hand this utopia can be viewed as endorsing a more cooperative ideology (an idea developed by the branch of Saint-Simonianism led by Enfantin). This utopia encompasses, then, both the myth of industrialism, the myth of work and productivity that we have now more or less unmasked, and also the idea of the convergence of forces beyond their present antagonism, the idea that antagonism is not fundamental and that instead a certain unanimity of all those who work is possible.

Saint-Simon's orientation raises, second, the idea of the end of the state. This notion may be a more popular one; it is still a utopia for some today. Saint-Simon expresses this idea by predicting that the rule of government over the people will be replaced by the administration of things. The relation of submission between the ruled and the rulers will be replaced by rational administration. In his commentary on Saint-Simon, Engels notes this antigovernment component and speaks of it with some irony, saying that it is something about which there had recently "been so much noise," a reference to the influence of Bakunin (75–76). This question of the abolition of the state also returns in Lenin. Lenin tries to place in a certain order of succession the time when it is necessary to reinforce the state in order to destroy the enemies of socialism—this is the period of the dictatorship of the proletariat—and the time when the state will fade and disappear. The notion of the disappearance of the state owes much to Saint-Simon's ideas; it is channeled through Bakunin's program and remains part of the utopian horizon of orthodox Marxism. The rationalistic emphasis of Saint-Simon's utopia leads to an apology for industry, which is not so attractive, but also to the dream of the end of the state. The political body as a body of decision-making is to be replaced by the reign of intelligence and, finally, of reason.

Another point I would like to raise, again well identified by Engels, concerns the role of genius in the utopian situation that Saint-Simon describes. To put the issue in less dramatic terms, it is the question of the role of the political teacher or the political educator, the latter a term I myself have used elsewhere.[6] The idea is that politics is not only the practical task of professional politicians but involves a kind of intellectual midwifery, something Socrates foresaw. It is the the problem of the philosopher-king, which is quite a different type than Weber's charismatic leader. This person is neither the religious prophet nor the savior but really the educator, the political educator. Saint-Simon considered himself one such creative mind, someone who starts what I have called the chain reaction. Linked to this issue is the attempt to invent religion. Can we say that this aspiration is a real possibility, or is not religion always the result of long traditions? Is someone able to say that he or she founds a religion?

Finally, Saint-Simon's utopia must confront the crucial charge posed by Engels: its underestimation of the real forces of history (71) and, consequently, its overestimation of the power of persuasion by discussion. This is the same difficulty that I have with Habermas, namely, the assertion that finally the extension of discussion will be enough to change things. Saint-Simon thinks that the violent state may be dissolved by the poets; poetry may dissolve politics. This is perhaps the ultimate residue of his utopia. The conjunction between technocrats and poets may be the most striking aspect of Saint-Simon's project. The utopia does without revolutionaries but conjoins technocrats and passionate minds. We should note that this discussion of the role of passion in utopia is a partial presentation that makes its most complete sense only in conjunction with Fourier. In Fourier the element of passion will be both the starting point and the organizing center. I wonder whether Bacon also faced this problem of how to move and animate the social body when the starting point is a blueprint for society that lacks emotional support.

Our discussion of Saint-Simon's utopia brings us back to my basic hypothesis that what is at stake in ideology and in utopia is power. It is here that ideology and utopia intersect. If, according to my analysis, ideology is the surplus-value added to the lack of belief in authority, utopia is what unmasks this surplus-value. All utopias finally come to grips with the problem of authority. They try to show ways people may be governed other than by the state, because each state is the heir of some other state. I have always been amazed by the fact that power does not have much of a history; it is very repetitious. One power imitates another. Alexander tried to imitate the oriental despots, the Roman caesars tried to imitate Alexander, others tried to imitate Rome, and so on throughout history. Power repeats power. Utopia, on the other hand, attempts to replace power. Take, for example, the problem of sexuality. Here too the utopian concern is the problem of the relation of power. For utopias sexuality is not so much an issue about procreation, pleasure, or the stability of institutions as about hierarchy. The hierarchical element is typical of the worst Western traditions since perhaps the Neolithic age. The continual problem is how to end the relation of subordination, the hierarchy between rulers and ruled, by replacing it. The attempt is to find alternatives that work through cooperation and egalitarian relationships. This question extends to all kinds of our relations, from sexuality to money, property, the state, and even religion. Religion is revealed as such an issue when we consider that the only religions we know have institutions that rule religious experience through a structure and therefore a certain hierarchy. The deinstitutionalization of the main human relationships is finally, I think, the kernel of all utopias. Our question of Saint-Simon is whether this can be accomplished through the lead of scientists, industrialists, and artists.

We should also ask whether utopias deinstitutionalize relationships in order to leave them deinstitutionalized or in order to reinstitutionalize them in a supposedly more humane way. One of the ambiguities of utopia is that there are in fact two different ways to solve the problem of power. On the one hand the argument may be that we should do away with rulers all together. On the other hand the argument may be instead that we should institute a more rational power. The latter may lead to a compulsory system, the hypothesis being that since we have government by the best, by the wisest, we must therefore comply with their rule. The result is a tyranny by those who know the best. The idea of a moral or ethical power is very tempting. Thus, the utopia has two alternatives: to be ruled by good rulers—either ascetic or ethical—or to be ruled by no rulers. All utopias oscillate between these two poles.

What particularly interests me in the notion of utopia is that it is an imaginative variation on power. It is true that specific utopias make an effort to be consistent, often to the point of being obsessively coherent and symmetrical. As we saw in Saint-Simon, a house of reflection is balanced by a house of invention, and so on. History is not this coherent, so in this sense the utopia is antihistorical. Ultimately, though, it is the free variation of utopias which is more intriguing than their claim to consistency or their neurotic claim to noncontradiction. The result of reading a utopia is that it puts into question what presently exists; it makes the actual world seem strange. Usually we are tempted to say that we cannot live in a way different from the way we presently do. The utopia, though, introduces a sense of doubt that shatters the obvious. It works like the *epoché* in Husserl, when he speaks in *Ideas I* of the hypothesis of the destruction of the world—a purely mental experiment. The *epoché* requires us to suspend our assumptions about reality. We are asked to suppose that there is nothing like causality, and so on, and to see where these suppositions lead. Kant has this notion also; he asks what is coherent about a body that it can be described sometimes as red, sometimes as black and white, and so forth. The order which has been taken for granted suddenly appears queer and contingent. There is an experience of the contingency of order. This, I think, is the main value of utopias. At a time when everything is blocked by systems which have failed but which cannot be beaten—this is my pessimistic appreciation of our time—utopia is our resource. It may be an escape, but it is also the arm of critique. It may be that particular times call for utopias. I wonder whether our present period is not such a time, but I do not want to prophesy; that is something else.

18

Fourier

As we have seen, Saint-Simon's utopia anticipates the life that we now know; for us, his industrialist world is no longer a utopia. The only major difference between our time and Saint-Simon's utopia is that he thought the industrialist world would satisfy mainly the interests of the neediest, which is not the case today. In contrast, Fourier's utopia is much more radical. No one shows more clearly what a utopia is than Charles Fourier, who was a contemporary of Saint-Simon and wrote his major work between 1807 and 1836. Fourier is interesting because he pushes his utopia below not only the level of politics but even below the level of economics to the root of the passions. Fourier's utopia works at the level of the system of passions that rules every kind of social system. In a sense, this is the utopia that should be related to Hobbes, since Hobbes was the first to elaborate what he called a mechanics of passions and derived his political system from this insight. Thus, the question Fourier poses—the problem of how political institutions are connected with the system of passions that underlies social life—has a long history.

Fourier's orientation to utopia is intriguing, second, because he writes and lives on the borderline between the realizable and the impossible. (We can look to the realizability of Fourier's utopia in terms of both his own continual efforts and the efforts of others, particularly in the United States.) Fourier lived and wrote at this turning point of the utopia. As I shall discuss later in more detail, one of my general conclusions about utopia is that all utopias have the ambiguity of claiming to be realizable but at the same time of being works of fancy, the impossible. Between the presently unrealizable and the impossible in principle lies an intermediary margin, and this is precisely where Fourier's work may be located.

Fourier's approach to utopia is also significant because it combines freedom of conception with a rigidity of the utopia's pictures. That a great quantity of new ideas is always expressed in pictures of extreme detail is one of the enigmas of utopias. In Fourier this compulsion takes the form of an obsession with numbers, which is itself not rare among utopian thinkers. He makes exhaustive lists: he knows how many passions and how many distinct personality types there are, and he knows how many occupational divisions there will be in the harmonious city. He describes schedules, diets, the hours for awakening, the common meal, the construction of buildings; everything is forecast in great detail. The problem of utopias, then, is not only the margin between the unrealized and the impossible but also the margin between fiction, in a positive sense, and fancy, in a pathological sense. The utopian structure cheats our categorization of the difference between the sane and insane. It contests their clear-cut distinction. As we shall see, it is not easy to decide which of these two traits—sane or insane—to apply to Fourier's utopia itself.

In Dominique Desanti's *Les Socialistes de l'Utopie,* she entitles her chapter on Fourier "A Life in Fancy" ("Une Vie dans l'Imaginaire"). Fourier's works as a whole deserve this title. What is typically fanciful in Fourier is the use of inversion as a constant. Fourier wants to invert what we see in life and to say the contrary in the utopia. The utopia is an inverted image of what we see in "civilization," Fourier's pejorative term for society as a whole. The utopia is an inversion of what is in fact an inverted society. The contrast is between life in civilization, which is bad, and life in harmony, Fourier's utopian world. I was intrigued by Fourier's emphasis on the notion of inversion, which we have previously seen to be an apparently common concept or scheme of many thinkers in the nineteenth century. Hegel used this concept, Marx used it against Hegel, and the utopians used it against real life. This trait must have struck Fourier's contemporaries very strongly, since in his short presentation on Fourier in "Socialism: Utopian and Scientific," Engels credits Fourier precisely with this dialectical power of inversion. Engels says that Fourier "uses the dialectical method in the same masterly way as . . . Hegel" (77), which is quite a statement.

If Fourier is distinguishable from Saint-Simon, the reason does not rest in his views on industry. Fourier shared much of Saint-Simon's enthusiasm on this subject; he too was an industrialist, in the sense that his program for the emancipation of the passions, which is his real contribution, relies on a hypothesis of abundance. (This hypothesis may be why Fourier speaks so loudly to some present approaches.) Fourier wanted a more productive industrial order, and he was also concerned about the well-being of the poorest. On the latter point, he had some quite specific ideas: for example, he promoted the notion of a decent minimum income and advanced the notion of the right to work, an idea which has still not been accepted in this country. He also set forth the idea that work should be alternated, a proposal akin to Marx's conception of a life in which we do several things in the same day. The positions of work must be shifted so that no one becomes a robot of some task. Fourier invented a very precise way of accomplishing this organization of labor by combining free choice with compulsory rotation. All his ideas are calculated with great exactitude.

Fourier's target, however, is not industry but civilization. He makes the important distinction between the necessary development of industry to achieve certain goals and the way of life linked to it. (Whether this separation can be made is a major question for us today.) Fourier's concern, to put it in Marxist terms, is to develop new relations of production for productive forms. It is on the basis of this concern that he describes the present horrors of civilization. Engels greatly praises Fourier's description here, because he sees in Fourier the critique of civilization. Engels also makes a most interesting remark about Fourier at this point; he says that Fourier is a satirist (76). I was tempted by this comment to relate irony as a mode of discourse and utopia. There is an element of irony in utopia. The utopia seems to say something plausible, but it also says something that is crazy. By saying something crazy, it says something real. This point parallels my earlier comments about utopia being on the margin between the realizable and the impossible and on the margin between the sane (if fictional) and the insane (the pathological). Perhaps Wayne Booth should follow up on *A Rhetoric of Irony* with work on utopia.

When Fourier's critique shifts from industry's development to the way of life linked to it, this marks a radical shift in the utopian concern itself, since as I said by way of introduction, Fourier digs under the layers of political authority and economic organization to put in question their basis in the passions. What Fourier brings forth is a theory of passions which is deduced from a cosmology that he claims is Newtonian. Already this is the begining of something very crazy. Both Saint-Simon and Fourier claim to be Newtonian; for Saint-Simon, Newtonian law is the basis for a social physics, and for Fourier the key idea is that of attractions. I do not know what Fourier understood about physics and the mechanics of heavenly bodies, but he fastened upon Newton's term "attraction." For Fourier the cosmology of attraction is the sign of a harmony that must be recovered.

Fourier's cosmology puts attraction at the root of everything, and his contention is that his utopia is in fact in conformity with nature. This links Fourier once again to the eighteenth century, though not to the Encyclopedists but rather to their enemy, Rousseau. Fourier follows the lineage of Rousseau; the task is to uncover nature, which has been concealed by civilization. Fourier's idea is that attraction is a divine code which society must follow. (I shall return to the religious aspect of this thesis later.) The utopia claims to be a restoration of the primitive law. Thus, it is both progressive and regressive. The progression is in fact a regression to the divine law. This world view has nothing scientific about it but is merely a mythical connection from astral attractions to a social code of passionate attraction *(attraction passionnée.)* Fourier's theory is a code of social attraction and under this rubric he derives specific codes of incredible detail.

This program is so ambitious as to be impossible, but its intent is what remains intriguing: the idea of liberating emotional potentialities which have been concealed, repressed, and finally reduced in number, strength, and variety. One of the central aspects of civilization is that there are very few passions, and so the problem of the utopia is to redeploy the span of passions. Here Fourier's obsession with numbers makes sense. All his work is in a certain regard a rediscovery of possible passions which have been repressed. In the same way that Marx wrote on *The Poverty of Philosophy* as his response to Proudhon's *The Philosophy of Poverty,* Fourier is responding to the poverty of the passions. The impoverishment of the notion of the passions is what he struggles against. Fourier's code of social attractions is not a code of rule but on the contrary a code for displaying the entire spectrum of passions under the combinatory laws of attraction. He has, for example, twelve fundamental passions, and they circle around what he characterizes as the pivotal drive for unity, which has the same position as justice in the Platonic structure. This drive for unity Fourier calls harmonism, the passion for harmony. This passion for harmony integrates passions which are for the most part social passions. (The exceptions are the five senses, which Fourier includes among the passions.) Three of these passions, the three distributive passions that rule social life, deserve special mention. The first is named the "alternate." In French it is the adjective *papillonne,* from the butterfly. This passion is the need for variety, whether in one's occupations or in one's relationships with various partners; it is the multiplication of relationships with a multiplication of partners. Fourier has been read here as a prophet of free love, and this was in fact his claim. The second distributive passion is called the composite passion, and it connects people's sensual and spiritual pleasures. The third is the cabalistic passion, which is the taste for intrigues and conspiracy and is the root of discussion. Again, this whole is supported by a theory of basic movements, orientations, and attractions.

Fourier's project is therefore to introduce a revolution in the passions. Life in civilization has repressed them and reduced their number. We might say that Fourier's project is an archeology of forgotten passions, which to a certain extent anticipates Freud's description of the id. In a sense, then, Fourier's work is a metapsychology of the id, if one that also gives a direction to politics, since the task of politics is to multiply and to amplify pleasures and joys. The multiplication of occupational divisions reflects Fourier's concern for the resurrection of the passions. There is a hint of this in the young Marx when he says that the humanization of nature and the naturalization of human being will be a resurrection of nature. This theme disappeared later in Marx—it was absent even by the time of *The German Ideology*—but it has returned in Marcuse and some modern branches of German and American naturalism. The idea is that nature has been enslaved, both outside ourselves and within ourselves, and so the salvation of nature is at once our task and our possibility. Once again we see that this project is not in the line of the Enlightenment but rather that of Rousseau. In Desroche's chapter on Fourier, he presents this perspective as the Edenic myth, the Edenic myth of harmony according to the principle of attraction. The presupposition held in common with Rousseau is that the passions are virtues and that civilization is what has transformed passions into vices. The problem is to liberate the passions from the vices, to release the vices from moral condemnation, even from moral assessment, in order to recuperate the underlying passions.

The aspect of Fourier's utopia that I would like to focus on is its religious component. Discussion of this problem will raise the larger question whether all utopias are not in some sense secularized religions that are also always supported by the claim that they found a new religion. The spiritual location of utopia is between two religions, between an institutionalized religion in decline and a more fundamental religion that remains to be uncovered. The utopian element is the argument that we may invent a religion based upon the remnants of the old religion, and my question is whether this combination of an antireligious trend and a search for a new religion from within the ruins of classical religion is an accidental or a permanent trait of utopia. The religious component of utopia is a strong factor throughout Fourier's work.

For Fourier the religious element is significant both negatively and positively. Negatively, Fourier's constant target is the preaching of hell. (Fourier may be accurate that the preaching of hell was central to the Catholic church in France during his lifetime, though I do not know what he would say about the present day when it seems that in many denominations this preaching has basically expired.) Fourier is so strongly against this preaching of hell, because for him the notion of Eden is extremely important. He wants to retain the notion of Eden as a claim that we may return before the alleged catastrophe of the fall. His problem is to develop a politics that would have as its aim a return before the fall. In turn, he sees the preaching of hell as the symbol of a whole structure, not only of religion but of the whole repressive structure of civilization. When he describes the modern city as hell, it is a hell on earth that mirrors the hell which is preached. There are two hells and they are the image of one another.

Fourier considers institutional religion to be fundamentally traumatizing because it is based on the image of God as essentially a cruel tyrant. It is in response to this image that Fourier calls himself an atheist. He has many pages where he speaks of the necessary combination of atheism and theism. His approach is not very dialectical, though, in the sense that it is a mere clash between two claims each advocated with the same strength. Fourier is a very religious man, and he thinks that humanity is fundamentally religious, but his religious approach is maintained through an atheistic attitude to God as tyrant. His atheism is the denial of this God who represents, to Fourier's mind, the divinization of privation. Fourier advocates instead the divinization of delight, which for him would be Eden. In one satirical passage, Fourier says that paradise as described by the preachers must be a much sadder place than life on earth, because it offers only something to see—white robes—and something to hear—celestial music—but nothing to eat and no sexual love.[1] Paradise, he says, is not very interesting! In fact, paradise as it is preached is a shadow of hell. Fourier's characterization is an intriguing comment on the reduction, throughout its history, of religion's symbolism by its own institutions.

The positive side of religion is expressed by the fact that for Fourier attraction is a divine code. The invocation of God is as strong as its denial. Fourier speaks, for example, about attraction as a compass, a " 'magic pointer in the hands of God by which he gets by incitations of love and pleasure what man gets only by violence' " (quoted in Desroche, 102). He says that his methodological accusation of God is an inner component of a " 'reasoned faith' " (quoted in Desroche, 103). There is something very modern to this approach. I myself try to speak elsewhere about the necessary juxtaposition of suspicion and recollection.[2] In a sense, Fourier is the prophet of this difficult paradox.

Most of Fourier's critical pages are directed against a stance he calls half atheist and half faith. This attack is against "the philosophers," by which he means not Kant or Plato but the French philosophers—Diderot, Voltaire, and so on. For Fourier, "the philosophers" were only half-atheists, because they were deists. They did not go far enough. Voltaire, for example, conceives of God as a clockmaker. This mechanistic God is completely alien for Fourier; it is an aspect of hell. Fourier's attack against deistic rationalism is very similar to Rousseau's.

Similarly, religion as he knows it is itself only half-witnessing—*demi-témoin*—because it has, according to him, forgotten, concealed, and betrayed the revelation of humanity's social destiny—namely, social harmony. The fact that the churches do not preach social harmony is a sign of their betrayal. Preaching about the good passions has been replaced by preaching about morals. For Fourier morals exemplify the infection of faith by the concept of hell. God is thereby lowered, he says, to the industrial realm of our duties. The wise have betrayed and buried the memory of lost happiness. Against a religion of austerity he preaches a religion of pure love and imagination. The poverty of religion and the religion of poverty are the same.

The religious overtone of Fourier's proclamations raises an issue about utopia as a whole: to what extent is utopia's futurism fundamentally a return? Fourier comments quite often that what he advocates is not a reform but a return, a return to the root. He has many pages on the topic of forgetfulness. This theme is also prevalent in Nietzsche and in others such as Heidegger; the idea is that we have forgotten something, and consequently our problem is not so much to invent as to rediscover what we have forgotten. In a sense all founders of philosophies, religions, and cultures say that they are bringing forth something that already existed.

Even the Greeks, who considered themselves the civilized and their predecessors the barbaric, had the idea that there were wise people in the past who knew. A certain myth about Egypt existed in Greece; the Egyptians represented this memory. Thus, when Plato presents new ideas, he says that he offers a *palaios logos,* an ancient logos. The new logos is always an ancient logos. Similarly, a common feature today of the futuristic attitude in Africa, from what I understand, is that it links itself to the recovery of a past which has been lost not only because of colonialism but through the process of civilization. The idea is to liberate a lost power.

This process of return has often been coupled with the schema of inversion. The oblivion or forgetfulness was an inversion, and so we must invert the inversion. The return is a re-turn. As I have mentioned, this notion of the turn, *die Kehre,* is not rare in modern philosophies, Heidegger being a good example. When the return is simply an inversion, though, this is the weak aspect of this conceptualization. The return takes the form of a mere inversion of alleged vices into virtues, and so we have a mere replacement by the contrary.

This reversal also has its humorous aspects. In Fourier we find a plea for pride, lewdness, avarice, greed, anger, and so forth. He also proffers some curious pages on opera; he thinks that opera should replace the religious cult. Fourier sees in opera a convergence of action, song, music, dance, pantomime, gymnastics, painting, and so on, and this for him is the religious meeting. It is a parable of passional harmony, a kind of ceremony of worship. One question we need to ask is whether Fourier's utopia is simply a literal reversal, a mere turning of vices into virtues, or an ironic one. As Engels also remarked, the element of irony in Fourier cannot be downplayed.

Fourier's ultimate expression of the religious imprint on everything is his advocacy of a regime of delight. I do not know whether Fourier's vision is feasible or instead doomed to failure, but he is the prophet of the idea that pleasure may be religious. Fourier's book, *Le Nouveau Monde Amoureux* (The New Amorous World), is an exploration, a speculation on the combinatory possibilities of sexual love under the law of passional attraction, and this law, we remember, is a divine code. Some may view Fourier's book as pornographic (and indeed it was suppressed by his disciples and first published only in 1967), but its religious element cannot be dismissed. In it Fourier combines fantasy, love, and worship. To transpose Habermas' expression, we might say that the problem is no longer discussion without boundary and constraint but fantasy and love without boundary and constraint. The identification with God resides in the element of enthusiasm, the enthusiasm of love, what Fourier calls the " 'passion of unreason' " (quoted in Desroche, 145). This image of God is the opposite of the clockmaker God of deism. God is the enemy of uniformity, Fourier says, and love is the spring of this passion of unreason.

I am particularly intrigued by Fourier's notion of passion, because what seems to be denied or undermined by this religion of passions, this divinization of passions, is the structure of power. This observation brings us back once more to my hypothesis that ideology and utopia converge finally on one fundamental problem: the opaque nature of power. In Fourier the problem of power is undercut by the renaissance of love, a resurrection of love. Fourier's utopia does not provide a political answer but rather denies that politics is the ultimate question. The problem is not how to create the good political state but how either to exist without the state or to create a passion-infused state. The utopian element is the denial of the problematic of work, power, and discourse—three areas all undermined by Fourier's problematics of passion.

In concluding the lectures on utopia, I would like to say a few last words about why I have chosen Saint-Simon and Fourier as creators of significant utopias, why I have chosen to explore their more practical utopias rather than other, merely literary ones. One reason for my choice lies in Mannheim. I was attracted precisely by the paradox in Mannheim that what characterizes utopia is not an inability to be actualized but a claim to shatter. The capacity of utopia to break through the thickness of reality is what interested me. I did not choose to examine a utopia like Thomas More's, because while his utopia is an alternative to reality, More says clearly that he has no hope that it will be implemented. As a vehicle for irony, utopia may provide a critical tool for undermining reality, but it is also a refuge against reality. In cases like these, when we cannot act, we write. The act of writing allows a certain flight which persists as one of the characteristics of literary utopias. A second reason for my bias or preconception in choosing practical over literary utopias is perhaps less visible. The utopias I have examined parallel my other studies on fiction. Fictions are interesting not when they are mere dreams outside reality but when they shape a new reality. I was intrigued, then, by the parallelism between the polarity of picture and fiction and that of ideology and utopia. In a sense all ideology repeats what exists by justifying it, and so it gives a picture—a distorted picture—of what is. Utopia, on the other hand, has the fictional power of redescribing life.

I would now like to make some last remarks on the lectures as a whole. What makes discussion about utopia difficult is that finally the concept has the same ambiguity as ideology, and for similar reasons. Because the concept of utopia is a polemical tool, it belongs to the field of rhetoric. Rhetoric has a continuing role because not everything can be scientific. As Althusser himself says, most of our life in fact is ideological in that sense—we could say utopian too—because this element of deviance, of taking distance from reality, is fundamental. In the same way that ideology operates at three levels—distortion, legitimation, and identification—utopia works at three levels also. First, where ideology is distortion, utopia is fancy—the completely unrealizable. Fancy borders on madness. It is escapism and is exemplified by the flight in literature. Second, where ideology is legitimation, utopia is an alternate to the present power. It can be either an alternate to power or an alternate form of power. All utopias, whether written or realized, attempt to exert power in a way other than what exists. I see even the utopias' sexual fantasies—such as Fourier's—as research not so much about the human instincts as about the possibilities of living without hierarchical structure and instead with mutuality. The concept of attraction is antihierarchical. At this second level utopia's problem is always hierarchy, how to deal with and make sense of hierarchy. At a third level, just as the best function of ideology is to preserve the identity of a person or group, the best function of utopia is the exploration of the possible, what Ruyer calls "the lateral possibilities of reality."[3] This function of utopia is finally the function of the nowhere. To be here, *Da-sein,* I must also be able to be nowhere. There is a dialectic of *Dasein* and the nowhere. In "The Seventh Elegy" of the *Duino Elegies* Rilke says: *Hiersein ist herrlich,* to be here is glorious. We must modify this sentiment and say both that to be here is glorious and that to be elsewhere would be better.

Without closing too quickly the problematics by this schema—schemas are very dangerous—I would say that this polarity between ideology and utopia may exemplify the two sides of imagination. One function of imagination is surely to preserve things by portraits or pictures. We maintain the memories of our friends and those we love by photographs. The picture continues the identity while the fiction says something else. Thus, it may be the dialectics of imagination itself which is at work here in the relation between picture and fiction, and in the social realm between ideology and utopia. It is to recognize these larger dynamics that I have constantly stressed that we must dig under the surface layer, where the distortions of ideologies are opposed only to the fallacies of fancy. At this surface layer we find only an apparent dichotomy of uninteresting forces. When we dig down, we reach the level of power. For me the problem of power is the most intriguing structure of existence. We can more easily examine the nature of work and discourse, but power remains a kind of blind point in our existence. I join Hannah Arendt in my fascination with this problem.

When we dig even further, we reach our final interest, which proceeds beyond the level of mutual labeling and even beyond that of power to the level where the imagination is constitutive. In contrast to the stage of distortion, where expressions are mutually exclusive, the expressions of the constitutive function are not exclusive. The deeper we dig under appearances, the closer we come to a kind of complementarity of constitutive functions. The ruling symbols of our identity derive not only from our present and our past but also from our expectations for the future. It is part of our identity that is open to surprises, to new encounters. What I call the identity of a community or of an individual is also a prospective identity. The identity is in suspense. Thus, the utopian element is ultimately a component of identity. What we call ourselves is also what we expect and yet what we are not. This is the case even if we speak, with Geertz and others, of the structure of identity as a symbolic structure, because as Geertz points out, we can differentiate between "models of" and "models for." "Models of" look toward what is, but "models for" look toward what should be according to the model.[4] The model may reflect what is, but it may also pave the way for what is not. It is this duality of faces that may be constitutive of imagination itself. As I have tried to suggest, it is a duality reflected not only as ideology and utopia but also, as we see in the arts, as picture and fiction.

I would term my analysis of ideology and utopia a regressive analysis of meaning. My claim is that this approach is not an ideal typical analysis but rather a genetic phenomenology in the sense proposed by Husserl in his *Cartesian Meditations*. This method allows us to reach a level of description without being outside the interconnections between ideology and utopia. A genetic phenomenology attempts to dig under the surface of the apparent meaning to the more fundamental meanings. The effort is to recognize the claim of a concept which is at first sight merely a polemical tool. I attempt to make the concept more honest.

As we close these lectures on ideology and utopia, I want to comment on the status of these reflections, and consider whether they can avoid being ideological and utopian themselves. This, we remember, was the paradox confronted by Mannheim. My own conviction is that we are always caught in this oscillation between ideology and utopia. There is no answer to Mannheim's paradox except to say that we must try to cure the illnesses of utopia by what is wholesome in ideology—by its element of identity, which is once more a fundamental function of life—and try to cure the rigidity, the petrification, of ideologies by the utopian element. It is too simple a response, though, to say that we must keep the dialectic running. My more ultimate answer is that we must let ourselves be drawn into the circle and then must try to make the circle a spiral. We cannot eliminate from a social ethics the element of risk. We wager on a certain set of values and then try to be consistent with them; verification is therefore a question of our whole life. No one can escape this. Anyone who claims to proceed in a value-free way will find nothing. As Mannheim himself asserted, anyone who has no projects or no goals has nothing to describe and no science to which he or she can appeal. In a certain sense my answer is fideist, but for me it is only an avowal of honesty to admit that. I do not see how we can say that our values are better than all others except that by risking our whole life on them we expect to achieve a better life, to see and to understand things better than others.

Even with this answer, though, it still may seem that we run the danger of being totally captured by whatever ideology it is that orients us. As we recall, Mannheim responded to this problem by distinguishing between relativism and relationism. He argued that he was not a relativist but a relationist. His contention was that if we have a large enough viewpoint, we can see how the various ideologies reflect limited positions. Only the breadth of our view liberates us from the narrowness of an ideology. This, we noted, is a kind of Hegelian claim, because Hegel's project was exactly to overcome the varieties of human experience by encompassing them within a whole. Each part of our experience then makes sense in its place within the whole. We can locate a certain ideology as part of the global picture. This stance, however, is linked once again to the problem of the uninvolved onlooker, who is in fact the absolute *Geist*. The Absolute Knowledge of Hegel becomes the value-free onlooker. Mannheim advances the idea of the intellectual who is not involved in the struggle for power and who understands everything. I would rather say that we cannot remove ourselves from the ideological circle, but we are also not entirely conditioned by our place in the circle. We know that Mannheim's paradox exists only because we have the capacity for reflecting on our situation; this is the capacity Habermas called *Selbstreflexion*. People are not completely caught in an ideology in another sense, because a common language implies the existence of exchange, some neutralization of narrow prejudices. This process of suspicion which started several centuries ago has already changed us. We are more cautious about our beliefs, sometimes even to the point of lacking courage; we profess to be only critical and not committed. I would say that people are now more paralyzed than blind. We know that it may be our ideology that causes us to react as we do.

In yet another sense Mannheim's paradox is not the last word, because when we consider the history of ideas, we recognize that the great works of literature and other disciplines are not merely expressions of their times. What makes them great is their capacity to be decontextualized and recontextualized in new settings. The difference between something which is purely an ideology reflecting one particular time and something which opens outward to new times is that the latter does not merely mirror what presently exists. A great part of our culture is nourished by projective ideas which are not only expressions, or even concealed expressions, of the times in which they were set forth. We can read a Greek tragedy precisely because it is not simply an expression of the Greek city. We do not care about the Greek city; the economy of ancient Athens is dead, but its tragedies are alive. They have the projective capacity to speak for readers or hearers who are not its contemporaries, who are not its original audience. The ability to address oneself beyond one's immediate audience to an unknown audience and the ability to speak for several time periods proves that important ideas are not merely echoes. They are not merely reflections in the sense of mirroring. We should apply the same criterion to ourselves. The utopian element has always displaced the ideological element.

Any analysis that attempts to explore the nature of historical change may find it difficult to proceed when the possibility of an all-encompassing view is no longer available. In response to this difficulty, Mannheim talks of a criterion of appropriateness. This criterion is rather difficult to apply, but it may be our only alternative. For Mannheim the problem is that the noncongruence of ideology and utopia must not go too far, because if it does it will either lag behind or move too far ahead of historical change. Ideology is finally a system of ideas that becomes obsolete because it cannot cope with present reality, while utopias are wholesome only to the extent that they contribute to the interiorization of changes. The judgment of appropriateness is the way to solve this noncongruence problem. It is a concrete judgment of taste, an ability to appreciate what is fitting in a given situation. Instead of a pseudo-Hegelian claim to have a total view, the question is one of practical wisdom; we have the security of judgment because we appreciate what can be done in a situation. We cannot get out of the circle of ideology and utopia, but the judgment of appropriateness may help us to understand how the circle can become a spiral.

Notes

EDITOR'S INTRODUCTION

1. *The Symbolism of Evil* (1967 [1960]); *Freud and Philosophy* (1970 [1965]). Here and throughout the notes to the introduction, the volume's year of publication appears within parentheses, the year of first publication, where different, within brackets.

2. *History and Truth* (1965 [2d ed., 1964]); *Political and Social Essays* (1976). The essays in both volumes generally were written in earlier parts of Ricoeur's career. With the exception of two articles in the latter volume (both from 1973), all articles date from 1967 or before. A more recent volume of Ricoeur's essays, *Hermeneutics and the Human Sciences* (1981), includes essays with social scientific interests—a theory of action, history as narrative, and proof in psychoanalysis—but only one essay, "Science and Ideology," directly addresses the questions of social and political theory that are the concern here.

3. In an interview with Peter Kemp, Ricoeur acknowledges and explains his silence about social and political matters during the past several years. He adds, though, that his silence has been only with regard to practice and not to theory, because his articles on ideology and utopia have continued his contribution to social and political theory. See Paul Ricoeur, "L'Histoire comme Récit et comme Pratique," *Espirit* (June N.S., 1981), 6:155–65.

Ricoeur's articles on ideology and utopia foreshadow the more thorough and systematic presentation in the lectures and include: "Science and Ideology," mentioned in the previous note and originally published in French in 1974; "Can There Be a Scientific Concept of Ideology?" in Joseph Bien, ed., *Phenomenology and the Social Sciences* (1978), pp. 44–59 [1974–75]; L'Herméneutique de la Sécularisation: Foi, Idéologie, Utopie," *Archivio di Filosofia* (1976) 46(2–3):49–68 [translated in very abbreviated form in "Ideology, Utopia, and Faith," *The Center for Hermeneutical Studies* (1976), 17:21–28]; and "Ideology and Utopia as Cultural Imagination," in Donald M. Borchert, ed., *Being Human in a Technological Age* (1979) pp. 107–26 [1976].

A secondary literature has recently started to appear in response to these articles. See John van den Hengel, "Faith and Ideology in the Philosophy of Paul Ricoeur,"

Eglise et Théologie (1983), 14:63–89; Robert Sweeney, "Value and Ideology," *Analecta Husserliana* (1983), 15:387–406; John B. Thompson, "Action, Ideology, and the Text," in *Studies in the Theory of Ideology* (1984), pp. 173–204; Tom Rockmore, "Idéologie Marxienne et Herméneutique," *Laval Théologique et Philosophique* (1984), 40(2):161–73. See also George A. Kendall, "Ideology: An Essay in Definition," *Philosophy Today* (1981), 25:262–76, especially p. 262 *n*.

For an annotated chronology of Ricoeur's writings on ideology and utopia, see the bibliography at the end of the present volume.

4. For Ricoeur's response to Althusser, refer to his participation in a discussion of Althusser's *Lenin and Philosophy,* in *Bulletin de la Société Française de Philosophie* (1968), 62(4):161–81. Ricoeur's comments appear on pages 161–68. For Ricoeur's previous work on Habermas, see "Ethics and Culture," *Political and Social Essays,* pp. 243–70 [1973], and "Hermeneutics and the Critique of Ideology," *Hermeneutics and the Human Sciences,* pp. 63–100 [1973].

5. See, e.g., *Freud and Philosophy,* p. 35.

6. For Ricoeur's other work on Marx, see "Le *Marx* de Michel Henry," *Esprit* (1978), 2:124–39; "Rückfrage und Reduktion der Idealitäten in Husserls 'Krisis' und Marx' 'Deutscher Ideologie,' " in Bernhard Waldenfels, Jan M. Broekman, and Ante Pažanin, eds., *Phänomenologie und Marxismus,* 3:207–39.

7. The full title of the work is *Freud and Philosophy: An Essay on Interpretation.* The original French title is even more revealing, as the English title and subtitle are reversed: *De L'Interpretation: Une Essai sur Freud.*

8. This does not mean that religious, psychological, or linguistic interests in Ricoeur are subsumed under a philosophic interest. Neither is it to argue that particular essays cannot have these other interests as their subject matters. Ricoeur is most fundamentally a philosopher, however, and his work has a philosophic orientation that cannot be reduced to religious, psychological, or linguistic inspiration.

9. Some indications of Ricoeur's social and political stances do appear, however. See his criticism of Althusser's response to the 1968 Soviet invasion of Czechoslovakia in lecture 8 and his comments on the American ideology in lecture 15.

10. Paul Ricoeur, "Action, Story, and History: On Re-reading The Human Condition," *Salmagundi* (1983), 60:60. Ricoeur has many references to the importance in his work of a philosophical anthropology. See, e.g., *Fallible Man* (1965) [1960]; and *The Conflict of Interpretations* (1974 [1969]). See also lecture 9.

11. Because Ricoeur's interest in Marx and Marxism is methodological rather than historical, his analysis stops with *The German Ideology*. For Ricoeur this text is the foundation for all Marx's specifically Marxist works. Ricoeur wants to develop a model that relates ideology to reality, and this model is located in the Marx of *The German Ideology* (even though Marx generally places the two concepts in opposition). In contrast, Marx's *Capital* reflects a methodological abstraction, because its discussion of political economy abstracts from the roles of individual human agents. Certain passages in *Capital—e.g.,* on the fetishism of commodities—may reflect Marx's earlier model, but more generally this work advances the model

of classical Marxism, one that opposes ideology to science. Ricoeur maintains that the most complete presentation of this latter model is located in Althusser, and consequently he does not discuss its other Marxist variants.

Ricoeur does express an interest in analyzing Lukács, but this discussion is limited owing to time constraints and Ricoeur's attention to method instead of specific historical figures (see lecture 7).

12. Ricoeur urges an interpretation of Marx that has him view human beings not only in their totality but as a totality. Economic categories are not the sole basis for human activity or human alienation. Production is not first an economic concept but one pertaining to human creativity in general. The role of consciousness is not rejected but said to be more properly understood as one part of the living individual and so not autonomous. The concept of alienation may have been abandoned in *The German Ideology* but only because it belonged to an idealistic vocabulary. The concept's nonidealistic intent can be recovered if we talk of human self-activity and the loss of this self-activity. To conceive of class as an ultimate cause is to fall prey to the terms of estrangement, because a concept like class is an abstraction objective only in the time of the division of labor. In support of a reading of Marx oriented to the role of totality, Ricoeur refers to Lukács and Sartre, and he says that the influence of Engels and Lenin on Marxism obscured this perspective (lecture 4). Only the category of totality preserves the many dimensions of the concept of production; in classical Marxism the notion is reduced to a mere economic concept.

13. Karl Marx, *The German Ideology* (1970), p. 47. See lecture 5.

14. Interestingly enough, Althusser does not presume that the march of history leads inevitably to the sole reign of science; on the contrary, he says it is utopian to think that science will ever totally replace ideology. Ideology has a persisting function as a necessary illusion; it has the ability—which science does not—to help us make sense of our lives. Ideology is something that we could not face the difficulties of life without. In the lectures Ricoeur comments at some length on Althusser's positive assessment here of the role of ideology. See lecture 8.

15. This criticism of Mannheim's emphasis on noncongruence may be contrasted with Ricoeur's comments in his introductory lecture.

16. Ricoeur also demonstrates that Weber slights the role of claim and belief in some of the types of authority to which he does attend. One prime example is legal authority. Ricoeur asserts that legal power maintains some features of traditional and charismatic power, despite Weber's contention that legal authority is purely rational. What makes legal power a power says Ricoeur, "may be finally borrowed always from the two other kinds of power" (lecture 12). Belief is also a factor here, Ricoeur maintains, because "Acceptance is the belief on which legality lies."

This criticism implicates Weber's analysis of ideal types. As Ricoeur points out, Weber's ideal types are characterized by a "prejudice toward rationality" (lecture 11). He examines the charismatic and traditional types not on their own basis but in relation to the legal and bureaucratic type. Rather than being value-free, Weber's analysis expresses "all his expectations about the nature of rationality in society" (lecture 12).

17. See note 4.

18. See Thomas McCarthy, *The Critical Theory of Jürgen Habermas* (1978), especially pp. 207–13.

19. The quotation is taken from Clifford Geertz, "Ideology as a Cultural System," *The Interpretation of Cultures* (1973), p. 208.

20. Paul Ricoeur, "The Tasks of the Political Educator," *Political and Social Essays,* pp. 271–93 [1973].

21. On the relation between ideology, utopia, and religious faith, see "L'Herménetique de la Sécularisation" and, for an abridged translation, "Ideology, Utopia, and Faith."

22. *Time and Narrative,* p. ix. *Time and Narrative* is a three-volume work. The first two volumes have appeared in French (1983, 1984) and English (1984, 1985). Hereafter, all references to *Time and Narrative,* volumes 1 and 2, will be noted, respectively, by the abbreviations "TN" and "TN2."

23. All references to *The Rule of Metaphor* will appear in the text with the abbreviation "RM." For a summary of Ricoeur's argument in this text, see Paul Ricoeur, "The Metaphorical Process as Cognition, Imagination, and Feeling," *Critical Inquiry* (1978), 5:143–59.

24. See also RM:197. On the concept of the "metaphoric," Ricoeur cites Hans-Georg Gadamer, *Wahrheit und Methode* (1960), pp. 71, 406 ff.; translated as *Truth and Method* (1975), pp. 67, 388 ff.

25. "Can There Be a Scientific Concept of Ideology?" p. 51.

26. "Science and Ideology," p. 231.

27. See also Paul Ricoeur, "Mimesis and Representation," *Annals of Scholarship* (1981), 2(3):20.

28. Throughout the volumes of *Time and Narrative,* the "dominant category" is the "mimesis of action" (TN2:153).

Ricoeur's vocabulary in the quoted passages from pp. 57–58 of *Time and Narrative* calls to mind his article "La Structure Symbolique de l'Action," *Actes de la 14e Conference de Sociologie des Religions* (1977), pp. 29–50. Ricoeur now rejects as inadequate, however, the vocabularly proposed there. See TN:243 *n.* 5.

29. Paul Ricoeur, "Explanation and Understanding: On Some Remarkable Connections Among the Theory of the Text, Theory of Action, and Theory of History," *The Philosophy of Paul Ricoeur,* p. 165. For a more expansive discussion, see Paul Ricoeur, " 'Logique Herméneutique'?" in Guttorm Fløistad, ed., *Contemporary Philosophy* (1981), pp. 179–223. Ricoeur repeats the lines just quoted on p. 209 of this article. In *Time and Narrative,* Ricoeur develops his argument still further and says that understanding and explanation are now an obsolete vocabulary, his preference instead being the terms "nomological explanation" and "explanation by emplotment" (TN:181).

30. In a more formal statement of the dialectic here, Ricoeur says:

> I shall attempt to show that the possibility of speculative discourse lies in the semantic dynamism of metaphorical expression, and yet that speculative discourse can respond to the semantic potentialities of metaphor only by providing it with the resources of a domain of articulation that properly belongs to speculative discourse by reason of its very constitution. (RM:259)

Ricoeur's statement recalls his formulation fifteen years earlier in the conclusion to *The Symbolism of Evil:* "The symbol gives rise to thought." This aphorism, Ricoeur comments, says two things: "the symbol gives; but what it gives is occasion for thought, something to think about" (348). What we need, Ricoeur continues, is therefore "an interpretation that respects the original enigma of the symbols, that lets itself be taught by them, but that, beginning from there, promotes the meaning, forms the meaning in the full responsibility of autonomous thought" (349–50).

The specific setting for the formulation in *The Symbolism of Evil* is religious symbolism. In a more recent article, Ricoeur says that a hermeneutics of religious discourse is the circular process involving "the moment of immediacy," "figurative mediation" (stories, symbols), and "conceptualization." See Paul Ricoeur, "The Status of *Vorstellung* in Hegel's Philosophy of Religion," in Leroy S. Rouner, ed., *Meaning, Truth, and God* (1982), pp. 70–88.

31. "Can There Be a Scientific Concept of Ideology?" p. 59.

32. "Science and Ideology," p. 243.

33. "Can There Be a Scientific Concept of Ideology?" p. 57.

34. See, e.g., Gadamer, *Truth and Method;* Emilio Betti, "Hermeneutics as the General Methodology of the *Geisteswissenschaften,*" in Josef Bleicher, *Contemporary Hermeneutics* (1980), pp. 51–94 [1962]; E. D. Hirsch, Jr., *Validity in Interpretation* (1979 [1967]) and *The Aims of Interpretation* (1976).

35. See Paul Ricoeur, "Construing and Constructing" (review of Hirsch, *The Aims of Interpretation*), *Times Literary Supplement* (February 25, 1977), p. 216. For Hirsch's response to critics such as Ricoeur, see E. D. Hirsch, Jr., "Meaning and Significance Reinterpreted," *Critical Inquiry* (1984), 11:202–25, esp. p. 210.

36. Paul Ricoeur, "La Raison Pratique," in Theodore F. Geraets, ed., *Rationality Today* (1979), p. 241 (my trans.). See also "Science and Ideology," p. 224, and lecture 10.

37. Paul Ricoeur, "History and Hermeneutics," in Yirmiahu Yovel, ed., *Philosophy of History and Action* (1978 [1974 conference]), p. 6. (This article is not exactly the same as one by the same title published in the *Journal of Philosophy* [1976] 73:683–95.) Ricoeur's statement here seems to parallel similar observations already noted about the relation between the metaphoric and the speculative. Both the speculative and the theoretical have a certain autonomy, yet their possibility rests on the dynamism of the metaphoric and the practical.

38. See Paul Ricoeur, "Objectivation et Aliénation dans L'Expérience Historique," *Archivio di Filosofia* (1975), 45(2–3):27–38. See also Paul Ricoeur, "Aliénation," *Encyclopedia Universalis* (1968), 1:660–64.

In the lectures Ricoeur has an important comment on the distinction at issue here, claiming that we must distinguish between the meaning and use of ideological structures, and in particular between their constitutive meaning and their ideological use. Taking Habermas' example of the ideological function of science and technology in modern capitalist society, Ricoeur says that this situation does not entail necessarily that science and technology "are constitutively ideological but rather that they are being used ideologically" (lecture 9).

To raise as a question the relation between meaning and use also brings to the forefront another context where this terminology is prominent, that of the analytic philosophy of language. But whereas in the lectures Ricoeur's point is to differentiate within ideology the constitutive from the distortive, the question posed for analytic philosophy is how can it distinguish between the ideological and what it holds to be constitutive.

39. Paul Ricoeur, "Imagination in Discourse and in Action," *Analecta Husserliana* (1978), 7:3.

40. Paul Ricoeur, "The Function of Fiction in Shaping Reality," *Man and World* (1979), 12:130. On the following page of the same article, Ricoeur equates imagination with the basic "metaphoric."

41. For the development of Ricoeur's theory of the imagination, see "Imagination in Discourse and in Action," "The Function of Fiction in Shaping Reality," and "Sartre and Ryle on the Imagination." The last appears in Paul A. Schilpp, ed., *The Philosophy of Jean-Paul Sartre* (1981), pp. 167–78.

The distinctions being drawn do not entail that reproductive and productive imagination—and hence ideology and utopia—are simple polarities, entirely autonomous one from the other. Instead, reproductive and productive fall along a common spectrum of the imagination. A return to Ricoeur's description of the tension between the metaphor and the speculative clarifies this point. While the speculative—the drive toward univocity—has a certain autonomy, its possibility nevertheless depends on the dynamism of the metaphoric. Its interpretation cannot be literal—in the sense of originary, proper, nonmediated—because no nonmetaphoric location is available. Similarly, ideology is not a literal reproduction of some social given, both because social action is always mediated symbolically and because ideology is symbolic and interpretive itself. We may say, then, that both ideology and utopia are imaginative in a productive sense, but ideology falls on the more reproductive end of this spectrum. As Ricoeur notes, ideology and utopia are both "practical fictions" ("The Function of Fiction in Shaping Reality," p. 123).

Time and Narrative provides a basis for a further extension of this comment. While both ideology and utopia are fictions (which is not equivalent, as we shall see, to being false), we cannot reduce even productive imagination to the merely fictional. Ricoeur calls the "configurational act" necessary for the emplotment of historical or fictional narrative a "grasping together" of the story's incidents. This act draws from the "manifold of events the unity of one temporal whole" (TN:66). Ricoeur goes on to say that this act of producing the configurational act can be compared to the work of the productive imagination (TN:68). He later insists, however, that he does not consider fiction to be synonymous with "imaginary construction," precisely because "The latter is an operation common to history and to the fictional narrative . . ." (TN:267 *n.* 1). If even history can be called an act of productive imagination, then surely ideology—itself already admittedly a fiction—must be called an act of productive imagination too. This reinforces that reproductive imagination must be considered part of the larger field of (productive) imagination.

42. "History and Hermeneutics" (1978), p. 9.

43. In *Time and Narrative,* volume 2, Ricoeur's discussion of fiction correlates closely with the utopian role described here. Fiction provides us "distance" from our times (155). "What indeed are these possible objects if not fictions . . .?" (76). The fictional experience constitutes a kind of "transcendence within immanence" (6).

44. Ricoeur's views here might be profitably compared to those of Thomas Kuhn in the philosophy of science. See, e.g., Kuhn, *The Structure of Scientific Revolutions* (1970 [1962]); "Metaphor in Science," in Andrew Ortony, ed., *Metaphor and Thought* (1979), pp. 409–19; "Preface," *The Essential Tension* (1977).

45. Ricoeur argues at the point in the lectures just quoted, for instance, that Althusser's framework of infrastructure and superstructure is built on a metaphor of the relation between a base and an edifice. Ricoeur challenges this metaphor of a "base" with another metaphor, about what is "basic" for human beings.

46. On Ricoeur's depiction of the relation between the study of imagination and the poetics of the will, see "Imagination in Discourse and in Action," p. 3.

As originally envisaged, Ricoeur's philosophy of the will was an enterprise that would proceed in three stages. First was a study of the essential—eidetic—structure of human being-in-the-world. This was completed in *Freedom and Nature* (1966 [1950]). Second was a study of the empirics of actual existence, a stage itself divided into two parts: first, on humanity's existential possibilities (particularly fallibility); and second, on humanity's actual experiences (in particular, the experience of evil). This stage was represented, respectively, by *Fallible Man* (1965 [1960]) and *The Symbolism of Evil* (1967 [1960]). The third stage was the projected poetics, which is yet incomplete.

Those interested in more summary presentations of the published stages may want to look at the first three articles in *The Philosophy of Paul Ricoeur* (1978), an anthology of his essays. The best secondary source on Ricoeur's work up to 1970 is Don Ihde's *Hermeneutic Phenomenology: The Philosophy of Paul Ricoeur* (1971).

47. "L'Histoire comme Récit et comme Pratique," p. 165. Ricoeur's statement is worth quoting at length:

> despite appearances, my single problem since beginning my reflections has been creativity. I considered it from the point of view of individual psychology in my first works on the will, and then at the cultural level with the study on symbolisms. My present research on the narrative places me precisely at the heart of this social and cultural creativity, since telling a story . . . is the most permanent act of societies. In telling their own stories, cultures create themselves. . . . It is true that I have been silent from the point of view of practice, but not at all at the theoretical level, because the several essays I have already published on the relation between Ideology and Utopia are entirely at the center of this preoccupation.

> [malgré les apparences, mon unique problème depuis que j'ai commencé à réfléchir, c'est la créativité. Je l'ai pris du point de vue de la psychologie individuelle dans mes premiers travaux sur la volonté, puis sur le plan culturel avec l'étude des symbolismes. Mes recherches actuelles sur le récit me placent précisément au coeur de cette créativité sociale, culturelle, puisque raconter . . . est l'acte le plus permanent des sociétés. En se racontant elles-mêmes, les cultures se créent elles-mêmes. . . . J'ai été silencieux, oui, du point de

vue de la pratique et de l'engagement, mais pas du tout sur le plan théorique, car les quelques écrits que j'ai déjà publiés sur le rapport entre Idéologie et Utopie sont tout à fait au centre de cette préoccupation.]

48. Paul Ricoeur, "Poetry and Possibility," *Manhattan Review* (1981), 2(2): 20–21.

49. Paul Ricoeur, "Creativity in Language," *The Philosophy of Paul Ricoeur,* pp. 132–33 [1973].

50. Ricoeur's language recalls his response to structuralism, evidenced in several of the essays in his book *The Conflict of Interpretations.*

This language also returns us to the ineradicably symbolic character of human action. As Ricoeur comments later, "there is no human experience that is not already mediated by symbolic systems, and, among them, by narratives." Paul Ricoeur, "Narrative and Hermeneutics," in John Fisher, ed., *Essays on Aesthetics: Perspectives on the Work of Monroe C. Beardsley* (1983), p. 157.

51. Ricoeur adds elsewhere: "It is not even certain that Heidegger's substitution of truth as manifestation for truth as adequation responds to what mimesis demands of our thinking about truth. For is it still a matter of manifestation, there where there is a fitting production?" "Mimesis and Representation," p. 31.

52. *Time and Narrative* 2:160.

53. See, respectively, RM:247 ff.. and TN:42, 226. See also Paul Ricoeur, *The Reality of the Historical Past* (1984).

54. "Mimesis and Representation," p. 30. See also RM:306.

55. "Ideology, Utopia, and Faith," p. 28.

56. "Ethics and Culture," p. 269.

57. Indicating that utopia and ideology are themselves not separable, Ricoeur maintains that identity may also be prospective (see lecture 18).

58. *Freud and Philosophy,* p. 35.

59. On this point Geertz's anthropology of culture may be subject to the same criticisms as Gadamer's hermeneutics. Ricoeur's differentiation from Geertz here is implicit in the lectures—particularly in his recourse to Habermas before introducing Geertz—but not discussed directly. For Ricoeur's criticism of Gadamer, see "Ethics and Culture" and "Hermeneutics and the Critique of Ideology."

60. The theme of totality is itself another important theme in Ricoeur's work, one that he addresses in the lectures in his analysis of Marx. This theme relates back to Ricoeur's quest for a philosophical anthropology, the project I referred to in the beginning of this introduction. At a more ontological level, Ricoeur defines the possibility of totality as "the search for a non-generic unity for the meanings of being" (RM:272), a thesis he derives from Aristotle. Ricoeur discusses this theme in relation to Aristotle on pp. 259–72 of *The Rule of Metaphor.* See also Paul Ricoeur, *Etre, Essence et Substance chez Platon et Aristote* (1982 [1957]). This thesis preserves the notion of totality while also preserving the understanding that the unity is not deduced from some common—nonsymbolic—origin but is more a result of family resemblance, to use the Wittgensteinian terminology.

61. "Ideology, Utopia, and Faith," p. 21. The same passage appears in "L'Herméneutique de la Sécularisation," p. 51.

1. INTRODUCTORY LECTURE

1. For purposes of style, Ricoeur's terminology throughout the lectures will usually refer either to social or cultural imagination but not to both at the same time. This stylistic convenience should not obscure the fact that the form of imagination Ricoeur is concerned with in these lectures is decidedly both social and cultural. The social, says Ricoeur,

> has more to do with the roles ascribed to us within institutions, whereas the cultural involves the production of works of intellectual life. The social seems to arise from the difference in various languages—and surely in French—between the social and the political. The political focuses on the institution of the constitutional, the sharing of power, and so on, whereas the social encompasses the different roles ascribed to us by varying institutions. The cultural, on the other hand, has more to do with the medium of language and the creation of ideas. (Conversation with the editor)

2. These lectures comprised Ricoeur's other course in the Fall quarter 1975 at the University of Chicago. The title of the course was "Imagination as a Philosophic Problem."

3. As Ricoeur will make clear later in this lecture, the term "function" is used quite differently than it is in sociological functionalism. At issue is precisely what functionalism does not attend: how ideology and utopia actually work, how they operate. As Ricoeur will elucidate, this is quite different from functionalism's attention merely to causes and determinants and their resultant patterns or uniformities.

4. Listed in the bibliography. See also the discussion of Parsons and Shils and the discussion of strain theory in Clifford Geertz, "Ideology as a Cultural System," *The Interpretation of Cultures,* pp. 197–99, 203–7.

5. See Geertz, *The Interpretation of Cultures,* p. 194.

6. Paul Ricoeur, "Science et Idéologie," *Revue Philosophique de Louvain* (1974), 72:326–56; now translated as "Science and Ideology," *Hermeneutics and the Human Sciences,* 222–46.

7. Geertz's own reference here is to strain theory alone. Page numbers throughout the remainder of this first lecture refer to Geertz's "Ideology as a Cultural System" in *The Interpretation of Cultures.*

8. Geertz, ibid., p. 193, citing F. X. Sutton et al., *The American Business Creed,* pp. 3–6.

9. Kenneth Burke, *The Philosophy of Literary Form.*

10. These lectures comprised Ricoeur's part of a course co-taught with David Tracy on "Analogical Language," offered Spring Quarter 1975 at the University of Chicago.

11. Ricoeur questions just how adequate genetic codes are as templates for the organization of organic processes. As noted a few lines earlier in the text, if it were not for the flexibility of our biological existence, the cultural system would be unnecessary.

12. The order cited in this paragraph has been changed from Ricoeur's original presentation in lecture. It has been made congruent with the order actually occur-

ring in the ideology lectures, something quite different from the order originally proposed here. Changes in the order of presentation and in the choice of figures occur as follows:

Proposed order (from original lecture.) Ideology as:

1. Distortion: Marx, German Marxists (Horkheimer, Habermas), French Marxists (Althusser), Mannheim.
2. Integration: Geertz, Erikson, Runciman.
3. Legitimation: Weber.

Actual Order. Ideology as:

1. Distortion: Marx, Althusser, Mannheim.
2. Legitimation: Weber, Habermas.
3. Integration: Geertz.

Horkheimer, Erikson, and Runciman are all dropped as central figures in the actual lectures. (In the original introductory lecture, reference is made to Erikson's chapter on ideology in *Identity: Youth and Crisis* and to Runciman's *Social Theory and Political Practice*.) Horkheimer is mentioned again only tangentially, Erikson is briefly referred to two or three times, and Runciman is not noted again at all.

The reader may note that Ricoeur's introductory presentation of ideology in this first lecture—a movement from distortion to integration to legitimation—follows the order originally proposed for the remaining ideology lectures.

13. The relative difference in the amount of treatment given ideology and utopia in this first lecture parallels the difference in the lectures as a whole. Of the eighteen lectures, only three focus on utopia, one each on Mannheim, Saint-Simon, and Fourier.

14. See note 2.

2. MARX: THE *CRITIQUE OF HEGEL* AND THE *MANUSCRIPTS*

1. See Joseph O'Malley, "Editor's Introduction," to Marx, *Critique of Hegel's "Philosophy of Right,"* pp. xxvii ff. While Ricoeur emphasizes the transformative method as the main critical approach in the *Critique,* O'Malley notes two other critical techniques also employed by Marx: a straightforward textual analysis and a historico-genetic method of criticism (p. xxvii).

2. Marx's quotation may be found in Hegel's *Philosophy of Right,* p. 162. The interjection is Ricoeur's.

3. MARX: THE "FIRST MANUSCRIPT"

1. See Sigmund Freud, "Obsessive Actions and Religious Practices," *Standard Edition,* 9:115–27.

4. MARX: THE "THIRD MANUSCRIPT"

1. "What is decisive is not to get out of the circle but to come into it in the right way." Martin Heidegger, *Being and Time,* p. 195.

2. Even after this expansion of Ricoeur's argument, readers may find it difficult to accept his view about the separability in Marx of material and spiritual estrangement. This reaction seems supported by lines like the following, which appears in Marx's text at the end of the extended quotation of Ricoeur's previous paragraph. As quoted by Ricoeur, Marx says: "Religious estrangement as such occurs only in the realm of consciousness, of man's inner life, but economic estrangement is that of real life. . . ." What Ricoeur does not say is that the quoted sentence ends: "its transcendence [economic estrangement's] therefore embraces both aspects" (136). Marx's derivation of religious estrangement from economic estrangement seems plain.

As Ricoeur only anticipates in his discussion here of totality, though, this characterization is not adequate. Ricoeur will return to the point later in discussing Althusser's depiction of the tension between infrastructure and superstructure and will demonstrate that Marxists have attempted to talk about an infrastructural basis while allowing the superstructure—which includes religion—a certain autonomy, one that reacts back on the basis. Ricoeur concludes that Althusser does not admit what his analysis makes patent: that the infrastructure/superstructure model is not revived but defeated. Ricoeur's discussion of Marx here seems to make a similar claim: Marx shows that the derivation of estrangement—including religious estrangement—is not univocal. Estrangement in the realm of consciousness cannot be subsumed under economic estrangement, i.e., under estrangement in "real life." Different realms have a certain autonomy of their own and can only be comprehended together under the notion of totality.

3. See Roger Garaudy, *Karl Marx: The Evolution of His Thought.*

4. *Emanzipation* is the word in the original German text, and this term, Ricoeur explains, has a clear kinship with the classical theological term *Erlösung,* which means deliverance—deliverance from Egypt, from slavery, and so on. While redemption *(Erlösung)* is often thought to possess simply a spiritual meaning, such an interpretation neglects the term's root as the act whereby a slave is liberated, set free—emancipated. Ricoeur refers to the vocabulary noted in Westermann, *Handbook to the Old Testament.* (Note based on conversation between Ricoeur and the editor.)

5. See Martin Heidegger, *What Is Philosophy?,* p. 95.

5. MARX: *THE GERMAN IDEOLOGY* (1)

1. As Shlomo Avineri points out, Marx himself never used the term "historical materialism" to describe his own approach. See Shlomo Avineri, *The Social and Political Thought of Karl Marx,* p. 65.

6. MARX: *THE GERMAN IDEOLOGY* (2)

1. See Paul Ricoeur, *Freud and Philosophy,* pp. 32–36.

2. Michel Henry, *Marx,* now available in English in abridged form, as *Marx: A Philosophy of Human Reality.* Ricoeur reviews Henry's book in a separate article: "Le *Marx* de Michel Henry," *Esprit* (1978), 2:124–39. Some other comments of Ricoeur on Henry are included in a discussion that appears following Henry's article, "La Rationalité selon Marx," included in Theodore F. Geraets, ed., *Rationality Today,* pp. 116–29. The general discussion of Henry is on pp. 129–35; Ricoeur's comments are on pp. 133–35. Henry's article was presented at an October 1977 conference.

7. ALTHUSSER (1)

1. See Eugen Fink, "Les Concepts Operatoires dans la Phénoménologie de Husserl," in *Husserl,* pp. 214–30.

9. ALTHUSSER (3)

1. In reviewing this statement, which appeared in his notes but was not delivered in lecture, Ricoeur commented that it raised an issue which the lectures do not resolve:

> The status of this proposition is itself a problem. It's the problem of trying to have a discourse about the human condition, the problem of the status of the sociology of knowledge and, beyond that, of any philosophical anthropology which claims to address itself to basic phenomena. Any discourse about humankind that claims to assess historical achievement has great difficulty situating itself. It's the problem of historicism, because historicism is exactly this quandry: if everything is historical, is the proposition that makes this statement historical also? I don't think that we can escape the claim that even if the human situation changes historically, it nevertheless changes within the limit of phenomena which can be identified as having a certain permanence. Perhaps we can say with Gadamer that propositions like these are themselves caught in the process of interpretation, a process that is always self-correcting and never claims to be in a position to see the whole. The question will return in the lectures when I say that ideology and utopia cure one another. (Conversation with the editor)

On Ricoeur's last remark, see the final lecture, which discusses Ricoeur's assessment of his own methodological stance. This problem of the self-referentiality of methodological propositions also reappears in Ricoeur's discussion of Weber in lecture 11.

Ricoeur also noted that one of his more recent works, an essay on Hannah Arendt, directly addresses this issue. He added:

> The argument of Arendt is that finally the claim of the Nazis and any tyranny is that they can mold humankind according to the ideology of the dominating group. The only resistance, she maintains, is to say that there is something beyond the famous statement that "everything is permitted." It is not by chance that Arendt wrote *The Human Condition,*

because for her it was an act of resistance to tyranny. She argued, for example, that labor, work, and action are not the same; they resist a leveling off. (Conversation with the editor)

See Ricoeur's preface to the French reissue of Hannah Arendt, *Condition de l'Homme Moderne*. An abbreviated version of this essay has appeared in English, but it does not include the section Ricoeur discusses here. See Paul Ricoeur, "Action, Story, and History: On Re-reading *The Human Condition*," *Salmagundi* (1983), no. 60, pp. 60–72.

10. MANNHEIM

1. For references to Nietzsche's discussion of *Redlichkeit,* see Karl Jaspers, *Nietzsche,* pp. 202–5. This text has been translated into English, but its page references to Nietzsche's works have been deleted. See Karl Jaspers, *Nietzsche: An Introduction to the Understanding of His Philosophical Activity,* pp. 201–4.

11. WEBER (1)

1. Paul Ricoeur, "Science et Ideologie," *Revue Philosophique de Louvain* (1974), 72:328–56. This article has now been translated and appears as "Science and Ideology" in Paul Ricoeur, *Hermeneutics and the Human Sciences,* pp. 222–46.

12. WEBER (2)

1. While Weber does not include class in his list of basic concepts, he does discuss the concept elsewhere in *Economy and Society*. See part 1, chapter 4, "Status Groups and Classes," and part 2, chapter 9, section 6, "The Distribution of Power within the Political Community: Class, Status, Party." The latter also appears in *From Max Weber,* the volume of Weber essays edited by Gerth and Mills.

13. HABERMAS (1)

1. For an expanded treatment of the relation between ideology, utopia, and religion, see Paul Ricoeur, "L'Herméneutique de la Sécularisation: Foi, Idéologie, Utopie," *Archivio di Filosofia* (1976), 46(2–3):49–68. An abridged translation of this article is available as "Ideology, Utopia, and Faith," *The Center for Hermeneutical Studies* (1976), 17:21–28.

15. GEERTZ

1. In the final lecture Ricoeur clarifies this description, saying that a regressive method "attempts to dig under the surface of the apparent meaning to the more fundamental meanings."

17. SAINT-SIMON

1. Frederick Engels, "Progress of Social Reform on the Continent," in Karl Marx and Frederick Engels, *Collected Works,* 3:394. Interestingly, in the same passage Engels commends *Fourier*'s writings as social *philosophy.*

2. In a passage in part 3 of *The German Ideology,* Marx says that he finds in Fourier's work "a vein of true poetry." This approval has a circumscribed context, however. Fourier's system may have been the most imaginative in comparison to Cabet's, Owen's, and so on, and all of these systems did have propaganda value at the beginning of the communist movement, but with the development of the Party, Marx says, "these systems lose all their importance and are best retained purely nominally as catchwords." Karl Marx, *The German Ideology* (Pascal ed.), p. 87.

3. Here and for the rest of this lecture, Engels' citations refer to "Socialism: Utopian and Scientific."

4. Henri de Saint-Simon, *Social Organization, the Science of Man, and Other Writings.* References to this volume will be cited in the text as "Saint-Simon."

5. This quotation of Saint-Simon is taken from Henri Desroche, *Les Dieux* Rêvés, p. 69. Future references to this volume will be cited as "Desroche"; all translations of Desroche are by Ricoeur.

6. Paul Ricoeur, "The Tasks of the Political Educator," *Political and Social Essays,* pp. 271–93.

18. FOURIER

1. See Henri Desroche, *Les Dieux Rêvés,* pp. 119–20, quoting Fourier. References to this volume will be cited in the text as "Desroche." Throughout this lecture, all translations of direct quotations are by Ricoeur.

2. See, e.g., Paul Ricoeur, *Freud and Philosophy,* pp. 32–36.

3. Raymond Ruyer, *L'Utopie et les Utopies,* p. 9.

4. Clifford Geertz, "Religion as a Cultural System," *The Interpretation of Cultures,* p. 93.

Bibliography

THE READINGS

Althusser, Louis. *For Marx*. Trans. Ben Brewster. New York: Vintage Books, 1970. Republished, London: Verso Editions, 1979 [distributed in U.S. by Schocken] (same pagination as 1970).

—— *Lenin and Philosophy*. Trans. Ben Brewster. New York: Monthly Review Press, 1971.

Desroche, Henri. *Les Dieux Rêvés*. Paris: Desclée, 1972.

Engels, Friedrich. "Socialism: Utopian and Scientific." In Karl Marx and Friedrich Engels, *Basic Writings on Politics and Philosophy,* pp. 68–111. Ed. Lewis S. Feuer. Garden City, N.Y.: Doubleday, 1959.

Fourier, Charles. *Design for Utopia*. Trans. Julia Franklin; intro. Charles Gide. New York: Schocken, 1971.

Geertz, Clifford. *The Interpretation of Cultures*. New York: Basic Books, 1973.

Habermas, Jürgen. *Knowledge and Human Interests*. Trans. Jeremy J. Shapiro. Boston: Beacon Press, 1972.

Mannheim, Karl. *Ideology and Utopia*. Trans. Louis Wirth and Edward Shils. New York: Harcourt, Brace, and World, 1936.

Marx, Karl. *Critique of Hegel's "Philosophy of Right."* Ed. and intro. Joseph O'Malley. Cambridge: Cambridge University Press, 1970.

—— *The Economic and Philosophic Manuscripts of 1844*. Ed. and intro. Dirk J. Struik. New York: International Publishers, 1964.

Marx, Karl and Frederick Engels. *The German Ideology,* Part 1. Ed. and intro. C. J. Arthur. New York: International Publishers, 1970.

Saint-Simon, Henri de. *Social Organization, the Science of Man, and Other Writings*. Trans. and ed. Felix Markham. New York: Harper and Row, 1964.

Weber, Max. *Economy and Society*. 2 vols. Ed. Guenther Roth and Claus Wittich. Berkeley: University of California Press, 1978 [1968].

CHRONOLOGY OF RICOEUR'S WORKS ON IDEOLOGY AND UTOPIA

"Herméneutique et Critique des Idéologies." *Archivio di Filosofia* (1973), 43(2–4):25–61. English: "Hermeneutics and the Critique of Ideology." In *Hermeneutics and the Human Sciences,* pp. 63–100. Ed. and trans. John B. Thompson. Cambridge: Cambridge University Press, 1981. This article is not an elaboration of Ricoeur' own views on ideology but rather an examination of Gadamer (hermeneutics) and Habermas (the critique of ideology).

"Science et Idéologie." *Revue Philosophique de Louvain* (1974), 72:328–56. English: "Science and Ideology." In *Hermeneutics and the Human Sciences,* pp. 222–46. Ed. and trans. John B. Thompson. Cambridge: Cambridge University Press, 1981.

"Can There Be a Scientific Concept of Ideology?" *Phenomenological Sociology Newsletter* (1974–75), 3(2):2–5, 8; 3(3–4):4–6. Reprinted in Joseph Bien, ed., *Phenomenology and the Social Sciences,* pp. 44–59. The Hague: Martinus Nijhoff, 1978. This article extensively parallels "Science and Ideology."

Lectures on Ideology and Utopia. Delivered at the University of Chicago, fall 1975.

"L'Herméneutique de la Sécularisation: Foi, Idéologie, Utopie." *Archivio di Filosofia* (1976), 46(2–3):49–68. Presented at a symposium June 1976. English: "Ideology, Utopia, and Faith." *The Center for Hermeneutical Studies* (1976), 17:21–28. Presented at a colloquy November 1975. The English text is a very abbreviated version of the French.

"Ideology and Utopia as Cultural Imagination." *Philosophic Exchange* (1976), 2(2):17–28. Reprinted in Donald M. Borchert, ed., *Being Human in a Technological Age,* pp. 107–26. Athens, Ohio: Ohio University Press, 1979. This article in part parallels the first lecture in *Lectures on Ideology and Utopia.*

"L'Imagination dans le Discours et dans l'Action." In Savoir, Faire, Espérer: Les Limites de la Raison, 1:207–28. Brussels: Facultés Universitaires Saint-Louis, 1976. English: "Imagination in Discourse and Action." *Analecta Husserliana* (1978), 7:3–22. Sections on ideology and utopia extensively parallel "Ideology and Utopia as Cultural Imagination."

"La Structure Symbolique de l'Action." *Actes de la 14e Conference de Sociologie des Religions,* pp. 29–50. Paris: Centre Nationale de la Recherche Scientifique, 1977. Pages 48–50 discuss the concept of ideology.

"Ideologie und Ideologiekritik." In Bernhard Waldenfels, Jan M. Broekman, and Ante Pažanin, eds., *Phänomenologie und Marxismus,* 1:197–233. Frankfurt: Suhrkamp, 1977. English: "Ideology and Ideology Critique." In Waldenfels, et al., *Phenomenology and Marxism,* pp. 134–64. Trans. J. Claude Evans, Jr. Boston: Routledge and Kegan Paul, 1984. This article is almost exclusively a presentation of parts of "Science and Ideology" and "Hermeneutics and the Critique of Ideology."

"Rückfrage und Reduktion der Idealitaten in Husserls 'Krisis' und Marx' 'Deutscher Ideologie.' " In Bernhard Waldenfels, Jan M. Broekman, and Ante Pažanin, eds., *Phänomenologie und Marxismus,* 3:207–39. Frankfurt: Suhrkamp, 1978.

RICOEUR WORKS CITED

"Action, Story, and History: On Re-reading *The Human Condition.*" *Salmagundi* (1983), no. 60, pp. 60–72.

"Aliénation." *Encyclopaedia Universalis* (1968), 1:660–64.

"Can Fictional Narratives Be True?" *Analecta Husserliana* (1983), 14:3–19.

"Can There Be a Scientific Concept of Ideology?" In Joseph Bien, ed., *Phenomenology and the Social Sciences,* pp. 44–59. The Hague: Martinus Nijhoff, 1978.

The Conflict of Interpretations. Ed. and intro. Don Ihde. Evanston, Ill.: Northwestern University Press, 1974.

"Construing and Constructing." (Review of E. D. Hirsch, Jr., *The Aims of Interpretation.*) *Times Literary Supplement,* February 25, 1977, p. 216.

"Creativity in Language." In *The Philosophy of Paul Ricoeur,* pp. 120–33. Ed. Charles E. Reagan and David Stewart. Boston: Beacon Press, 1978.

"Ethics and Culture." In *Political and Social Essays,* pp. 243–70. Ed. David Stewart and Joseph Bien. Athens, Ohio: Ohio University Press, 1974.

Etre, Essence et Substance chez Platon et Aristote. Paris: Société d'Edition D'Enseignement Supérieur, 1982.

"Explanation and Understanding: On Some Remarkable Connections Among the Theory of the Text, Theory of Action, and Theory of History." In *The Philosophy of Paul Ricoeur,* pp. 149–66. Ed. Charles E. Reagan and David Stewart. Boston: Beacon Press, 1978.

Fallible Man. Trans. and intro. Charles Kelbley. Chicago: Henry Regnery, 1965.

Freedom and Nature: The Voluntary and the Involuntary. Trans. and intro. Erazim V. Kohák. Evanston, Ill.: Northwestern University Press, 1966.

Freud and Philosophy: An Essay on Interpretation. Trans. Denis Savage. New Haven: Yale University Press, 1970.

"The Function of Fiction in Shaping Reality." *Man and World* (1979), 12:123–41.

"Hermeneutics and the Critique of Ideology." In *Hermeneutics and the Human Sciences,* pp. 63–100. Ed. and trans. John B. Thompson. Cambridge: Cambridge University Press, 1981.

Hermeneutics and the Human Sciences. Ed. and trans. John B. Thompson. Cambridge: Cambridge University Press, 1981.

"L'Herméneutique de la Sécularisation: Foi, Idéologie, Utopie." *Archivio di Filosofia* (1976), 46(2–3):49–68.

"L'Histoire comme Récit et comme Pratique." (Interview with Peter Kemp.) *Esprit* (June 1981), 6:155–65.

"History and Hermeneutics." In Yirmiahu Yovel, ed., *Philosophy of History and Action,* pp. 3–20. Dordrecht, Holland: D. Reidel, 1978. Paper presented at the First Jerusalem Philosophical Encounter, December 1974.

"History and Hermeneutics." *Journal of Philosophy* (1976), 73(19):683–95.

History and Truth. Trans. and intro. Charles A. Kelbley. Evanston, Ill.: Northwestern University Press, 1965.

"Ideology and Utopia as Cultural Imagination." *Philosophic Exchange* (1976), 2(2):17–28.

"Ideology, Utopia, and Faith." *The Center for Hermeneutical Studies* (1976), 17:21–28.

"Imagination in Discourse and Action." *Analecta Husserliana* (1978), 7:3–22.

" 'Logique Herméneutique'?" In Guttorm Fløstad, ed., *Contemporary Philosophy,* 1:179–223. The Hague: Martinus Nijhoff, 1981.

"Le *Marx* de Michel Henry." *Esprit* (1978), 2:124–39.

"The Metaphorical Process as Cognition, Imagination, and Feeling." *Critical Inquiry* (1978), 5:143–59.

"Mimesis and Representation." *Annals of Scholarship* (1981), 2(3):15–32.

"Narrative and Hermeneutics." In John Fisher, ed., *Essays on Aesthetics: Perspectives on the Work of Monroe C. Beardsley,* pp. 149–60. Philadelphia: Temple University Press, 1983.

"Objectivation et Aliénation dans l'Expérience Historique." *Archivio di Filosofia* (1975), 45(2–3):27–38.

"Poetry and Possibility." (Interview with Philip Fried.) *Manhattan Review* (1982), 2(2):6–21.

Political and Social Essays. Ed. David Stewart and Joseph Bien. Athens, Ohio: Ohio University Press, 1974.

"Préface." In Hannah Arendt, *Condition de l'Homme Moderne,* pp. i–xxviii. Paris: Calmann-Lévy, 1983.

"La Raison Pratique." In Theodore F. Geraets, ed., *Rationality Today,* pp. 225–41. Ottawa: University of Ottawa Press, 1979. Discussion pp. 241–48. Presented as part of a symposium, October 1977.

The Reality of the Historical Past. Milwaukee: Marquette University Press, 1984.

"Rückfrage und Reduktion der Idealitaten in Husserls 'Krisis' und Marx' 'Deutscher Ideologie.' " In Bernhard Waldenfels, Jan M. Broekman, and Ante Pažanin, eds., *Phänomenologie und Marxismus,* 3:207–39. Frankfurt: Suhrkamp, 1978.

The Rule of Metaphor. Trans. Robert Czerny et al. Toronto: University of Toronto Press, 1977.

"Sartre and Ryle on the Imagination." In Paul A. Schilpp, ed., *The Philosophy of Jean-Paul Sartre,* pp. 167–78. La Salle, Ill.: Open Court Press, 1981.

"Science and Ideology." In *Hermeneutics and the Human Sciences,* pp. 222–46. Ed. and trans. John B. Thompson. Cambridge: Cambridge University Press, 1981.

"The Status of *Vorstellung* in Hegel's Philosophy of Religion." In Leroy S. Rouner, ed., *Meaning, Truth, and God,* pp. 70–88. Notre Dame, Ind.: University of Notre Dame Press, 1982.

"La Structure Symbolique de l'Action." *Actes de la 14e Conference de Sociologie des Religions,* pp. 29–50. Paris: Centre Nationale de la Recherche Scientifique, 1977.

The Symbolism of Evil. Trans. Emerson Buchanan. Boston: Beacon Press, 1969.

"The Tasks of the Political Educator." In *Political and Social Essays,* pp. 271–93. Ed. David Stewart and Joseph Bien. Athens, Ohio: Ohio University Press, 1974.

Time and Narrative, vols. 1 and 2. Trans. Kathleen McLaughlin and David Pellauer, Chicago: University of Chicago Press, 1984, 1985.

For a complete Ricoeur bibliography, see Frans D. Vansina, *Paul Ricoeur: Bibliographie Systématique de ses Ecrits et des Publications Consacrées a sa Pensée (1935–1984). A Primary and Secondary Systematic Bibliography (1935–1984).* Louvain-la-Neuve: Editions de l'Institut Supérieur de Philosophie, 1985.

SECONDARY WORKS CITED

Althusser, Louis. "Lénine et la Philosophie." *Bulletin de la Société Française de Philosophie* (1968), 62(4):125–61; discussion, 161–81.

—— *Essays in Self-Criticism.* Trans. Grahame Lock. Atlantic Highlands, N.J.: Humanities Press, 1976.

Anscombe, G. E. M. *Intention.* Ithaca, N.Y.: Cornell University Press, 1957.

Apel, Karl-Otto. *Towards a Transformation of Philosophy.* Trans. Glyn Adey and David Frisby. Boston: Routledge and Kegan Paul, 1980.

Arendt, Hannah. *Eichmann in Jerusalem: A Report on the Banality of Evil.* New York: Penguin Books, 1976.

—— *The Human Condition.* Chicago: University of Chicago Press, 1958. French: *Condition de l'Homme Moderne.* Trans. Georges Fradier; pref. Paul Ricoeur. Paris: Calmann-Lévy, 1983.

—— *The Origins of Totalitarianism.* New York: Harcourt Brace Jovanovich, 1973.

Avineri, Shlomo. *The Social and Political Thought of Karl Marx.* Cambridge: Cambridge University Press, 1968.

Bachelard, Gaston. *The Philosophy of No.* Trans. G. C. Waterson. New York: Orion Press, 1968.

Bacon, Francis. *New Atlantis.* Oxford: Clarendon Press, 1974.

Betti, Emilio. "Hermeneutics as the General Methodology of the *Geisteswissenschaften.*" In Josef Bleicher, *Contemporary Hermeneutics,* pp. 51–94. London: Routledge and Kegan Paul, 1980.

Bloch, Ernst. *Thomas Münzer als Theologe der Revolution.* Frankfurt: Suhrkamp, 1969.

Booth, Wayne C. *A Rhetoric of Irony.* Chicago: University of Chicago Press, 1974.

Burke, Kenneth. *The Philosophy of Literary Form: Studies in Symbolic Action.* Baton Rouge: Louisiana State University Press, 1941; 2d ed., 1967.

Cabet, Etienne. *Voyage en Icarie.* Paris: Slatkine, 1979.

Campanella, Tommaso. *The City of the Sun.* Trans. A. M. Elliott and R. Millner. West Nyack, N.Y.: Journeyman Press, 1981.

Desanti, Dominique. *Les Socialistes de l'Utopie.* Paris: Payot, 1970.

Engels, Friedrich. *Anti-Dühring.* Trans. Emile Burns; ed. C. P. Dutt. New York: International Publishers, 1976.

—— "Progress of Social Reform on the Continent." In Karl Marx and Frederick Engels, *Collected Works,* 3:392–408. New York: International Publishers, 1975.

Erikson, Erik H. *Childhood and Society.* New York: W. W. Norton, 1950; 2d ed. revised and enlarged, 1963.

—— *Identity: Youth and Crisis.* New York: W. W. Norton, 1968.

Eurich, Nell. *Science in Utopia: A Mighty Design.* Cambridge: Harvard University Press, 1967.

Fackenheim, Emil L. *The Religious Dimension in Hegel's Thought.* Boston: Beacon Press, 1970.

Feuerbach, Ludwig. *The Essence of Christianity.* Trans. George Eliot. New York: Harper and Row, 1957.

Fichte, J. G. *The Science of Knowledge.* Trans. and ed. Peter Heath and John Lachs. Cambridge: Cambridge University Press, 1982.

Fink, Eugen. "Les Concepts Operatoires dan la Phénoménologie de Husserl." In *Husserl,* pp. 214–30. Paris: Minuit, 1959 [1957 conference]. German: "Operative Begriffe in Husserls Phänomenologie." *Zeitschrift für Philosophische Forschung* (1957), 11:321–37.

Fourier, Charles. *Le Nouveau Monde Amoureux.* Ed. Simone Debout-Oleszkiewicz. Paris: Anthropos, 1967.

—— *The Utopian Vision of Charles Fourier.* Trans., ed., and intro. Jonathan Beecher and Richard Bienvenu. Columbia: University of Missouri Press, 1983.

Freire, Paulo. *Pedagogy of the Oppressed.* Trans. Myra Bergman Ramos. New York: Seabury Press, 1970.

Freud, Sigmund. *Civilization and Its Discontents.* Trans. and ed. James Strachey. New York: W. W. Norton, 1962.

—— *The Ego and the Id.* Trans. Joan Riviera; revised and newly ed. by James Strachey. New York: W. W. Norton, rev. ed., 1962.

—— *The Future of an Illusion.* Trans. W. D. Robson-Scott; translation rev. and ed. James Strachey. Garden City, N.Y.: Doubleday, 1964.

—— *Moses and Monotheism.* Trans. Katherine Jones. New York: Vintage Books, 1967.

—— *New Introductory Lectures on Psychoanalysis.* Trans. James Strachey. New York: W. W. Norton, 1966.

—— *The Interpretation of Dreams.* Trans. James Strachey. New York: Basic Books, 1956.

—— "Obsessive Actions and Religious Practices." In *The Standard Edition of the Complete Psychological Works of Sigmund Freud,* 9:115–27. Trans. and ed. James Strachey. London: Hogarth Press, 1959.

—— "Psycho-analytic Notes on an Autobiographical Account of a Case of Paranoia." [The Schreber case.] In *The Standard Edition of the Complete Psychological Works of Sigmund Freud,* 12:3–84. Trans. and ed. James Strachey. London: Hogarth Press, 1958.

—— "The Unconscious." In *The Standard Edition of the Complete Psychological Works of Sigmund Freud,* 14:159–204. Trans. and ed. James Strachey. London: Hogarth Press, 1957.

Gadamer, Hans-Georg. *Truth and Method.* Trans. Garret Burden and John Cumming. New York: Seabury Press, 1975.

Garaudy, Roger. *Karl Marx: The Evolution of His Thought.* Trans. Nan Apotheker. Westport, Ct.: Greenwood Press, 1976.

Goldmann, Lucien. *The Hidden God.* Trans. Philip Thody. New York: Humanities Press, 1964.

Gramsci, Antonio. *Selections from the Prison Notebooks.* Ed. and trans. Quintin Hoare and Geoffrey Nowell Smith. New York: International Publishers, 1971.

Habermas, Jürgen. *Theory and Practice*. Trans. John Viertel. Boston: Beacon Press, 1974.

Hegel, G. W. F. *Hegel and the Human Spirit: A Translation of the Jena Lectures on the Philosophy of Spirit (1805–6)*. Trans. Leo Rauch. Detroit: Wayne State University Press, 1983.

—— *Logic*. (Part 1 of the *Encyclopaedia of the Philosophical Sciences*.) Trans. William Wallace. Oxford: Clarendon Press, 1975.

—— *Phenomenology of Spirit*. Trans. A. V. Miller. Oxford: Clarendon Press, 1977.

—— *Philosophy of History*. Trans. J. Sibree. New York: Dover Publications Press, 1952.

—— *Philosophy of Right*. Trans T. M. Knox. New York: Oxford University Press, 1967.

Heidegger, Martin. *Being and Time*. Trans. John Macquarrie and Edward Robinson. New York: Harper and Row, 1962.

—— *The Essence of Reasons*. Trans. Terrence Malic. Evanston, Ill.: Northwestern University Press, 1969.

—— *What Is Philosophy?* Trans. and intro. William Klubach and Jean T. Wilde. New Haven: College and University Press, 1956.

Henry, Michel. *L'Essence de la Manifestation*. Paris: Presses Universitaires de France, 1963.

—— *Marx*. Paris: Gallimard, 1976. English (abridged): *Marx: A Philosophy of Human Reality*. Trans. Kathleen McLaughlin. Bloomington: Indiana University Press, 1983.

—— "La Rationalité selon Marx." In Theodore F. Geraets, ed., *Rationality Today*, pp. 116–29. Ottawa: University of Ottawa Press, 1979.

Hess, Moses. *Philosophische und Sozialistieche Schriften 1837–1850: Eine Auswahl*. Berlin: Akademie-Verlag, 1980.

Hirsch, E. D., Jr. *The Aims of Interpretation*. Chicago: University of Chicago Press, 1976.

—— *Validity in Interpretation*. New Haven: Yale University Press, 1967.

—— "Meaning and Significance Reinterpreted." *Critical Inquiry* (1984), 11:202–25.

Husserl, Edmund. *Cartesian Meditations*. Trans. D. Cairns. The Hague: Martinus Nijhoff, 1960.

—— *The Crisis of European Sciences and Transcendental Phenomenology*. Trans. and intro. David Carr. Evanston, Ill.: Northwestern University Press, 1970.

—— *Ideas. General Introduction to Pure Phenomenlogy*. Trans. W. R. Boyce Gibson. New York: Collier Books, 1962.

Huxley, Aldous. *Brave New World*. London: Chatto and Windus, 1970.

Hyppolite, Jean. *Genesis and Structure of Hegel's "Phenomenology of Spirit."* Trans. Samuel Cherniak and John Heckman. Evanston, Ill.: Northwestern University Press, 1974.

Ihde, Don, *Hermeneutic Phenomenology: The Philosophy of Paul Ricoeur*. Evanston, Ill.: Northwestern University Press, 1971.

Jaspers, Karl. *Nietzsche*. Berlin: Walter de Gruyter, 1947. English: *Nietzsche: An Introduction to the Understanding of His Philosophical Activity*. Trans. Charles

F. Wallraff and Frederick J. Schmitz. Tucson: University of Arizona Press, 1965.
Kant, Immanuel. *Critique of Pure Reason.* Trans. Norman Kemp Smith. New York: St. Martin's Press, 1965.
Kendall, George H. "Ideology: An Essay in Definition." *Philosophy Today* (1981), 25:262–76.
Kon, Igor S. *Filosofskij Idealizm i Krizis Buržuaznoj Istoričeskoj Mysli* [Philosophical Idealism and the Crisis in Bourgeois Historical Thinking]. Moscow, 1959. German: *Die Geschichtsphilosophie des 20. Jahrhunderts. Kritischer Abriss.* Trans. Willi Hoepp. Berlin: Akademie-Verlag. 2 vols. 2d ed., 1966.
Kuhn, Thomas S. *The Essential Tension.* Chicago: University of Chicago Press, 1977.
—— "Metaphor in Science." In Andrew Ortony, ed., *Metaphor and Thought,* pp. 409–19. Cambridge: Cambridge University Press, 1979.
—— *The Structure of Scientific Revolutions.* Chicago: University of Chicago Press, 1962; 2d ed., enlarged, 1970.
Lacan, Jacques. *Ecrits,* 2 vols. Paris: Editions du Seuil, 1966. English: *Ecrits: A Selection.* Trans. Alan Sheridan. New York: W. W. Norton, 1977.
Lenin, Vladimir I. *State and Revolution.* New York: International Publishers, 1932; 2d ed., 1971.
Lukács, Georg. *History and Class Consciousness.* Trans. Rodney Livingstone. Cambridge: MIT Press, 1971.
Marcuse, Herbert. *One-Dimensional Man.* Boston: Beacon Press, 1971.
Marx, Karl. *Capital,* vol. 1. Trans. Samuel Moore and Edward Aveling. New York: International Publishers, 1967.
—— *Grundrisse.* Trans. Martin Nicolaus. New York: Vintage Books, 1973.
—— *The Poverty of Philosophy.* New York: International Publishers, 1936.
Marx, Karl and Frederick Engels. *The German Ideology,* Parts I and III. Ed. R. Pascal. New York: International Publishers, 1963 [1947].
McCarthy, Thomas. *The Critical Theory of Jürgen Habermas.* Cambridge: MIT Press, 1978.
Moltmann, Jürgen. *Theology of Hope.* Trans. James W. Leitch. New York: Harper and Row, 1967.
More, Thomas. *Utopia.* New York: W. W. Norton, 1975.
Mumford, Lewis. *The Story of Utopias.* New York: Viking Press, 1968.
Orwell, George. *1984.* New York: Oxford University Press, 1984.
Owen, Robert. *The Book of the New Moral World.* London: J. Watson, 1849.
Parsons, Talcott. "An Approach to the Sociology of Knowledge." In James E. Curtis and John W. Petras, eds., *The Sociology of Knowledge,* pp. 283–306. New York: Praeger, 1970.
—— *The Social System.* New York: Free Press, 1964.
Plato. *The Collected Dialogues.* Ed. Edith Hamilton and Huntington Cairns. Princeton: Princeton University Press, 1961.
Proudhon, Pierre-Joseph. *Système de Contradictions Economiques, ou Philosophie de la Misère.* In *Oeuvres Completes,* vol. 1. Paris: Slatkine, 1982.
Riasanovsky, Nicholas V. *The Teachings of Charles Fourier.* Berkeley: University of California Press, 1969.

Rilke, Rainer Maria. *The Selected Poetry of Rainer Maria Rilke*. Trans. and ed. Robert Hass. New York: Random House, 1982.

Rockmore, Tom. "Idéologie Marxienne et Herméneutique." *Laval Théologique et Philosophique* (1984), 40(2):161–73.

Runciman, W.G. *Social Theory and Political Practice*. Cambridge: Cambridge University Press, 1963.

Ruyer, Raymond. *L'Utopie et les Utopies*. Paris: Presses Universitaires de France, 1970.

Saint-Simon, Henri de. *New Christianity*. Trans. J. E. Smith. London: B. D. Cousins and E. Wilson, 1834.

—— *Oeuvres*. Geneva: Slatkine, 1977.

—— *The Political Thought of Saint-Simon*. Trans. Valence Ionescu; ed. Ghita Ionescu. New York: Oxford Univeristy Press, 1976.

—— *Selected Writings on Science, Industry, and Social Organization*. Trans. and ed. Keith Taylor. London: Croom Helm, 1975.

Sarte, Jean-Paul. *Critique of Dialectical Reason*. Trans. Alan Sheridan-Smith; ed. Jonathan Rée. Atlantic Highlands, N.J.: Humanities Press, 1976.

Schutz, Alfred. *The Phenomenology of the Social World*. Trans. George Walsh and Frederick Lehnert. Evanston, Ill.: Northwestern University Press, 1967.

Shils, Edward. "Ideology and Civility: On the Politics of the Intellectual." *Sewanee Review* (1958), 66:450–80.

Skinner, B. F. *Walden II*. New York: Macmillan, 1976.

Sutton, F. X., S. E. Harris, C. Kaysen, and J. Tobin. *The American Business Creed*. Cambridge: Harvard University Press, 1956.

Sweeney, Robert. "Value and Ideology." *Analecta Husserliana* (1983), 15:387–401.

Thompson, John B. "Action, Ideology, and the Text." In *Studies in the Theory of Ideology*, pp. 173–204. Cambridge: Polity Press, 1984.

van den Hengel, John. "Faith and Ideology in the Philosophy of Paul Ricoeur." *Eglise et Théologie* (1983), 14:63–89.

Weber, Max. *From Max Weber*. Trans. and ed. H. H. Gerth and C. Wright Mills. New York: Oxford Unversity Press, 1958.

—— *The Protestant Ethic and the Spirit of Capitalism*. Trans. Talcott Parsons. New York: Charles Scribner's Sons, 1958.

—— *The Theory of Social and Economic Organization*. Trans. A. M. Henderson and Talcott Parsons; ed. and intro. Talcott Parsons. New York: Free Press, 1947.

Weil, Eric. *Philosophie Politique*. Paris: Vrin, 1956.

Wells, H. G. *A Modern Utopia*. Lincoln: University of Nebraska Press, 1967.

Westermann, Claus. *Handbook to the Old Testament*. Trans. and ed. Robert H. Boyd. Minneapolis: Augsburg Publishing House, 1967.

Whorf, Benjamin Lee. *Language, Thought, and Reality*. Cambridge: MIT Press, 1956.

Wittgenstein, Ludwig. *Philosophical Investigations*. Trans. G. E. M. Anscombe. New York: Macmillan, 1953; 2d ed., 1958; 3d ed., 1969.

—— *Tractatus Logico-Philosophicus*. Trans. D. F. Pears and B. F. McGuinness. London: Routledge and Kegan Paul, 1963.

Index